# Research Methods for Sport Management

Research methods courses have become a compulsory component of most degree programmes in sport management. This is the first introductory research methods textbook to focus exclusively on sport management. Through the use of examples, cases and data taken from the real world of sport management it opens up a traditionally dry area of study, helping the student to understand the vital importance of sound methodology in their studies and subsequent professional practice.

The book covers the full range of quantitative and qualitative methods across the whole span of the research process, from research design and the literature review to data analysis and report writing. Every chapter contains a range of useful features to aid student learning, including summaries, discussion questions and guides to further resources, as well as examples drawn from contemporary sport around the world. *Research Methods for Sport Management* is an essential course text for all sport management students and an invaluable reference for any sport management professional involved in operational research.

**James Skinner** is a Professor of Sport Business and Director of the Institute for Sport Business at Loughborough University, London, UK. His research interests are in drugs in sport, culture strategy, leadership and change, sport and social capital, and research methods for sport management.

**Allan Edwards** is Head of Sport and Exercise Science at the University of Canberra, Australia. His research interests include qualitative research methodology, high performance sport management and sport marketing.

**Ben Corbett** is a sport management PhD candidate and lecturer at Griffith University, Australia. His research interests include organizational strategy and change, high performance management, and sport event legacy.

# Foundations of Sport Management

*Series Editor:*
David Hassan, University of Ulster at Jordanstown, UK

*Foundations of Sport Management* is a discipline-defining series of texts on core and cutting-edge topics in sport management. Featuring some of the best known and most influential sport management scholars from around the world, each volume represents an authoritative, engaging and self-contained introduction to a key functional area or issue within contemporary sport management. Packed with useful features to aid teaching and learning, the series aims to bridge the gap between management theory and practice and to encourage critical thinking and reflection among students, academics and practitioners.

Also available in this series

**Managing Sport Business: An Introduction**
*David Hassan and Linda Trenberth*

**Managing Sport: Social and Cultural Perspectives**
*David Hassan and Jim Lusted*

**Managing High Performance Sport**
*Popi Sotiriadou and Veerle De Bosscher*

**Routledge Handbook of Sport and Corporate Social Responsibility**
*Kathy Babiak, Juan Luis Paramio-Salcines and Geoff Walters*

**Sport Governance: International Case Studies**
*Ian O'Boyle and Trish Bradbury*

**Research Methods for Sport Management**
*James Skinner, Allan Edwards and Ben Corbett*

# Research Methods for Sport Management

James Skinner, Allan Edwards and Ben Corbett

Routledge
Taylor & Francis Group

LONDON AND NEW YORK

First published 2015
by Routledge
2 Park Square, Milton Park, Abingdon, Oxon OX14 4RN

and by Routledge
711 Third Avenue, New York, NY 10017

*Routledge is an imprint of the Taylor & Francis Group, an informa business*

*British Library Cataloguing-in-Publication Data*
A catalogue record for this book is available from the British Library

*Library of Congress Cataloging-in-Publication Data*
Skinner, James.
Research methods for sport management / James Skinner, Allan Edwards,
Benjamin Corbett.
pages cm – (Foundations of sport management)
1. Sports administration – Research. I. Edwards, Allan. II. Corbett,
Benjamin. III. Title.
GV713.S573 2014
796.06'9 – dc23
2014017175

ISBN: 978-0-415-57255-2 (hbk)
ISBN: 978-0-415-57256-9 (pbk)
ISBN: 978-0-203-85612-3 (ebk)

Typeset in Perpetua
by Florence Production Limited, Stoodleigh, Devon, UK

Printed and bound in Great Britain by
TJ International Ltd, Padstow, Cornwall

# Contents

# CONTENTS

# Figures

# Tables

# Abbreviations

| | |
|---|---|
| ABA | American Basketball Association |
| ANCOVA | analysis of covariance |
| ANOVA | analysis of variance |
| APA | American Psychological Association |
| AR | Action Research |
| ARU | Australian Rugby Union |
| AWS | Amazon Web Services |
| BRICS | Brazil, Russia, India, China, South Africa |
| CA | conversation analysis |
| CAQDAS | Computer Assisted/Aided Qualitative Data Analysis |
| CDA | critical discourse analysis |
| CLS | critical legal studies |
| CMC | computer mediated communication |
| CRT | critical race theory |
| CSR | corporate social responsibility |
| DA | discourse analysis |
| DV | dependent variable |
| EAR | Emancipatory Action Research |
| ESPN | Entertainment and Sports Programming Network |
| FIFA | Federation of International Football Association |
| GT | grounded theory |
| ICC | International Cricket Council |
| IRB | International Rugby board |
| IRC | Internet relay chat |
| IV | independent variable |
| KIM | knowledge and information management |
| LIFE | Leisure Involvement For Everyone |
| MANOVA | multivariate analysis of variance |
| MCD | membership categorization device |
| NASCAR | National Association of Stock Car Racing |
| NBA | National Basketball Association |

| NCAA | National Collegiate Athletic Association |
|------|------------------------------------------|
| NFL | National Football League |
| NOOC | naturally occurring online community |
| ORC | online research community |
| PAAS | Participant authored audiovisual stories |
| PAR | Participatory Action Research |
| QDA | qualitative data analysis |
| QRU | Queensland Rugby Union |
| RSS | Really Simple Syndication or Rich Site Summary |
| SCR | surf company representatives |
| SFS | sponsored female surfers |
| SPSS | Statistical Package for the Social Services |
| SRP | standarized relational pairs |
| WNBA | Women's National Basketball Association |

# Part 1

# Overview of the Sport Management Research process

# Chapter 1

# Basic principles of Sport Management Research

## WHAT IS SPORT MANAGEMENT RESEARCH?

Sport managers strive for organizational improvement and this requires an ability to identify problems, to address these and search for potential solutions. To achieve this, sport managers can spend a great deal of time evaluating other people's research, deciding what the strengths and weaknesses are in each case, and hoping to apply their conclusions to their own reading and to the procedures they follow in their research. The world of sport, however, poses many unique and novel problems that are not experienced in business, government or charity work – for example very few managers will ever deal with an employee who can prove they are the best in the world at their job. As such, sport managers, perhaps even more than other types of manager, need to look carefully at the claims of others, judging for themselves whether or not those claims are convincing and reliable. To do that, they need to understand the process by which other researchers have come to their conclusions, and this means understanding both their methodologies and the intellectual frameworks within which they have operated.

In this book the concept of research means the systematic *collection*, *analysis* and *interpretation of data to answer a certain question or solve a problem*. All the italicized words attach specific meaning in the steps of actually developing and executing a research project. At its basic level, research is a way of investigating problems with the aim of finding solutions to those problems, or at least raising questions and issues that future researchers will investigate. The same is true of Sport Management Research, which devises questions relating to specific problems or issues in the field, and then devises methods by which these problems or issues can be answered (or at least better understood). This process is important because it can add knowledge about sport management issues, improve sport management practices, inform sport management policy issues and become a catalyst for complex thinking, informed communication and toleration for competing paradoxes.

## WHAT MAKES SPORT MANAGEMENT RESEARCH DIFFERENT?

Sport management is a nexus. The discipline was rooted and grown in university Health or Exercise Science departments that saw the need to study and educate 'sport people' in sport organization governance (i.e. the management of high performance development systems and grassroots club participation). As sport management expanded, alliances with business researchers and courses became more common to the point that business schools began to offer a sport management degree. There are numerous universities that offer a sport management degree, yet it continues to spread across business and health schools, highlighting the interdisciplinary connection.

As Smith and Stewart (2010) described, sport has been divided between two opposite viewpoints, but actually lies somewhere in the middle:

> At one extreme, sport is viewed as a unique cultural institution with a host of special features wherein the reflexive application of standard business practices not only produces poor management decision making, but also erodes its rich history, emotional connections, tribal links, and social relevance. At the other extreme, sport is seen to be nothing more than just another generic business enterprise subject to the usual government regulations, market pressures and customer demands, and is best managed by the application of standard business tools that assist the planning, finance, human resource management and marketing functions. (p. 1)

It is not hard to suggest from this statement that the sport purists (born in the Health Science Schools) side with the first extreme, and the management purists (born in Business Schools) side with the second extreme. The truth does lie in the middle, with theory and research frameworks from health and business borrowed, adapted or amalgamated in the study of sport issues.

The convergence of disciplines occurs not just between health and business schools, but also within the business school disciplines. Economics, marketing, strategy, finance, organizational behaviour, sustainability, human resources, law and politics to mention some, are all topics a sport management researcher can both simultaneously apply to existing business theory and diverge within a unique sport context. While sport often, and more frequently, operates in a business setting, there are significant theoretical and practical variations that require a sport management researcher to alter traditional business viewpoints. For example, can a model designed to explore marketing practices to business 'customers' easily transition to study sport 'fans'? The sport management discipline offers researchers a wide variety of business studies within the inimitable and complex contexts of sport. Smith and Stewart (2010) noted the following special features of sport that separate it from institutionalized business principles:

- the fusion of loyalty, identification and irrational optimism;
- the tension between winning and profit-making;
- transforming the sport-field into a workplace;
- the dilemma of corporate sport;
- the need to balance variable quality against competitive balance;
- the crucial importance of setting up structures for collaborative behaviour among competing interests;
- supply chain restrictions (i.e. on-field performance);
- managing the fishbowl-experience of players;

- managing players as income earning assets;
- the confounding influence of league structures.

Finally, sport management offers a connection to other disciplines, such as tourism, entertainment and leisure. The globalization of sport and the continued rise of mega-sport events affects tourism, and the principles of tourism can be applied to sport tourists – whether it be direct and indirect tourism, triple bottom line (economic, social, environmental) impacts or the legacy left by showcasing host regions. Sports have always been entertainment for the masses, competing against other forms of arts, music and films. However, they also converge closer than ever in the new millennium with sport often combining with other entertainment options to leverage additional viewers. Entertainment is a form of leisure, but the connections to leisure extend further, and range from spectatorship to community sport participation.

## WHY DO SPORT MANAGEMENT RESEARCH?

Research and reflection are essential in any discipline if that discipline is to grow in a positive and beneficial way. Thomas, Nelson and Silverman (2005) asserted:

> one of the primary distinctions between a discipline or profession and trade is that the trade deals only with how to deal with something, whereas the discipline or profession concerns itself not only with how but also with why something should be done in a certain manner and why it should even be done (p. 6).

The same authors go on to discuss some of the problems associated with research and its applicability to practitioners and professionals in sport management: problems directly affecting Sport Management Research and sport management practitioners. In particular, they discuss the language and jargon of research, which can be at times too technical, too unfamiliar and, dare we say, too 'academic'. Additionally, practitioners may not always see the relevance to the work they are actually undertaking. These are all concerns that the sport management researcher should heed before embarking on their research project. They should ask some important questions of themselves: Is this topic relevant? Who will benefit from this research? If the answers to these questions are that the topic is of relevance only to the researcher, and the researcher her/himself is the primary beneficiary of the research outcome, then serious consideration should be given before proceeding down this particular path.

Sport Management Research can add important information to the discipline's knowledge base. Such information, where relevant, can be drawn on by other researchers, practitioners, policy makers, and even other stakeholders such as club members, athletes, fans, existing and potential sponsors, advertisers, marketers and any other interested member of the general public. For the researcher, a particular research study may be on a topic or issue previously ignored, or perhaps on a 'new' topic that had never been considered before. The research may also build on previous research studies, providing results to confirm or extend the previous study, or even to question its findings. This is true of any academic discipline and sport management is no exception. A research report might provide a study that has not been

**5**

conducted and thereby fill a void in existing knowledge. It can also provide additional results to confirm or disconfirm results of prior studies.

Research can assist in advancing organizational practices through suggesting new ideas to improve organizational effectiveness and efficiencies. It can help practitioners evaluate approaches that they hope will work in their own management settings and at a broader level create relationships between sport managers who may be trying out similar ideas in different locations. Research also informs conversations, for example by influential policy makers, which might directly impact on sport managers. For example, policy decisions relating to drugs in sport or the funding of youth sport in deprived areas. Research can help the policy makers weigh up various perspectives and make informed decisions: decisions that therefore should be fair, contextualized, responsible and (hopefully) effective.

## TRENDS IN SPORT MANAGEMENT

We have set forth what makes Sport Management Research different and the reasons for conducting Sport Management Research. But what are the current trends in sport management that a future researcher has the opportunity to study? Some broad environmental trends have opened research opportunities to many of the same disciplines we discussed above, and include technological advancements, commercialization and globalization. Each of these trends affects sport, and often in different ways than in business or health. In addition, each trend compounds with the others creating a complex web of pressures for change.

Technological advancements have made the quantity and quality of sport engagement swell. It is easier than ever (and will continue to get easier) to watch sport on television, computers and mobile devices. This has led to a global audience for many sport teams and leagues, increasing the commercialization of these properties. Fan engagement via the Internet, especially on social media websites, provides an opportunity to build stronger relationships with a global audience and expand sponsorship sales. However, the global demand drives up player costs and broadcast rights fees – which are also increased because the quantity and quality of offsite spectating is reducing the growth rate in onsite spectating. Gate receipts, formerly the largest revenue generator for sports, have fallen behind broadcast rights as primary income for many top level leagues.

Globalization and technological advances are beginning to shift the balance of power from traditional commercialized sporting regions (i.e. North America, Europe) to largely populated regions (i.e. South America, Asia Pacific). The rise of the economically emerging BRICS nations (Brazil, Russia, India, China, South Africa) in the global sport market adds significant opportunity to develop sport. Mega-events are targeting these nations, with the International Olympic Committee recently awarding bids to China (Beijing, 2008), Russia (Sochi, 2014), and Brazil (Rio de Janeiro, 2016), and the Federation of International Football Association (FIFA) awarding the World Cup bids to South Africa, 2010 and Brazil, 2014.

Technology, globalization, and commercialization may be the principal trends; however they are not the only trends affecting sport management. Researchers have the opportunity to study other trends, including modernization of sport organization governance, regulatory changes, innovative equipment and merchandizing, demographic changes (i.e. aging populations, change in employment patterns, increasing diversity), sport for development and many more. More recently, the management of doping has been in the forefront of Sport Management Research.

## TYPES OF SPORT MANAGEMENT RESEARCH

In this book we refer to two main types of research: *basic research* and *applied research*. These are, in effect the 'extremes' of the research continuum with basic research being at one end and applied research at the other, as their methods and applicability to the sport management practitioner are so diverse. In the field of sport management, research is generally not only basic or applied, but often a combination of both.

Basic research is theoretical in nature, and deals with theoretical problems. It looks to try and make sense of the world and the way in which the world operates. In general, the research takes place in a controlled setting such as a laboratory, but for the sport manager this could be an interview room or any other venue where the researcher can control the conditions under which the research takes place. In this situation, the results of research may have little direct application for the sports manager (i.e. a team manager or government health promoter). The research may yield important data for the researcher and other academics interested in the same theory or problem. However, the form in which the research is reported/conveyed, i.e. academic journals, and the types of data collected make it unlikely to be of direct relevance to a sport management setting. Applied research on the other hand takes place in the real world, or real world settings such as the sporting organization, and therefore, if undertaken well, can produce results that are relevant to the sport management practitioner and can be implemented back within the specific sporting organization to improve practice. Most Sport Management Research is neither purely applied nor purely basic, but incorporates some aspects of both.

The second way of classifying research projects involves looking at the distinctive methodological features of the research. These are: (1) organizational and design concerns such as whether or not the proposed research is exploratory or highly structured; and (2) the conceptual and theoretical frame of reference that will guide the research – that is, qualitative or quantitative research.

Manheim and Rich (1995) define *exploratory research* as:

> research intended only to provide greater familiarity with the phenomena one wants to investigate so that one can formulate more precise research questions and perhaps develop hypotheses. Such studies can be essential when a sport management researcher is investigating new phenomena or phenomena that have not been studied before (p. 89).

In contrast, *structured research* refers to a research process that follows a relatively familiar patterned arrangement. For example, in a structured study, the researcher organizes or *structures* what one is looking for according to a protocol that guides him/her in terms of 'What to look for, the order in which to make observations and the way to record the results' (p. 202).

As a future sport management researcher, it is necessary to understand the various types of research that exist as it can influence your research questions and your research design. When you have completed this text it will become clear how the type of research you engage with affects the way it can be interpreted, reported and utilized.

## SPORT MANAGEMENT RESEARCH METHODOLOGIES

To begin, we would argue that there is no one best research approach. The sport management researcher will determine which approach will be most effective for the resolution of their specific research question, and this is often determined by the nature of the question or topic being investigated. The research methodology chosen will generally be influenced by the philosophical beliefs of the researcher, as well as the resources available to conduct the research – including available participants and the research site. Undertaking research from a quantitative, qualitative or mixed methods perspective affects the approach to the research process itself.

### A quantitative approach to Sport Management Research

It has been suggested that quantitative approaches to Sport Management Research have historically dominated the discipline (Amis and Silk, 2005). Quantitative research is a type of research in which the researcher decides what to study, asks specific, narrow questions, collects quantifiable data from participants, analyses these numbers using statistics and attempts to conduct the inquiry in an unbiased, objective manner. Creswell (2008) sees three main features of quantitative research that are prevalent today:

- collecting and analysing information in a numeric form;
- collecting scores and then using them to measure the performance or attributes of individuals and organizations;
- procedures and processes by which groups are compared or by which factors common to individuals or groups are related through experiments, surveys, correlation studies and other methods. (p. 48)

In general terms, when employing this approach the researcher will look at trends or variables whose relationship can be defined in a quantifiable manner. For example, variables such as gender or age, and attitudes towards a specific type of behaviour such as illicit drug use in sport, or undesirable off-field behaviour, could be studied to determine whether there is a relationship between the two and whether one variable influences another.

### A qualitative approach to Sport Management Research

Under qualitative research 'the researchers attempt to understand the behaviour and institutions by getting to know well the persons involved, their values, rituals, symbols, beliefs and their emotions' (Nachimas and Nachimas, 1992, p. 287). Qualitative research presents an alternative to the traditional form of quantitative research. Creswell (2008) sees the current characteristics of qualitative research as:

- A recognition by researchers that they need to listen to the views of research participants;
- A recognition that researchers need to ask general, open questions and collect data in those places where people live and work;
- A recognition that research can advocate for change and better the lives of individuals. (p. 51)

Qualitative research has been constantly evolving, with the development of naturalistic inquiry, or constructivism, to emphasize the importance of the participant's view; to take into account the setting or context in which the participants expressed those views; and to look at the meanings that people assigned to different issues. During the 1980s and 1990s, types of qualitative research design emerged including case studies, grounded theory research and narrative inquiry, along with the emergence of qualitative computer software programs for data analysis – examples include NVivo and Qualysis.

In the 1990s and 2000s researchers have seen the emergence of participatory and advocacy practices in qualitative research, themes that express concern for the needs of individuals in lower social classes, racial groups and women. These themes called for researchers to report, as part of their research, their own personal biases, values and assumptions. It cast research into politics in which it considered the rights of women, gays, lesbians, racial groups and different classes in our society – all traditionally under-represented in mainstream sport – and honoured different viewpoints during both the writing and the reading of qualitative reports. It also spoke about qualitative data collection procedures in which inquirers were sensitive to participants, actively collaborated with them (rather than studying them) and respected the dignity of each individual who offered data for research.

## A mixed method approach to Sport Management Research

With the mixed method approach, the sport management researcher decides to collect both quantitative data (quantifiable data) as well as qualitative data (images, interviews, stories). This is not merely a process of collecting two distinct types of data – quantitative and qualitative – the researcher needs to merge, integrate, link or embed both separate types of data.

One form of mixed method design that can be successfully utilized by the sport management researcher is *triangulation mixed methods*. In a *triangulation* study the researcher gathers both quantitative and qualitative data, analyses both datasets separately, compares the results from the analysis of both datasets, and makes an interpretation as to whether the results support or contradict each other. The direct comparison of the two data sets by the researcher provides a more reliable perspective on the problem being studied: a 'triangulation' of data sources.

The strength of this design is that it combines the advantages of each form of data – i.e. quantitative data provides for generalizability whereas the qualitative data offers information about the context or setting. This design enables a researcher to gather information that uses the best features of both quantitative and qualitative data collection. It can be difficult, however,

**9**

to transform one form of data into the other form in order to integrate and compare data. Additionally, even if integration of the data is possible, inconsistent results may emerge, making it necessary to collect additional data or revisit the collected databases to reconcile the differences.

What the above discussion indicates is that as a potential sport management researcher there are a number of methodologies and approaches that you can choose to employ. Before you can do this, however, you need to have a sound understanding of each method as well as the knowledge of how to implement a research study that may employ one of these methods. We devote much of this text to providing you with this knowledge, as we believe such knowledge is essential for sport managers in the twenty-first century.

## RESEARCH PARADIGMS

We believe that it is important that sport management researchers understand research paradigms and that they have an understanding of the major frameworks that they will come across in their reading. This is because it is not a matter of having a theory and putting it into practice, nor of doing something and deriving a theory from it, but of both theory and practice happening simultaneously, interactively and continuously. Understanding the range of possible frameworks, and how others have used them is key to understanding your own processes of thought. Paradigms can be considered as ways of seeing the world in terms of perceiving, understanding and interpreting a theory, explanation, model or map. Edwards and Skinner (2009) believed that most sport management researchers have an intellectual framework that governs the way they perceive the world, and their own place within it, even if they are unable to articulate just what that framework is.

This paradigm, or framework, shapes research from the beginning to the end, because it provides the structure within which choices (including the initial choice of a research subject) are made. This framework comes partly from the institutional setting within which research takes place – the position taken by employers or those who commissioned the research, or by supervisors, by the department within which researchers work and by the university/college that employs them. Part of it will come from the personal position of the sport management researcher which may have been shaped by their biography of experiences as well as their previous education, political and religious beliefs, gender, sexual preference, race and/or class affiliations. So your choice of a research topic, its conduct and its results will be governed by your own beliefs about your understanding of what constitutes knowledge and knowing.

Research paradigms can shape our thinking (and research) processes as they allow us to understand what kinds of knowledge are possible, and how we can ensure they are both adequate and legitimate (Maynard and Purvis, 1994). As an introduction to this way of thinking, we will touch on three research paradigms: (1) objectivism, (2) constructivism and (3) subjectivism.

Objectivism suggests there is an objective reality and things exist irrespective of observers. Understandings and values are objectified in those being researched, and if we go about it 'the right way' we can discover objective truth. We often associate objectivism with positivism, as both approaches sense the bases of valid knowledge and suggest that knowledge is advanced through careful observation and experiment. It is argued that theory is universal and not context bound. Such approaches search for an invariant causal relationship and imply that there is a body of scientific knowledge waiting to be found through rigorous objective research often referred to as the 'scientific method'.

Constructivism suggests there is no universal objective truth 'awaiting discovery' and that there is no meaning without mind and therefore truth/meaning is not discovered but constructed. Truth (meaning) comes into existence in, and out of, our engagement with our unique realities. Constructivist approaches include interpretivism, which suggests that life is explained in terms of multiple interacting factors and that cause and effect are mutually interdependent. Humans make sense of their world by construing or constructing and therefore it is impossible to have complete objectivity. We need to understand each individual in context and not pursue general laws, as the world is composed of tangible and intangible multifaceted realities that are best studied holistically. In this light, inquiry is value laden as values influence the framing, conduct and focusing of the research problems. Similarly, the constructivist approach can be seen in critical approaches to research that acknowledge that a great deal of life cannot be personally controlled. Interpretations of reality only make sense against a background of social rules, practices and beliefs. Critical approaches argue that research must involve the reformulating, or 'resymbolizing', of events through constructing rather than through discovery, recording or transmitting. In critical approaches, including feminism and queer theory, the fundamental aim is liberation and emancipation.

Finally, subjectivism suggests that truth (meaning) comes into existence in, and as a product of, our engagement with our world realities as there is no reality 'out there'. Meaning cannot originate in an interaction between humans and their world realities, since the latter are not valid. Subjectivism is associated with the post-structural and postmodern domains. These domains reject faith in reason, rationality and belief in evolutionary progress. They seek to challenge the authority of convention and science and examine the ideological underpinnings of convention and science. Researchers who work within these domains argue that knowledge claims must be set within the conditions of the contemporary world and embrace multiple perspectives of race, class, gender, age, sex orientation and other group affiliations. As such they acknowledge and recognize the importance of different discourses and of marginalized people, and reject meta-narratives or universals that hold true everywhere. For post-structuralists it is through the deconstruction of texts that researchers are able to expose contradictions, inconsistencies and concealed hierarchies of power/oppression.

## HYPOTHETICAL CASE EXAMPLE: RESEARCH INTO THE CULTURE OF DRUGS IN SPORT

Members of a rugby team have been identified as taking performance enhancing drugs. Following a series of media stories, 'leaks', suspensions and even a prosecution, the team's management wish to know whether the culture of drug taking remains endemic in their team. They commission you to research the team's cultural beliefs towards drug taking.

The three frameworks above would take a very different approach to this question.

An objectivist (or positivist) would seek to measure the team's culture, as objectively as possible, perhaps using validated questionnaires – on the grounds that if it cannot be objectively observed/measured then it is not 'real'. Likewise, the objectivist approach would seek to use universally applicable theories of team culture to frame the issue and interpret any data generated.

A constructivist (or interpretivist) would seek to understand the unique and immeasurable way in which the team's culture is constantly constructed and reconstructed by its members. While no universally 'valid' theory can be applied, rules describing the transmission of beliefs and attitudes could be described and used to identify key individuals, groups and networks that might allow a successful intervention to prevent/reduce drug taking.

A subjectivist would reject the possibility of either applying a general theory or generating a unique theory for this particular social group. Instead, the subjectivist might seek to participate in the group's processes and interactions, with a view to influencing attitudes and beliefs (as well as personally experiencing their content and transmission). While the 'system' may be influenced and experienced, no objective knowledge about it can be generated or extracted, and at best the researcher's experiences will form any resultant 'data'.

Which approach do you most agree with, and why?

We shall explore research paradigms later in this text, as Sport Management Research embraces a diverse array of practices driven by varying knowledge constituting assumptions. This eclecticism legitimizes distinctive perspectives and research agendas yet identifies a need to be concerned about how and why in particular social contexts certain research practices are deemed valuable while others are discounted as valueless aberrations.

## STRUCTURE OF THE BOOK

From the above discussion it is clear that the field of Sport Management Research is diverse, complex and constantly evolving. Key to dealing with the complexity of the sport management environment is the ability to undertake research. In the following chapters we set out a framework for the sport management researcher to be able to do this, as well as provide an insight into the different approaches and methods that can be used by the sport management researcher. Through this understanding we hope that you will be able to answer important questions and investigate issues of relevance to both the sport management researcher and the sport management practitioner in order to provide potential solutions to emerging problems in the world of Sport Management Research. In Chapter 2 we present an overview of the research process, beginning with an overview of the three research paradigms discussed in this book: qualitative, quantitative and mixed methods. Chapter 3 continues the discussion of the research process by looking at how a sport management researcher identifies their research problem, conducts a review of the literature and, importantly, considers the ethical implications of the research study to be undertaken.

Part 2 of this book examines qualitative research processes. Chapter 4 examines different qualitative data collection techniques and their applicability to the field of Sport Management Research. Chapter 5 then explores techniques of qualitative data analysis, including trends, and methods of determining validity. The following chapters then discuss particular qualitative methodologies that have the potential to be utilized by sport management researchers. Chapter 6 looks at Action Research, and the iterative cycle of plan, act, observe and reflect (and plan again based on the outcome of the first cycle), which the sport management researcher will undertake from within the organization. Chapter 7 discusses case study method and how it allows the researcher to delve into a real-life context and produce a rich description from which to understand the situation. Deconstruction and its applicability to the study of sport management literature are discussed in Chapter 8. The discussion of discourse analysis and ethnomethodology in Chapter 9 looks at how these methodologies discover 'ways of being' and how people make sense of themselves and others in everyday life, and how these methodologies can be applied to Sport Management Research in real and practical ways. Chapter 10 looks at traditional ethnography, including some emerging ethnographies such as autoethnography, netnography, ethnodrama and phenomenography, and discusses the applicability of these emerging ethnographies to Sport Management Research. Chapter 11 discusses the concept of gender as a methodology. In particular, the concepts of feminism and queer theory are examined, and we discuss the impact these theories could have on the sport management environment. Narrative inquiry and the stories sport management researchers can tell is the focus of Chapter 12. We examine narrative inquiry as a qualitative research methodology and look at the capacity it has to bring to the field of Sport Management Research an understanding of the unique experiences of sport managers. Chapter 13 addresses phenomenology and looks at how this enables the sport management researcher to gain an understanding of the lived experience of those in the sport management field. The final chapter in this section, Chapter 14, looks at emerging qualitative approaches. Here we examine some of the key features of social network theory, whiteness studies, race/critical race theory, disability studies, visual sociology and participant authored audiovisual stories. Additionally this chapter looks at postcolonialism and globalization and discusses how the process of globalization has impacted on world sport.

Part 3 of the book examines quantitative research processes. Chapter 15 begins with an overview of research design for a quantitative study and looks at the most common quantitative designs used by sport management researchers. This chapter also introduces the concepts of descriptive and inferential statistics. Chapter 16 examines data collection methods for a quantitative study and looks at different statistical techniques. We then discuss the principles of sampling and provide examples of a number of sampling techniques that can be used by the sport management researcher, and finally we will introduce some foundation statistical techniques and provide a greater understanding of the place of statistics in Sport Management Research. Quantitative data analysis techniques are discussed in Chapter 17. Statistical software packages are introduced, as are the processes of coding and different ways of presenting the data. Chapter 18 follows on from our earlier discussion of inferential statistics defining the nature and purpose of inferential statistics, and arguing that these statistical methods go further than just describing data: they attempt to determine whether differences or relationships are real due to chance and allow us to infer any such differences to populations. In Chapter 19 correlation and regression analysis is addressed, and we discuss in general terms how the relationships between two or more variables can be explained through the use of statistical techniques. Chapter 20 looks at how the researcher can determine difference among groups and we examine the criteria we use to establish which inferential test should be chosen to effect an appropriate analysis. In the final chapter in this section, Chapter 21, chi-square and Spearman's rho are discussed, both of which are non-parametric tests that are used when you have serious violations of the assumptions required to perform parametric statistical tests.

The final section of the book, Part 4, looks at alternative approaches to Sport Management Research. In Chapter 22 we examine mixed methods approaches to research and look at some of the ways this can be applied to Sport Management Research. Chapter 23 discusses the emerging framework of Research 2.0, and whether this can be adapted to Sport Management Research 2.0.

## Chapter 2

# The Sport Management Research process

## LEARNING OUTCOMES

By the end of this chapter you should be able to:

- compare qualitative, quantitative and mixed methods research approaches;
- discuss the importance of developing a research process;
- explain the basic steps involved in formulating a research process;
- reflect on the differences between qualitative and quantitative research process, and the possible overlaps with a mixed methods approach;
- describe some methods by which a research plan should be evaluated.

## KEY TERMS

*Qualitative research* – research that seeks to provide understanding of human experience, perceptions, motivations, intentions and behaviours based on description and observation, utilizing a naturalistic interpretative approach to a subject and its contextual setting.

*Quantitative research* – research based on traditional, more formal scientific methods, which generates numerical data and usually seeks to establish straightforward causal relationships between two or more variables, using statistical methods to test the strength and significance of the relationships.

*Mixed methods research* – a style of research that adopts research procedures that are typically applied in both quantitative and qualitative studies.

*Research plan* – a detailed description of the procedures that will be used to investigate your topic or problem.

## KEY THEMES

- What are some of the basic differences between qualitative, quantitative and mixed methods approaches?
- How does the research process differ in each of the approaches?

## CHAPTER OVERVIEW

This chapter makes explicit the notion that, when undertaking any research study or investigation, careful and methodical planning on the part of the sport management researcher is required (Edwards and Skinner, 2009). From the outset, the sport management researcher must carefully plan every step of the research process – from formulating the initial question, conducting a review of the literature, refining the research question(s), formulating the research design and determining the methodology to be used. This chapter will look at the different ways the sport management researcher can approach the development of their research plan from the perspective of a quantitative, qualitative or mixed methods approach.

## INTRODUCTION

This chapter is our attempt to distinguish between three research methodology paradigms, in terms of the type of data they generate. A *paradigm* is a perspective based on a set of assumptions, concepts and values that are held by a community of, in this case, sports management researchers. For most of the twentieth century, the *quantitative* paradigm was dominant. During the 1980s, the *qualitative* paradigm came of age as an alternative to the quantitative paradigm, and was often conceptualized (sometimes wrongly) as the polar opposite of quantitative research – after all, all research seeks to answer questions and improve our understanding of phenomena. Finally, as the 'gap' between qualitative and quantitative methods was questioned and closed, mixed-methods research became the legitimate third paradigm, in particular following the publication of the *Handbook of Mixed Methods in Social and Behavioral Research* (Tashakkori and Teddlie, 2003).

## QUANTITATIVE RESEARCH

*Quantitative research* generates numerical, comparable data that, in sports management at least, often entails the use of large-scale survey methodologies, such as questionnaires or structured interviews. If a researcher has stopped you at a stadium or if you have responded to an online survey, in most cases, it falls under the umbrella of quantitative research. Economic impact of a sporting event is a common quantitative study used in sport management, and is often accomplished by in-stadia and/or online surveys of attendee spending. This type of research reaches many more people, but the contact with those people is much quicker than it is in qualitative research. Surveys, however, are not the only available option; Creswell (2009) outlined five different categories of quantitative research designs: experimental; quasi-experimental; single subject experiments; correlation; and survey research. In reality, however, it is often very difficult to conduct controlled experiments in the sport management setting – leaving questionnaires and correlational research as perhaps the most pragmatic quantitative options. As a rule of thumb, quantitative research is often associated with deductive approaches: testing existing theories by using them to make predictions that can then be compared, as impartially as possible, to real and 'accurate' measurements.

## QUALITATIVE RESEARCH

Researchers who use *qualitative research* for their studies are interested in understanding, exploring and discovering. They use interviews and focus groups, analyse documents, observe behaviours in groups, investigate culture and look for trends and patterns in the data they collect. For example, teams often use focus groups to gain valuable data from the local community before undergoing new stadium construction. The data collected is then analysed to find trends in what the community prefers in a new stadium (e.g. seat plans, food outlets), where and how the stadium can be built to minimize disruptions (e.g. noise, traffic), and what other ways the community desires to use the stadium and surrounding facilities outside of team competitions. Under the umbrella of qualitative research, there are many different methodologies, some of which are discussed in later chapters. As a rule of thumb, qualitative research is often associated with inductive approaches: building theories and explanations where none (or nothing suitable) currently exist.

## MIXED METHODS RESEARCH

*Mixed methods research* adopts procedures from both quantitative and qualitative studies, often seeking to balance out the weaknesses of using either approach in isolation. The purpose of these designs is to build upon the synergy and strength that exists between quantitative and qualitative methods, in order to more fully understand a given phenomenon than would be possible using either quantitative or qualitative methods alone. As a rule of thumb, mixed methods studies, like their qualitative counterparts, tend to be deployed in situations where exploration is necessary – open-mindedly detecting and attempting to explain trends in a data set. Continuing the example above, stadium developers often use a mixed methods approach during the tender process. Quantitative methodologies assist in projecting economic, social and environmental impacts of a new stadium, followed by qualitative methodologies that uncover community preferences and influences for those impacts.

## THE RESEARCH PROCESS

Performing research can be challenging, and the sport management researcher beginning a research project with only a blank sheet of paper might feel quite overwhelmed. 'Getting organized' and developing a process can provide a clear pathway that will both guide the research project and offer the researcher some peace of mind. The following section will provide a model research process that can be used as a guide for accomplishing your research project or dissertation. It will discuss research methods and provide a comprehensive graphical model that can be used as a guide to quick-start your research effort. A research process can be defined as a detailed description of the procedures that will be used to investigate your topic or problem. In general, a research plan will include the following two key elements that, between them, encapsulate the ideas and methods the sport management researcher may use:

1   a detailed presentation of the steps to be followed in conducting the study – i.e. an overall view of what, when, where, how and why for performing the research;

**17**

2    a strong idea of how each step will inform the next – i.e. how the literature review
     will frame neat research questions and formulate clear research questions, and how
     the methods and analysis will answer these research questions.

A number of textbooks provide a highly similar overview of a typical research methodology
and, in some cases, the philosophical assumptions underpinning it. For example, Creswell
and Plano-Clark (2010) outlined a typical seven-step process and demonstrated how this
process frames the construction of reports of research studies (see Figure 2.1).
     Using Creswell and Plano-Clark's procedure as a basis for developing a research strategy,
a new eight-step process can be evolved, specific to sports management. The process should
include the steps illustrated in Figure 2.2.

## Unpacking the research process

The research process outlined in Table 2.1 addresses both the research process and a number
of subsequent options in a matrix format, with rows representing the steps in the process
and columns representing those elements in the research designs. The model allows researchers
to locate where they are in the process and compare research designs, options for methods,
analysis and interpretation. The expectation is that having this tool as a map might guide
decision making within the research process, as well as alleviating any confusion experienced

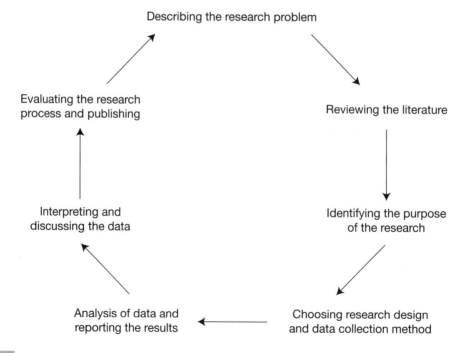

**Figure 2.1**  *The seven steps of research proposals*

Source: Creswell and Plano-Clark (2010, p. 67)

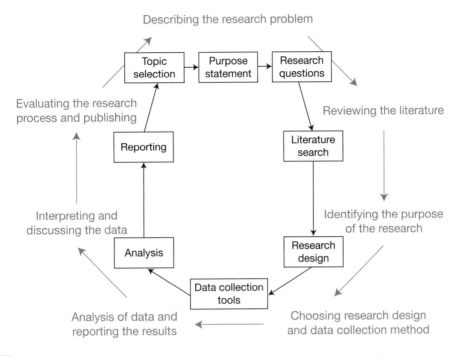

**Figure 2.2** *Mapping a process for Sports Management Research*

by novice sport management researchers. Planning, executing and reporting the research process can all be supported by making reference to the matrix provided here.

While the sequence looks linear in the process, in actual practice there is a great deal of iterative or recursive effort, circling back, to refine and revise earlier steps. It is also important to note that, depending upon the research design, some of the linear/sequential steps can actually occur simultaneously (e.g. data collection and analysis). However, regardless of this real-life 'truth', the writing of proposals and reporting of the process tend to follow quite a common structure and format.

## Preparing the research proposal

The *research proposal* is a document one typically writes with a view to gaining funding, supervision, or to have one's project formally approved (e.g. by an ethics board). Typically, once a research proposal is completed and approved the researcher will be required to follow the proposal submitted just like a contractual obligation. Developing a written research proposal forces the sport management researcher to think through every aspect of the study. However, 'best laid plans' don't always survive exposure to reality, particularly the more exploratory forms of research mentioned above, and with the approval of supervisors or funders, it can be acceptable to change the plan in response to new and interesting findings.

**Table 2.1** *The research process*

| Research designs | Qualitative research | Quantitative research | Mixed methods research |
|---|---|---|---|
| Topic selection | Topic assumes reality is constructed by individuals involved in the research (subjective). Researcher and their biases may be known to participants in the study. | Topic assumes something can be measured objectively. Researcher and their biases are not known to participants in the study (double blind studies). | Objective and subjective researcher characteristics may be known to participants. |
| Purpose statement | Seek to gain an in-depth understanding of what a particular situation, phenomenon or experience means to individuals, groups or cultures. | Test hypotheses, look at cause and effect and make predictions. | Combines rationales. |
| Research question | A *qualitative* research question asks a question about some process, issue, or phenomenon that is to be explored. Uses words such as explore, discover and construct. | A *quantitative* research question is an interrogative sentence that asks a question about the relation that exists between two or more variables. Uses words such as describe, explain and predict. | A mixed method approach seeks to examine a problem or a detailed understanding of a central phenomenon as well as describing at least two variables and a conjectured relationship between them. |
| Literature search | The literature tends to play a minor role in suggesting a specific research question to be asked but justifies the importance of studying the research problem. | The literature tends to provide a major role through suggesting the research questions to be asked. It also justifies the research problem and creates the need for the direction (purpose statement and research question or hypothesis) of the study. | The literature tends to be directive and supportive of both qualitative and quantitative questions/ hypotheses. |
| Research methodology and design | Uses inductive logic. Categories emerge from the informants and lead to patterns or theories that help to explain a phenomenon. Study of behaviour in a natural environment. Designs include narrative, phenomenology, ethnographic, case study, grounded theory approaches. | Uses deductive logic. Concepts, variables and hypotheses are chosen before the study begins. Study of behaviour under controlled conditions isolates causal effects. Designs include experimental, quasi-experimental, single subject experiments, survey and correlation approaches. | Study of behaviour in a natural environment as well as under controlled conditions. |

| | | | |
|---|---|---|---|
| Data collection | *Qualitative* researchers use various types of interviews (including focus groups), observation and field work approaches, and/or examine documents and artefacts (including photos, letters, diaries). | *Quantitative* researchers use surveys, specific measurement tools or instruments; set up control groups; test hypotheses and look for relationships among variables or set up processes for identifying predictions. | Data from open-ended responses, interviews, participant observations, field notes, reflections and precise measurements using structured and validated data collection instruments. |
| Data analysis | Exploratory or bottom–up: the researcher generates a new hypothesis and theory from the data collected. Identifies patterns, features, themes. Data analysis includes a variety of approaches (axial coding, analysis of themes, thick description, structural description, personal bracketing), depending on the type of study being conducted (i.e. narrative, phenomenological, grounded theory, case study or ethnographic study). | Confirmatory or top-down: the researcher tests the hypothesis and theory with the data. Studies use analysis approaches that include the use of descriptive, correlation and inferential statistics. Data analysis is a discrete process that occurs after all of the data has been collected. | Identifies patterns, features and themes as well as statistical relationships. |
| Reporting the results | Narrative report with contextual description and direct quotations from research participants. For *qualitative* research reports, the purpose of the project and the nature of the themes being addressed provide a process for the report. Researchers tend to take a subjective (reflexive) and biased approach. Reflexivity means researchers tend to reflect on their own biases, assumptions and values in the context of the research. Particular or specialized findings that are less generalizable. | Statistical report with correlations, comparisons of means and statistical significance of findings. For *quantitative* research reports, the steps of the quantitative research method are used as the structure of the report. Generalizable findings that can be applied to other populations. | Research reports tend to use flexible, emerging structures and evaluate criteria. Researchers tend to also take an objective unbiased approach. |

## Research proposal purpose

In light of the above requirements to gain supervision, funding and ethical approval, the research proposal has several core purposes:

1   A research proposal should contain all the key elements involved in the *research process* and include sufficient information for the readers to evaluate the proposed study.
2   A research proposal is a *planning tool*: a map or sketch of activities to be executed, resources to be employed and a time frame to be adhered to.
3   A research proposal serves the function of *convincing* people of the value of the proposed work by showing them how the research will make a difference to the world, or by identifying a dilemma in existing theory that the research will help resolve.
4   A research proposal *demonstrates the expertise of the researcher* in a particular area of study by summarizing, comparing and integrating all the relevant theory and existing research pertaining to a specific topic.
5   A research proposal seeks to *demonstrate competency* to carry out the proposed study by describing an appropriate and feasible research method.

Research proposals come in different formats, as different universities, funders and governing bodies will place a different emphasis on certain elements of the research process. For example, some will emphasize scientific rigour, while others might emphasize accessibility and dissemination of findings. Likewise, the process may vary for qualitative and quantitative projects. Tables 2.2 and 2.3 outline a generic proposal and then potential variations when writing qualitative and quantitative proposals.

## THESIS PROPOSAL FORMAT

Although every proposal is unique, they all aim to persuade the reader of one 'big idea'. This central claim is otherwise referred to as the *'thesis'*; hence a research thesis usually refers to the development of one central claim. This tendency is reflected in research degree requirements that ask candidates to demonstrate a 'significant original contribution to knowledge, and/or to the application of knowledge within the field of study'.

With this in mind, the following thesis proposal templates include elements regarding publication, media and/or communication/dissemination of one's project with a writing and communications focus. This template is offered as a guide that may require adaptation based on your research goals. Consult with the appropriate supervisors as you adapt and develop this to your specific thesis project.

## Quantitative methods and the thesis

A thesis using quantitative methods may be seen as a formal application of the scientific method to test certain hypotheses, answer specific questions, examine relationships between/among variables and generalize the results. The focus of this type of thesis may be theoretical or applied.

**Table 2.2** *A generic template for writing a research proposal*

1 Overview of the study
   - Introduction to the study
   - Background to the study

2 Statement of the research problem
   - The qualitative paradigm format
   - The quantitative paradigm format

3 Research objectives/aims

4 Research questions

5 Research hypotheses

6 Research rationale

7 Scope of the study

8 Literature review

9 Conceptual process

10 Definitions, delimitations and limitations

11 The nature of the necessary evidence

12 Selecting a research methodology
   - The qualitative paradigm
   - The quantitative paradigm
   - The mixed methods paradigm

13 Results and their dissemination

14 Budgeting

15 Referencing

**Table 2.3** *Typical differences between qualitative and quantitative research proposals*

| Qualitative research proposal | Quantitative research proposal |
| --- | --- |
| Identify the general research issue | State the hypothesis |
| Explain how the researcher intends to gain entry to the research site | Determine the participants |
| Identify the participants | Select measuring instruments |
| Estimate the time that will be spent in the field | Choose a specific research design |
| Determine the best ways to collect data | Specify procedures to conduct the study |
| Identify appropriate ways to analyse the data | Stipulate the statistical techniques |

The basic research methodologies of a university thesis using quantitative methods are listed and described in Table 2.4, briefly, to give you an idea of what is involved when tackling a quantitative research thesis.

**Table 2.4** *Typical methodologies adopted within quantitative research projects*

| Research method | Description |
| --- | --- |
| Experimental research | Investigates the effect of the manipulation of one or more independent variable(s) on a dependent variable. This is accomplished by exposing one or more experimental (treatment) groups and comparing the results to one or more control (non-treatment) group(s). Random assignment of subjects to the groups is essential in this design. |
| Quasi-experimental research | Allows the investigator to 'approximate' the conditions of experimental research in a setting that does not allow random assignment to experimental and/or control groups or control and/or manipulation of all important variables. Attention must be given to internal and external validity in this design. |
| Causal-comparative (ex post facto) research | Investigates possible cause-and-effect relationships by identifying some existing consequence (dependent variable) and going back through the data (or time) to search for plausible causal factors (independent variables). |
| Correlational research | Investigates the extent to which variations in one variable are related to variations in one or more other variables. |
| Case and field research | Studies intensively the background, current status and environmental interactions of a given unit. A unit may be described as an individual, group, institution or community. |
| Historical research | Allows the investigator to reconstruct a historical event objectively and accurately in its own unique setting. |
| Philosophical research | Tries to find in the subject matter (philosophical position) a basis for comparison, classification, interpretation or generalization. |
| Theoretical research | Presents a detailed description of a 'theoretical model' that describes the interrelationships among all important variables related to the behaviour under investigation. |

In quantitative research there is a typical chapter structure. This structure may vary depending on the research, the supervisor's preference or a particular university's preferred approach (although this is rare). In general terms, however, the quantitative thesis structure is outlined in Table 2.5.

## Qualitative methods and the thesis

Qualitative research seeks answers to questions that are not easily quantified, such as those involving an individual's experience, different social settings and the individuals who inhabit those settings. Qualitative researchers are most interested in how humans make sense of their surroundings through symbols, metaphors, rituals, social structures, social roles and so forth. Qualitative methods emphasize measures that are intentionally unobtrusive.

Creswell (2007) identifies five approaches to qualitative research that encompass specific data collection and analysis tactics; these approaches are outlined in Table 2.6.

**Table 2.5** *A typical chapter structure for a quantitative research thesis*

|  | Quantitative thesis format |
| --- | --- |
| Chapter 1 | Introduction:<br>General statement of the problem, background of the problem, significance of the problem, definition of terms as necessary. |
| Chapter 2 | Review of relevant literature:<br>Comprehensive review of articles relevant to the study. This review justifies, to some extent, the researcher's methodology and provides a rationale for research. |
| Chapter 3 | Design:<br>Specific statement of the problem hypotheses to be tested, general methodology, including analytical procedures, population/sample instrumentation, if any. |
| Chapter 4 | Results:<br>Findings and interpretations of data. |
| Chapter 5 | Summary:<br>Conclusions, limitations of the study and recommendations for further research. |

**Table 2.6** *Typical methodologies adopted within qualitative research projects*

| Research approach | Description |
| --- | --- |
| Narrative approach | Focuses on the analysis of stories portrayed by an individual through text or discourse. It includes collecting stories, reporting experiences described and chronologically ordering the experiences. |
| Phenomenological approach | Focuses on the common conscious experience of a phenomenon shared by multiple people. It describes the essence of how and what the participants experience without additional explanation or analysis. |
| Grounded theory approach | Focuses on a large sample of interpretations regarding a process, action or interaction. Interpretations provide the data from which to generate a theory about the phenomenon. |
| Ethnographic approach | Focuses on the shared patterns of behaviour, beliefs and language developed among a group of people. Research describes how the culture works through the analysis of shared values. |
| Case study approach | Focuses on the values, behaviours and interactions within a bounded system. The report describes themes based on detailed data collection from the specific case. |

Most recent qualitative research includes such methods as: case studies; observation of experiments in natural settings; interviewing; historical analysis (historiography); and analysis of documents/texts. A suggested format for a thesis based on qualitative methods is outlined in Table 2.7. Exceptions, revisions and modifications to this format are acceptable.

**Table 2.7** *A typical chapter structure for a qualitative research thesis*

| | Qualitative thesis format |
|---|---|
| Chapter 1 | Introduction:<br>Orientation of the study, stating the research problem and placing it into theoretical and/or historical context. |
| Chapter 2 | Literature review:<br>Comprehensive review of articles relevant to the study, justifying, to some degree, the researcher's own methodology. |
| Chapter 3 | Methodology:<br>• Explanation of how research was accomplished: what the data consisted of; how the data were collected, organized and analysed. Justification for the analytic strategy.<br>• Participants: who the subjects were, how they were selected, what steps were taken to protect them from risks.<br>• Nature of data: e.g. interview, ethnography, videotapes, etc., and how data was selected.<br>• Description of research setting: validity and reliability of the research data may depend on the appropriateness of the setting selected. |
| Chapter 4 | Findings and results:<br>• Findings refer to what the data actually are.<br>• Results offer interpretations and analyses of these data. |
| Chapter 5 | Summary:<br>Conclusions, limitations of the study and recommendation for further research. |
| References | Referencing format normally applied is APA. |

## Features of a mixed methods thesis

A mixed methods approach will choose a mixture of the features above from both qualitative and quantitative approaches that will suit the research problem being studied. In this format, the researcher brings together various elements of qualitative and quantitative research formats. A more detailed typical format of a mixed research proposal is given below to allow you to identify the different quantitative and qualitative components of the study.

1  Introduction
   a)  Statement of the problem
   b)  Purpose of the study (including rationale for mixing quantitative/qualitative statements)
   c)  Research questions (quantitative/qualitative)
   d)  Literature review (separate section, if quantitative)
   e)  Scope and limitations of the study
2  Procedures/methods
   a)  Characteristics of mixed method research
   b)  Type of mixed methods design (including decisions involved in its choice)
   c)  Visual model and procedures of the design
   d)  Data collection procedures (types of data, sampling strategy)

e)   Data analysis and validity procedures

f)   Role of the researcher

3   Anticipated ethical issues

4   Significance of the study

5   Preliminary pilot findings

6   Expected outcomes or advocacy/participatory changes (including empowerment)

7   Appendices

## Using a self-evaluation checklist

A quick checklist of typical tasks to be completed will assist in focusing the research and will allow you to check you have not missed anything important. An example of such a checklist is outlined in Table 2.8.

# CONCLUSION

The sport management researcher will approach the development of their research process from the perspective of either a quantitative, qualitative or mixed methods approach. Regardless of the approach, the sport management researcher must carefully plan every step of the research process, from formulating the initial question, conducting a review of the literature, refining the research question(s), to formulating the research design and determining the methodology to be used. To enhance our understanding of the research process further we need to look at how a sport management researcher identifies their research problem, conducts a review of the literature and, importantly, considers the ethical implications of the research study to be undertaken. This is the focus of our next chapter.

# REVIEW QUESTIONS

Undertaking any research study or investigation requires careful and methodical planning on the part of the sport management researcher.

- Identify one type of research study where quantitative research methodologies would be most effective.
- What might be some of the advantages of using a mixed methods approach?
- What would a typical research plan look like for your project, and can you start to formulate a proposal for it?

# SUGGESTED EXTENDED READING FOR STUDENTS

Edwards, A. and Skinner, J. (2009). *Qualitative research in sport management*. Oxford: Elsevier.

**Table 2.8** *Self-evaluation checklist*

*Questions*

1    Thesis topic
- Is the topic clear and well defined?
- Does it involve a problem, question or hypothesis that sets the agenda and points precisely to what needs to be explored or discovered?

2    Literature review
- Have you accessed the most recent literature of relevance to your topic, as well as seminal sources from the past?
- Do you refer to major books, articles, artefacts? Since quality is more important than quantity, how well have you selected your material?
- Does the literature review hang together, to show how the ideas and findings have developed, or is it merely a shopping list of books and articles?
- Is the review critical? Does it briefly evaluate, showing how your dissertation fits into what is mistaken or lacking in other studies? The literature review should provide a critically appraised context for your studies.

3    Theoretical underpinnings
- Does theory permeate the structure from beginning to end; from statement of problem to conclusion? Are you asking yourself a key question, presenting a thesis or defending a statement? Be clear about your approach.
- Theory is the framework of your study – not a luxury. Your thesis will be judged, in part, by how well you express and critically understand the theory you are using, and how clearly and consistently it is connected with the focus and methodology of your dissertation.

4    Methodology
- Is your choice of methods and research techniques well suited to the kind of problem you are studying? Methods work if they provide a persuasive response to your question, positive or negative.
- Is your description of the methods you have adopted clear enough to take a blueprint and replicate?

5    Results
- Are your findings faithful to what you actually found – do you claim more than you should? Don't 'massage' your evidence or findings.
- Have you provided enough evidence to make a convincing case?
- Have you presented everything directly relevant to the question in such a way that the reader doesn't have to flip back and forth to make their own connections?
- Are results or findings clearly and accurately written, easy to read, grasp and understand?

6    Conclusions
- Have you answered the question 'so what?' What should we do with your findings and conclusions? What do they imply?
- Findings don't speak for themselves – they need to be analysed. Have you explained what your findings mean and their importance, in relation to theory and practice?

## Chapter 3

# Identifying the research problem, conducting a literature review, and ethical considerations

## LEARNING OUTCOMES

By the end of this chapter you should be able to:

■ identify the research problem;
■ distinguish between inductive and deductive reasoning;
■ describe the process for conducting a literature review;
■ identify major ethical considerations involved in Sport Management Research;
■ describe some potential conflicts of interest related to Sport Management Research.

## KEY TERMS

*Inductive reasoning* – from data to theory – where individual observations that appear to be linked allow the researcher to formulate models and theories that might explain the pattern observed.

*Deductive reasoning* – from theory to data – testing theoretical explanations by isolating the predictions that they make about reality, and testing whether these predictions are accurate.

*Hypothesis* – a clear statement of what observations or effects will be observed if the theory is correct ($H_1$, 'research' hypothesis), or if the theory is incorrect ($H_0$, the 'null' hypothesis).

*Delimitations* – restrictions imposed by the researcher to ensure that the experiment remains controlled, so that s/he can be more confident that the specific things they examined caused the changes they observed.

*Basic research* – highly constrained experiments, often conducted in lab conditions with strict delimitations, which therefore loses immediate social significance. Delivers a 'pure' test of theory, but may not translate into 'real-life' settings.

*Applied research* – addresses immediate problems for improving practice and is evaluated on the basis of its contribution to the solution of immediate problems.

*Literature review* – a critical comprehensive reporting of any existing literature that is relevant to the study being conducted by the researcher.

*Research problem* – a concise and clear statement that provides the context for the research study, and that generates specific research questions that the research study aims to answer.

*Ethics* – a set of principles of right conduct, and the rules and standards governing the actions of a person. Generally, ethical principles exist to ensure the protection of research participants, the researchers themselves, the universities/institutes overseeing the research, and the discipline as a whole.

*Integrity* – steadfast adherence to a strict moral or ethical code.

*Beneficence* – the state of being beneficial.

*Consent* – acceptance or approval of what is being done or planned by another. Where possible, informed consent (giving consent in the full knowledge of planned actions and likely consequences) is viewed as preferable to simple consent.

*Coercion* – compelling by force of authority, by deceit or by the use of inappropriate incentives or punishments.

*Conflict of interest* – competing interests that may undermine the researcher's pursuit of 'pure knowledge', for example financial links to companies interested in 'proving' a particular result.

## KEY THEMES

- What is a research problem?
- What are different types of research?
- What is a literature review?
- Where does the sport management researcher get research ideas from?
- What are the legal and ethical considerations that need to be considered by the sport management researcher?

## CHAPTER OVERVIEW

It is an important part of the research process for the sport management researcher to precisely identify the area they want to investigate. To do this, they must first critically examine what has been published in the area, and this process will help them to work out how they should go about conducting the investigation (and why). Once the researcher has determined these things then it is possible to address the first part of a research thesis – the introduction. This chapter looks at the various ways in which the sport management researcher can determine a suitable research topic/question.

## INTRODUCTION

Many sport management problems may not be appropriate for a research study. They may simply be trivial issues that do not require further investigation – such as, are there more blonde haired football players than those with brown hair in the draft? It is very unlikely that answering this question would provide meaningful insight into sport management. The sport management researcher should avoid trivial research problems, as well as those studies that lack any theoretical relevance. If there is no theoretical framework to inform or guide a study (deductive) and any study designing one (inductive) would struggle to fit alongside existing research, then we need to ask serious questions about the benefit of doing the study. For example, many wristbands that claim to improve performance would require an entirely new branch of physics to explain how they work – so should a sport management researcher concern themselves with this? The final type of problems that the sport management researcher will *avoid* are those where a research topic is 'saturated' and any new studies are either purely replication or do not add meaningful knowledge to the body of literature.

With a literature base that is still emerging in sports management it can sometimes seem that the harder a researcher tries to think of a research topic/question, the more the researcher might feel that their study has already been done. This frustrating experience is the reason why the success of research depends largely on taking a great deal of care during the preliminary preparation of the project (i.e., you'd rather solve this issue early on than find out you've been beaten to the punch after you've collected and analysed your data).

### Selecting the research problem

A research problem involves accurately capturing a key issue regarding existing knowledge – for example: a gap, a deficiency, a contradiction or an uncertainty. As a good rule of thumb, the sport management researcher should ensure that their statement of the problem captures the *who*, the *what*, the *where*, the *when* and the *why* of the problem situation. Good studies often establish the *how* as well. The statement of the problem is a specific and accurate synopsis of the overall purpose of the study, and having read it, any interested reader should immediately understand the relevance and importance of your proposed study.

There are certain criteria that should be taken into consideration when selecting a research problem:

*Workability*: Is the contemplated study within the limits and range of your resource and time constraints? Will you have access to the necessary sample size to generate the numbers required (e.g. to enable statistical comparisons)? Is there reason to believe you can come up with an 'answer' to the problem? Is the methodology that you have planned appropriate, manageable and understandable?

*Critical mass*: Is the problem of sufficient magnitude and scope to fulfil the requirements of your course and level of study? Will it deliver findings of sufficient significance? Will it 'fill' your specified word limit?

*Interest*: Are you interested in the problem area, specific problem and potential solution? Does it relate to your background and career interest? Does it 'turn you on'? Will you learn useful skills from pursuing it? Generally, if you are going to spend 6–12 months (or more) investigating a problem, you had best be interested in the answer.

*Theoretical value*: Does the problem fill a gap in the literature? Will others recognize its importance? Will it contribute to advancement in your field? Does it improve the 'state of the art'? Is it publishable?

*Practical value*: Will the solution to the problem improve sport management practices? Are real-life sports managers and CEOs likely to be interested in the results? Will future research be changed or informed by the outcomes? Will your own research practices be likely to change as a result?

## Finding a problem

There are many problem situations that may give rise to research. Bless, Higson-Smith and Kagee (2006) suggest that research problems can be classified according to the motives or interests that drive them, using the following criteria: observation of reality, theory, previous research, practical concerns and personal interest.

1   *Observation of reality* denotes that research questions may be developed by researchers' observations of everyday life, usually observations that require exploration and explanation.

2   *Theory* may, for example, denote conflicting theoretical positions, i.e. two theories to explain the same phenomenon, or theories that make wholly contradictory predictions. Such conflicts present an ideal opportunity for researchers.

3   *Previous research* can also identify conflicting findings and observations, leading to uncertainty about which theory or management practice is 'best'. Rather than leaving such conflicts unresolved, such contradictory (or 'equivocal') findings present ideal opportunities for sports management researchers.

4   *Practical concerns* usually arise from sport managers and practitioners (such as the management trainers). Practical concerns are generally driven by problems experienced in the everyday practice of sports managers, rather than being motivated by conflicts between theories or findings.

5   *Personal interest* describes the very real and normal situation, that researchers have their own special areas of interest, and that their interest inspires their research topics – for example, the desire to follow a career in that field, or a friend or family member who has been affected in some way.

Additionally as a researcher in sport management you should:

■   be aware of the research being done at your institution. If possible be aware of research being undertaken by colleagues or fellow researchers at other institutions;

■   be alert to any controversial issues that may arise in your area of interest;

■   be aware of what is *big* in sport management at the moment – e.g. drugs in sport, salary cap, corruption?

■   discuss the potential research with your peers, lecturers, PhD students.

Where they exist, read a review paper covering your topic (i.e. a paper that uses other research findings as its 'data') and from there read any relevant research studies from the reference list. From the search you should make a list of research questions that appear unanswered. Try to balance your research question with your capabilities and experience. It shouldn't be too hard or too easy.

A general process for developing a research problem may involve the following processes:

- outline the general context of the problem area;
- highlight current key theories, concepts and ideas in this area;
- establish what appear to be the underlying assumptions of this area;
- question why the issues identified are important/relevant;
- establish whether there is anything that needs to be solved.

Read around the area (subject) to get to know the background and to identify unanswered questions or controversies, and/or to identify the most significant issues for further exploration.

Clearly specifying the problem is important because it provides a foundation for the research objectives, the methodology, the work plan and budget etc. (e.g. how much money can you justifiably request for the project?). Additionally, a clearly stated research problem makes it easier to find information and reports of similar studies and enables the researcher to clearly explain why the proposed research project should be undertaken. The research problem is a key element of research, and Table 3.1 contains several questions that help determine the feasibility of the research problem.

**Table 3.1** *Criteria for testing the feasibility of the research problem*

Is the problem of current interest in Sport Management Research?

Will it be possible to apply the results in sport management practice?

Does the research contribute to sport management theory?

Will the research identify new problems and lead to further research for sport managers?

Is the research problem important for sport managers?

Will it be practically possible to undertake the research?

Will it be possible for another researcher to repeat the research?

Is the research free of any ethical problems and limitations?

Will it have any value to the field of sport management?

Do you have the necessary knowledge and skills to do the research? Are you qualified to undertake the research?

Is the problem important to you and are you motivated to undertake the research?

Is the research viable in your situation?

Do you have the necessary support for the research?

Will you be able to complete the project within the time available?

Do you have access to the facilities and support the research requires?

## INDUCTIVE AND DEDUCTIVE REASONING

*Inductive reasoning* is where we attempt to explain individual observations that appear to co-occur or 'conjoin' by proposing a mechanism or theory (Figure 3.1). Induction begins from particular observations and builds towards broader generalizations. The classic example is that if a person only ever observes men in senior sport management positions, they will induce a 'rule' that all senior sport managers are men. This also illustrates the inherent weakness of inductive reasoning, as a single female senior sport manager disproves the rule, and this is why we must test theories once they have been generated through induction. Following induction, the progression from the level of 'proposed theory' to that of 'substantiated' theory requires many individual studies that test the specific hypotheses offered by your new theory. This approach is more likely to utilize qualitative methodologies.

*Deductive reasoning* obtains specific hypotheses (predictions) from a theory (Figure 3.2). This involves the use of logical if–then type rules to arrive at a set of expected observations.

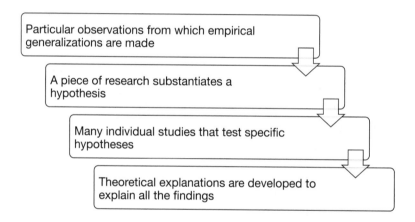

**Figure 3.1** *Inductive reasoning*

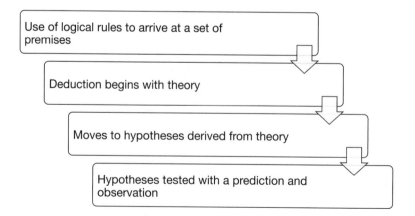

**Figure 3.2** *Deductive reasoning*

For example: Rule 1: All sport marketers are creative. Rule 2: Michelle is a sport marketer. Deduction: Michelle is creative. Deduction begins with theory and then develops specific, testable hypotheses derived from theory, and then tests these hypotheses by making careful and accurate observations.

This approach to testing and theory is often referred to as the hypothetico-deductive method and since it emphasizes hypotheses, prediction and testing, is sometimes held to be the *par excellence* of science. As explained above, theories are used to derive testable predictions, or hypotheses, and then observations are carefully collected to test these predictions. Both forms of reasoning, inductive and deductive, are useful – although the inductive approach tends to be used more in humanities-based research and adopts a qualitative methodology, while the deductive approach tends to be used more in 'hard science' areas and adopts more quantitative methodologies. For example, a sport management researcher may predict that watching the Olympic Games inspires more youth participation in Olympic sports. How might the researcher quantitatively test this hypothesis?

## PURPOSE OF THE LITERATURE REVIEW IN IDENTIFYING THE PROBLEM

A major part of developing the research problem is reading what has already been published about the problem. As indicated earlier, the first step in identifying a problem is locating a series of studies from the literature, and then deciding which studies relate to your chosen topic. To do this successfully the sports management researcher must know how to locate information and then how to use it. If the researcher does this correctly then the knowledge generated can stimulate inductive reasoning – that is, the researcher may attempt to locate and synthesize all relevant literature on a topic to develop a more general explanation or a theory to explain certain phenomena. For example, the sport management researcher might induce that participation in sport leads to greater social cohesion, which will create better communities. Once this has been accomplished the researcher might also discuss their thoughts with peers and fellow researchers/experts to eliminate any unproductive or unpromising approaches.

### Developing hypotheses

Hypotheses are logically derived from previous theories and research findings. For example, a theory (or a new modification to a theory) may make a prediction that has not yet been tested, or alternatively one may make predictions based on the findings of recent similar studies. The 'research hypothesis' always predicts what will happen if the theory is correct, while the null hypothesis always predicts what will be seen if there is no pattern. This is discussed in more detail in Chapter 18.

### Developing the method

The purpose of developing the method is to effectively evaluate the hypothesis. If the method is planned and pilot-tested appropriately, the study's outcome will allow the hypothesis to be evaluated. One could even argue that the researcher has 'failed' when the results of the study are blamed on methodological problems. A review of the literature is very helpful in identifying successful methods, for example recent studies examining the same topic, or other studies that have attempted to use the same experimental design. It is a good idea to pilot-test any unusual methods to determine whether the method answers the specific question asked, and delivers useable data. Otherwise the researcher may find out too late that their method does not answer the question, and their contribution to sport management literature will be undermined.

## BASIC LITERATURE SEARCH STRATEGIES

There is no single right way to undertake a literature search. The search will depend considerably on the researcher's familiarity with the topic. If the researcher has virtually no knowledge about a particular topic, the starting point and sequence will be different from that of somebody already quite familiar with the literature. Most researchers will go straight to a computer to start a literature search. This can certainly be useful, but there are two major weaknesses that the researcher must consider:

1   Generally, only more recent references are available for computer searching, depending on the database used (and in many cases you might still need to go and find a paper copy for older 'classic' references rather than simply clicking on a link).
2   Getting the necessary background and broad overview of the problem from individual studies can be difficult, as many database searches tend to only give individual studies – leaving you as the researcher to evaluate which studies are truly relevant to your own study.

Talk to the reference librarian at your library for guidance in undertaking the literature search.

The review of literature is generally undertaken in two stages: stage one involves a general overview of the relevant area using secondary sources (i.e. books, book chapters and reviews that will give you a broad overview of the area); while stage two involves a more specific and structured review involving primary sources (i.e. to help identify specific research problems and opportunities to contribute). Primary sources are ultimately the most valuable tool for the researcher in that the information is first-hand. Most primary sources in a literature review are peer reviewed journal articles. In sport management some of these journals include: *Sport Management Review*, *Journal of Sport Management*, *European Sport Management Quarterly*, *International Journal of Sport Management*, *International Journal of Sport Communication* and the *International Journal of Sport Management and Marketing*. Dissertations are also primary sources, however dissertations may be difficult to locate as they are often only stored in a university library. Typical databases for searching sport management studies include: Index Medicus (medline); Psychinfo; ERIC; Sports Discus; and of course, the bibliographies of any good articles that you do find. Online search engines, such as Google Scholar, are fast becoming a user-friendly online tool to search many databases at once.

## Literature searching and the Internet

There is no question that the Internet (and its associated hardware) has significantly changed the methodologies of qualitative research. Searching the Internet for resources; using software to manage citations; interviewing participants over the Internet; using dialogues and interactions online as data; and even using online software to analyse your data are all now part and parcel of much scholarship in Sports Management Research. While the Internet can be a valuable and time-effective means of gathering information, sport management researchers must recognize that just because it is available on the Internet, and even if the website looks professional and authoritative, the information contained there is often unreliable or politically motivated. It is essential that the researcher determine the validity and authenticity of information retrieved via the Internet (Denzin and Lincoln, 2005).

### *Some questions to consider regarding website information*

Most government agencies have websites that offer copies of recent reports and policies, whether for free or at a cost. For example, the Australian Sports Commission and Sport England are two such websites. These websites can be a useful source of information as one can at least be sure that the source is original and, in all likelihood, quite influential. Electronic journals are generally very useful, particularly if they are peer reviewed and receive 'impact factors' and indexing. However, you should be wary of websites and blogs that seem to 'replicate' the format of proper journals offering inaccurate, erroneous or fabricated information. As the primary researcher, it is your job to evaluate any and all documents that you use carefully. In general though when using the web as a source for information you may want to ask yourself the following questions:

- Whose website is it? Is it a well-known and reputable organization?
- Is it a reputable individual's website? Be cautious and consider the credibility of the individual who is operating and maintaining the website.
- Is the material dated? Can it be referenced formally using the Harvard system?
- Can the information be corroborated?

## SIX STEPS IN THE LITERATURE SEARCH

If we move away from the basics, there are relatively formal and specific steps to follow that will help to ensure a high-quality literature review:

*Step 1: Write the problem statement.* As discussed above, one can begin by trying to specify what research questions are being asked, and which are the most relevant/important. For example, a sport management researcher might want to find out whether the way that sport managers are trained influences their ethical attitudes. More specifically, the researcher wishes to examine the difference between the 'traditional' management approach of focusing on the economic bottom line versus a triple bottom line management approach. By carefully defining the research problem, the researcher will be able to keep the literature search within reasonable limits. While you may progress through numerous drafts of a problem statement, always try to write the statement as completely (and as concisely) as you can very early in the literature review.

*Step 2: Collate secondary sources.* As noted above, these will offer you a broad oversight of the area so you can begin to 'get your bearings' and navigate around.

*Step 3: Determine descriptors.* What are some of the key words and phrases that relate to your research question?

*Step 4: Search, evaluate and collect primary sources.* Original studies are those that have collected their own data, rather than reviewing the studies of others.

*Step 5: Read and record literature.* While arduous and sometimes very boring, this is the 'meat' of your task in preparing a literature review, and key tasks to guide your reading should include: forming a statement of problem; considering the characteristics of subjects that you will need; the types of measures and instruments you may need to source; the independent and dependent variables in your own study; the experimental design and statistical/ interpretative analyses used; the way you will report findings; and potential questions for further study.

*Step 6: Write the literature review.* A review of literature is not a mere list or summary of books and articles that the researcher has read. Instead, a literature review combines the most significant aspects of the works one has consulted. It is a *combination* and *synthesis* in the form of *an integrated description* of the field of study. In reviewing literature, the reviewer must show awareness of the most important and relevant theories, models, studies and methodologies and should indicate how these are relevant to one's project, and evaluate how these works are similar to and/or different from one's own research.

The literature review serves several important functions. It ensures the production of original work; it acknowledges the contribution of previous works; it demonstrates critical ability to evaluate literal materials; it rationalizes the importance of the problem being studied; it defines the boundaries of the research project; it establishes the size and extent of the research project; it considers the procedures and the instruments that can/should be used in the research project; it casts the 'problem' in a better perspective through a better understanding of the underlying theory in an attempt to render it 'solvable'; it helps to ensure you avoid the unnecessary (non-purposeful) repetition of research already undertaken.; it assists you in evaluating the significance of your own findings (i.e. at the end of the study); it helps to formulate and justify hypotheses and research questions; and it allows the researcher to carry out work more purposefully. In fact a good literature review can be pretty inspirational, believe it or not!

A literature review normally has an introduction, a body (with relevant research organized and synthesized), a summary and conclusions. It is important to include in the literature review a description of the work being done, being critical where necessary. Summarize the main facts and conclusions that emerge, synthesizing to produce main themes, directions/ trends, contradictions etc., and point out those areas in the field that are still inadequately covered.

It is increasingly a good idea to use a software program such as EndNote when conducting the literature review as this will assist you throughout the preparation of your final article or report, by managing your references and producing an 'instant' reference list at the end.

## RECENT CASE EXAMPLE: REVIEW OF SPORT MANAGEMENT LITERATURE

*The following article is an example of how literature review has been used in the past by researchers in Sport Management Research. The interested reader may wish to find/download and read the article for further insights.*

Hostile takeover or joint venture: Connections between institutional theory and sport management research. Washington, M., and Patterson, K. D. W. (2011). *Sport Management Review, 14*(1), 1–12.

Washington and Patterson reviewed the literature on institutional theory as it is often used in Sport Management Research. After a comprehensive analysis of primary sources and summarizing the common concepts, they concluded that sport management researchers have a limited use of all the concepts. They found that sport management studies lack breadth and depth in the concepts of institutional change and organizational field dynamics, and that the use of institutional theory could and should be extended to explore other neglected sport management problems. For example, they suggest that institutional theory may assist in understanding the emergence or decline in sport institutions (i.e. teams, brands and marketing methods).

## ANNOTATED BIBLIOGRAPHY

Developing an annotated bibliography is another procedure to organize research information. Many academic organizations/schools require this highly simplified literature review as part of the initial research process. What the annotated bibliography will display is that the researcher has read and understands the materials gathered. It also identifies critical research issues that directly support the study topic, such as research designs, methodology, samples and findings. For example, a sport management researcher may put together an annotated bibliography on organizational change. This may include the more generic studies on organizational change before eventually being narrowed to those research projects that have examined organizational change in sporting organizations.

## PRESENTING A QUALITATIVE RESEARCH PROBLEM

As noted above, qualitative research tends to address very different topics and questions to quantitative research. It lends itself to inductive research projects, and also to subjects where the main phenomena being studied are very difficult to measure accurately, such as an organizational culture or the processes of managerial change. Creswell (2009) suggested the following guidelines for writing qualitative research questions: (a) present one or two central research questions followed by sub-questions; (b) relate the central research question to the specific qualitative strategy of inquiry; (c) begin the research question with 'what', 'how', 'why', 'what if'; (d) where possible, focus on a single phenomenon or concept; (e) use exploratory verbs: discover, seek to understand, explore a process; (f) use non-directional language (delete words that suggest quantitative study with a directional orientation: affect, influence, impact, determine, cause etc.); (g) be open, and expect that the research questions will evolve and change during the study consistent with the emerging design.

## PRESENTING A QUANTITATIVE PROBLEM

A key aspect of a quantitative study that is quite unique from qualitative approaches, is that the researchers must identify the different *variables*. These variables include the independent variable (IV) – which the experimenters control and vary on purpose, usually by specific amounts, to examine differences in the dependent variable (DV) – which varies in response to the specified changes in the IV, and these changes are measured by the experimenter. In simple terms, we simply measure the effects of making specific changes. We must also consider the role of categorical variables – independent variables that cannot be manipulated (e.g. gender, age). Researchers usually record things such as age, gender and social status to see whether they influence the impact of the IV on the DV, i.e. to determine whether the cause and effect relationship of the independent and dependent variables is different in the presence of the categorical variable or variables.

Finally, we must carefully consider the impact of extraneous variables. These can affect the relationship between independent and dependent variables but are not included, measured or controlled. The possible influence of extraneous variables is usually talked about in the discussion section, especially if attempts to balance them out (randomization, large samples) or control them (constrained/closed lab conditions) may have failed. For example, you could speculate that improving the governance of an organization may improve sporting performances, but this overlooks the impact of extraneous variables such as other teams improving, good or bad 'luck' and injuries.

The researcher decides which variables to manipulate and control. One can control the possible influence of one variable by keeping it out of the study. Thus, the researcher chooses not to assess a variable's possible effect on a relationship between the independent and dependent variables, so this variable is controlled. So, for example, in the above study of organizational governance, failing to measure other teams' investment and performance levels, or only having a very loose measure of team performance (such as simple win:loss records), would mean that the effects of extraneous variables are missed. Rarely are the variables labelled as such in the actual problem statement. As a good rule of thumb, the researcher should identify the independent and dependent variables, and at least discuss how other variables were accounted for and controlled.

## PRESENTING THE HYPOTHESIS: TYPES OF HYPOTHESES

As well as being either experimental or null, hypotheses can be classified in terms of their derivation: inductive or deductive. An inductive hypothesis might be arrived at by speculating, and 'stitching together' different theories to make a novel prediction. A deductive hypothesis is a clear and logical consequence of the theory: 'if the theory is right then this should happen'.

A research hypothesis will state the expected results. For example, a sport manager involved in the fitness industry could hypothesize that the distance from the fitness centre is more influential in determining regular attendance than the types of activities offered. The null hypothesis will state what will be observed if 'nothing unusual' is happening. So, for example, if you predicted a positive correlation between distance-to-gym and usage, the null hypothesis would be 'no relationship' and *not* a negative correlation (which would mean the closer you live, the less you use the gym). This is a common mistake made by undergraduate students. Crucially, the statistics are testing that the null hypothesis can be rejected, and *not* that the experimental hypothesis is 'true'. Rejecting the null does not automatically mean the 'alternate' hypothesis is true, it might mean some other effect that we didn't think of has happened too.

## HYPOTHESES AND THE RESEARCH PROBLEM

With respect to the relationship between a hypothesis and a research problem, both hypothesis testing and addressing the research problem contribute to the body of knowledge, for example by supporting or refuting an existing theory. However, a hypothesis differs from a problem. A problem is formulated in the form of a question; it serves as the basis or origin from which a hypothesis is derived. Thus, a hypothesis is not on the same level with a research problem. A hypothesis is a derivative of a problem, and the same problem could precipitate many different hypotheses and tests. Besides this understanding of their relationship that one is born out of the other, a problem (question) cannot be directly tested, whereas a hypothesis can and should be tested and verified (De Wet, Monteith, Steyn and Venter, 1981).

## Purpose and function of hypotheses

Hypotheses have several very important functions related to the research project as well as general knowledge building:

- They provide direction towards resolution of a problem. It is a scheme that points towards what can be done and how problems can be solved.
- They *offer explanations for the relationships between those variables that can be empirically tested.*
- Their development helps to ensure *the researcher has sufficient background knowledge to enable him/her to make suggestions in order to extend existing knowledge.*
- They *give direction to an investigation.*
- They can *structure the next phase in the investigation.*

## Formulating hypotheses

Because hypotheses give structure and direction to research, the following aspects should be kept in mind when formulating a hypothesis:

■ Hypotheses can only be formulated after the researcher has gained enough knowledge regarding the nature, extent and intensity of the problem. A hypothesis is formulated after the problem has been stated and the literature study has been concluded. It is formulated when the researcher is totally aware of the theoretical and empirical background to the problem.

■ Hypotheses are tentative statements/solutions to be tested, derived from explanations of the formulated problem.

■ The research problem does not have to consist of one hypothesis only. The type of problem area investigated, and the extent that encircles the research field are the determining factors on how many hypotheses will be included in the research proposal.

Hypotheses cannot be formulated in qualitative research because qualitative research is conducted for description, exploration and discovery. Instead of hypotheses, qualitative researchers pose research questions and some of these research questions even emerge as the study progresses. On the other hand, while a qualitative researcher is in the field, some hypotheses may be inductively generated and later tested. Further discussion with examples of hypothesis testing is taken up in Chapter 18.

## DEFINITIONS

The researcher must define every term that is directly associated with the study. The *operational definition* is the observable phenomenon that enables the researcher to empirically test whether or not the predicted outcomes can be supported. If the researcher is going to conduct a study that involves a measure of sponsorship effectiveness, then they must operationally define sponsorship effectiveness and must also provide some observable evidence of changes in its effectiveness. Owing to the exploratory and technical nature of research, the definitions you need are very rarely the same as those in the dictionary. For example, management skills, abilities and talent can all appear very similar in everyday language, but can have very specific meanings in Sport Management Research as established by the definition attached to them.

## ASSUMPTIONS, DELIMITATIONS AND LIMITATIONS

*Assumptions* assume that certain conditions exist. The fewer assumptions included in a research problem the better. For example, a study in sport management that compares management training methods must assume that the trainers involved are capable of promoting learning (and that the trainee managers are capable of learning). If this assumption is not made then the study would be impossible, yet if it is untrue then the whole study becomes worthless. Furthermore, in a learning study the researcher must assume that the sample selection (for example, *random selection*) results in a *normal distribution* with regard to learning capacity (these italicized terms are discussed in Part 3). For example, a study designed to access spectators' attitudes towards violence and sport is based on the assumption that this attitude can be reliably measured. Furthermore, you need to be able to assume that the respondents will respond truthfully. One frequently overlooked aspect of research is the assumptions made by statistical tests. These often involve the distribution of data, the number of participants etc. and if you do not check they have been met then you may end up making spurious claims.

*Delimitations* are boundaries that the researcher sets to limit the generalizability of findings. They are imposed by the researcher in the scope of the study. For example, in a study dealing with the attitude of individual sport athletes to doping, the researcher may choose to restrict the selection of subjects to just two or three sports, simply because all individual sports cannot be included in one study. Thus the researcher delimits the study.

*Limitations* are possible shortcomings or influences that cannot be controlled or are the results of the delimitations imposed by the researcher. If we limit the previous study of individual-sport athletes to just two sports there is an immediate limitation with respect to how well these represent all individual sports and therefore the generalizations that can be made from the research. The researcher should not be overzealous in searching for limitations as it may devalue the study too much in the eyes of the research community. An example of a limitation is that a sport organization might only allow the researcher to collect data during a certain time of the regular season, or that selected participants might not answer truthfully or at all. In setting out the limitations, Pajares (2007) suggested that the researcher should think about one's analysis, the nature of self-report, one's instruments and the sample. In other words one should think about threats to internal validity that may have been impossible to avoid or minimize and explain. Further discussion of this is taken up in Part 3 of the book.

Table 3.2 can be used to help you identify some common sources of limitations in quantitative and qualitative research.

**Table 3.2** *Identifying limitations*

| Quantitative research | Qualitative research |
| --- | --- |
| State the limitations of your study. | Describe the limitations of your study. |
| Did the sampling frame coincide with the targeted population or sub-population? | What related phenomena, events, or questions were not examined – by original plan or due to unexpected barriers? |
| Were the response rates and item-completion rates substantially less than 100 per cent? | What access did the researcher seek but was unable to gain? |
| Were the informed consent materials likely to have biased some responses? | How were informants selected, and how might that have biased or limited the information that was collected from them? |
| Were measurement scores less than highly reliable and valid? | How did requirements for protection of humans perhaps adversely affect the study? |
| Were the experiments perhaps biased with 'experimenter effects'? | How did the researcher's presence perhaps affect the phenomena being studied? |
| Did quasi-experiments and statistical modelling fail to control for viable competing hypotheses? | |
| Were the assumptions of the statistical procedures not fully met? | |
| Did the low power from small sample sizes perhaps contribute to few statistically significant results? | |

## WHY DO WE NEED TO CONSIDER ETHICAL CONSIDERATIONS IN SPORT MANAGEMENT RESEARCH?

Historically, ethical issues and the politics associated with research have not been as influential or as high on the research agenda as they are at present. The morality of conducting research and methodological approaches in specific areas has undergone many critiques across disciplines as have the purpose and benefits behind research. The focus for some sport management researchers has been on research that benefits disadvantaged groups or individuals. In some research studies it is important to consider the balance of power between the researcher and the researched. To protect all participants, ethical policy and standard procedures are required. The following section explains research ethics, the importance of research ethics and the concerns with relation to valuing the data obtained through research against valuing the potential interference of the participants involved in the research.

## WHAT ARE RESEARCH ETHICS

Ethics are a set of principles of right conduct, and the rules and standards governing the actions of a person; they define what is or is not legitimate or moral. Internationally, codes of behaviour and legal considerations exist so as to provide fixed rules and principles for researchers. However, sport management researchers will often face conflicts in their principles and must weigh up the benefits of the knowledge to be obtained from the research versus the rights of those taking part in the research study.

Research ethics provide protection of vulnerable populations, maintenance of professionalism, risk management standards, and ensure public support for research. In the design and conduct of human research, research ethics need to be seen as an integral component of the research process. Ethical considerations need to be considered in every phase of the research study.

Some of the ethical violations that could occur, either consciously or unconsciously include: violating agreements of disclosure; violating confidentiality of participants; invoicing for work not done, or excessive charges; misrepresentation of the results of the study; deceptive interactions with participants (ignoring informed consent); and disregarding legal liability for risks. All violations can come at a cost, to either the participants and/or the sport management researcher. As such, McMillan and Schumacher (2006, pp. 142–145) outline several principles for conducting ethical research. These include: (1) the lead researcher (primary investigator) must ensure the ethical treatment of all study subjects, human or animal, and compliance with all controlling government policies; (2) study subjects and any parents or guardians (if subjects are minors) should be honestly informed as to the study's purpose, benefits, risks (physical or psychological harm or discomfort) and time frames; (3) informed consent agreements must encompass an explicit consent to participate, acknowledgment of being informed of any risk or risk potential, a signed statement by the subject acknowledging the risks or risk potential including an understanding that participation is voluntary and that they have the right to exit the study at any time; (4) the disclosure of subject information, information that could potentially identify a subject, must be kept confidential, unless disclosure is required by law; and (5) privacy issues should be addressed. For example, upon completion of a study, if it is clear that documented potential or probable benefits have been withheld from some individuals these individuals should be offered the benefits they were denied.

## CONCLUSION

This chapter discussed the processes that underpin a research study or investigation. It has identified that ideas for research can be obtained from numerous sources. Once the research topic has been identified the sport management researcher needs an understanding of research planning, what constitutes a literature review and strategies to complete one. A systematic approach to research that is guided by well-constructed questions will allow the sport management researcher to not only identify what happens, but how it happens, and also, importantly, why it happens.

This chapter has also offered an overview of the ethics process and its implications for Sport Management Research. There are many times when the researcher faces difficult choices and will need to weigh up the benefits of the research against any possible harm caused to participants. A system of research ethics serves to guide the researcher in making the moral choices that will ultimately benefit both the research and the participants.

## REVIEW QUESTIONS

It is an important part of the research process for the sport management researcher to identify the area they want to investigate. With a basic understanding of this process, answer the following questions:

- Identify three ways in which the sport management researcher can determine suitable research topics.
- How can the sport management researcher identify what has already been published in their area of interest?
- What are the implications of conducting a basic research study as opposed to an applied research study?

The design of the research study, including the formulation of ideas, questions, reviewing the literature and the research plan itself are the essential first steps for the sport management researcher intending to undertake research. Now, having an overview of this process, attempt to answer the following question:

- Is the Internet a primary and reliable source of literature and/or information for the sport management researcher?

Research ethics, central to the design of the research study, are necessary to protect the right of the sport management researcher, to ensure the research participants are not placed at any risk of harm, and to reduce the likelihood of legal action against researchers and their institution. With this understanding, attempt to discuss the following scenario.

■ Discuss the ethical concerns associated with investigating the impact of a new sport development programme on elite junior athletes.

## SUGGESTED EXTENDED READING FOR STUDENTS

National Commission for the Protection of Human Subjects of Biomedical and Behavioral Research. (1979). *The Belmont Report. Ethical principles and guidelines for the protection of human subjects of research*. Washington, DC: National Institutes of Health. Available at: *http://ohsr.od. nih.gov/guidelines/belmont.html*

Nkwi, P., Nyamongo, I., and Ryan, G. (2001). *Field research into social issues: Methodological guidelines*. Washington, DC: UNESCO.

# Part 2

# Qualitative research for sport management researchers

## Chapter 4

# Qualitative data collection in Sport Management Research

## LEARNING OUTCOMES

By the end of this chapter you should be able to:

■ describe the major types of data collection in Sport Management Research;
■ understand the different qualitative data collection methods employed in Sport Management Research;
■ identify data collection methods suitable for use in Sport Management Research.

## KEY TERMS

*Participant observation* – the researcher observes the research study site by direct participation in the study.

*Focus groups* – small groups of participants share their thoughts about a specific topic of research.

*Direct observation* – the noting and recording of actions and behaviours, events and activities at the research site.

*Fieldwork* – where the researcher engages in the research study in the natural setting of the topic of study, as opposed to a controlled environment.

## KEY THEMES

The key questions raised in this chapter are:

■ How does the sport management researcher determine the most applicable data collection methods to utilize?
■ Which interview techniques are more suitable for the Sport Management Research study?
■ When are focus groups a preferable approach for data collection?

## CHAPTER OVERVIEW

The data collection phase is devoted to gathering the data for the research and organizing it, so that it can be properly analysed. This chapter covers the four basic types of qualitative data collection: observations, interviews, documents and audiovisual materials.

## DATA COLLECTION TECHNIQUES

Creswell (1998) indicated that there are *four* basic types of qualitative data collection:

1   observations (ranging from nonparticipant to participant);
2   interviews (ranging from semi-structured to open-ended);
3   documents (ranging from private to public); and
4   audiovisual materials (comprising materials such as photographs, compact discs and videotapes).

In recent years, new forms of data collection have emerged consisting of journaling in narrative story writing, utilizing text from email messages, and observation through videotapes and photographs (Creswell, 1998). In addition, Denzin and Lincoln (2005) suggested data collection using techniques such as the analysis of artefacts and cultural records, the use of visual materials and the use of personal experience. For instance, a biography, the portrait of an individual's life, is made from documents, interviews and possible observations (Creswell, 1998).

## 1 Observations

Observational techniques are methods by which individuals gather first-hand data on the policies, programmes, projects, processes or behaviours being studied. They provide researchers with an opportunity to collect data on a wide range of behaviours, to capture a great variety of interactions, and to openly explore the evaluation topic. Observation entails the systematic noting and recording of actions and behaviours (both verbal and non-verbal), events and objects in the location or group being researched. Observations can be useful during both the *formative* and *summative* phases of research. Table 4.1 summarizes some of the key discussion concerning the use of observations in qualitative research.

### The role of the observer

There are various methods for gathering observational data, depending on the nature of a given research project. The extent to which full participation is possible (and/or desirable) will depend on the nature of the project and its participants, the political and social context, the nature of the evaluation questions being asked and the resources available.

> The ideal is to negotiate and adopt that degree of participation that will yield the most meaningful data about the program given the characteristics of the participants,

the nature of staff–participant interactions, and the sociopolitical context of the program.

(Patton, 1990, p. 209)

**Table 4.1** *Advantages and disadvantages of observations*

*Advantages*

- Researcher conducts fieldwork to understand situation/context
- Researcher may be able to identify unanticipated outcomes from an 'insider' perspective
- Are usually unstructured and flexible
- Observations give insight into the behaviour of individuals and groups

*Disadvantages*

- High levels of observer expertise may be necessary in various settings
- Observer presence may contaminate data
- Selective perception of observer may compromise data
- Observer has little control over the setting and may not get quality data
- Behaviours observed may not be an accurate representation of actual setting
- Fieldwork may be expensive and time consuming
- Training is critical

There are two generally recognized observation techniques: *direct* and *participant*. *Direct observation* is privileged in the scientific or positivist paradigm, as it is believed to be more objective and protect the neutrality of the researcher. In contrast, *participant observation*, which evolved in the field of anthropology, is more aligned with the naturalistic paradigm that argues that total objectivity is neither possible nor desirable.

## DIRECT OBSERVATION

The researcher observes without engaging or interacting with the situation or environment they are observing, in the belief that they are not disturbing the environment and are able to maintain neutrality and objectivity in the process. For example, a sport management researcher may quietly and inconspicuously observe the engagement/non-engagement of fans with sponsorship activation booths outside a sporting event. There are critiques of this belief that point out that once researchers appear on the scene, total objectivity and therefore, control of bias, is no longer possible as the presence of the researcher alone will automatically influence people's behaviour. Engaging in observation – where the participants are unaware of the researcher's presence – raises ethical concerns, as participants may not have given informed consent for the observation to occur.

## PARTICIPANT OBSERVATION

As the name 'participant' suggests, the researcher participates in the activities of the persons being observed rather than being an aloof observer. The researcher has two roles – as

**51**

observer and as participant. The researcher participates as much as possible in the daily life of the subjects while also carefully observing everything he or she can about it. Volunteering at a sport event is one way to enable participant observation. Through this, the researcher is seeking to gain what is called an 'emic' perspective of the native's point of view or the insider's perspective. The researcher records detailed field notes, conducts interviews based on open-ended questions and gathers whatever site documents might be available, and these items form the data in the study.

The role of the researcher in participant observation also involves variations in *overt* or *covert* dimensions. In terms of the *overt*, participants in the field are fully aware who the observer is and that observations are being conducted together with a complete explanation of the study. By contrast, in a *covert* position, participants are not informed or aware of anything occurring. Researchers need to be aware of ethical considerations around covert observation and the absence of informed consent on the part of the unaware (and perhaps even unwilling) research participants. Hammersley and Atkinson (1983) suggested that there is the danger of the researcher 'going native'. This often means being too involved or having too close a rapport with the person or persons being observed to the extent that the researcher loses objectivity, or rather (given objectivity is not always the aim of such studies), loses the ability to achieve the study's aims. For example, a researcher sent to covertly observe a culture of illicit doping in a sport team may be seduced by the success of winning, and perhaps the money/fame and status. This researcher might then be very unwilling to report on the team, or may fabricate data to help exonerate the team from any wrongdoing.

### RECORDING OBSERVATIONAL DATA

Observations are carried out using a carefully developed set of steps and instruments. The observer is more than just an onlooker, but rather comes to the scene with a set of target concepts, definitions, and criteria for describing events. While in some studies observers may simply record and describe, in the majority of evaluations, their descriptions are, or eventually will be, judged against some criteria or expectations.

Observations are usually guided by a *structured protocol*. The protocol can take a variety of forms, ranging from describing events to a checklist or a rating scale of specific behaviours/activities that address the study's question-of-interest. The use of a protocol helps to ensure that all observers are gathering the pertinent information and (with appropriate training) applying the same criteria in the evaluation (i.e., improving the instrument's *reliability*). The *protocol* should usually prompt the observer to: describe the setting; identify the participants in the setting; describe the role of the researcher in the setting; document the interactions in the setting; and assess the exact behaviours and events that form the focus of the study.

### Fieldwork

Fieldwork involves the researcher working for long periods of time in a natural setting. Field relations are the complex relationships the researcher develops with others (for example, gatekeepers who help to allow/arrange access, and the research participants themselves) while in the field. Whereas volunteering for a single sport event was an example of participant observation, volunteering over the course of the year in the event office would be considered fieldwork. These relationships have logistical, procedural, ethical and political dimensions (Schwandt, 2001).

## FIELD NOTES

Field notes are frequently used to provide more in-depth background or to help the observer remember salient events (for example key emotions during a data collection, or vital information that was provided outside the formal 'observation'/recording). Field notes contain the description of what has been observed. The descriptions must be factual, accurate and thorough, without being judgemental and cluttered by trivia. The date and time of the observation should be recorded, and everything that the observer believes to be worth noting should be included. No information should be trusted to future recall, as human memory is famously unreliable. The ideal observation process is supported and contextualized by keeping systematic and analytical field notes. During the data collection phase the researcher typically keeps four types of field notes, as described by Richardson (2000):

1  *methodological notes* on issues and decisions pertaining to the research process, such as coding labels and participant criteria;
2  *observational notes* collected during observations made while attending the above mentioned events and interviews;
3  *analytical notes* noting assumptions and the process of data analysis and interpretation; and
4  *general field notes* that include anecdotal information such as contacts made for future reference.

The use of technological tools, such as a battery-operated tape recorder or dictaphone, laptop computer, camera or video camera, can make the collection of field notes more efficient and the notes themselves more comprehensive. Informed consent must almost always be obtained from participants before any observational data are gathered, and the participants must be informed where their data will be kept, how long for, and how it will be used *before* they give consent (covert studies create a problem in this respect, and the 'solution' is normally agreed by negotiation with a suitable ethics board).

## RECENT CASE EXAMPLE: OBSERVATION

*The following article is an example of how observation has been used in the past by researchers in Sport Management Research. The interested reader may wish to find/download and read the article for further insights.*

Transforming sport and identity in the post-apartheid South African nation-state. Maralack, David Mark. (2010). Unpublished doctoral dissertation, University of Minnesota.

In his dissertation Maralack examined processes of state restructuring and nation-state building in post-apartheid South Africa through the lens of sport policies and institutions. The post-apartheid state used sports to nurture post-apartheid identity, overcome economic inequalities and racial cleavages, and foster civic participation at the same time.

To complete his study Maralack used a diverse set of methods including document analysis, participant observation and interviews to assess the efficacy of sports policies in transforming sport, identities and nation building at national and local levels.

It is essential that the sport management researcher employs good observational practices when using this method. These practices include: (a) careful documentation of the following: the degree and quality of participation of individuals and groups; all aspects of the setting; the personal interactions between individuals and groups; the body-language of participants and the physical setup of the house or meetings and gatherings; the informal interactions before, during and after discussions and meetings, and during breaks; (b) a critical attitude involving: continual questioning of own assumptions and biases; cross-checking; reflexivity; and (c) video and photographs that may be useful in certain circumstances as they offer relatively objective and accurate recordings of events.

## 2 Interviews

The use of interviews as a data collection method begins with the assumption that the participants' perspectives are meaningful, knowable and able to be made explicit. An interview, rather than a paper and pencil survey, is selected when interpersonal contact is important and when opportunities for follow-up of interesting comments are desired.

The most utilized data collection method in qualitative research studies is the interview. Two schools of thought exist with respect to interview type. Most authors classify qualitative interviews into three types: *structured interviews*, *unstructured interviews* and *semi-structured interviews*. Other researchers propose only two types of interviews in qualitative research: *structured interviews*, in which a carefully worded questionnaire is administered; and *in-depth* interviews, in which the interviewer does not follow a rigid form but simply lets the conversation flow. The following discussion outlines the use of the term interview by both schools of thought.

*Structured interviews*, sometimes called standardized interviews, are used in quantitative research and involve the researcher asking the same set of questions, in the same order, using the same words, to different interviewees. Structured interviews are convenient for comparing different interviewees' answers to the same questions, and when a team of researchers is involved in conducting the interviews. For instance, structured interviews may offer a source of comparison of sponsor message recall, drawing on both the subject matter and feelings generated for a particular message. This is especially helpful when several researchers are testing recall from numerous study participants.

Burns (1997) suggests there are several disadvantages to this method of interviewing. First, the researcher has no flexibility to determine the beliefs, feelings, attitudes and perceptions of the respondent beyond those elicited by the predetermined response categories. Second, in using a structured interview, the interviewer must become a neutral standardized medium wherein questions are presented without bias or subjectivity. As a result, the method fails to acknowledge the inherent human-ness of the interviewer. Finally, the detachment and impersonal approach required can prevent trust and rapport from developing between the interviewer and the respondent, meaning important data (such as the participant's real feelings on a matter) may be lost.

*Semi-structured interviews* (sometimes referred to as focused interviews) involve a series of open-ended questions based on the topic areas the researcher wants to cover. The open-ended nature of the question stays true to defining the topic under investigation, as well as providing opportunities for both interviewer and interviewee to discuss some topics in more detail. If the interviewee has difficulty answering a question or provides only a brief response, the interviewer can use cues or prompts to encourage the interviewee to consider the question further. In a semi-structured interview the interviewer also has the freedom to probe the interviewee to elaborate on the original response or to follow a line of inquiry introduced by the interviewee. Because of the nature and context of many qualitative sport management studies, semi-structured interviews are the most common form of interviewing in the discipline. The major disadvantage of semi-structured interviews, if one is seeking to generate objective or comparable data, is that the researcher is vulnerable to the interpretations and subjective insights of the informant.

*Unstructured interviews* (sometimes referred to as 'depth' or 'in-depth' interviews) have very little structure at all. The interviewer goes into the interview with the aim of discussing a limited number of topics, sometimes as few as one or two, and frames the questions on the basis of the interviewee's previous response. Although only one or two topics are discussed they are covered in great detail. Unstructured interviews are exactly what they sound like – interviews where the interviewer wants to find out about a specific topic but has no structure or preconceived plan or expectation as to how they will deal with the topic. The difference with semi-structured interviews is that in a semi-structured interview the interviewer has a set of broad questions to ask and may also have some prompts to help the interviewee but the interviewer has the time and space to respond to the interviewee's responses. The major disadvantage of unstructured interviews is that the researcher is vulnerable to being dragged 'off topic' by the responses of the interviewee, as responses that often seem like a natural part of the conversation may, when analysed, be totally irrelevant to the actual research question.

All three types of interview can be used in combination (Patton, 1990). For example, after conducting structured interviews, researchers could follow up with semi-structured interviews, and perhaps even extend to using unstructured interviews or, conversely, they may start with unstructured interviews to relax the interviewees, and move to a semi-structured interview format.

## In-depth interview

As indicated previously, some researchers propose only *two* types of interview approaches in qualitative research: *structured interviews* and *in-depth interviews*. In *structured interviews* (as above) the emphasis is on obtaining answers to carefully phrased questions. Interviewers are trained to deviate as little as possible from the question wording to ensure uniformity of interview administration. In contrast, an in-depth interview is a dialogue between a skilled interviewer and an interviewee. Its goal is to elicit rich, detailed material that can be used in analysis (Lofland and Lofland, 1995). In-depth interviews are characterized by extensive probing and open-ended questions. Typically, the project evaluator prepares an interview guide that includes a list of questions or issues that are to be explored and suggested probes for following up on key topics. The guide helps the interviewer pace the interview and make interviewing more systematic and comprehensive. Lofland and Lofland provide guidelines for preparing interview guides, conducting the interview with the guide and writing up the interview. Poor interviewing skills, poor phrasing of questions or inadequate knowledge of the subject's culture or frame of reference may result in a data collection that obtains little useful information. There are also a number of factors to consider when determining the setting for an interview, these are detailed in the following text box.

## FACTORS TO CONSIDER IN DETERMINING THE SETTING FOR INTERVIEWS (BOTH INDIVIDUAL AND GROUP) INCLUDE THE FOLLOWING:

- Select a setting that provides privacy for participants.
- Select a location where there are no distractions and it is easy to hear respondents speak.
- Select a comfortable location.
- Select a nonthreatening environment.
- Select a location that is easily accessible for respondents.
- Select a facility equipped for audio or video recording.
- Stop telephone or visitor interruptions to respondents interviewed in their office or homes.
- Provide seating arrangements that encourage involvement and interaction.

### Recording interview data

Interview data can be recorded on tape (with the permission of the participants) and/or summarized in notes. As with observations, detailed recording is a necessary component of interviews since it forms the basis for analysing the data. Typical procedures for recording and analysing the data are as follows. First, the interviewer listens to the tapes and writes a verbatim account of the interview. Transcription of the raw data includes word-for-word quotations of the participant's responses as well as the interviewer's descriptions of the participant's characteristics, enthusiasm, body language and overall mood during the interview. The major advantages of this transcription method are its completeness and the opportunity it affords for the interviewer to remain attentive and focused during the interview. The major disadvantages are the amount of time and resources needed to produce complete transcriptions and the inhibitory impact tape recording has on some respondents.

Alternatively, another procedure for recording interviews draws on notes taken by the interviewer or assigned note-taker. This method is called 'note expansion'. As soon as possible after the interview, the interviewer listens to the tape to clarify certain issues and to confirm that all the main points have been included in the notes. This approach is recommended when resources are scarce, when the results must be produced in a short period of time, and when the purpose of the interview is to get rapid feedback from members of the target population. The note expansion approach saves time and retains all the essential points of the discussion. In addition to the drawbacks pointed out above, a disadvantage is that the interviewer may be more selective or biased in what he or she writes, and the method of expanding notes is very likely to generate unreliable and incorrect data.

Finally, the interviewer may use no tape recording, but instead takes detailed notes during the interview and draws on memory to expand and clarify the notes immediately after the interview. This approach is useful if time is short, the results are needed quickly and the evaluation questions are simple. The drawbacks noted above are at their most pronounced, however, if this method is used, and real care must be taken to record the outcomes of the interview. The key practices to employ in qualitative interviews are outlined in the following text box.

## GOOD PRACTICE IN QUALITATIVE INTERVIEWS:

Probing and cross-checking

■ questions or topics are tailored to different informants and stages of enquiry, making use of findings from previous interviews;

■ informants can be identified progressively to explore a range of different types of knowledge and perspectives;

■ findings are reduced to understandable patterns using qualitative analysis and/or diagrams;

■ findings are validated by cross-checking with other questions and information from other informants.

Good interpersonal skills

■ sensitivity to the respondents' mood, body language, time constraints and the different cultural norms that may shape these;

■ ability to really listen to answers, and to probe and cross-check in a thorough but sensitive manner;

■ taking notes in a discrete, non-threatening way that does not interrupt the flow of conversation;

■ tape recording is often a possibility;

■ using humour and personal experience to bring up sensitive issues or to challenge a response.

Careful documentation

■ continually examining one's own biases;

■ as far as possible quoting an interviewee's exact words and making clear where the interviewer's own analysis and interpretation has been added.

## Qualitative interview analysis

Once the interview data has been recorded and transcribed then it is ready for analysis. Creswell (2009, pp. 185–189) developed six steps as a process of qualitative interview analysis. These six steps include:

Step 1: Organize and prepare the data for analysis (for example, by carefully coding participants' ages, backgrounds and roles).

Step 2: Read through all the data for familiarization.

Step 3: Begin detailed analysis with a coding process (examples follow later, as they depend on the exact methodology chosen).

Step 4: Use the coding process to generate a description of the setting or people as well as themes for analysis.

Step 5: Advance how the description and themes will be represented in the qualitative narrative.

Step 6: Make an interpretation or meaning of the data.

Face-to-face structured, semi-structured and unstructured interviews are some of the most effective procedures used by the sport management researcher. There are also several more specialized forms, including ethnographic interviewing, phenomenological interviewing, elite interviewing, focus-group interviewing, and interviewing children – each requires particular levels of expertise and guidance.

## RECENT CASE EXAMPLE: INTERVIEW TECHNIQUES

*The following thesis is an example of how interviews have been used in the past by researchers in Sport Management Research. The interested reader may wish to find/download and read the article for further insights.*

> Interviews with Surf Company Representatives. Franklin, R. (2011). Unpublished doctoral dissertation, Griffith University.

The researcher's personal contacts and networks within the surfing industry initially made the process of gaining permission to conduct the research less problematic. To gain insight into the branding, sponsorship perceptions and management practices by the Big Three surf companies, the researcher utilized a combination of both structured and semi-structured interview approaches to approach and interview representatives from each surf company. The representatives also named as 'marketing' and/or 'team managers' in charge of women's surfing within the selected companies were targeted because of their experience and understanding of the area to be researched. An initial phone call was made to each surf company by the researcher. This served as a means of introduction to the research topic and to also ascertain which person would be best to provide information about management practices of the company. Once identified, the representatives were contacted by phone and a meeting time or phone interview was set up. A structured format was found more useful when undertaking the surf company representative interviews as a tool to gain a comparative sense of their role within the company and to complement questions sent via email. The interview began with the researcher initiating a conversation about their background and their role within the particular surf company. A typical question was:

> How long have you been involved with this company and what is your main role with regard to female surfers?

As the interview progressed, a more semi-structured interview approach was introduced. A general discussion about their surfing experience, time spent and their role in the company led to more probing questions requiring specific information aimed at extending developing themes, one example being:

> Does your company believe female lifestyle marketing and sponsorship is becoming a more valuable investment and if so, does your company have a main strategic direction with regard to public and media image for your sponsored female surfers?

Following these interviews a company profile was developed by the researcher using relevant surf websites, to provide initial background information about the individual surf company and brand. Once completed, an individual company profile was sent to each representative for verification and for them to append any additional information they felt necessary.

## Focus groups

Sometimes it is preferable to collect information from groups of people rather than from a series of individuals. Focus groups are (usually semi-structured) interviews with a number of participants that aim to explore a specific set of issues. Focus group discussions (or group interviews) capitalize on group interaction and communication to generate data. Focus group discussions can help researchers explore and clarify views in ways that are not possible or accessible in one-to-one interviews. A sport management researcher may gather eight to ten fans of a team and through a series of open-ended questions, encourage discussion around issues important to fans in their own vocabulary, and explore their priorities. Tables 4.2 and 4.3 provide a summary of other issues to consider when planning to use focus groups in your research. Factors to consider when choosing focus groups are included in Table 4.3.

## Validity and reliability of the research interview

Interviews can be conducted individually (one-to-one) or as a group. The validity and reliability of the data collected from the interview varies with the type of interview employed, as well the experience of the interviewer. Some approaches to research reject 'validity' and

**Table 4.2** Characteristics of a focus group

1   The recommended size of a group is six to ten people.

2   Several focus groups should be run in any research project.

3   The members of each focus group should have something in common, characteristics that are important to the topic of investigation.

4   Focus groups are usually specially convened groups. It may be necessary or even desirable to use pre-formed groups but difficulties may occur.

5   Qualitative information is collected that makes use of participants' feelings, perceptions and opinions.

6   Using qualitative approaches in focus groups requires certain skills. The researchers require a range of skills: group skills in facilitating and moderating, listening, observing and analysing.

**Table 4.3** Factors to consider when choosing focus groups

| Factors to consider | Use focus groups when . . . |
| --- | --- |
| Group interaction | interaction of respondents may provide deeper insight and richer data. |
| Sensitivity of subject matter | subject matter is not too sensitive to prevent respondents from withholding information. |
| Extent of issues | the volume of issues to cover is not too extensive. |
| Continuity of information | a single subject area is being examined in depth. |
| Observation | it is desirable for stakeholders to hear what participants have to say. |
| Logistics | an acceptable number of target respondents can be assembled in one location. |
| Cost and training | quick turnaround is critical, and funds are limited. |
| Availability of qualified staff | focus group facilitators are able to control and manage groups. |

Source: Adapted from Krueger (1994) *Focus Groups: A Practical Guide for Applied Research*

'reliability' outright, whereas others seek to conduct interviews that can make some sort of claim to these.

*Validity* in interviewing refers to the formation of suitably operationalizing constructs and ideas. Edwards and Skinner (2009) indicated that interviewing attempts to achieve construct validity through three tactics. *First*, triangulation of interview questions is usually established in the research design stage by two or more carefully worded questions that look at the subject matter under investigation from different angles. *Second*, the interview method usually contains an inbuilt negative case analysis whereby, in each interview and before the next, the technique explicitly requires that the interviewer attempt to disprove emerging explanations

---

## RECENT CASE EXAMPLE: THE INTERVIEW

*The following article is an example of how interviews have been used in the past by researchers in Sport Management Research. The interested reader may wish to find/download and read the article for further insights.*

Qualitative analysis of NASCAR fan identity. Halloran, Erin M. (2010). Doctoral dissertation, Temple University. AAT 3390493

The purpose of this research study was to provide a rich and thick description of what it means to be a NASCAR (National Association of Stock Car Racing) fan. Specifically, the researcher examined how NASCAR fans create their sport fan identity, how being a NASCAR fan influences their overall identity, and the social and cultural aspects associated with being a NASCAR fan. The participants consisted of 12 (10 male and 2 female) self-identified NASCAR fans in attendance at one of three races (Daytona 500 at Daytona International Speedway in Daytona Beach, FL; Samsung/RadioShack 500 at Texas Motor Speedway in Justin, TX; or the Richmond 400 at the Richmond International Raceway (RIR) in Richmond, VA) during the 2006 NASCAR Nextel Cup Series season. Interviews were transcribed verbatim and analysed, yielding four major themes. The themes that emerged included: (a) entry into NASCAR, (b) being A NASCAR Fan, (c) 'ya'll NASCAR fans': fan camaraderie, and (d) win on Sunday. . . sell on Monday.

---

interpreted in the data (Dick, 1990). *Finally*, the flexibility of the approach allows the interviewer to re-evaluate and redesign both the content and process of the interview programme, thus establishing content validity.

*Reliability* in interviewing refers to how consistently a technique measures the concepts it is supposed to measure, enabling other researchers to repeat the study and attain similar findings. Edwards and Skinner (2009) suggested that reliability is usually achieved through four tactics: *first*, reliability is attained through the structured process of interviews. *Second*, reliability is achieved through organizing a structured process for recording, writing and interpreting data. *Third*, research reliability is often achieved through comparison of the research findings between the interviewer and interviewee (sometimes called 'member checking'). *Finally*, the use of a planning committee to assist in the design and administration of the interview programme is another way that reliability can be achieved (Guba and Lincoln, 1994).

## 3 Documents

Lincoln and Guba (1985) defined a document as any written or recorded material not prepared for the purposes of the evaluation or at the request of the inquirer. Creswell (2009) added that the term 'document' includes not just texts, but also sound, photos, videos and any materials that carry relevant messages. Guba and Lincoln (1981) suggested that documents can be divided into two major categories: *public records* and *personal documents*.

**61**

*Public records* are materials created and kept for the purpose of attesting to an event or providing an account (Lincoln and Guba, 1985). Public records can be collected from outside (*external*) or within (*internal*) the setting in which the evaluation is taking place (i.e. through an internal audit or by employing a more neutral organization). Examples of *external* records in sport management are attendance and statistics reports, newspaper archives and records that can assist an evaluator in gathering information about relevant trends in branding, ticket sales, athletic performances and the like. *Internal* records include documents such as transcripts, historical accounts, institutional mission statements, annual reports, budgets, reports, minutes of meetings, internal memoranda, policy manuals, institutional histories, catalogues, handbooks, official correspondence, demographic material, mass media reports and presentations.

*Personal documents* are first-person accounts of events and experiences. These include diaries, portfolios, photographs, artwork, schedules, scrapbooks, letters to the paper, etc. Personal documents can help the evaluator understand how the participant sees the world and what she or he wants to communicate to an audience. Collecting data from documents is relatively invisible to, and requires minimal cooperation from persons within the setting being studied. As such, the ethical issues around consent are usually handled by an ethics committee instead of approaching the individual concerned.

The use of document collection has a number of advantages and disadvantages. Some of these are outlined in Table 4.4.

Three distinctions among documents are usually made. The first distinction is made between *primary sources* and *secondary sources*. Primary sources have a direct relationship with those who are studied. They include letters, diaries and reports. Secondary sources are transcribed or edited from primary sources and may include errors that the transcribing and editing processes made.

**Table 4.4** *Advantages and disadvantages of document studies*

*Advantages*

- Freely available in most circumstances
- Usually an inexpensive source of data
- Provide contextual background
- Provide opportunity for study of trends over time
- Unobtrusive

*Disadvantages*

- Documentation may be incomplete
- In some cases there may be inaccuracy and questionable authenticity of data
- Searching for documents may pose challenges
- Analysis of documents may be time consuming
- Access may be difficult

The second distinction is made between public and private documents. In a sport organization public documents may include newsletters and minutes of meetings. Private documents would include the details of tenders and commercial in-confidence documents. The third distinction is made between *solicited* and *unsolicited* documents. Solicited documents are produced with requests of the researchers. For example, researchers can ask participants to keep diaries in which users write down reflective thoughts and comments. *Unsolicited* documents are naturally produced and later taken by researchers; examples include personal diaries and letters.

## Systematic data collection of documents

Altheide (2000, p. 291) lists six steps to follow in order to carry out systematic data collection of documents:

1 Pursue a specific problem to be investigated;
2 Become familiar with the process and context of the information source;
3 Become familiar with examples of relevant documents, noting the format in particular and select a unit of analysis, for example, each article;
4 List several items or categories to guide data collection and draft a protocol (data collection sheet);
5 Test the protocol by collecting data from several documents;
6 Revise the protocol and select several additional cases to further refine the protocol.

Like most research, qualitative document collection is not separate from data analysis. This is an interpretive process. As part of the dual process of collection and analysis Altheide (1996, pp. 23–44) developed a twelve step process model involving five stages of qualitative document analysis, as follows:

STAGE 1 – DOCUMENT STUDY DEVELOPMENT
Step 1: Pursue a specific problem to be investigated.
Step 2: Become familiar with the process and context of the information source; explore possible documents of information.
Step 3: Select a unit of analysis.

STAGE 2 – PROTOCOL DEVELOPMENT AND DATA COLLECTION
Step 4: List several items to guide data collection and draft a protocol.
Step 5: Test the protocol by collecting data from several documents.
Step 6: Revise the protocol and select several additional cases to further refine the protocol.

STAGE 3 – DATA CODING AND ORGANIZATION
Step 7: Arrive at a theoretical sampling rationale and strategy.
Step 8: Collect the data, using preset codes, if appropriate, and many descriptive examples. Keep the data with the original documents, but also enter data in a plain text word-processing

format for easier search–find and text coding. Make appropriate adjustments to other data. Complete data collection.

### STAGE 4 – DATA ANALYSIS
Step 9: Perform data analysis, including conceptual refinement and data coding. Read notes and data repeatedly and thoroughly.
Step 10: Compare and contrast 'extremes' and 'key differences' within each category or item. Make textual notes. Write brief summaries or overviews of data for each category.
Step 11: Combine the brief summaries with an example of the typical case as well as the extremes. Illustrate with materials from the protocols for each case.

### STAGE 5 – FINAL REPORT
Step 12: Integrate the findings with your interpretation and key concepts in another draft.

An example of a sport management researcher utilizing document analysis could be a study of the salary cap breach by the Melbourne Storm National Rugby League team in Australia in 2010. The *first stage* (steps one to three) was to find online newspaper articles based on the questions about the salary cap regulations designed for document analysis. This involved selecting a unit of analysis (e.g. each article). In terms of sources of information being used in this study, 12 articles were primary sources, 27 articles were secondary sources, and 31 articles were tertiary sources. According to Merriam (1998), primary sources are 'those in which the originator of the document is recounting first-hand experience with the phenomenon of interest. The best primary sources are those recorded closest in time and place to the phenomenon by a qualified person' (p. 122). Secondary sources are reports of a phenomenon by those who have not directly experienced the phenomenon of interest; these are often compiled at a later date (Merriam, 1998). Interestingly, the same article could be categorized as primary or secondary or tertiary depending upon the purpose of the study (Merriam, 1998). Tertiary sources comprise information that is the distillation and collection of primary and secondary sources.

The *second stage* (steps four to six) was to list several items to guide data collection and draft a protocol. Miles and Huberman's (1994) document summary form was used to develop the protocol. Based on the uniqueness of this study, other items such as emerging themes and important quotations were added to the protocol. The protocol was then tested by collecting data from several documents, and revising the protocol and selecting several additional documents to further refine the protocol.

The *third stage* (steps seven to eight) included data coding and organization. In this stage, it involves collecting the data, using preset codes (Miles and Huberman, 1994), keeping the data with the original documents, but also entering data in a table format for easier search–find and text coding. A midpoint analysis was conducted about halfway to two-thirds through the documents to permit emergence, refinement or collapsing of additional themes.

The *fourth stage* (steps nine to eleven) included conceptual refinement and data coding. Notes and data were reviewed thoroughly three times. Fifty-two online newspaper articles, totalling 78 pages were reviewed. In this stage, comparisons and contrasts were conducted on the 'extremes' and 'key differences' within each category or item. Textual notes and brief summaries or overviews were made on the data for each category. The last stage (step 12) was to integrate the findings with the researcher's interpretation and key concepts.

---

**RECENT CASE EXAMPLE: DOCUMENT ANALYSIS**

*The following article is an example of how document analysis has been used in the past by researchers in Sport Management Research. The interested reader may wish to find/download and read the article for further insights.*

Unfiltered? A content analysis of pro athletes' 'Twitter' use. Shockley, Justin. (2010). Masters dissertation, East Tennessee State University.

Shockley studied popular social networking sites such as 'Twitter' to argue that athletes no longer communicate with the general public solely through traditional media outlets such as newspapers. Social networking sites such as 'Twitter' allow athletes to directly communicate with mass audiences. This direct communication raises several questions with regard to dynamics of communication and uses of Internet portals. A *content analysis* examined professional athletes' 'Twitter' posts to help answer these questions.

## 4 Audiovisual materials (comprising materials such as photographs, compact discs and videotapes)

Creswell (1998) indicated that one type of qualitative data collection includes audiovisual materials comprising materials such as photographs and videotapes. Visual documents are records of events that have occurred in the past (Barthes, 1981). It has also been noted that photographs and videos speak a language of emotion and meaning (Denzin, 2004). According to Denzin (2004, p. 240), four narratives or meaning structures exist in any set of photographs and videos. These four meaning structures are:

1    The visual text;
2    The audio text, including what photographers say about their photographs;
3    The narrative that links the visual and audio text into a coherent story, or framework; and
4    The interpretations and meanings the viewer bring to the visual, audio, and narrative texts.

Documents from photographs and video clips may be analysed using Collier and Collier's (1986) principles of critical analysis of visual documents. As Collier and Collier suggested, these guidelines are provisional, and should fit to the needs of the researcher.

### Phase one: 'Looking and feeling'

a)    Observe the visual documents as a totality.
b)    Look and listen to the materials. Let them talk to you. Feel their effects on you. Record these feelings and impressions.
c)    Write down questions that occur to you. Note patterns of meaning.

**65**

*Phase two: 'What question are you asking?'*

a)   State your research question.
b)   What questions does the text claim to answer?
c)   How does it represent and define key cultural values? And
d)   Inventory the evidence, note key scenes and images.

*Phase three: 'Structured microanalysis'*

a)   Do a scene by scene, microanalysis, transcribe discourse, describe scenes, and take quotes from the text.
b)   Form and find patterns and sequences.
c)   Write detailed descriptions.
d)   How does the text represent objective reality, handle facts, represent experience, and dramatize truth?
e)   Keep a focus on the research question.
f)   Identify major moments in the film/text when conflicts over values occur. And
g)   Detail how the film/text/image takes a position on these values.

*Phase four: 'Search for patterns'*

a)   Return to the complete record.
b)   Lay out all the photographs, or view the film in its entirety.
c)   Return to the research question. How do these documents speak to and answer your question?
d)   Contrast realist and subversive reading of the text.
e)   Write an interpretation, based on the principles of interpretation discussed above. (Collier and Collier, 1986, pp. 178–179)

## EXAMPLES OF DATA COLLECTION STRATEGIES

Table 4.5 outlines a possible sequence of data collection.

---

### HYPOTHETICAL CASE

A recent trend in rugby union has been the increased globalization of professional rugby contracts. Most rugby national governing bodies have had a policy of only selecting players for the national team if they play in the domestic competition. The rationale for selecting only domestic players is to keep the domestic competition at a high level in order to maintain spectatorship, the main financial driver for professional rugby union governing bodies. With countries such as France and Japan offering the highest wages, more and more players are forgoing national team selection in order to make a better living overseas. This has caused

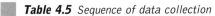

**Table 4.5** *Sequence of data collection*

| Time frame | Data collection method | Description |
| --- | --- | --- |
| Over the period from 2007–2010 | Preliminary observations | Provide insight and sensitivity to the organisational and procedural structures of surf companies and sponsored competitions |
| Over the period from 2007–2010 | Field notes | Taken throughout the fieldwork to clarify observations and interviews at events and surfing competitions |
| Over the period from 2007–2010 | Documents and visual data | Collection and initial analysis of newspaper articles, surfing magazines articles and photos, reports to gain grounding and understanding about research topic |
| January and June 2009 and 2010 | Preliminary discussion | Conducted with female surfers at competition sites |
| January and June 2009 and 2010 | Consent package and survey Sponsored female surfers | Given out to each female surfer at competition sites |
| January 2010 | Email to surf company representatives | Initial email to introduce researcher, provide consent package and suggested structured interview questions |
| February 2010 April 2010 May 2010 | Semi-structured interviews Sponsored surfers | Conduct semi-structured and in-depth interviews with selected sponsored female surfers |
| March 2010 | Unstructured interviews at Divas of Surfing Night | Questions about sponsorship asked at Divas of Surfing Night Casual conversations with participants at the event |
| February 2010 | Interviews with company representatives | Conduct in-depth interviews in person or via phone with surf company representatives |
| Over the period from 2007–2010 | Casual conversations with members of the surfing community | Casual conversations at surfing events took place with spectators, parents of surfers and organizers of events |
| September 2010 | Follow-up observations | Focus on specific items to clarify themes and confirm whether data collected from previous observations are typical or unique |
| December 2010 | Follow-up interviews and emails | To confirm data from previous interviews, check understanding and meanings and practices and clarify any discrepancies between the data collection methods |

Source: Franklin (2012, p. 203)

some national governing bodies to reconsider the domestic competition rule in order to stay competitive in international competitions by selecting the top players available globally, and not limiting selection to domestic players. One research question that may be addressed from this growing trend is: to what extent do stakeholders value a national competition over national team success (or vice-versa)?

Case questions:

1   What research method(s) could you utilize to answer that research question?
2   How might you focus the research question to enable easier data collection?
3   What other research questions come to mind under this scenario? Would answering those research questions require the same data collection? How would they be different?

## CONCLUSION

This chapter has examined the data collection methods that can be utilized to acquire data, and to address the research aims. *Four* basic types of qualitative data collection: (a) observations (ranging from nonparticipant to participant), (b) interviews (ranging from semi-structured to open-ended), (c) documents (ranging from private to public), and (d) audiovisual materials (comprising materials such as photographs, compact discs and videotapes) were discussed in detail.

## REVIEW QUESTIONS

Data collection is the process of collecting or gathering information pertaining to a specific research topic that will be used by the sport management researcher in the later process of analysis to formulate theories, produce recommendations or contextualize events and activities in the sport management setting. With this in mind:

■   Distinguish between the different forms of observation and interviews and how these might be used by the sport management researcher.
■   Discuss how documents can be used by the sport management researcher to collect specific data. Provide examples of the documents a sport management researcher may use in their research.

## SUGGESTED EXTENDED READING FOR STUDENTS

Creswell, J. W. (2007). *Qualitative inquiry and research design: Choosing among five approaches* (2nd edn). Thousand Oaks, CA: Sage.
Edwards, A. and Skinner, J. (2009). *Qualitative research in sport management*. Oxford: Elsevier.
Krueger, R. A. (1994). *Focus groups: A practical guide for applied research*. Thousand Oaks, CA: Sage Publications.

# Chapter 5

# Qualitative data analysis in Sport Management Research

## LEARNING OUTCOMES

By the end of this chapter you should be able to:

- define what is qualitative data analysis;
- explain and compare approaches in analysing qualitative data;
- describe two trends that attempt to explain the purpose of qualitative data analysis;
- code and develop categories in qualitative data analysis;
- identify key methods in the coding process;
- understand the use of Computer Assisted/Aided Qualitative Data Analysis (CAQDAS).

## KEY TERMS

*Modes of analysis* – the process by which the researcher reviews the data collected with the aim of making sense of it so that evidence can be obtained to answer the research question.

*Triangulation* – examining the consistency of information generated by different data collection techniques, or examining different data gathered by the same collection technique.

*Coding* – the organization of raw data into conceptual categories.

## KEY THEMES

- What is coding?
- What is Computer Assisted/Aided Qualitative Data Analysis?

## CHAPTER OVERVIEW

Qualitative data is mostly in the form of words, phrases, sentences and may include visual images, audio and video recordings. Qualitative data is often a mass of words obtained from recordings of interviews, field notes of observations and analysis of documents as well as reflective notes of the researcher. This mass of information has to be organized, summarized, described and interpreted. In sports management research, where the material of the most interest is often not in the form of quantifiable numbers, but rather people's opinions and experiences, qualitative data may be extremely relevant and useful. This chapter discusses qualitative data analysis (QDA) for the sport management researcher.

## WHAT IS QUALITATIVE DATA ANALYSIS (QDA)?

Qualitative data analysis (QDA) is the range of processes and procedures whereby we move from the qualitative data that have been collected into some form of explanation, understanding or interpretation of the people and situations we are investigating.

Replicating a previous theme in the book, when conducting research, there is a choice between two fundamental research approaches: *induction* and *deduction*. The *inductive approach* moves from empirical observations to conclusions that are finally developed into theories. Hence, the research process begins with collecting data with the aim of using that data to develop theories or improve existing ones. The *deductive approach*, on the other hand, uses existing theories as guiding frameworks, which will offer categories and a predetermined structure for the analysis. In principle this should lead to a more detailed understanding of a theory, for example, or an understanding of how sports managers actually apply the theory in practice.

Some research attempts to strike a balance between *inductive* and *deductive* approaches. According to Patel and Davidson (2003), such a combination is referred to as an *abductive* approach. Hence, where an existing theory seems relevant, but may need 'fleshing out' with details, an abductive approach may allow the theoretical framework to be maintained while the rich and detailed data allows new insights to be gained into how it might apply.

## ANALYSING QUALITATIVE DATA

Like quantitative data, qualitative data can be classed as *primary* or *secondary*. Primary data consists of text that has been collected directly from participants, such as individual interviews, group discussions or participant observation. This type of data is collected by the researcher(s) and is usually in the form of written notes or transcriptions of tape-recorded discussions. Secondary data is collected from secondary sources such as letters, diaries, case notes/ histories, agendas and policy documents (all highly applicable to sport management situations) as well as published or unpublished research material. Once the origins of the data are established, interpretation can occur in two ways:

1   by establishing and applying a theoretical position or positions through which the data is viewed and compared (deductive); and

2   by creating ideal types or theoretical categories that provide a structure for analysis (inductive) (Grbich, 1999, p. 149).

Analysis is usually seen as an ongoing process that begins from the moment research questions are confirmed and secondary material sources directly related to the topic or issues are reviewed. Analysis continues throughout the data collection phase until the presentation of the findings.

## METHODS OF DATA ANALYSIS IN QUALITATIVE SPORT MANAGEMENT RESEARCH

Some of the most relevant methods of data analysis for Sport Management Research are presented in Table 5.1. Some of these methods are discussed in more detail later in this book.

**Table 5.1** Data analysis methods in qualitative Sport Management Research

| Mode | Description | Uses |
|---|---|---|
| Hermeneutical analysis | Hermeneutics is the study of interpretation theory and can be either the art of interpretation, the theory and practice of or interpretation. There are various forms of hermeneutics (traditional, contemporary and philosophical). One can frequently find reference to the 'hermeneutic circle': that is, relating the whole to the part and the part to the whole. | These approaches might be used when trying to 'reverse engineer' the intentions, sociocultural zeitgeists or political parties behind key documents or policies. |
| Exegesis | The terms exegesis and hermeneutics are sometimes used interchangeably because exegesis focuses primarily on the written text. | |
| Semiotics | Semiotics is primarily concerned with the meaning of signs and symbols in language. The foundation idea is that words/signs can be assigned to primary conceptual categories, and these categories represent important aspects of the theory to be tested. The importance of an idea is revealed in the frequency with which it appears in the text. | |
| Phenomenology/ Heuristic analysis | Provides insight into how people make sense of the world they live in. | These approaches might be used in attempting to understand the experiences of participants in a sports initiative or programme, or perhaps those who dropped out. |
| Narrative analysis | Understanding/researching the way people make meaning of their lives as narratives. | |

**Table 5.1** continued

| Mode | Description | Uses |
|------|-------------|------|
| Typology | A classification system, taken from patterns, themes, or other kinds of groups of data. | These approaches allow a researcher to bring order and sense to an area or phenomenon that may initially appear complex and chaotic. |
| Taxonomy | The practice and science of classification. | |
| Constant comparison/ Grounded theory | Comparing codes to find consistencies and differences. | These approaches are highly applicable as concepts begin to take shape from the data, and require you to try and propose how the new concepts are linked, or relate to each other. |
| Analytic induction | Systematic examination of similarities between various social phenomena in order to develop concepts or ideas. | |
| Content analysis | Content analysis is a research technique for making replicable and valid references from data to their contexts. The researcher searches for structures and patterned regularities in the text and makes inferences on the basis of these regularities. | |
| Logical analysis/ Matrix analysis | Uses flow charts, diagrams, etc. to pictorially represent the data, as well as written descriptions to provide an outline of generalized causation, logical reasoning process, etc. | |
| Quasi-statistics | Counts the number of times something is mentioned in field notes as very rough estimate of frequency. | In some circumstances, the number of times a word or phrase is mentioned may be a key issue, in which case counting frequency (or perhaps, in what context the word/phrase is used) may be a relevant approach. |
| Event analysis/ Microanalysis | Emphasis is on finding precise beginnings and endings of events by finding specific boundaries and things that mark boundaries or events. Specifically oriented towards film and video. | In situations where a specific event or story is of interest, often critical moments, catastrophes or 'breakthroughs', then analysing the specific event may be highly informative. |
| Conversation analysis | In conversation analysis, it is assumed that the meanings are shaped in the context of the exchange. The researcher immerses themselves in the situation to reveal the background of practices. | Sometimes researchers wish to analyse natural conversations or natural 'discourse', rather than structured question–answer type data. It may be, for example, that people speak very differently (and more honestly) in this circumstance, and that very different data might be generated. |
| Discourse analysis | Discourse analysis builds on both content analysis and conversation analysis but focuses on 'language games'. A language game refers to a well-defined unit of interaction consisting of a sequence of verbal moves in which turns of phrase, the use of metaphor and allegory all play an important part. | |

## PROCEDURAL RIGOUR

Two major trends have been identified in the debate about rigour and validity in qualitative research:

- the *exclusive trend*, for which the qualitative paradigm is so radically different from the quantitative paradigm that a new language must be used to express its rigour and validity (Guba and Lincoln, 1981, 1982, 1989);
- the *inclusive trend*, which argues that the credibility of qualitative research can only be widely accepted if the language of mainstream (quantitative) research is maintained, although operationalized to meet the new conditions and circumstances (Yin, 1994; Morse, Barret, Mayan, Olson, Spiers and Hon, 2002; Creswell, 2009).

The following discussion outlines both these trends and their applicability for Sport Management Research.

### Exclusive trend

The proponents of the exclusive trend claim that the terms 'validity' and 'reliability' from quantitative research do not make sense in qualitative research, so they should be replaced. Trochim and Donnelly (2008) described the belief of some researchers that a purpose of the qualitative approach is to reject validity since no single reality exists. However, instead of seeking objective reliability and validity, alternative criteria for validating qualitative research may include 'credibility, transferability, dependability and confirmability' (p. 149). Table 5.2 compares these criteria against those most commonly used in quantitative research that are discussed further in the next section.

**Table 5.2** *Criteria commonly used in validating qualitative and quantitative research*

| Quantitative research | Qualitative research |
|---|---|
| Internal validity | Credibility – can the research findings be trusted? Was the process robust and transparent? |
| External validity | Transferability – do the findings extend to other areas and offer useful insights for others? |
| Reliability | Dependability – are the findings repeatable, or would other researchers report similar interpretations? |
| Objectivity | Confirmability – is there any way of testing the findings for 'truth'? Even if the study cannot be repeated, is there an auditable trail we can follow from raw data to final analysis? |

#### Trustworthiness

Trustworthiness is the umbrella term coined by Lincoln and Guba (1985). They use this term to refer to a set of criteria that have been offered for judging the quality or goodness of qualitative enquiry. Lincoln and Guba and subsequently many others have argued that these criteria are more appropriate than the traditional quantitative criteria of validity and reliability. There are four major components that comprise trustworthiness criteria, these are: *credibility*, *transferability*, *dependability* and *confirmability*.

*Credibility* in qualitative research is like internal validity in quantitative research. Credibility involves ensuring that the participants, setting and processes are accurately identified and described for the research to be meaningful. Techniques for establishing credibility include: prolonged engagement, persistent observation, triangulation, peer debriefing, negative case analysis, referential adequacy and member checking. For example, a sport management researcher investigating concussion policies in a football team may enhance credibility by interviewing several people at different levels and positions in the organization to encompass any different and consistent viewpoints.

*Transferability* exists when the results can be applied to other contexts. The researcher describes in detail the context and underlying assumptions of the research (thick description), so that transferability is possible, but the person who transfers the results to a different context is responsible for the transfer. The notion of transferability raises the question, 'can we apply these findings to other contexts or groups of people?' or, 'will fans of one sport studied have similar viewpoints or actions of fans in other sports?'

All steps of the methods used to collect and analyse data should be documented and traceable in order to allow for *auditability* (Padgett, 2008). To reduce *researcher bias*, a process of reflexivity, or a systematic self-awareness, where the researchers would reflect on their analysis of the data and discuss the differences in coding after cross-checking, is important.

*Dependability* emphasizes the stability of the data over time. Dependability is often another word for reliability. It is when the researcher attempts to account for changing conditions in the phenomenon chosen for the study as well as changes in the design created by increasingly refined understanding of the setting. Dependability in qualitative research is often achieved by the researcher allowing cross-checking of codes (also known as inter-coder agreement or inter-rater reliability) by other research experts to see whether these experts would code in the same way as the researcher (Creswell, 2009); as a sport researcher, if you have coded interviews with team trainers, coaches and athletes that reflect particular values over doping allegations, by then asking an external expert to code segments of the interviews tests dependability if those same particular values arise. The researcher must be able to account for the permanently changing context in which the research takes place, describing any changes that occur and how these changes affect the research.

*Confirmability* demonstrates that the inquiry is free of bias, values and prejudice, i.e. that the data interpretations and outcomes are rooted in contexts and persons apart from the researcher and are not mere products of the researcher's imagination. The researcher must document the procedures, so that others can check and recheck the data throughout the study. Techniques that may be used to strengthen confirmability include: prolonged engagement, persistent observation, peer debriefing, negative case analysis and triangulation. Continuing the example above, if the researcher has a biased opinion of doping in sport and allows that bias to creep into the coding process, they may 'uncover' values from the trainers, coaches and athletes that match their own values. A first external expert may code the data to test dependability, and a second external expert may code portions of the data to confirm the findings.

After the study, a data audit or external audit should be conducted by a researcher not involved in the research process, to examine both the process and product of the research study. This process 'will ensure the truth value of the data' (Creswell, 2009, p. 199).

## Inclusive trend

Many interpretations exist within the inclusive trend. The approach discussed here is proposed by Creswell (2009). According to Creswell, *qualitative validity* refers to the different procedures the researcher employs to ensure findings are accurate, whereas *qualitative reliability* refers to whether a particular research approach is consistent across different projects and different researchers. *Qualitative generalization* is a term that is not often discussed in contexts of qualitative research, since the findings achieved from qualitative research methods are normally not intended for generalization (Creswell, 2009). The following discussion will outline this trend.

## QUALITATIVE VALIDITY

Creswell (2009) recommended the use of multiple strategies that enhance the researcher's ability to assess the accuracy of findings, as well as convince the readers of that accuracy. According to Creswell, one advantage of qualitative research can be high validity. *Validity,* in Cresswell's interpretation means that 'the researcher checks for the accuracy of the findings' (p. 190) by using multiple strategies to enhance the researcher's ability to evaluate the precision of findings. Creswell also suggested that 'good qualitative research contains comments by the researchers about how their interpretation of the findings is shaped by their background' (p. 192). Creswell specifically listed a series of steps to avoid validity threats for qualitative research. He argued that it is a prime imperative to check for the 'accuracy of the findings' (p. 196) and he listed eight strategies to avoid validity issues that should also improve the researcher's capability to evaluate the truthfulness of the given information. These are: (1) triangulation; (2) member checking; (3) rich, thick description; (4) avoidance of researcher bias; (5) negative case analysis; (6) prolonged engagement; (7) peer debriefing; and (8) external auditing. These strategies are explained in the following passages using a sport management context.

## 1 Triangulation

Triangulation can be achieved by collecting data using different sources, different settings and at different times. Burns (1997) postulated that triangulation leads to verification and validation of qualitative analysis in two ways: first, by examining the consistency of information generated by different data collection techniques; and second by examining the consistency of different information within the same technique. Triangulation is regarded as the best way to reduce the likelihood of misinterpretation with the target to clarify meaning and verifying

**75**

the repeatability of an observation or interpretation. Denzin and Lincoln (1998) identified four basic types of triangulation:

- *Data-source triangulation*: The use of different types of data sources in a study. For example, a sport researcher may corroborate the strategic direction of a national sport organization by triangulating data from interviews, documents, and archive records.
- *Investigator triangulation*: The use of different researchers or evaluators. The main purpose is to eliminate any bias inherent in using a single observer in the collection, analysis, and discussion of data.
- *Theory triangulation*: The use of multiple perspectives to interpret a single set of data.
- *Methodological triangulation*: Involves the use of multiple techniques to study a single problem. (p. 46)

When analysing data, ensuring that the triangulation methods above are covered will give the researcher an added measure of validity in the final reporting of results.

## Crystallization vs triangulation

Denzin and Lincoln (1994) indicate that 'triangulation arises from the traditions of navigation in which a point in space can be located precisely through three directions' (p. 15). Richardson (2000) argued the approach to research using triangulation assumes that 'data are fixed objects that can be understood precisely' (p. 929). However, Richardson (2000) suggested that postmodernism views the world from more than three sides and proposes the central imagery for 'validity' is not the triangle but rather the crystal (i.e. more perspectives will offer more insights). Cooky (2006, p. 66) postulated that 'a postmodern epistemological perspective rejects triangulation on the grounds that objective reality cannot be captured' and proposed 'inclusion of multiple data collection methods adds rigor, depth, complexity and richness to any inquiry'. It has been suggested that using triangulation in a postmodern context does not acknowledge that 'human subjects and histories of their action and technologies are dynamic, always in motion and always changing' (Edwards and Skinner, 2009, p. 146).

Richardson (2000) viewed crystallization as 'deconstructing the traditional idea of validity and providing the reader with a deepened, complex, thoroughly partial, understanding of the topic' (p. 929). Crystallization, in this way refers to the material that is filtered through to the researcher as a participant–observer and partial 'insider'. This metaphor considers data as both 'fragmented and seen through the prism of perception as dispersed reflections of the phenomena' (Richardson and Lockridge, 2004, p. 240). Therefore, interpretation of data in this approach depends upon the crystal or the lens that the researcher looks through at that given time.

According to Richardson and Lockridge (2004, p. 240), 'crystals and prisms . . . reflect externalities and refract within themselves, creating different colors, patterns, arrays, casting off in different directions. What we see depends on our angle of response.' Furthermore, 'instead of locating the data precisely, recognition is directed towards methods that shape the data that is perceived. What is perceived is not the "data" in any raw form, but the refractions of that data' (p. 240). They also explain that 'crystallization, without losing structure, deconstructs the traditional idea of "validity"' (p. 240).

From this perspective the researcher adopts the metaphor of the 'crystal' as a more valid approach to conceptualizing the fragmented 'truth' and contextualizing data. This approach also recognizes that validity is less about questioning whether or not the study 'measures what was supposed to be measured' or even that it 'saw what was meant to be seen' (Fine, 1994, p. 72). Rather, Reinhartz (1992) believes that 'as long as the researcher is self-aware, whatever happens is useful data' (p. 68). Therefore, it is the responsibility of the researcher in any qualitative study to consider the filters, lenses and crystals surrounding their work, and this can clarify the researcher's understanding of the subject matter.

## 2 Member checking

Member checking is often viewed as an important procedure for verifying findings and ensuring that they are valid and meet the trustworthiness criterion of *confirmability*. Member checking is also referred to as *respondent validation*. Lincoln and Guba (1985) described member checks as 'the most crucial technique for establishing credibility' (p. 314) in a research study. In Sport Management Research, the validity process consists of taking data and interpretations back to the participants in the study so that they can confirm the credibility of the information and the researcher's interpretations.

In member checking, researchers systematically check the data and the narrative account with participants. This may involve, for example, a focus group of fans reviewing the findings on season ticket purchase motivation, or those fans viewing the raw data (for example, transcriptions or observational field notes) and commenting on their accuracy.

Throughout this process, the researchers ask participants whether the themes or categories make sense, whether they are developed with sufficient evidence, and whether the overall account is realistic and accurate (Creswell, 2009). In turn, researchers incorporate participants' comments into the final narrative. In this way, the participants add credibility to the qualitative study by having a chance to react to both the data and the final narrative.

This process has been criticized, first, on the grounds that it is not clear how the procedure actually helps establish the truth of findings, and second, that implementing a member check may introduce bias, leading to respondents changing their original opinions. For example, fans may be swayed by other fans' motivations to purchase after reading and reflecting on a focus group transcript. Member checks are therefore valued just as much for their ethical impact as for their *epistemological* contribution, wherein it is simply courteous to feedback findings to those who have given their time and knowledge to the research project. The current view is that member checking, like many of the other processes here, does not necessarily lead to confirmation of the findings on its own, but is a useful way of generating more data and insights.

## 3 Rich, thick description

Another procedure for establishing credibility is rich, thick description. According to Denzin (1989): 'thick descriptions are deep, dense, detailed accounts . . . thin descriptions, by contrast, lack detail, and simply report facts' (p. 83). The purpose of a thick description is that it creates a level of trust in the data, so that the reader can see and feel how well the quotes have been analysed and organized. The process of writing using thick description is to provide as much detail as possible. It may involve describing a small slice of interaction, experience or action; locating individuals in specific situations; bringing a relationship or an interaction alive between two or more persons; or providing a detailed rendering of how people feel (Denzin, 1989). So, instead of just describing themes related to match fixing from several data sources, the sport management researcher might explicitly describe the emotions, context, and dialogue of the interview sessions with team managers affected by match fixing. According to Creswell (1998), this allows the reader to make decisions regarding transferability based on shared characteristics. This is done by providing detailed accounts of the participants and the setting. Rich, thick descriptions allow the reader to see connections and patterns (as well as the researcher). Creswell (1998) highlighted that rich, thick description allows the reader to make decisions regarding transferability because the writer describes in detail the participants or settings under study. With such detailed description, the researcher enables readers to transfer information to other settings and to determine whether the findings can be transferred 'because of shared characteristics' (p. 203).

## 4 Avoidance of researcher bias

Creswell (1998) asserted that avoiding, or at least clarifying, researcher bias from the outset of a study is a validity issue. In this strategy, the sport researcher notes past experiences, biases, prejudices and orientations that may influence the study. For example, if the researcher was an athlete who personally experienced a drastic change in team policies that affected their career, this should be noted if they are studying post-athletic career pathways for athletes. Hatch (2002) also advised researchers to submit a self-disclosure statement detailing any potential biases that may be relevant to the topic of the study. McMillan (2004) added that attributes of the researcher such as age, gender, race, hostility and physical appearance may influence research results. Two strategies to avoid researcher bias are *reflexivity* (researcher self-awareness and self-reflection) and *researcher journaling* (detailed and timely documentation of the researcher thoughts). *Reflexivity* is a validity procedure whereby researchers report on (and may even try to modify) personal beliefs, values and biases that may shape their inquiry. This validity procedure uses the lens of the researcher but to reflect on the social, cultural and historical forces that shape their interpretation.

## 5 Negative case analysis

According to Strauss and Corbin (1990), negative case analysis enhances rigour in qualitative research and is used in the quest for verification. A negative case analysis is an ongoing and deliberate attempt to refute or challenge developing themes/ideas. Negative case analysis refers to the process of testing out sampling strategies and/or analysis to look for alternative explanations or different cases that are in contrast to the researcher's own theories or explanations. This is part of a well-established approach known as *analytic induction*.

Negative case analysis may involve a re-examination of every case, after the initial analysis is completed, to see whether the characteristics or properties of the emergent themes were applicable to all cases. It is argued that in addition to developing your explanation, if you have explored any alternative explanations, your own explanation will have much wider theoretical significance (Mason, 1996).

## 6 Prolonged engagement

Another validity procedure is for researchers to stay at the research site for a prolonged period of time. Fetterman (1989) contends that 'working with people day in and day out for long periods of time is what gives ethnographic research its validity and vitality' (p. 46 – noting, of course, that not all research is ethnographic). During repeated observation, the sport management researchers build *trust* with participants, find gatekeepers to allow access to people and sites, establish rapport so that participants are comfortable disclosing information, reciprocate by giving back to the people being studied, which allows the sport researcher to challenge their own preconceptions of the research environment.

Being in the field over time solidifies evidence because researchers can check out the data and their hunches and compare interview data with observational data. It is not a process that is systematically established, but constructivists recognize that the longer they stay in the field, the more the different perspectives will be heard from participants and the better the understanding of the context of participant views. In practice, prolonged engagement in the field has no set duration, but as an example, a sport management researcher could easily spend from four months to a year with a team, incorporating an entire season and even the off-season.

## 7 Peer debriefing

A peer review or debriefing 'is a process of exposing oneself to a disinterested peer in a manner paralleling analytical sessions and for the purpose of exploring aspects of the inquiry that might otherwise remain only implicit within the inquirer's mind' (Lincoln and Guba, 1985, p. 308). A peer reviewer provides support, plays devil's advocate, challenges the researchers' assumptions, pushes the researchers to the next step methodologically, and asks hard questions about methods and interpretations (Lincoln and Guba, 1985). In the peer debriefing strategy, the lens for establishing credibility is someone external to the study, and a critical paradigm is operating because of the close collaboration between the external reviewer and the qualitative researcher. This procedure is best used over time during the process of an entire study. Peer debriefers can provide written feedback to sport researchers or simply serve as a sounding board for ideas. The ultimate purpose of peer debriefing, contended Lincoln and Guba (1985), is to enhance the credibility, or truth value, of a qualitative study, by providing 'an external check on the inquiry process' (p. 301). Peer debriefing is particularly advisable because of a distinctive characteristic of qualitative research: the researcher-as-instrument. Individual researchers are the primary means for data collection and analysis. As such, each researcher brings a different combination of subjective knowledge, skills and values to the research endeavour. Researchers must come to know their unique characteristics as research tools and to understand how their subjectivity affects the conduct and results of their research. *Researcher subjectivity* is often equated with bias and seen as something to be avoided.

## 8 External auditing

The last method of verification employed is an external audit. In establishing an *audit trail*, researchers provide clear documentation of all research decisions and activities. An audit trail is established by sport management researchers documenting the inquiry process through journaling and memoing, keeping a research log of all activities, developing a data collection chronology and recording data analysis procedures clearly.

External auditing is a procedure that is useful for determining both dependability and confirmability. It is a procedure whereby an independent third party can review the documents and records of the process and activities of the research project. In doing so, the independent third party is able to make a judgement about the dependability of procedures employed by the researcher and the extent to which the findings are confirmable.

An external auditor examines both the process and the product, assessing accuracy and determining whether the findings, interpretations and conclusions are supported by the data (Creswell, 1998). The external auditor is usually skilled in qualitative research and is not connected to the study in any way. The external auditor examines this documentation with the following questions in mind: are the findings grounded in the data? Are inferences logical? Is the category structure appropriate? Can inquiry decisions and methodological shifts be justified? What is the degree of researcher bias? What strategies were used for increasing credibility? (Schwandt and Halpern, 1988).

## APPROPRIATE PREPARATION (SKILL/KNOWLEDGE LEVEL) OF THE RESEARCHER

Morse and Richards (2002) stated 'any study is only as good as the researcher' (p. 168). This statement holds true even more so for qualitative research, as the *researcher is the instrument* (p. 168). Therefore, being prepared in qualitative methods prior to the undertaking of a qualitative study is essential.

Table 5.3 outlines Cresswell's (1998) verification processes, as applied to a study evaluating social capital in community sport organizations. When considered as a whole, a researcher should attempt to employ the majority if not all of these procedures.

## QUALITATIVE RELIABILITY

*Reliability is* commonly used in relation to the question of whether the measures devised for concepts in the social sciences are consistent. *Qualitative reliability* differs from validity in that reliability indicates the 'researcher's approach is consistent across different researchers and different projects' (Creswell, 2009, p. 190).

**Table 5.3** *Verification processes for qualitative research*

| | |
|---|---|
| Prolonged engagement and persistent observation | Data was collected for over six months in the field from various community sport groups. |
| Triangulation | Data was used from documents, interviews and community focus groups to assess the validity of findings. |
| Peer review and debriefing | The researcher(s) should regularly reflect on the data and discuss emerging propositions and interpretations from the data. Researchers who are not engaged in fieldwork in specific settings are able to adopt the role of 'critical friend', giving feedback and probing for alternative interpretations. |
| Negative case analysis | Community sport organizations were asked for disconfirming evidence. |
| Clarifying researcher bias | The researcher(s) should operate in a *reflexive* manner from the project's outset. Reports should clarify assumptions about the research goals and about how support to community sport groups should be organized. |
| Member checks | The data collected, its analysis, the interpretations of it and the conclusions drawn should be given back to research participants so that they can judge the accuracy and credibility of the accounts. |
| Rich, thick description | Reports should be detailed descriptions of the research settings. |
| External auditing | An external auditor from a government agency could examine the research process to determine whether the findings, interpretations and conclusions drawn are consistent. |

Source: Adapted from Creswell (1998)

In order to do this, Creswell (2009) and Yin (2009) suggested documentation of as many steps of the procedure as possible and other reliability procedures, including cross-checking codes, checking transcripts and writing definitions of codes, and constantly comparing data with those definitions of the codes. The following procedures can be used as a means of ensuring reliability for single researcher studies: (1) ensure appropriate preparation (skill/knowledge level) of the researcher; (2) ensure appropriate review of the literature; (3) ensure coding reliability; and, (4) ensure transcripts do not contain obvious errors (Creswell 2009, p. 190). Gibbs (2007) similarly suggests the following reliability procedures: (1) check transcripts for mistakes; (2) check the persistence of the meaning of the codes; (3) coordinate communication among coders; and (4) cross-check codes developed by different researchers.

Other reliability control measures used included having backup copies of both recorded interviews and transcripts. In addition, repetition of certain questions may lead to misinterpretation of the findings, and should be clarified during and after the interviews. This probing is also a technique of getting a deeper understanding of responses.

## QUALITATIVE GENERALIZABILITY

Generalizability is a term that is not discussed often in contexts of qualitative research, since the findings achieved from qualitative research methods are normally not intended for generalization (Creswell, 2009). Therefore *'qualitative generalization* is a term that is used in a limited way . . . since the intent of this form of inquiry is not to generalize findings . . . "particularity" rather than "generalizability" is the hallmark of qualitative research' (pp. 192–193). Generalizability can also be referred to as *external validity*. Threats to external validity occur if the researcher develops inaccurate inferences from the sample and generalizes these findings to the larger population.

## Data analysis and representation

In order to deal with data analysis and representation, Creswell (2007, p. 148) suggested three strategies should be employed. These are: Step 1: Preparing and organizing the data; Step 2: Reducing the data into themes through a process of coding and condensing the codes; and Step 3: Representing the data in figures, tables or a discussion. Similarly Creswell (2009) provides data analysis guidelines. These steps are interrelated and not always visited in the order presented. These guidelines or six step data analysis process include: (1) transcription; (2) thematic labelling; (3) coding process; (4) individual and cross-case analysis; (5) conceptual model development; and (6) data 'sense-making' (theory extensions). These stages shall now be discussed.

## 1 Transcription

Transcription is the process of converting audio recorded data or handwritten field notes obtained from interviews and observations into verbatim form (i.e. written or printed) for easy reading. After transcription, it is necessary to organize your data into sections that are easy to retrieve.

## 2 Thematic labelling

Bogdan and Biklen (1982) defined qualitative modes of analysis as 'working with data, organizing it, breaking it into manageable units, synthesizing it, searching for patterns, discovering what is important and what is to be learned, and deciding what you will tell others' (p. 145). Qualitative researchers tend to use inductive analysis of data, meaning that the critical themes emerge out of the data. Qualitative analysis requires some creativity, for the challenge is to place the raw data into logical, meaningful categories; to examine them in a holistic fashion; and to find a way to communicate this interpretation to others. This process is called thematic labelling.

## 3 Coding process

Coding is the process of examining the raw qualitative data in the transcripts and extracting sections of text units (words, phrases, sentences or paragraphs) and assigning different codes or labels so that they can easily be retrieved at a later stage for further comparison and analysis, and the identification of any patterns. Strauss and Corbin (1990) identified the following types of coding: *open coding* and *axial coding*. Coding will be discussed in more detail later in this chapter.

## 4 Individual and cross-case analysis

This process involves applying the thematic framework to all transcripts systematically and annotating the textual data with codes.

## 5 Conceptual model development

This is the process of developing individual matrices for each key theme and entering coded sections of text (plus identifiers) into appropriate charts.

## 6 Data sense making (theory extensions)

This involves using the charts to map the range and nature of responses, create typologies, identify associations between themes and attempt explanations.

## CODING DATA

*Codes* are tags that categorize the data collected during a study to assign meanings to them. Coding is the first stage to providing some form of logical structure to the data. Coding makes it easier to search the data, make comparisons and identify patterns that require further investigation. Codes can be based on themes, topics, ideas, concepts, terms, phrases or keywords found in the data, but they can also correspond to passages of audio or video recordings and to parts of images. Codes should be valid, that is they should accurately reflect what is being researched, where possible they should be mutually exclusive (in that codes should be distinct, with no overlap) and they should be exhaustive, that is, all relevant data should fit into a code.

A suggested framework for undertaking coding includes:

1 The data is carefully read, all statements relating to the research question are identified, and each is assigned a code, or category. These codes are then noted, and each relevant statement is organized under its appropriate code, either manually or on computer, along with any notes or memos that the researcher wishes to add of their own. This is referred to as *open coding* (Strauss and Corbin, 1990). During open coding, the researcher must identify and tentatively name the conceptual categories into which the phenomena observed will be grouped. The goal is to create descriptive, multidimensional categories that form a preliminary framework for analysis. For example, when working with transcripts from interviews on sport for development in rural communities, some open codes might include 'raising awareness', 'connection', 'driver of change' and 'quality of life'. Words, phrases or events that appear to be similar can be grouped into the same category. These categories may be gradually modified or replaced during the subsequent stages of analysis that follow.

**83**

As the raw data are broken down into manageable chunks, the researcher must also devise an *audit trail* – that is, a scheme for identifying these data chunks according to their speaker and the context. Qualitative research is characterized by the use of 'voice' in the text; that is, participant quotes that illustrate the themes being described.

2 The next stage of analysis involves re-examination of the categories identified in stage 1 to determine how they are linked, a complex process sometimes called *axial coding* (Strauss and Corbin, 1990). The discrete categories identified in open coding are compared and combined in new ways as the researcher begins to assemble the 'big picture'. In the sport for development example, open codes of 'raising awareness' and 'driver of change' may be linked through common passages in the transcripts. The purpose of coding is to not only describe but, more importantly, to acquire new understanding of a phenomenon of interest. Therefore, causal events contributing to the phenomenon, descriptive details of the phenomenon itself and the ramifications of the phenomenon under study must all be identified and explored. During axial coding the researcher is responsible for building a conceptual model and for determining whether sufficient data exists to support that interpretation.

3 Once the first two stages of coding have been completed, the researcher should become more analytical, and look for patterns and explanation in the codes. Questions should be asked such as: Can I relate certain codes together under a more general code? Can I organize codes sequentially? Can I identify any causal relations?

4 The fourth stage is that of *selective coding*. This involves reading through the raw data for cases that illustrate the analysis, or explain the concepts. The researcher should also look for data that is contradictory, as well as confirmatory. For example, selective coding can include finding direct quotes from participants that relate how sport first raises awareness of a development issue through meaningful gatherings, then is a catalyst for changing that issue by ongoing education tied to the sport events.

Lewins, Taylor and Gibbs (2005) provide a detailed list of the kinds of things that can be coded (see Table 5.4).

## MEMOING

While coding data, the researcher can aid in the maximization of the validity and reliability of the analysis process by writing *memos*. These are the ideas that occur to the researcher while coding the data, for example, concerning explanation, theorizing or other ideas about the data. They can be extremely helpful in trying to make sense of the data at a later date. Memos can be written directly on the transcripts, or the researcher can keep a record of them elsewhere. Making memos as detailed as possible can help with later analysis.

### Recursive abstraction

Some qualitative datasets are analysed without coding. A common method here is *recursive abstraction*, where datasets are summarized, those summaries are then further summarized, and so on. The end result is a more compact summary that would have been difficult to accurately discern without the preceding steps of distillation.

**Table 5.4** *What can be coded*

Behaviours, specific acts

Events – short once in a lifetime events or things people have done that are often told as a story

Activities – these are of a longer duration, involve other people within a particular setting

Strategies, practice or tactics

States – general conditions experienced by people or found in organizations

Meanings – a wide range of phenomena at the core of much qualitative analysis. Meanings and interpretations are important parts of what directs participants' actions

Participation – adaptation to a new setting or involvement

Relationships or interaction

Conditions or constraints

Consequences

Settings – the entire context of the events under study

Reflexive – researcher's role in the process, how intervention generated the data

Source: Lewins, Taylor and Gibbs (2005)

A frequent criticism of recursive abstraction is that the final conclusions are several times removed from the underlying data. While it is true that poor initial summaries will certainly yield an inaccurate final report, qualitative analysts can respond to this criticism. They do so, like those using coding method, by documenting the reasoning behind each summary step, citing examples from the data where statements were included and where statements were excluded from the intermediate summary.

## Mechanical techniques

*Content analysis* is a procedure for the categorization of verbal or behavioural data, for purposes of classification, summarization and tabulation. The content can be analysed on two levels. The basic level of analysis is a descriptive account of the data: this is what was actually said with nothing read into it and nothing assumed about it, e.g. 'I would never pay to see a WNBA (Women's National Basketball Association) game.' Some texts refer to this as the manifest level or type of analysis. The higher level of analysis is interpretative: it is concerned with what was meant by the response, what was inferred or implied, e.g. does this participant not like basketball? Women's sports? Or has a preference to spend money on other entertainment options? Additional context may be required to interpret the original statement. It is sometimes called the latent level of analysis.

Content analysis researchers frequently rely on computers to scan and sort large sets of qualitative data. At their most basic level, mechanical techniques rely on counting words, phrases or coincidences of tokens within the data. Mechanical techniques are particularly well suited for a few scenarios. One such scenario is for datasets that are simply too large for a

**85**

human to effectively analyse, or where analysis of them would be cost-prohibitive relative to the value of information they contain. Another scenario is when the chief value of a data set is the extent to which it contains certain adverse events within a lengthy journal data set or searching for mentions of a sport brand in positive reviews of sport marketing. A large variety of coding schemes exist, as well as many CAQDAS tools – such as NVivo and ATLAS.ti – used to assist in coding and in helping to organize the resulting patterns. These will be examined in the final section of this chapter.

## APPROACHES TO QUALITATIVE DATA ANALYSIS

Qualitative data analysis involves various *approaches*. Two of these are outlined below.

The *grounded theory* approach offers something intended to be a rigorous approach in generating theory from qualitative data. Grounded theory is an 'inductive' approach in the analysis of qualitative data in which theory is systematically generated from data. The grounded theory approach is used for theory building. The main feature of the grounded theory procedure is the use of the *constant comparison technique*. Using this technique, categories or concepts that emerge from one stage of analysis are compared with categories or concepts that emerge from the previous stage. This approach is discussed in detail in the next chapter.

Another approach to qualitative data analysis is called *framework analysis* (Ritchie and Spencer, 1994). In contrast to the grounded theory procedure, framework analysis was explicitly developed for applied research. In applied research, the findings and recommendations of research need to be obtained within a short period to become adopted. The general approach of framework analysis shares many of the common features with the grounded theory approach discussed earlier. This approach to qualitative data analysis allows the researcher to set the categories and themes from the beginning of the study. However, this approach also allows for categories and themes that may emerge during data analysis that the researcher had not stated at the beginning of the study. Once the categories or themes have been predetermined, specific pieces of data are identified that correspond to the different themes or categories. Charts can be either *thematic* for each theme or category across all respondents (cases) or by *case* for each respondent across all themes. An example of these charts is provided in Table 5.5 and 5.6.

**Table 5.5** *Example thematic chart*

| Theme | Case 1 | Case 2 |
|---|---|---|
| Crisis communication | 'The salary cap breach effected was a real surprise and we went into damage control.' | 'The media jumped all over the story and we had nowhere to hide.' |

**Table 5.6** *Example case chart*

|  | Theme 1 | Theme 2 |
| --- | --- | --- |
|  | Social media marketing | Sponsorship |
| Case 1 | 'Social media has changed the way we function as sport marketers.' | 'The role of sport sponsorship has changed since the Tiger Woods scandal.' |

## COMPUTER ASSISTED QUALITATIVE DATA ANALYSIS SOFTWARE

Computer Assisted/Aided Qualitative Data Analysis (CAQDAS) is the use of computer software to aid qualitative research such as transcription analysis, coding and text interpretation, recursive abstraction, content analysis, discourse analysis, grounded theory methodology, etc. CAQDAS can assist the sport management researcher in the modes of analysis process by searching, organizing, categorizing and annotating textual and visual data. CAQDAS saves time and effort in data management by extending the ability of the researcher to organize, track and manage data. The transparency and reliability of the data analysis processes may enhance the credibility of the research processes. The use of CAQDAS is not without controversy. Table 5.7 summarizes some of the contentious issues.

**Table 5.7** *Advantages and disadvantages of CAQDAS*

*Advantages*

- Efficient
- Uniform
- Prestige in using computing
- Allows for focused and detailed analysis
- Facilitates rigour and transparency
- Makes qualitative data more scientific
- Time-saving
- Ability to analyse larger sets of data
- More substantive analysis
- Data analysis remains the intellectual, interpretive and creative work of the researcher

*Disadvantages*

- Inflexible
- Not hands-on
- Distracts from ideas, emphasizes words
- Reification of the researcher and data
- Advocates the positivist or quantitative approach
- CAQDAS should support rather than replace manual data analysis
- Segments of text are removed from the whole, thus creating a loss of perspective
- Considerable time constraint in mastering the software in order to free the researcher to perform in-depth analyses and interpretation of the data
- CAQDAS is for coding, not analysis

CAQDAS has also been criticized for favouring the grounded theory approach (Coffey, Holbrook and Atkinson, 1996). In the grounded theory approach the process of coding is the fundamental task that needs to be satisfied first before any further processes can be carried out. Table 5.8 summarizes the various approaches to analysis.

**Table 5.8** Summary of comparative analysis process

| Grounded theory method | CAQDAS | Manual |
| --- | --- | --- |
| Open coding | Creation of codes as free nodes by sentence or paragraph description/ summary of sentences or paragraph | Creation of codes based by paragraph description/summary of paragraph |
| Axial coding | Re-reading of codes/free nodes and re-arrangement according to theme/ categories/tree nodes Creation of hierarchies by "drag" and "drop" | Re-reading of codes generated and rearrangement according to theme/ category – cutting and pasting |
| Selective coding | Re-reading of codes and categories and selection of category that most represents the cumulated categories Higher hierarchies of the tree nodes are established to show the selected codes | Re-reading of codes and categories and selection of category that most represent the cumulated categories |

Source: Based on Strauss and Corbin (1990)

Despite ongoing debate around the advantages and disadvantages of CAQDAS, many researchers now use CAQDAS, but often only for the purpose of coding alone, and go back to the manual methods for the theory-building stage; thus ensuring that the benefits of automation are reaped and its shortcomings are avoided.

## CAQDAS SELECTION

Weitzman and Miles (1995) classified this software into five categories. These are: (1) text retrievers; (2) textbase managers; (3) code and retrieve programs; (4) code-based theory builders; and (5) conceptual network builders. Fielding and Lee (2002) later identified three generations of CAQDAS. *First generation* software consisted of word processing and database software that allowed a researcher to search for specific text strings, but did not allow for encoding the data. *Second generation* software provided additional capability to encode the data, retrieve data by those codes and add memos to the encoded text. Second generation CAQDAS is commonly referred to as code and retrieve software. *Third generation* CAQDAS has added the ability to create complex families or networks of codes to support theory building. In most cases, third generation CAQDAS packages are represented by the latest versions of the industry leading products such as ATLAS.ti® and are classified as code-based theory builders. Other prominent CAQDAS products, classified as conceptual network builders, provide linking and graphic capabilities, but may lack coding and database management features. Third generation CAQDAS is very complex software and a significant learning curve is necessary for mining its full potential for qualitative research.

The CAQDAS networking project lists the following tools a CAQDAS program should have: content searching tools; coding tools; linking tools; mapping or networking tools; query tools; writing and annotation tools. Selection of a suitable CAQDAS package requires the researcher to understand the purpose of the study, expected results and the available timeline in which to perform the study. Once CAQDAS becomes applicable to a particular study or research problem, various packages must be evaluated and an appropriate CAQDAS package selected. Selection criteria may be different depending on the group in which a specific qualitative researcher resides. Students and other qualitative researchers may be directed to use a particular CAQDAS package as part of a university's standard software application suite. Some researchers may require more than one CAQDAS package. Training on the software is recommended. Appropriate usage of CAQDAS can then free the researcher from the burden of managing the raw data and allow him or her time to delve into the data and observe emergent themes and patterns as they develop.

There are a number of well-known CAQDAS packages. Some of the packages take some time to learn, even with specialized instruction. The sport management researcher needs to weigh up the pros and cons of taking the time to learn such a package before deciding on a particular approach. The software packages range in the level of sophistication, and if intending to utilize a CAQDAS package, the sport management researcher should seek a package that has the tools that suit the research style, rather than just the package that offers the greatest functionality. If a sport management researcher is likely to be undertaking a considerable amount of qualitative research over a reasonable period of time, then it may be worthwhile learning one of the packages. On the other hand, if the researcher is engaged in a one-off piece of research, then we would recommend manual analysis. For a comprehensive overview and comparison of different CAQDAS packages, visit the WinMax website: www.winmax.de/english/linkse.htm

## CAQDAS PACKAGES FOR SPORT MANAGEMENT RESEARCH

The following discussion examines some popular CAQDAS packages utilized in Sport Management Research.

### Qualitative data analysis with ATLAS.ti

ATLAS.ti is a computer program that supports the qualitative analysis of large bodies of textual, graphical, audio and video data. It offers a variety of tools for accomplishing the tasks associated with any systematic approach to 'soft' data, for example, material that cannot be analysed by formal, statistical approaches in meaningful ways. In the course of such a *qualitative analysis* ATLAS.ti helps to uncover the complex phenomena hidden in data in an exploratory way. The main strategic modes of operation can be termed 'VISE': visualization, integration, serendipity and exploration.

**89**

## Qualitative data analysis with NVivo

NVivo is a multifunctional software system for the development, support and management of qualitative data analysis (QDA) projects. It is used in a wide range of research for handling non-numerical unstructured data by processes of indexing, searching and theory building. NVivo transforms the way data is viewed (from static to dynamic) in a way that makes relationships between categories more visible by using text formatting and hyperlinks to other documents and categories.

## Qualitative data analysis with Leximancer

Leximancer is a sophisticated qualitative analysis of textual data. This software tool automates the analysis of concepts in the text, creating visualization maps of the concepts and the relationships between them. The key capabilities of the Leximancer software provides a means for generating and recognizing themes, including themes that might otherwise have been missed or overlooked if the data had been manually coded (Crofts and Bisman, 2010). Table 5.9 represents the proposed benefits of this software analysis system.

**Table 5.9** The benefits of Leximancer

| Leximancer benefits | Author/s |
| --- | --- |
| It is implemented as a commercial-quality program, is easy to use and 'has been evaluated for stability, reproducibility and correlative validity' | Stockwell, Colomb, Smith and Wiles, 2009, p. 425; Smith and Humphreys, 2006 |
| As an automated form of content analysis, it is able to discover underlying core associations without being influenced by human biases in the coding process or by the expectation bias from the coder's personal knowledge | Isakhan, 2005; Michael, Fusco and Michael, 2008; McKenna and Waddell, 2007 |
| It has established a role in content analysis as a means for discovering 'unexpected meaningful connections' through its automated objective analysis process | Dann, 2010, p. 149 |

Crofts and Bisman (2010) claim 'a distinct advantage for the researcher in using the concept map, rank-ordered concept lists and text query options is the ability to read instances of specific concepts to understand their relationships with one another' (p. 319). An example of a concept map from research by Franklin (2012) on sponsored female surfers is provided as an example (Figure 5.1).

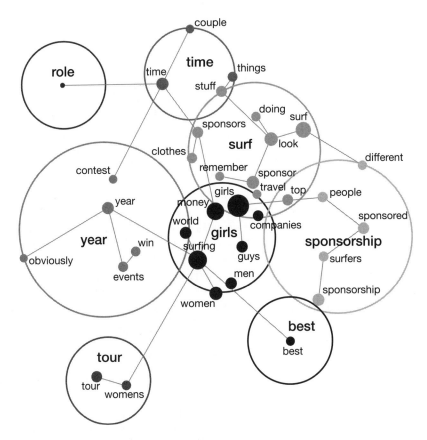

**Figure 5.1** *Combined sponsored female surfers' themes and concepts*

*Leximancer phases of analysis*

Franklin (2012) organized data into two individual sets, one set from the responses to interviews with surf company representatives and the other from interviews with sponsored female surfers. The analysis of data from interviews with surf company representatives (SCR) and sponsored female surfers (SFS) is divided into six phases as presented in Table 5.10.

## SUMMARY ON CAQDAS

The final decision on using Computer Assisted Qualitative Modes of Analysis Software (CAQDAS) is left to the confidence and expertise of the sport management researcher. If a researcher does reject the use of CAQDAS for analysis, then it should not immediately be assumed that the quality of analysis is inferior. Provided the mode of analysis is carried out correctly then there should be little difference in the quality of analysis.

**Table 5.10** *Leximancer phases of data analysis*

| Phase | Description | Action |
|---|---|---|
| First phase SCR | Familiarization with the data | Immersion in the raw data, e.g. preview company profiles and Internet websites, listening to audio recordings and transcribing interviews, reviewing the observations and field notes, noting initial ideas |
| First phase SFS | | Immersion in the raw data, e.g. preview female surfer profiles and Internet websites, listening to audio recordings and transcribing interviews, reviewing the observations and field notes, noting initial ideas |
| Second phase SCR | Searching for overall themes | Uploading the combined surf company files into Leximancer to identify key concepts and themes |
| Second phase SFS | | Previewing survey data for relevant themes and quotes Uploading all transcribed interview data from SFS into Leximancer to identify key concepts and themes |
| Third phase | Reviewing themes | Checking themes relative to observations, field notes and content analysis of other material |
| Fourth phase | Defining and naming themes | Ongoing analysis to refine specifics of each theme Reviewing data to extract relevant quotes and literature review to identify links |
| Fifth phase | Producing the findings | The final opportunity for analysis Selection of vivid, compelling extract examples, final analysis of selected extracts, relating back to analysis of research questions and literature, producing findings of the analysis |
| Sixth phase | Searching for individual themes | Uploading individual company files into Leximancer to identify key individual company concepts and themes (Repeat phases 2, 3, 4 and 5) |

Source: Adapted from Braun and Clarke (2006, p. 87) and Stewart (2010, p. 38)

## HYPOTHETICAL CASE

1  Read the text below: 'Tiger Woods apology transcript'.
2  Consider the research topic: 'Sport celebrity bad behaviour effects on stakeholders'.
3  Consider the research question: 'How can athletes mend the relationship with sponsors in the wake of scandal?'
4  After reading the article once, go back and open the code to identify the main actors, themes and key relationships.

## TIGER WOODS 2010 APOLOGY TRANSCRIPT

Many of you in the room are my friends. Many of you in this room know me. Many of you have cheered for me, or worked with me, or supported me, and now, every one of you has good reason to be critical of me.

I want to say to each of you, simply, and directly, I am deeply sorry for the irresponsible and selfish behavior I engaged in.

I know people want to find out how I could be so selfish and so foolish. People want to know how I could have done these things to my wife, Elin, and to my children. And while I have always tried to be a private person, there are some things I want to say.

Elin and I have started the process of discussing the damage caused by my behavior. As she pointed out to me, my real apology to her will not come in the form of words. It will come from my behavior over time. We have a lot to discuss. However, what we say to each other will remain between the two of us.

I am also aware of the pain my behavior has caused to those of you in this room. I have let you down. I have let down my fans. For many of you, especially my friends, my behavior has been a personal disappointment. To those of you who work for me, I have let you down, personally and professionally. My behavior has caused considerable worry to my business partners.

To everyone involved in my foundation, including my staff, board of directors, sponsors, and most importantly, the young students we reach, our work is more important than ever. Thirteen years ago, my dad and I envisioned helping young people achieve their dreams through education. This work remains unchanged and will continue to grow. From the Learning Center students in Southern California, to the Earl Woods Scholars in Washington, DC, millions of kids have changed their lives, and I am dedicated to making sure that continues.

But, still, I know I have severely disappointed all of you. I have made you question who I am and how I have done the things I did. I am embarrassed that I have put you in this position. For all that I have done, I am so sorry. I have a lot to atone for.

But there is one issue I really want to discuss. Some people have speculated that Elin somehow hurt or attacked me on Thanksgiving night. It angers me that people would fabricate a story like that. She never hit me that night or any other night. There has never been an episode of domestic violence in our marriage. Ever.

Elin has shown enormous grace and poise throughout this ordeal. Elin deserves praise, not blame. The issue involved here was my repeated irresponsible behavior. I was unfaithful. I had affairs. I cheated. What I did is not acceptable. And I am the only person to blame. I stopped living by the core values that I was taught to believe in.

I knew my actions were wrong. But I convinced myself that normal rules didn't apply. I never thought about who I was hurting. Instead, I thought only about myself. I ran straight through the boundaries that a married couple should live by. I thought I could get away with whatever I wanted to. I felt that I had worked hard my entire life and deserved to enjoy all the temptations around me. I felt I was entitled. Thanks to money and fame, I didn't have far – didn't have to go far to find them. I was wrong.

I was foolish. I don't get to play by different rules. The same boundaries that apply to everyone apply to me. I brought this shame on myself. I hurt my wife, my kids, my mother, my wife's family, my friends, my foundation, and kids all around the world who admired me.

I've had a lot of time to think about what I have done. My failures have made me look at myself in a way I never wanted to before. It is now up to me to make amends. And that starts by never repeating the mistakes I have made. It is up to me to start living a life of integrity.

I once heard – and I believe it is true – it's not what you achieve in life that matters, it is what you overcome. Achievements on the golf course are only part of setting an example. Character and decency are what really count. Parents used to point to me as a role model for their kids. I owe all of those families a special apology. I want to say to them that I am truly sorry.

It is hard to admit that I need help. But I do. For 45 days, from the end of December to early February, I was in inpatient therapy, receiving guidance for the issues I'm facing. I have a long way to go. But I've taken my first steps in the right direction.

As I proceed, I understand people have questions. I understand the press wants me to – to ask me for the details of the times I was unfaithful. I understand people want to know whether Elin and I will remain together. Please know that as far as I'm concerned, every one of these questions and answers is a matter between Elin and me. These are issues between a husband and a wife.

Some people have made up things that never happened. They said I used performance-enhancing drugs. This is completely and utterly false.

Some have written things about my family. Despite the damage I have done, I still believe it is right to shield my family from the public spotlight. They did not do these things. I did. I have always tried to maintain a private space for my wife and children. They have been kept separate from my sponsors, my commercial endorsements, when my children were born, we only released photographs so they . . . so that the paparazzi could not chase them.

However, my behavior doesn't make it right for the media to follow my two and a half-year-old daughter to school and report the school's location. They staked out my wife and pursued my mom. Whatever my wrongdoings, for the sake of my family, please leave my wife and kids alone.

I recognize I have brought this on myself. And I know above all I am the one who needs to change. I owe it to my family to become a better person. I owe it to those closest to me to become a better man. That is where my focus will be. I have a lot of work to do. And I intend to dedicate myself to doing it.

Part of following this path for me is Buddhism, which my mother taught me at a young age. People probably don't realize it, but I was raised a Buddhist, and I actively practiced my faith from childhood until I drifted away from it in recent years. Buddhism teaches that a craving for things outside ourselves causes an unhappy and pointless search for security. It teaches me to stop following every impulse and to learn restraint. Obviously, I lost track of what I was taught.

As I move forward, I will continue to receive help because I have learned that is how people really do change. Starting tomorrow, I will leave for more treatment and more therapy.

I would like to thank my friends at Accenture and the players in the field this week for understanding why I am making this – these remarks today. In therapy, I have learned that looking at – the importance of looking at my spiritual life and keeping it in balance with my professional life. I need to regain my balance and be centered so I can save the things that are most important to me: my marriage and my children.

That also means relying on others for help. I have learned to seek support from my peers in therapy, and I hope someday to return that support to others who are seeking help.

I do plan to return to golf one day. I just don't know when that day will be. I don't rule out that it will be this year. When I do return, I need to make my behavior more respectful of the game.

In recent weeks, I have received many thousands of emails, letters and phone calls from people expressing good wishes. To everyone who has reached out to me and my family, thank you. Your encouragement means the world to Elin and me. I want to thank the PGA Tour, Commissioner [Tim] Finchem and the players for their patience and understanding while I work on my private life. I look forward to seeing my fellow players on the course.

Finally, there are many people in this room and there are many people at home who believed in me. Today, I want to ask for your help. I ask you to find room in your hearts to one day believe in me again. Thank you.

## CONCLUSION

This chapter has explained the principles and techniques that should underpin qualitative data analysis. It began by discussing the analysis of qualitative data and an appropriate framework that can be used in organizing that analysis. It identified two major trends in the debate about rigour and validity in qualitative research (*exclusive trend* and *inclusive trend*). The stages in qualitative analysis were then discussed. Finally, Computer Assisted Qualitative Data Analysis Software (CAQDAS) and how it can assist the sport management researcher in the modes of analysis process was discussed.

## REVIEW QUESTIONS

The process of modes of analysis aims to provide the sport management researcher with the opportunity to make sense of the data so that evidence can be obtained that can then be used to answer the research question. With a basic understanding now of the modes of analysis process, attempt to answer the following questions:

- What are the three types of coding, and at what stage of the coding process would they be employed?
- Identify some advantages and disadvantages to the use of CAQDAS over completely manual modes of analysis processes.

## SUGGESTED EXTENDED READING FOR STUDENTS

Creswell, J. W. (2009). *Research design: Quantitative, qualitative and mixed methods approaches.* New York: Sage.

Edwards, A., and Skinner, J. (2009). *Qualitative research in sport management.* Oxford: Elsevier.

Padgett, D. (2008). *Qualitative methods in social work research.* Los Angeles, CA: Sage.

## Chapter 6

# Action Research and Sport Management Research

## LEARNING OUTCOMES

By the end of this chapter you should be able to:

■  identify the origins of Action Research as a means of understanding variation in the contemporary literature;

■  define, compare and contrast the distinguishing bases of Action Research;

■  develop a review of the key features associated with Action Research;

■  describe the range of practical methods associated with Action Research;

■  consider the ethical challenges associated with Action Research;

■  consider the specific application of Action Research methodologies to community health initiatives.

## KEY TERMS

*The Action Research cycle* – the steps of plan, act, observe and reflect.

*Emancipatory Action Research* – seeks to bring together action and reflection, theory and practice through a participatory democratic process aimed at developing practical solutions to issues.

*Participatory Action Research* – involves the participation of those who may be affected by the outcomes of research in decision making at all stages of the research process. It is often used for liberationist inquiry or development research with disadvantaged communities.

## KEY THEMES

■  How is Action Research self-reflective?

■  What are the key differences between emancipatory and participatory Action Research?

## CHAPTER OVERVIEW

This chapter explores a key qualitative methodology that can be utilized by sport management researchers. Action Research is cyclic, or iterative, in nature and the researcher using this methodology will generally be working from within the organization to continually plan, act, observe and reflect, based on the outcome of the first cycle.

## WHAT IS ACTION RESEARCH (AR)?

Action Research is based on a philosophical stance that focuses on the way knowledge is acquired, interpreted and what outcomes can be expected. It is grounded on the foundations of naturalistic inquiry and phenomenology. Through the systematic participatory approach of Action Research, the lived experiences of participants are explored to find meaning and understanding that, with reflection, can translate to learning that is a basis for action.

Considered qualitative research, Action Research seeks action to improve practice and study the effects of the action that was taken. In Action Research, the implementation of solutions occurs as an actual part of the research process. There is no trying to generalize the findings of the study, as is the case in quantitative research studies.

According to Heron and Reason (1997), Action Research is similar to constructivist research methods but it adds the important ontological components of cooperation and experiential knowing, affirming 'the primary value of practical knowing in the service of human flourishing' (p. 274). This framework acknowledges self-reflection as part of a participatory worldview (Heron and Reason, 1997). They further suggest that 'to experience anything is to participate in it, and to participate is both to mold and encounter; hence, experiential reality is always subjective–objective' (p. 278). Having an understanding of this allows for appreciation of the lived experience and insights of all research participants or stakeholders of a system. It is an emancipatory, postmodern methodology, equalizing all people involved in the process of change. It is argued that Action Research also increases accountability and quality (Catelli, 2001; Hart, 1996; Schön, 1991). Hart suggests that Action Research is problem focused, context specific, participative, involves change and intervention geared to improvement, and is a process based on a continuous interaction between research, action, reflection and evaluation.

To summarize the above views, Action Researchers believe that complex social systems and social situations cannot be reduced for meaningful study; and as such, Action Research is a process of making sense of and understanding complex interactions and systems. Action Research is therefore highly suitable to sport managers as sport organizations inherently involve unique and complex interactions and systems. The cycle of plan, act, observe and reflect represents actions that any sport manager should be engaging with on a regular basis to allow them to draw out understandings for others to learn from.

## THE EVOLUTION OF ACTION RESEARCH

Action Research as we currently understand it evolved from a range of sources. While Reason and Bradbury (2001) offered the warning that 'we doubt if it is possible to provide one coherent history of Action Research' (p. 3), most histories of the field tend to start with the view that

Action Research originated out of innovative work within *The Group Dynamics* movement in social psychology in the 1940s; and in particular by Kurt Lewin (Carr and Kemmis, 1986; Hart and Bond, 1995).

The process begins, according to Lewin (1948), with the researcher setting down a general idea of what he or she wants to achieve. The next step involves gathering information about the present situation, which allows the researcher to formulate 'an "overall plan" of how to reach the objective, and [to make] a decision in regard to the first step of action' (p. 205). This stage is followed by a series of phases, each involving 'circles' of action, evaluation, reflection, fact-finding, modifying the original plan and planning the next action. Lewin likens the process to a spiral staircase, where the steps ultimately lead to achievement of the desired outcome.

MacTaggart (1991) identified Lewin's work as first generation Action Research, which developed through the late 1950s in the educational sphere in America. MacTaggart discusses how the process evolved with second generation Action Research developing within Britain from the 1960s through to the 1980s. The third generation originated in the 1980s with a call for a more critical basis within Australia and Europe. Finally, the fourth generation emerged in Australia with emancipatory Action Research as the culmination of the previous three generations. It was here that the influences of the work of the German philosopher and sociologist Jurgen Habermas began to filter into Action Research. The fourth generation of Action Research owes much of its origins to the previous generations.

Throughout this period Action Research has not been without its criticisms. The most significant being the challenge of defining the term and the lack of consistent approaches. The lack of consistent methodology enables such a wide range of interpretations to be made that it becomes difficult to evaluate and critique the rigour of an Action Research project. Practitioners can have difficulties applying a methodology that can be used in a number of different ways, which poses potential problems for the practitioner and may lead to lack of confidence in the results by those who are interested in the outcomes.

Despite these criticisms it is now generally accepted that Action Research has a number of key features, which are outlined in Table 6.1.

**Table 6.1** *Features of Action Research*

| Feature | Explanation |
| --- | --- |
| Problem-aimed | Research focuses on a special situation in practice. Action Research is aimed at a specific problem recognizable in practice. |
| Collective participation | All participants (for instance the researchers and persons standing in the practice) form an integral part of Action Research with the exclusive aim to assist in solving the identified problem. |
| Type of empirical research | Action Research is characterized as a means to change the practice while the research is going on. |
| Outcome of Action Research | Action Research is characterized by the fact that problem solving, seen as renewed corrective actions, cannot be generalized, because it should comply with the criteria set for scientific character. |

Source: Jacob *et al.* (2012)

## ACTION RESEARCH ASSUMPTIONS

A major difference between Action Research and other forms of research is that Action Researchers insist that research processes, research outcomes, and the application of results to problem solving are inextricably linked (Greenwood and Levin, 1998). Action Researchers accept that a particular outcome is realized through the intersection of environmental conditions, a group of people and a variety of historical events, including the actions of the participants (Greenwood and Levin, 1998). From this perspective, all explanations of present situations are actually accounts of historical moments and particular causes acting on particular organizations in specific contexts. The Action Researcher understands the uniqueness of an Action Research project and is aware of the limitations of generalizing outcomes to other situations and organizational contexts.

The role of *theory* in Action Research is to explain how what happened was possible and took place, to lay out possible scenarios for the future and give good reasons for the ones that seem to be probable outcomes. As Bate, Khan and Pye (2000) note, the methodology of Action Research doesn't emphasize prediction; it focuses instead on allowing what needs to happen, to happen. From a political perspective, Action Researchers believe that research results should be useful for participants in gaining increased control over their own situation, and that the research questions should be influenced by everyone involved in the study (Greenwood and Levin, 1998). For example, empowering concussion sufferers and medical personnel with knowledge of concussion treatment and prevention increases their ability to pressure sport bodies to change policies. Furthermore, it is critical to involve those groups in each stage of the Action Research, from research question development to interpretation of results to enacting the outcomes. It is preferable that participants be involved in the research process as it is not a technique applied by one person on others, but a process that is co-managed by the interested parties (Dick, 2002). This is what makes Action Research a particularly useful tool for sport organizational research. The characteristics that underpin the approach (see Table 6.2) lend themselves to its application in sport organizations as sport organizations are complex social settings with numerous stakeholders with an inherent interest in its organizational practices.

**Table 6.2** *Characteristics of Action Research*

- Focus on a particular social setting
- Collaboration/dialogue with others to identify the issues and to collect and analyse data
- Deliberate intervention into the operation of the status quo
- Processes of research lead to the construction of knowledge and theory (and political action)
- Testing of knowledge and theory by feeding information back into changes in practice
- Evaluation of changes through further cycles of action and reflection
- Opening of theories and knowledge to wider scrutiny through publication, information dissemination and application by others in their own situations

# ESTABLISHING A STRATEGY FOR ACTION RESEARCH

According to McLean (1995), a strategy for Action Research involves three stages: conceptualization, implementation and interpretation. While the conceptualization and interpretation stages demand skills that are part of the researcher's general skills, the implementation stage is dependent on the other stages.

## Conceptualization

The first stage in the Action Research process is conceptualization, which requires that the specific process to study is selected. Furthermore, it is important to consider what results are expected from the process, the outcome and how the input might promote the outcome. In this perspective, Action Research is the process of determining whether the conceptualization was achieved. McLean (1995) stressed that the process of carefully considering the input and outcome brings up a clearer understanding that leads to new ideas of how the process can be improved.

## Implementation

The stage of implementation consists of three components: measurement of the outcomes, identifying a standard of comparison and comparing current performance with the standard (McLean, 1995). This is the most technical phase of the Action Research process; and through the participation of the researcher, the implementation will be smoother.

## Interpretation

Interpretation is the final stage in the Action Research process (McLean, 1995). In this phase judgements are made about the effectiveness of the observed company. Here, findings of the implementation stage are brought together with the findings from the conceptualization stage. Furthermore, it is during the interpretation stage that judgements can be made about the effectiveness of the practice and whether it produces better results than the theories involved in the topic. In order to achieve the best results possible in the interpretation stage, it is crucial that the research effectively evaluates the implementation phase.

Despite Action Research having three clearly defined stages, sport managers, however, can have difficulties with Action Research because as a methodology it lacks a consistency in its approach. Applying a methodology that can be used in a number of different ways poses potential problems that may lead to lack of confidence in the results by those who are interested in the outcomes. Sport managers therefore need to consider a raft of issues before embarking on an Action Research project. An overview of these issues is presented in Table 6.3.

**Table 6.3** *Issues of Action Research for the sport management researcher to consider*

- Who will you involve?
- What issues/questions will you focus on?
- What steps in the process will you put in place next?
- How will you collect data/information?
- How will you track/analyse it/identify emerging issues?
- What resources do you need?
- What skills/knowledge do you need?

## THE ACTION RESEARCH PROCESS

According to Kemmis and Grundy (1997), there are three conditions necessary for Action Research to exist:

■ A project takes as its subject matter a social practice, regarding it as a strategic action susceptible to improvement.

■ The project proceeds through a spiral of cycles of planning, acting, observing and reflecting with each of these activities being systematically and self critically implemented and interrelated.

■ The project involves those responsible for the practice in each of the moments of the activity, widening participation in the project gradually to include others affected by the practice and maintaining collaborative control of the process.

Two criteria appear as fundamental to Action Research: the *cyclic process* and *the research partnership*. Noffke and Stevenson (1995) discuss the cyclical nature of Action Research:

> As a research method, Action Research is cyclical, that is, it does not progress from an initial question to the formulation of data collection, analysis and conclusion . . . The process does not end, as with traditional notions of research, with richer understandings of education for others to implement; rather it aids in the ongoing process of identifying contradictions which, in turn, help to locate spaces for ethically defensible, politically strategic action. (pp. 4–5)

Action Research also emphasizes the concept of *co-researchers* and stresses the notion of partnership as fundamental to achieving more democratic research processes and realization of practical, relevant outcomes. Research is 'done with' not 'done to' participants. The researcher does not presume a position of power nor participate as an expert, but rather as an equal partner in a process of discovery. Knowledge and power is balanced; the sport researcher may have knowledge of the process but the participants have knowledge of the setting. Changes in position may occur as participants gain more understanding of the situation and participate in finding solutions. Action Research calls for reflection and analysis of knowledge and action by all participants and, consequently, has an educational function.

## THE ACTION RESEARCH CYCLE

In its simplest form the cyclical aspect of Action Research is outlined in Figure 6.1 and is presented as:

- Plan – develop a plan of critically informed action to improve what is already happening;
- Act – act to implement the plan;
- Observe – observe the effects of the critically informed action in the context in which it occurs;
- Reflect – reflect on these effects as the basis for further planning, subsequent critically informed action, [etc.] through a succession of stages (Kemmis and MacTaggart, 1988, p. 10).

In the cycle of 'plan, act, observe and reflect' of Action Research, reflection is a key theoretical component. From an analytic perspective the methodology endorses a *reflective* analytical approach. Gall, Borg and Gall (1996) note the analysis of data within an Action Research or critical theoretical research approach is reflective, rather than structural or interpretive. They state that, 'Reflective analysis is largely subjective and it is not possible to

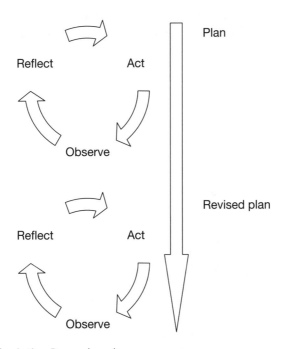

**Figure 6.1** *The Action Research cycle*

specify standard procedures for doing this type of data analysis' (p. 571). Furthermore critical researchers do not view data as something that contains facts that need to be 'discovered' or 'uncovered', but rather 'data is constructed during research, and if reflected upon is somewhat self-validating because it grasps and reflects reality' (Reid, 1997, p. 56). Returning to an earlier example, Action Research for concussion prevention and treatment is not about discovering a link between head impacts and brain damage, but rather finding amicable solutions to how concussions are perceived and implementing policy changes in dealing with concussion injuries.

Reason (1990) describes a cycle or loop of reflective analysis as 'moving to and fro between reflection and experience' (p. 45). This he suggests can be individually based, where each person operates individually and reflects upon their individual experiences, with ideally a group reflection at the very beginning or very end. Alternatively, it can be collective, where the researcher and participants 'always reflect together; and they always experience together . . . interacting as a group . . . What is essential here is to ensure that each person has a say in the reflective phase and is fully involved in the experience phase'(p. 45).

Reason (1990) suggests that the balance between reflection and experience be seen as critical in relation to validity. Too much experience will result in a 'supersaturated inquiry' or too much reflection can result in 'intellectual excess' (p. 48). After each experience phase, Reason (1990) suggests three lines of thought for reflection: the descriptive, the evaluative, and the practical. In the descriptive phase, the researcher describes 'what went on, framing lucid descriptions. When evaluating, they are judging how sound and well founded these descriptions are; that is, how well they cohere with the recollected, presented content of the experience phase' (p. 49). The practical phase entails – in light of the description and evaluation – 'what sort of content to explore in the next experience phase' (p. 50).

Streubert and Carpenter (1999, pp. 266–267) utilized five steps in the Action Research process. These steps include planning, action, evaluation, reflection and conclusions. Within each step are a number of stages the researcher must follow; these are identified below.

1   Planning
    i)   describe the procedures for selecting participants;
    ii)  describe the extent of collaboration between researchers and participants during the analysis phase;
    iii) describe strategies for data analysis;
    iv) involve participants in the interpretation;
    v)   description should reflect understanding of the educational situation;
    vi) action planning;
    vii) describe the planned change in detail;
    viii) describe the change implementation methods;
    ix) describe the method to evaluate the planned change;
    x)   all participants should be included in the action planning.
2   Action
    i)   implement the change in the practice setting where the problem occurred;
    ii)  specify the implementation period.

3   Reflection
  i)   specify methods for facilitating reflection;
  ii)  describe the results of reflection.
4   Evaluation
  i)   describe the strategies for evaluating the change;
  ii)  evaluate the process for implementing the change and the outcomes of the change;
  iii) evaluate the data evaluation methods for appropriateness to factors evaluated;
  iv)  include participants in the evaluation;
  v)   address the validity and reliability of quantitative findings and the trustworthiness of qualitative findings.
5   Conclusions, implications and recommendations
  i)   conclusions must reflect the findings;
  ii)  formulate theory from the findings;
  iii) describe findings in sufficient detail;
  iv)  discuss ethical and moral implications;
  v)   include recommendations for research, education and practice;
  vi)  describe the benefits participants gain from the study.

An alternative model of Action Research is provided by Dick (2000) who prefers the simple approach of action, critical reflection, action, critical reflection. For Dick, these are the essential features of Action Research. The reflection consists of a review of what has happened so far and deliberate planning for what will be done next. These cycles occur over a variety of time spans, ranging from entire programmes and beyond, down to moment-by-moment action. Dick (2000) emphasizes that there are 'cycles within cycles within cycles'. While the full range of Action Research models cannot be discussed in detail here, those developed by Lewin (1948), Greenwood and Levin (1998) and Gummesson (2000) are frequently referenced and provide representative examples of different approaches.

## MANAGING THE PRACTICAL NATURE OF THE RESEARCH PROCESS

In most practical terms, efforts have been made to define the practical elements required in the undertaking of the Action Research process. Kemmis and McTaggart (1988) list a range of 'principles of procedure' that have strong ethical components; these include:

- observing protocol;
- involving participants;
- negotiating with those affected;
- reporting progress;
- obtaining explicit authorization before observation starts;
- obtaining explicit authorization before files or data are examined;
- negotiating descriptions and others' point of view;
- obtaining explicit authorization before using quotations;

■ negotiating reports for various levels of publication;
■ accepting responsibility for maintaining confidentiality;
■ assuming authorization has been gained, retain the right to report your work;
■ making your principles of procedures binding and known (pp. 106–108).

They also offer a range of observations in getting started in Action Research, including:

■ participate yourself in the Action Research process;
■ get organized when initiating the process;
■ be content to start small;
■ articulate the main theme and establish agreement around it;
■ establish a time-line that sets the time period for the work;
■ arrange for supportive work-in-progress discussions;
■ be tolerant and supportive of all involved; be persistent about recording and monitoring;
■ plan for the longer haul in bigger issues of change;
■ register progress;
■ write up throughout the project;
■ be explicit about all progress made. (Kemmis and McTaggart, 1988)

## THE ROLE OF THE RESEARCHER IN ACTION RESEARCH

According to Webb (1990), traditional approaches to research involve 'smash and grab' – the researcher enters a situation, grabs the required data and leaves again. The Action Researcher attempts to work with participants on an equal basis. Action Researchers act as facilitators and are integral to the process. The participant status of the researcher is acknowledged in Action Research and is treated as a resource for the process.

Action Researchers achieve a balance of critique and support through a variety of actions, including direct feedback, written reflections, pointing to comparable cases and citing cases from the professional literature where similar problems, opportunities or processes have occurred. The Action Researcher needs to open up lines of discussion and be able to make evident the tacit knowledge that guides the local conduct.

Gronhaug and Olson (1999) observe that there are several challenges faced by Action Researchers. They must be able to make adequate observations and select and make use of other available data; interpret and make sense of the observations, which requires conceptualization and theory-building skills; plan and execute actions; and plan, collect, analyse and interpret data to examine the outcome of the action. This shows that Action Research presumes important skills regarding observing and interviewing (and other data collection techniques), adequate theoretical knowledge that allows for observation and interpretation, creativity and ability to construct explanations, methodological skills to examine outcomes of proposed action.

The types of roles that researchers take in their settings are a function of four factors (Adler and Adler, 1987): first, the conditions inherent in the setting that may affect the researcher's obtaining and maintaining access to the research setting. For example, if conducting Action

Research on fair athlete recruiting practices in the NCAA, the researcher may need access to private information on scouting at several institutions; and, if any foul play was occurring then that information might be even more difficult to access. Second, the researcher's abilities, identities, theoretical orientations, demographics and other personal factors can influence the research process. This includes the researcher's prior knowledge of the group members and degree of comfort with the people. Third, field researchers' roles may be affected by changes in the setting itself during the research period, including changes to group membership. Finally, researchers may undergo changes within themselves and therefore seek out new ways of collecting data (Adler and Adler, 1987).

## TYPES OF ACTION RESEARCH

There are a number of Action Research approaches available; however, there are two main ones that are applicable to Sport Management Research. These are Participatory Action Research and Emancipatory Action Research.

## Participatory Action Research (PAR)

Participatory Action Research (PAR) is research in which there is collaboration between the study participants and the researcher in all steps of the study: determining the problem, the research methods to use, the analysis of data, and how the study results will be used. The participants and the researcher are co-researchers throughout the entire research study.

Early developments in PAR transpired in the 1950s in America; however, it was not really taken seriously until the 1980s. The purpose of PAR is to minimize power differences between researchers and constituents, increase the knowledge of participants and promote social change. PAR is associated with two aspects of learning theory: Kurt Lewin's Action Research (1951) principles (knowledge flows from taking action) as well as the work of Paulo Freire (*Pedagogy of the Oppressed*, 1970) in which he described a process of education for marginalized groups that involved mutual learning among teachers and students. The basic assumption of these approaches is that academic research should be used to reduce the harmful effects of oppression by involving members of powerless groups in the construction of knowledge, a critical examination of the world around them, and action to address social problems (Stringer, 1999). PAR also draws upon social constructionism and the work of postmodern theorists such as Michel Foucault who maintain that scientific knowledge often has little relevance in people's everyday lives, but instead serves to maintain existing institutional arrangements that limit power to members of economic, social and political elites (Rodwell, 1998).

PAR is participatory in that it expects and encourages the researcher and research participants to collaboratively engage in a strong degree of involvement and participation in the research process. It also questions the inequalities that are produced and maintained by the unequal power relations in our society (Pierce, 1995). In recognizing itself as a way to improve the social situation through intellectual effort (Popkewitz, 1984), the research approach therefore needs to be openly and explicitly committed to a more just social order and attempt to critique and question the status quo (Lather, 1986).

**107**

## Emancipatory Action Research (EAR)

Lather (1991) and Smith (1993) both contend that Action Research should be an attempt to translate critical thought into emancipatory action. To accomplish this, they suggest that Action Research needs to be deliberately interventionist, and not compromise this intervention by strictly adhering to a prescribed approach. Smith recognizes these two alternative directions that critical educational theory may follow (1993, p. 84). The first direction encompasses the aim of empowerment through utilizing research methods such as critical ethnography, policy analysis and text analysis as discussed previously (Smith 1993, p. 84). The second direction includes approaches that encompass the notions of participation, but also includes and makes explicit the commitment to action. Smith terms this 'Emancipatory Action Research' (EAR) to differentiate it from Participatory Action Research (1993, p. 84). In other words, it can be seen that perhaps there are two strands of Action Research, the participatory and the emancipatory. An objective of emancipatory research is therefore to enable the researcher and researched to work collaboratively in relation to the design, direction and conduct of the research (Kemmis and McTaggart, 1988).

According to MacTaggart (1991), EAR could be defined in two ways: first, as '[involving] a group of practitioners accepting responsibility for its "own emancipation" from the dictates of irrationality, injustice, alienation and unfulfillment'; second, as 'the activity of a self-leading group aimed at developing new practices and/or changing the constraints with a shared radical consciousness' (p. 30).

According to Carr and Kemmis (1986), the main points of EAR of equal importance include:

- bridging the gap between theory and practice;
- the epistemological understanding that the practitioners possess valid knowledge;
- participation and equality of those involved within the situation;
- practitioners critically reflecting on their own practices;
- the empowerment of the practitioners;
- democratically chosen actions are implemented;
- communication, which implies dialogues between participants; and
- a cyclic process of planning, action, observation and reflection. (p. 17)

The methodology is selected and employed by the practitioners themselves, implying it is situation specific. Accordingly, EAR is more than simple radical critique – it demands action.

Within the sphere of sport management EAR can serve the practitioners as an alternative to traditional methods of research and aid sport managers with improving their practices.

## CRITICISMS OF ACTION RESEARCH

Although we have noted that one of the key criticisms of Action Research is the lack of consistent approaches, it is important to address some of the other criticisms of Action Research. Badger (2000) identifies that Action Research is limited in its effectiveness as a strategy to manage change because of the lack of methodological rigour in this research method.

**Table 6.4** Criticisms of Action Research

- No external or internal validity
- Findings are context specific
- Lack of impartiality by researchers and dual role of researcher/participant
- Difficult to publish AR results
- Tendency for inexperienced researchers to focus entirely on planning, acting and observing phases and less upon theorizing
- Ethical responsibilities to other participants
- Length of projects – ongoing and evolutionary
- As Action Research has become an accepted and legitimate methodology, its potential for action may be diluted by applying processes, structures, stages and so forth
- Action Research that is non-participatory and non-interventionist is unable to measure up to its political, empowering or emancipatory purposes

There are also criticisms because a rigid methodology for Action Research does not exist. Each unique setting or organization requires a unique research method utilizing the researchers interpersonal and communication skills rather than a strict operationalized format. Other common criticisms are outlined in Table 6.4.

## CREDIBILITY AND RIGOUR IN ACTION RESEARCH

Greenwood and Levin (1998) define credibility in Action Research as the arguments and the processes necessary for having someone trust the research results. One type of credibility is when knowledge generated by a group is credible to that group. This is fundamentally important to Action Research because of the collaborative nature of the research process. Another type is external credibility which is knowledge capable of convincing someone who did not participate in the inquiry that the results are believable. Credibility is established through prolonged engagement, persistent observation, triangulation, diverse case analysis, participant debriefing, referential adequacy and member checking.

Stringer and Genat (2004) argue that credibility of an Action Research project may be further enhanced by the participation of stakeholders. Engaging sport managers as participants in the research minimizes the impact of the likelihood that the researcher will interpret events through their own interpretive framework. Bray, Lee, Smith and Yorks (2000) report on the merits of participative inquiry as a means of establishing validity, in which participants collaborate (work together), cooperate (accommodate each other) and actively engage in a process of inquiry to answer questions of importance to them.

Rigour in Action Research refers to how data are generated, gathered, explored and evaluated, and how events are questioned and interpreted through multiple Action Research cycles. According to Coghlan and Brannick (2001), the Action Researcher needs to show four things in order to demonstrate rigour: first, how the researcher engaged in the steps of multiple Action Research cycles and how these were recorded to reflect that they are a true

**109**

representation of what was studied; second, how the researcher challenged and tested his or her own assumptions and interpretations of what was happening continuously through the project, by means of content, process and premise reflection; third, how the researcher accessed different views of what was happening, which may have produced confirming and contradictory interpretations; and fourth, how the researcher's interpretations and diagnoses are grounded in scholarly theory and rigorously applied.

This perspective is supported by Dick (2000) who also acknowledges that it is the balance between critical reflection and flexibility that allows adequate rigour in Action Research to be achieved. Dick (2000) emphasizes that the most important source of rigour in research, including Action Research, is the vigorous and continuous search for disconfirming evidence. If an Action Research project is attempting to shift physical education pedagogy from a competitive sport platform to a theoretically 'ideal' participatory fitness platform, then the researchers (including the participants) should actively seek evidence that supports the competitive platform as ideal. Dick (2002) explains that there are several features of Action Research that allow it to pursue rigorous understanding. First, there is the involvement of all interested parties to provide more information about a situation. The information in the physical education pedagogy study might come from parents, students, educators, policy makers and academics, and no group should be treated with less regard than another. Second, the critical reflection in each cycle provides many chances to correct errors, especially when there are cycles within cycles. It should occur after initial interviews and conversations with each group, during and after test cycles of both competitive sport and participatory fitness platforms, and as a whole during the analysis of those tests. Third, within each cycle the assumptions underlying the plans are tested in action, which adds to the achievement of rigour. These cycles allow further opportunities to seek out disconfirming evidence. Dick (2014) summarizes by stating that:

> with access to these sources of rigor, Action Research is not a second-best methodology to be used when other methods don't suit. It is a rigorous alternative in its own right, better for some applications, worse for others. (p. 25)

Reason and Bradbury (2001) have identified five choice points for assessing the rigour of an Action Research. They are:

1   *Relationship* – the Action Research should be explicit in developing a praxis of relational participation; that is whether the Action Research group is set up to ensure maximum participation, whether best decisions are those that ensure maximum participation, whether less powerful people are helped by their participation in the inquiry.

2   *Practical outcome* – the Action Research should be guided by reflexive concern for practical outcomes. That is, the research is validated by participants' new way of acting in light of the work. At the end the participants should be able to say, 'That was useful. I am able to use what I have learned.'

3   *Extended ways of knowing* – the Action Research should be inclusive of a plurality of knowing. That is:

a) the Action Research should ensure conceptual–theoretical integrity. A well-written AR study should be such that it can be used by fellow inquirers with similar concern to 'see as if' and illuminate their own situation;

b) it should embrace ways of knowing beyond the intellect, that is, artful ways of expression such as song and dance, video, poetry and photography;

c) the AR should intentionally choose appropriate research methods. The choice of methods should be ecologically sensitive to the context in which it is being used.

4  Pay attention to what is *worthy of attention* – how do we decide where to put our effort?

At the heart of this process is to always ask the question 'What values do we hold vis-à-vis the value of work with which we engage?' Reason and Bradbury (2001) believe that:

> Since the AR community is committed to bring an attitude of inquiry towards questions of fundamental importance, we would do well to find ways to address the question of what purposes are worthy of more direct attention. It is worthwhile to articulate positive, life enhancing qualities in a situation and to amplify these than to seek problems and try to solve them. It is thus better to ask appreciative questions than critical questions. The emphasis should be to ask the right research questions so that we are convening a process that will generate the outcome we want. (p. 453)

5  *Enduring consequences* – the AR should emerge towards a new and enduring infrastructure. This means that the dyadic, small group micro engagement of people should manifest into an ongoing new patterning of behaviour at a macro level even after the Action Researchers have left the scene (Reason and Bradbury, 2001).

It should be noted however that Reason and Bradbury (2001) acknowledge that a given Action Research project cannot address all these points.

## VALIDITY OF ACTION RESEARCH METHODS

Researchers have identified a number of assumptions underlying the term 'validity'. Denzin and Lincoln (1998) in Stringer and Genat (2004) interpret validity in Action Research as, 'a text's call to authority and truth' (p. 49). Processes for establishing validity of the Action Research methodology are not widely established in the literature (Waterman, 1998). Action Research is fluid, flexible and very much contextually based. As a consequence, validity rests on the goals and specific methods utilized for knowledge discovery or agreed upon by those involved in the process and are recognized as an acceptable approach for achieving the study goals. This is an agreement between the researchers and sport managers, and may not affect other sport contexts. Mason (1996) believes that qualitative Action Research rests on the researchers' ability to demonstrate that concepts 'can be identified, observed, or "measured" in the way [the researcher says] they can' (p. 24).

**111**

Waterman, Tillen, Dickson and De Konig (2001) further suggest that Action Research needs to be judged according to its own terms: participatory work, aimed at change, and movement between reflection, action and evaluation. Badger (2000) claims that Action Research is not amenable to critique by the strategies used for other methodologies. He explains: 'the design of Action Research is led by the research problem rather than the requirements of a particular methodology, and may be affected by the dynamics of the situation itself' (p. 201).

Action Research seeks to construct an understanding of a dynamic, complex social world, situation or agency and, being essentially qualitative and naturalistic, it reveals subjective experiences of the participants and how they assess meaning in their world or situation. Taking a set of criteria proposed by Lincoln and Guba (1985), Stringer and Genat (2004) suggest validity is demonstrated through trustworthiness and is established by attaining credibility, transferability, dependability and confirmability. Stringer and Genat (2004) view validity as a question of quality and address issues of validity when they say: 'the truths emerging from naturalistic inquiry are always contingent (i.e. they are "true" only for the people, the time and setting of that particular study). We are not looking for "the truth" or "the causes", but "truths-in-context"' (p. 49).

They go on to explain that there are no objective measures of validity, so the underlying issue is trustworthiness, 'the extent to which we can trust the truthfulness or adequacy of a research project' (p. 50).

Coghlan and Brannick (2001, p. 10) have said that Action Research is evaluated within its own frame of reference and that questions of reliability, replicability and universality do not pertain to the Action Research approach. For them, an Action Researcher should be able to answer three questions:

- What happened? The relating of a good story.
- How do you make sense of what happened? This involves rigorous reflection on that story.
- So what? This most challenging question deals with the extrapolation of usable knowledge or theory from the reflection on the story.

Table 6.5 looks at how the researcher determines the level of validity in their findings.

**Table 6.5** Validity of findings from Action Research

How valid are the findings from Action Research?

- Action Research uses different measures of validity and reliability than other forms of research.
- Action Research values responsiveness over replicability meaning that 'credibility, validity and reliability in Action Research are measured by the willingness of local stakeholders to act on the results of the action research' (Greenwood and Levin, 1998).
- Documentation of an Action Research undertaking takes the form of a case study, and thus becomes a resource that other organisations can learn from and apply in their own contexts.

## APPLICATION OF ACTION RESEARCH IN SPORT MANAGEMENT

Action Research is based on the premise that other types of research that are based on empirical positivism are, by design, outside of the process. For example, to be able to understand the workings of a sport organization and to initiate change based on evaluation, research has to be done inside the sport organization. This requires participation on the part of the internal and external stakeholders themselves. This method encourages involvement and buy-in by those most affected by potential system changes. With the researcher being a part of the social reality being studied, interpretations are subjective but can be confirmed by other participants (Zuber-Skerritt, 1992).

From this perspective the sport management practitioners not only pose the research questions but search for and try out their own answers to those questions. Because the research is practitioner driven, it promotes the development of professionals and the body of knowledge on which they base their actions. In today's rapidly changing sport management environment, it is important that sport managers study their own practice and construct the new knowledge needed to answer their current questions and solve their own problems.

---

### RECENT CASE EXAMPLE: ACTION RESEARCH

*The following article is an example of how Action Research has been used in the past by researchers in sport management. The interested reader may wish to find/download and read the article for further insights.*

An action research inquiry into the Saanich initiative: Leisure involvement for everyone. Clarke, D. L. (2008). Unpublished doctoral thesis, Royal Roads University (Canada). MR69171

The Leisure Involvement For Everyone (LIFE) initiative was created to assist the economically disadvantaged residents of the Municipality of Saanich, British Columbia in benefiting from recreation programmes and services. Through the principles of Action Research, this project reviews LIFE and its current effectiveness and subsequently recommends modifications to improve the success as defined by stakeholders. The data analysis illustrates that there are currently many best practices, however looking to the future, a number of recommendations are made. These include defining and measuring success, considering new eligibility requirements, temporarily screening applicants, creating more flexibility within the programme, increased marketing, programming changes, streamlining of the application process and developing new ways to support staff.

---

## HYPOTHETICAL CASE

Upon observing the media's perception and promotion of women in sport, a researcher was inspired to conduct a brief study on the public's perceptions of women's sports. She surveyed a random sample to discover how many people watch women's sport and why. She also looked at secondary data for participation rates, revenues and expenses of men's and women's sports.

After interpreting the data, she noted a need to change these key areas:

A    make sport as beneficial to women as it is to men;

B    change parental perceptions of women in sport to allow more girls to participate;

C    women athletes should not be perceived as sex objects, and they should be given equal presence in media;

D    advertising should eliminate sporting women as sex symbols to reduce stereotypes;

E    calls for affirmative action (similar to workforce) and greater than Title IX to provide more sporting opportunities to women.

How would you design an Action Research project based on all or some these initial observations?

Which people or groups of people would you seek to participate in the study?

What outcomes would you expect?

What are some ways you might implement these outcomes?

How would you evaluate the results?

How would you know if the study was a success?

## CONCLUSION

Conducting Action Research within a sport management organization can be seen as problematic in relation to issues around conflict of interest, ethical considerations and the positioning of the researcher in relation to membership of the organization. Despite this, there is evidence to suggest that Action Research, by dealing with the realities of practice, is more likely to represent the 'truth' as compared to other research methods. The emancipatory and participatory models of Action Research would seem particularly applicable to the sport management field.

## REVIEW QUESTIONS

With a general understanding now of the emancipatory and participatory models of Action Research:

■   Identify the steps in conducting an Action Research study.

## SUGGESTED EXTENDED READING FOR STUDENTS

Brydon-Miller, M. (2008). Ethics and action research: Deepening our commitment to principles of social justice and redefining systems of democratic practice. In P. Reason and H. Bradbury (eds), *The SAGE handbook of action research: Participatory inquiry and practice* (pp. 199–210). Thousand Oaks, CA: Sage Publications.

Kemmis, S. (2010). What is to be done? The place of Action Research. *Educational Action Research, 18*(4 Dec), 417–427.

McNiff, J., Lomax, P., and Whitehead, J. (1996). *You and your Action Research project*. London: Routledge.

Pain, R., and Francis, P. (2003). Reflections on participatory research. *AREA, 35*(1), 46–54.

# Chapter 7

# What is case study research?

## LEARNING OUTCOMES

By the end of this chapter you should be able to:

- define what is a case study;
- justify the use of the case study method;
- differentiate between single and multiple cases;
- explain the steps in using the case study method.

## KEY TERMS

*Case study* – an empirical inquiry that investigates a contemporary phenomenon within its real-life context.

## KEY THEMES

- Do case studies have any practical relevance to Sport Management Research?

## CHAPTER OVERVIEW

The case study method is the investigation of a phenomenon in its real-world context using multiple empirical methods (Yin, 2003). Case studies are highly contextual in that they cover a specific time period of the phenomenon and involve a small number of participants. Researchers have typically used the case study method to analyse how and why particular events unfold or to compare how similar groups were impacted by a particular change. The rationale behind using the case study method is that it allows the researcher to delve into a real-life context and produce a rich description from which to understand the situation – which then allows for the opportunity to build theory.

Case studies may be utilized for qualitative, quantitative and mixed methods research. This chapter will focus on the application of case study to qualitative research, and in particular, Sport Management Research.

## DEFINING CASE STUDY

The term case study is often used interchangeably with 'field research', 'qualitative research', 'direct research', 'ethnographic studies' or 'naturalistic research'. Yin (1984) defined the case study research method as: 'an empirical inquiry that investigates a contemporary phenomenon within its real-life context; when the boundaries between phenomenon and context are not clearly evident; and in which multiple sources of evidence are used' (p. 23). Likewise, and perhaps more relevant to sport management, Yin (1994) defined a case study as: *'The essence of a case study, the central tendency among all types of case study is that it tries to illuminate a decision or set of decisions: why they were taken, how they were implemented, and with what result'* (p. 78, emphasis added). For Creswell (1998), a case study is an exploration of a bounded system that may be a programme, an event, an activity or a group of individuals.

## CASE STUDY AS A RESEARCH METHOD

Four different applications for case studies have been identified by Yin (1984):

1   To *explain*: (a) the causal links in real-life interventions that were too complex for the survey or experimental strategies; and (b) the particular case at hand with the possibility of coming to broader conclusions.
2   To *describe* the real-life context in which an intervention had occurred.
3   To *evaluate* an intervention in a descriptive case study.
4   To *explore* those situations where the intervention being evaluated has no clear, single set of outcomes.

In summary, case study is considered an *empirical inquiry* that investigates contemporary phenomena within its real-life context, especially when the boundaries between phenomena and context are not clearly evident. The case study inquiry copes with the technically distinctive situation in which there will be many more variables of interest than the data points. It relies on multiple sources of evidence, with data needing to converge in a triangulating fashion. As such, it benefits from the prior development of theoretical propositions to guide data collection and analysis.

Many sport management issues and principles occur in real-life contexts; situations that are often quite unique in terms of the problems faced, the tools/resources available, the organizational and political goals, and the experiences/philosophy of the practitioners involved. As such, a research methodology that explicitly accepts the uniqueness of each individual case

**117**

and seeks to use methods and analysis appropriate to that situation is highly applicable. In sport management as a researcher you would use case study as a methodology as it allows the researcher to provide a description of the complex environment within sport organizations and an understanding of social phenomena and real-life events that occur.

## CHARACTERISTICS OF A CASE STUDY

The 'characteristics' of a case study have been defined in many ways. The categories of intrinsic, instrumental and collective are used by Stake (1995). Merriam (1988) defines 'a qualitative case study as an intensive, holistic description and analysis of a single instance, phenomenon, or social unit' (p. 21). The case study can be a:

- descriptive qualitative case study;
- interpretive qualitative case study;
- evaluative qualitative case study.

Yin (1984) employs the terms exploratory, descriptive and explanatory. The similarities of the terms may be grouped thus: *intrinsic and descriptive*; *instrumental, interpretive and explanatory*; and *exploratory and evaluative*.

In essence, *descriptive and intrinsic* case studies describe in detail a particular case without forming hypotheses, making judgements or pitting against a theory. As stated by Stake (1995): 'the study is undertaken because one wants better understanding of this particular case . . . not because the case represents other cases . . . but because, in all its particularity and ordinariness, this case itself is of interest' (p. 88).

The *descriptive* case study can provide a basis for future comparison and theory building but it is not the primary reason for the study, the narrative account is.

---

### RECENT CASE EXAMPLE: DESCRIPTIVE CASE STUDY

*The following article is an example of how descriptive case study has been used in the past by researchers in Sport Management Research. The interested reader may wish to find/download and read the article for further insights.*

A case study of the use of risk management in NCAA compliance at a Division I Institution. Werner, M. R. (2006). Unpublished doctoral dissertation. Eastern Michigan University. Paper 97.

This case study's purpose was to describe an intercollegiate athletic department's risk assessment policies and procedures, with the intent to demonstrate the effects on compliance outcomes. The research utilized interview and document data, and concluded that the risk assessment was successful and could be modelled at other institutions to protect against NCAA compliance issues.

---

*Instrumental*, *interpretive* or *explanatory* case studies are more about interpreting or theorizing about the phenomenon (Merriam, 1988). The interpretive, explanatory or instrumental case study is more likely to look at the 'why' question and contain a far greater level of analysis and conceptualization than a descriptive case study.

---

### RECENT CASE EXAMPLE: INTERPRETIVE CASE STUDY

*The following article is an example of how interpretive case study has been used in the past by researchers in Sport Management Research. The interested reader may wish to find/download and read the article for further insights.*

> More than basketball: Determining the sport components that lead to long-term benefits for African-American girls. Olushola, J. O., Jones, D. F., Dixon, M. A., and Green, B. C. (2012). *Sport Management Review, 16*(2), 211–25.

This interpretive case study was conducted to examine a sport for development programme targeted at African-American girls. The results were interpreted that sport was a vehicle in increasing the educational attainment of the study participants.

---

*Evaluative* case studies, according to Merriam (1988), involve 'description, explanation and judgment' (p. 28). Although Yin (1994) does not ascribe evaluation as a specific type of case study, he does state the value and place of case study in evaluative research because case studies can explain, describe, illustrate and explore to form judgements about a programme, event or intervention.

---

### RECENT CASE EXAMPLE: EVALUATIVE CASE STUDY

*The following article is an example of how evaluative case study has been used in the past by researchers in Sport Management Research. The interested reader may wish to find/download and read the article for further insights.*

> The effects of a professional development programme on primary school teachers' perceptions of physical education. Harris, J., Cale, L., and Musson, H. (2011). *Professional Development in Education, 37*(2), 291–305.

This case study evaluated the impact of a physical education professional development programme aimed at primary school teachers. The programme was found to have a positive effect on the perceptions of physical education by the teachers, however had limited impact beyond perceptions.

---

## Descriptive vs explanatory case studies

The *descriptive* case study is associated with describing how the phenomenon exists in the everyday world. The aim of descriptive case studies is to provide enough detailed description so that a better understanding of the phenomenon is made, and one is able to develop new insights. Unlike the descriptive study, the *exploratory* case study not only aims to provide a description of the case, but also attempts to provide an explanation of the phenomenon.

## Single vs multiple case studies

Case study research may be conducted using single or multiple participants. The *single* case study design is intrinsic in nature and is useful for testing the 'applicability of existing theories to real world data' (Willig, 2001, p. 74). A single case design would be used when the focal case is used to test a well-formulated theory or the case represents an extreme or unique case. For example, studying the impact of changing the dates of FIFA World Cup in Qatar on a single nation's (e.g. Australia) professional football season.

The *multiple* case study design differs from the single case in that it does not just test existing hypotheses, but allows the sport management researcher to generate new hypotheses. That is, through the comparison of individual cases, the sport management researcher has the opportunity to develop and refine these new formulations. This means that the same study has two or more cases. What would the impact of changing the dates of the FIFA World Cup have on professional competitions in Europe, Asia and America? If it is found to have similar negative impacts in several global competitions, then the case against moving the dates is much more significant. As such, the evidence from multiple cases is often considered more compelling, which makes the overall study more robust. Undertaking a multiple case study, however, can require extensive resources and time beyond the means of a single researcher.

If you decide to use a multiple case study design each case must be chosen carefully and specifically. The cases should have similar results (a literal replication) or contrary results (a theoretical replication) predicted explicitly at the outset of the investigation. It is important in a replication process to develop a rich, theoretical framework. The framework needs to state the conditions under which a particular phenomenon is likely to be found (literal replication) and the conditions under which it is not likely to be found (theoretical replication). The individual cases within a multiple-case study design may be either holistic or embedded. When an embedded design is used each individual case study may in fact include the collection and analysis of quantitative data.

## USING THE CASE STUDY METHODOLOGY TO BUILD A THEORY

Case study research can be useful in *theory building*, as described in Table 7.1. Theories are initially based on a particular case or object. Mintzberg (1979) states that for a researcher to effectively build a theory, it needs to be clearly specified what kind of data is to be collected and how that data is to be systematically gathered. As highlighted by Eisenhardt (1989), 'the definition of the research questions, within a broad topic, permit the researcher to specify the kind of organisation to be approached . . . and the kind of data to be gathered' (p. 536).

This is in accordance with Yin's (1989, 1993) thinking, which confirms the importance that the research question plays in the overall design of the research. However, what about the role of a developed theory or the lack of one, within the research design?

While Eisenhardt (1989) is not wholly in favour of developing a theory prior to the data collection phase, Yin (1989) argues that: 'theory development prior to the collection of any case study data is an essential step in doing case studies' (p. 36). Yin highlights a number of steps in the process, including: (1) developing a theory from the reviewed literature;

**Table 7.1** *Theory building*

| Step | Activity | Reason |
|---|---|---|
| Getting started | Definition of research question<br>A priori constructs | Focuses efforts<br>Better grounding for *constructs* measures |
| Selecting cases | Neither theory nor hypotheses<br>Specified population<br>Theoretical, not random sampling | Retains theoretical flexibility<br>Constrains extraneous variation and sharpens external validity<br>Focuses efforts on theoretically useful cases |
| Crafting instruments and protocols | *Multiple data collection* methods<br>Qualitative and quantitative data combined | Strengthens grounding of theory by *triangulation* of evidence<br>Synergistic view of evidence<br>Fosters divergent perspectives, strengthens grounding |
| Entering the field | Overlap data collection and analysis, including field notes<br>Flexible and opportunistic data collection methods | Speeds analysis and reveals helpful adjustments to data collection<br>Allows researcher to take advantage of emergent themes and unique case features |
| Analysing data | Within case analysis<br>Cross-case pattern search using divergent techniques | Gains familiarity with data and preliminary theory generation<br>Forces researcher to look beyond initial impressions and see evidence through multiple lenses |
| Sharpening hypotheses | Iterative tabulation of evidence for each construct<br>Replication, not sampling, logic across cases<br>Search evidence 'why' behind relationships | Sharpens construct definition, validity and measurability<br>Confirms, extends and sharpens theory<br>Builds internal validity |
| Enfolding literature | Comparison with conflicting literature<br>Comparison with similar literature | Builds internal validity, raises theoretical level, and sharpens construct definitions<br>Sharpens generalizability, improves construct definition and raises theoretical level |
| Reaching closure | Theoretical saturation when possible | Ends process when marginal improvements become small |

Source: Eisenhardt (1989)

(2) defining the relationship between the variables within the theory; (3) defining the units of analysis; (4) the process of analysis; and (5) the criteria for interpreting the findings (pp. 33–35).

## Types of case study

A number of variations of case studies have been proposed. Table 7.2 outlines the various typologies associated with case study research.

**Table 7.2** Case study types and descriptions

| Case study type | Description |
| --- | --- |
| Illustrative case studies | Illustrative case studies describe a domain; they use one or two instances to analyse a situation. This helps interpret other data, especially when researchers have reason to believe that readers know too little about a programme. These case studies serve to make the unfamiliar familiar, and give readers a common language about the topic. The chosen site should typify important variations and contain a small number of cases to sustain readers' interest. |
| Exploratory case studies | Exploratory case studies condense the case study process: researchers may undertake them before implementing a large-scale investigation. Where considerable uncertainty exists about programme operations, goals and results, exploratory case studies help identify questions, select measurement constructs and develop measures; they also serve to safeguard investment in larger studies. |
| Critical instance case studies | Critical instance case studies examine one or a few sites for one of two purposes. A very frequent application involves the examination of a situation of unique interest, with little or no interest in generalizability. A second, rarer, application entails calling into question a highly generalized or universal assertion and testing it by examining one instance. This method particularly suits answering cause-and-effect questions about the instance of concern. |
| Programme effects case studies | Programme effects case studies can determine the impact of programmes and provide inferences about reasons for success or failure. |
| Prospective case studies | In a prospective case study design, the researcher formulates a set of theory-based hypotheses in respect to the evolution of an on-going social or cultural process and then tests these hypotheses at a predetermined follow-up time in the future by comparing these hypotheses with the observed process outcomes using 'pattern matching' (Campbell, 1966; Trochim, 1989) or a similar technique. |
| Cumulative case studies | Cumulative case studies aggregate information from several sites collected at different times. The cumulative case study can have a retrospective focus, collecting information across studies done in the past, or a prospective outlook, structuring a series of investigations for different times in the future. |
| Narrative case studies | Case studies that present findings in a narrative format are called narrative case studies. This involves presenting the case study as events in an unfolding plot with actors and actions. |
| Embedded case studies | A case study containing more than one sub-unit of analysis is referred to as an embedded case study (Yin, 2003). |

**Table 7.3** *Typology of case studies*

| Types of case | Usefulness |
|---|---|
| Unusual, extreme, or deviant cases | Useful in understanding puzzling cases that seem to break the rules, and why certain people or organizations seem to achieve particularly good or bad results. Useful in understanding the reasons for exceptionally good or bad performance. |
| Typical or average cases | Useful in understanding the situation of most people, communities and organizations. Findings may be replicable in other 'normal' situations. |
| Homogenous or similar cases | Useful in looking at particular sub-groups in depth, which may be important when many different types of people or activities are involved. |
| Varied or heterogeneous cases | Useful in exploring common or distinct patterns across great variance. Common patterns in such cases are likely to indicate core and central impacts of wider relevance, precisely because they occur across diverse groups. |
| Critical cases | Useful when a single case study can dramatically make a point; statements such as 'if it happens here it can happen anywhere' or 'if it doesn't work here it won't work anywhere' indicate that a case is critical. |
| Snowballing cases | One starts with a few cases and then selects others on the basis of the findings. Useful when the information to select all case studies is not available or is dependent on a greater understanding of the situation. |
| Convenience cases | Where case studies are chosen solely because it is easy – the information already exists, the site is very close, and so on. Generally a bad idea if these are the only or most important reasons for choosing case studies. |

Source: Roche, 1999 adapted from Patton, 1990.

Another typology of case studies is presented in Table 7.3, based upon the work of Roche (1999) and Patton (1990).

The following sections outline the processes involved in conducting case study.

## CASE STUDY PROTOCOL

Prior to the commencement of case study research it is recommended that a research protocol be established.

The protocol should include:

- an overview of the case study project (project, substantive issues, relevant reading);
- field procedures (how to gain access to interviewees, planning for sufficient resources, providing for unanticipated events etc.);
- case study questions (about individuals, multiple cases, entire study, normative questions about policy recommendations and conclusions).

## STEPS IN USING THE CASE STUDY METHOD

Yin (1994) identified the following steps in conducting any case study.

- The first relates to the *research questions*, which are most likely to be 'how' and 'why' questions. For example, why are there not more women on boards of national sport organizations?
- The second relates to the *unit of analysis*, which could be an individual, a group of individuals, or an organization. Are you studying the effects of adding a woman on the board? The woman herself? The governing body? An entire league?
- The third relates to *linking the data* collected with the research questions. Will the interview questions actually answer your research questions? Will interviewing players offer answers to why women are not equally represented on boards?
- The fourth relates to the *interpretation* of findings. A useful technique is 'pattern-matching' where data collected from the case may be related to some theoretical proposition. Will your findings corroborate or detract from gender equality theories? How can those theories help to interpret your findings?

The following research process is based upon the steps recommended by Tellis (1997).

### Step 1 Determine and define the research questions

In the initial stage of planning the researcher establishes a clear research focus by forming *research questions* about the problem (or situation) to be studied. This research focus could be a programme, an entity, a person or a group of people. The key purpose is to find answers to questions that begin with 'how' or 'why'.

It is important also that the researcher undertake a literature review when formulating the research questions and check what has been done previously to help determine how the study

---

### RESEARCH QUESTIONS

1   Propositions if any
2   Unit(s) of analysis
    - If your questions do not lead to the favoring of one unit of analysis over another, your questions are probably either too vague or numerous
    - To compare findings – definitions should not be too idiosyncratic
    - Do not consider closure permanent
    - Technique: discuss with colleague
3   Logic linking data to propositions
    - Currently there is no precise way of setting the criteria for interpretation
4   Criteria for quality

Yin (2003, 22–27)

---

will be designed, conducted and publicly reported. Research does not occur in a vacuum and it is the responsibility of the researcher to connect the research question to political, social, historical and personal issues.

## Step 2 Select the cases and determine data gathering and analysis techniques

### a) Selection of cases

The objective of case studies and qualitative research is not to be statistically representative in the manner of the formal random samples typical of quantitative studies. Alternatively, case studies 'draw a purposive sample, building in variety and acknowledging opportunities for intensive study' (Stake 2000, p. 446). Purposive sampling, or criterion-based selection (Maxwell 1996; Ritchie, Lewis and Elam 2003), bases the selection of study settings and participants on features and characteristics that will enable the researcher to gather in-depth information on the areas of research interest. This form of sampling is therefore purposeful and strategic (Maxwell 1996), with considerations of convenience and ease of access to study situations and participants given only secondary importance.

Researchers need to decide whether to:

- select 'single' or 'multiple' cases to study in depth;
- relate the selection of the case or cases back to the purpose of the study;
- identify the boundary around the case.

### b) Data gathering techniques

The key decision for a researcher is to determine in advance what evidence to gather and what analysis techniques to use with the data to answer the research questions.

The case study approach uses a range of techniques appropriate to a given context. It is important to note that this is unlike some other forms of research that employ a particular method of data collection or data analysis. A case study may employ a wide variety of data collection methods. Generally case studies will use qualitative methods of data collection. These include:

- *interviews*: the interview is an important technique for data collection and there are two forms of interview: closed or structured interviews and open-ended interviews. Open-ended interviews allow subjects to express themselves more freely and provide insight into events;
- *observations*: this could be direct observation of events and behaviours as well as participant-observation where the researcher is an active participant in the events being studied;

**125**

■ *documents*: these could be letters, memos, agendas, administrative documents, newspaper articles and any other relevant documents. Documents are useful for making inferences about events. Documents are communications between persons in the study;

■ *physical artefacts*: these are objects collected from the setting that could be products made by students and other individuals, the objects used such as tools or instruments. (Stake, 1995 and Yin, 1994)

Tellis (1997) indicates that the researcher must make sure the data gathering tools are used systematically and properly to ensure:

■ construct validity
■ internal validity
■ external validity
■ reliability.

The use of the terms validity and reliability is deemed by some researchers to be inappropriate in case study research in the qualitative paradigm (Sandelowski, 1996; Bergen and While, 2000). Other researchers have attempted to overcome this criticism of case study as illustrated in Tables 7.4 and 7.5:

**Table 7.4** *Positivist criteria for judging quality*

| Tests | Case study tactic | Phase of research |
| --- | --- | --- |
| Construct validity | • Multiple sources of evidence<br>• Establish chain of evidence | Data collection |
| | • Have key informants review draft case study reports | Composition |
| Internal validity | • Perform pattern matching<br>• Perform explanation-building<br>• Address rival explanations<br>• Use logic models | Data analysis |
| External validity | • Use theory in single case designs<br>• Use replication logic in multiple-case designs | Research design |
| Reliability | • Use case study protocol<br>• Develop case study database | Data collection |

Source: Yin (2003, p. 34)

**Table 7.5** *Interpretivist criteria for judging quality/credibility*

| Principles | Case study tactic | Phase of research |
|---|---|---|
| Hermeneutic | • Long periods of time between conducting cases, preparing drafts and drawing conclusions | Data collection |
| Contextualization | • Sufficient time to reconsider the context, check alternative interpretations and maintain an overall suspicion of the findings | Data collection |
| Interaction | • Researcher places themselves and subjects into a historical perspective, socially engaging in the process | Data collection |

Source: Klein and Myers (1999)

## Step 3 Prepare to collect the data

A key element in data collection is the use of *multiple sources* of evidence. The opportunity to use multiple sources of evidence in case studies far exceeds that in other research methods such as experiments or surveys and allows a researcher to address a broader range of historical and observational issues in order to gain a better understanding of a case and contribute to theorization. Furthermore, the use of multiple sources of evidence enables better triangulation of findings.

Maintaining *a chain of evidence* in the collection of data allows an external observer – the reader of the case study for example – to follow the derivation of any evidence from initial research questions to ultimate case study conclusions. The researcher also needs to prepare letters of introduction, establish rules for confidentiality and be prepared to revisit and revise the research design and the original set of research questions.

## Step 4 Collect data in the field

An important role for the researcher is to collect and store multiple sources of evidence comprehensively and systematically through the creation of a *case study database*. Four components should be contained in a *database* created for case study research:

- notes (including interview data)
- documents
- tabular materials (e.g. from surveys, structured interviews)
- narrative (stories, diaries).

Based on field notes the researcher may be able to identify patterns emerging or, alternatively, may need to reformulate or redefine the data collection strategy.

Yin (2003) suggests the following principles for data collection:

- ask good questions;
- be a good listener;
- be adaptive and flexible;
- have a firm grasp of the issues being studied;
- be unbiased by preconceived notions. (pp. 58–62, pp. 67–80)

## Step 5 Evaluate and analyse the data

Yin (1989) notes that in case study methodology, all the data needs to be available for other researchers to review. Yin (2003) notes that high quality evaluation and analysis require the researcher to:

- attend to all the evidence;
- address all major rival interpretations;
- address the most significant aspect of your case study;
- use their own prior, expert knowledge;
- examine the raw data using many interpretations in order to find linkages with the original research questions;
- categorize, tabulate and recombine data to address the initial research questions;
- treat the evidence fairly to produce analytic conclusions answering the original 'how' and 'why' research questions.

This process, although conducted independently, involves four steps. These are:

*Step 1*  The sport management researcher must immerse themselves in the data for the case (interviews and journals) through numerous readings.

*Step 2*  The sport management researcher must commence data reduction through coding emerging themes.

*Step 3*  Once the data is coded, the sport management researcher begins data interpretation.

*Step 4*  Once all case studies are analysed and written up, they are then compared by the sport management researcher for similarities and differences.

## Step 6 Prepare the report

The report of case studies should convince the reader that the researcher has examined all aspects of the subject studied and the boundaries of the case. The aim of the written report is to transform a complex issue into one that the reader can understand. It is also hoped that by reading the report, a reader will arrive at their understanding independent of the researcher.

*Case study report styles*

- linear-analytic – follows the sequence: problem, methods, findings of data collection and analysis, conclusion;
- comparative – the same kind of case is repeated two or three times. Alternative descriptions or explanations can be compared;
- theory-building – where case evidence is used to construct/ground a new theory;
- suspense – the result comes first, the reasons later.

Figure 7.1 summarizes the above six steps more broadly.

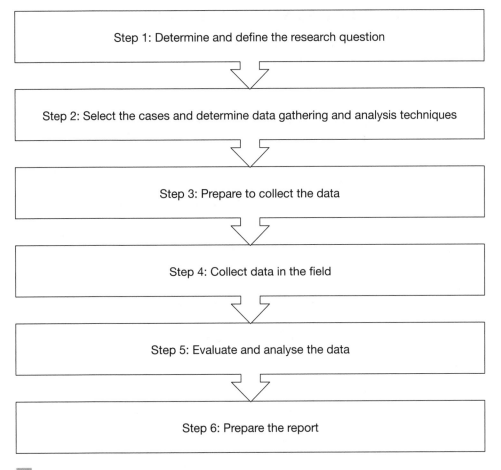

**Figure 7.1** *Steps in the case study method*

## ADVANTAGES AND DISADVANTAGES OF CASE STUDY APPROACH

Researchers including Marshall and Rossman (1995) and Yin (1994) believe that when the main purpose of the research project is exploratory, then a case study approach is an appropriate strategy. In particular, Yin (1994) asserts that the case study is appropriate for exploratory analysis when investigating contemporary phenomena within its real-life context, and when the boundaries between the phenomena and the context are not clear, as is often the case in sport management. Furthermore, case studies are the strategy of choice when the focus is on understanding the dynamics present within single settings, and when existing theory seems inadequate (Eisenhardt, 1989). The advantages and disadvantages of case studies for sport management researchers are summarized in Table 7.6.

## TRADITIONAL PREJUDICES AGAINST CASE STUDY RESEARCH

Table 7.7 outlines the traditional prejudices against case study research as outlined by Yin (2003). What follows then is a brief discussion on the counterpoint by various researchers.

**Table 7.6** *Advantages and disadvantages of case studies for sport management researchers*

*Advantages*

A single or small number of cases allows the sport management researcher to capture in-depth understanding of a sport environment.

A diversity of data collection methods can be utilized to understand the complexities of the sport environment.

The boundaries of the research such as time and context can be controlled by the sport management researcher to gain a full understanding of the sport situation.

Greater research flexibility allows the sport management researcher to choose from a range of research approaches.

The sport management researcher may use case study for a variety of purposes and for different cases.

The results of a case study investigation can inform theory development in sport management.

*Disadvantages*

It can result in overly complex theories.

It can be difficult to ensure external validity.

It can be difficult to conduct, effectively and efficiently.

No single approach can be deemed sufficient for the development of a sound theory.

The high risk of researcher bias.

Source: Parkhe (1993); Bailey (1992); Eisenhardt (1983); Yin (1994)

**Table 7.7** *Traditional prejudices against case study research*

*Traditional prejudices against case study research*

- Lack of rigour
- Little basis for generalization
- Takes too long and results in massive unreadable documents

Source: Yin (2003, pp. 10–12)

## 1 Rigour

*Case studies do not use standard methodologies; hence, they lack rigour.*

Case studies use multiple sources of data collection such as observation, interviews, archives and quantitative data. This ensures triangulation and provides stronger substantiation of constructs and hypotheses (Eisenhardt, 1989).

## 2 Generalizability

*Case studies are subjective, lack rigour and are not capable of arriving at generalization.*

An investigator's goal is to expand and generalize theories (analytic) and not to enumerate frequencies (statistical) (Yin, 1984). For case studies generalizability is determined by the strength of the description of the context. It is argued by other case study researchers that generalization is a redundant concept for case study research and analysis is based on the 'categorical aggregation of instances' (Bergen and While, 2000). More is learned about the 'particular' and the interpretation of these particulars is through an analytical generalization.

## 3 Data overload

*Case study involves collection of data from several sources. Thus, it accumulates a massive amount of data. The researcher has to analyse this massive amount of data. Case research is time consuming and may result in documentation overload.*

Multiple data collection and analysis is the strength of case research as it helps in understanding complex phenomena in their context. Case researchers always develop a strategy of time management and documentation overload.

### RECENT CASE EXAMPLE: CASE STUDY

*The following article is an example of how a case study has been conducted in the past by researchers in Sport Management Research. The interested reader may wish to find/download and read the article for further insights.*

Contextual influences and athlete attitudes to drugs in sport. Smith, A.C.T., Stewart, B., Oliver-Bennetts, S., McDonald, S., Ingerson, L., Anderson, A., Dickson, G., Emery, P., Graetz, F. (2010) *Sport Management Review, 13*, 181–197.

This article reports on 11 narrative-based case histories that sought to: (1) uncover the attitudes of players and athletes to drugs in sport, and (2) explore contextual factors influencing the formation of those attitudes as informed by social ecology theory.

## CONCLUSION

The aim of case study research is generalizing to theoretical propositions but not to populations. Sport management case studies may be epistemologically in harmony with experiences of others, and a natural basis for generalization. Although the case study method is valuable to sport management it is infrequently used as a method in Sport Management Research. Encouragement for its use in Sport Management Research as a method is given in order to investigate the day-to-day observations and interventions that constitute sport management practice. The benefits of using case study include: the research can be conducted in the natural setting, and because of this it is grounded or embedded and this allows for rich description (Woods, 1997; Yin, 2003). Case study as a research method can and does provide rich narrative data gathered by a variety of both qualitative and quantitative methods. Bounding or defining the case strengthens the methodology, design and validity. Inherent in the characteristics of case study is the sport management researchers' depth of interest and focus on the specificity or uniqueness of the case. This makes possible or allows for a detailed study of all aspects of an individual case or cases.

## REVIEW QUESTIONS

Case study as a method can be used to investigate the day-to-day observations and interventions that constitute sport management practice. With this in mind:

■ Provide an example of how a case study approach could be used in a sport management setting. Identify the limitations that may exist and how those limitations may be overcome.

## SUGGESTED EXTENDED READING FOR STUDENTS

Creswell, J. W. (1998). *Qualitative inquiry and research design: Choosing among five traditions.* Thousand Oaks, CA: Sage.

Merriam, S. B. (1988). *Case study research in education: A qualitative approach*. San Francisco, CA: Jossey-Bass.

Ritchie, J., Lewis, J., and Elam, G. (2003). Designing and selecting samples. In J. Ritchie and J. Lewis (eds), *Qualitative research practice: A guide for social sciences students and researchers*. London: Sage.

Yin, R. K. (2003). *Case study research, design and methods* (3rd edn). Newbury Park, CA: Sage.

Yin, R. K. (2011). *Applications of case study research* (3rd edn). Newbury Park, CA: Sage.

# Chapter 8

# Deconstruction and Sport Management Research

## LEARNING OUTCOMES

By the end of this chapter, you should be able to:

■ understand the basic concepts of deconstruction;
■ identify some of the key strategies with which to apply deconstruction in Sport Management Research.

## KEY TERMS

*Deconstruction* – 'involves the attempt to take apart and expose the underlying meanings, biases, and preconceptions that structure the way a text conceptualizes its relation to what it describes' (Denzin, 1994, p. 185).

## KEY THEMES

■ Can deconstruction be used as a research methodology in Sport Management Research?
■ What is deconstruction?

## CHAPTER OVERVIEW

This chapter explores Jacques Derrida's strategy of deconstruction as a way of understanding and critiquing sport management theory and practice. Deconstruction looks primarily at existing literature as opposed to direct interaction with an organization. Deconstruction seeks to locate and identify multiple interpretations within texts and to then dislocate the dominant discourse by examining the language and structure of the text – by what has been selected, and not selected, to create the structure.

## WHAT IS DECONSTRUCTION?

According to Saukko (2003) deconstruction is a theoretical perspective, a methodology and a method. Deconstructionism is closely associated with the work of Jacques Derrida. Derrida's work demonstrates a constant critical interrogation of texts. As Denzin (1994) asserted, deconstruction 'involves the attempt to take apart and expose the underlying meanings, biases, and preconceptions that structure the way a text conceptualizes its relation to what it describes' (p. 185).

Deconstruction is often associated with postmodernism. We argue that it is useful and relevant as a way of challenging the dominant paradigm of any discipline, including sport management. Because deconstruction is notoriously difficult to define, we offer a number of examples of deconstruction in action.

Deconstructionist features include: (1) *close reading of text* to demonstrate that any given text has irreconcilably contradictory meanings rather than a unified, logical whole; (2) the *aim* of deconstruction is *to criticize Western logic* but it arose as a response to *structuralism* and *formalism*; (3) seeing text as more radically *heterogeneous* than in a formalist way; (4) seeing works in terms of their *undesirability*; (5) regarding language as a *fundamentally unstable medium*; (6) the text is based only on the author's intentions; and (7) language and logic always being ruled by *hierarchical oppositions*.

In sport management deconstruction can facilitate further scholarly discussion by challenging the legitimacy and validity of those precepts and ideas generally accepted within the sport management academic community to be irrefutable. Think about Western culture's generalizable assumptions about women as sport fans and compare that to men as sport fans. In practice and in academia, sport managers and/or sport management researchers often use these stereotypes when exploring fan affiliation. These inherent attitudes and assumptions can be isolated and inferred using deconstructionist methodologies.

## DEFINING DECONSTRUCTION

One of the difficulties that many have with deconstruction is its unwillingness to be pinned down and precisely defined. We can see its elusive nature in Derrida's (1996) constant refusal to offer a definition: 'Deconstruction doesn't consist in a set of theorems, axioms, tools, rules, techniques, methods . . . There is no deconstruction, deconstruction has no specific object' (p. 218). Deconstruction challenges an author's attempt to privilege a theory, technique or model as a superior way to arrive at closure around knowledge. For example, deconstructing institutionalism (a common organizational change theory used in Sport Management Research) may reveal major limitations with an author's attempt to explain a national sport organization's response to change in board members, thus finding that institutionalism cannot explain the actions of the board to the extent the author argues. Thus, deconstruction particularly holds nothing sacred, seeks to question every assumption

**135**

and presupposition offered under the rubric of 'knowledge', and, most importantly, challenges any author[ity]'s claim to a 'method' of knowledge production that is privileged over others.

## THE DECONSTRUCTION METHOD

Deconstruction has often been presented and defended by its best proponents as neither a traditionally constituted philosophical system tending towards its own coherence and closure, nor an easily reproducible, stable method of inquiry or analysis (Wortham, 1998). Derrida himself refused to characterize deconstruction as a method, referring to it at different times as an 'experience' or a 'movement'. It has in innate exploratory nature. The experience of deconstructing a text is to work through the structured genealogy of its concepts, to determine from a certain external perspective that it cannot name or describe what this history may have concealed or excluded, constituting itself as history through this repression in which it has a stake. The goal of the 'deconstructor' is to challenge the text's claims to coherence, neutrality and objectivity.

Deconstruction cannot be sought in an instruction manual. It is a method to be followed regardless of context, discourse and purpose. Derrida's theoretical notions inform us of the broad purpose of deconstruction and of a general outline of its practice but there is no one way to 'do' it. Derrida's writings supply some general rules, some procedures that can be transposed by analogy, but these rules are taken up in a text that is each time a unique element and that does not let itself be turned totally into a method.

Though much has been referred to in recent years regarding deconstruction in postmodern research there is a noticeable scarcity of deconstruction strategies. Martin (1990, p. 355) provides a useful framework from which to begin the process of deconstruction:

- dismantling a dichotomy, exposing it as a false distinction;
- examining silences – what is not said;
- attending to disruptions and contradictions, places where the text fails to make sense;
- focusing on the element that is most alien to a text or a context as a means of deciphering implicit taboos – the limits to what is conceivable or permissible;
- interpreting metaphors as a rich source of multiple meanings;
- analysing 'double-entendres' that may point to an unconscious subtext, often sexual in content;
- separating group-specific and more general sources of bias by 'reconstructing' the text with iterative substitution phrases;
- exploring, with careful 'reconstructions' the unexpected ramifications and inherent limitations of minor policy changes;
- using the limitations exposed by 'reconstruction' to explain the persistence of the status quo and the need for more ambitious change programmes.

As a method, however, it is not without its advantages and disadvantages. These are outlined in Table 8.1.

**Table 8.1** *Advantages and disadvantages of deconstruction*

*Advantages*

- Subverts the privileged position of positivist theory
- Holds theory intellectually accountable
- Makes clear the fact that knowledge production is always a political act
- Examines silences – what is not said

*Disadvantages*

- Accusation of nihilism
- Derrida refuses to characterize deconstruction as a method
- Lack of definition
- Not a method of analysis

## RECENT CASE EXAMPLE OF DECONSTRUCTION

*The following article is an example of how deconstruction has been used in the past by researchers in Sport Management Research. The interested reader may wish to find/download and read the article for further insights.*

Interpreting policy language and managing organizational change: The case of the Queensland Rugby Union. Skinner, J., Stewart, B., and Edwards, A. (2004). *European Sport Management Quarterly*, 4(2), 77–94.

This article uses Derrida's (1976, 1978, 1981, 1982) postmodern theories of deconstruction and 'differance' to analyse organizational change in Queensland Rugby Union (QRU) during the 1990s. Specifically, it aims to examine the ways in which internal policy and planning documents produced by QRU were formulated, and subsequently interpreted by the many volunteer officials at the local and community level. Derrida's constructs provided a framework within which to explain the potential for policy and planning documents to produce fragmented organizational outcomes. This approach to the interpretation of texts proved a valuable tool for exploring the paradoxes, biases and contradictions in social and organizational behaviour. Data was collected through semi-structured interviews with individuals at differing functional levels within the QRU hierarchy. The interview data was supplemented by content analysis of policy and planning documents developed by the QRU. The results showed that policy and planning documents were not only interpreted differently at the different functional levels of the QRU, but when used to guide change, often met resistance that was not anticipated. The ambiguity of these documents therefore complicated the organizational change process because organizational sub-units frequently gave meanings to the text that were not intended by senior management.

## THE IMPORTANCE OF DECONSTRUCTION IN SPORT MANAGEMENT RESEARCH

Our purpose in introducing deconstruction to sport management is twofold. First, we believe that in the practice of sport management, and theorizing about that practice, deconstruction offers pedagogy for the critical reading of texts. It tends to be assumed, once a text achieves a canonical status, that the business of commentary is to seek out coherence and intelligibility, to justify the text on its own argumentative terms. Deconstruction, of course, does exactly the opposite and calls into question the 'coherence and intelligibility' of a text precisely on its own argumentative terms. Just because institutionalism is widely accepted in sport management, does it justly argue the points the sport management researcher has used it to argue?

Our second purpose is to subvert the privileged position of positivist theory as a theory of knowledge production. This influence is due to many factors; among them: (1) Sport management scholars' unwillingness to critically examine the political, ontological, metaphysical and epistemological assumptions that underlie research, and (2) Specific institutional arrangements for the production and dissemination of sport management knowledge that form a 'market' for Sport Management Research that is driven by factors beyond the intellectual competence of the research. Thus, Sport Management Research is less expansive and less intellectually rigorous than it could be. Our dual purposes, then, are designed to hold positivist theory intellectually accountable and to make clear the fact that knowledge production is always a political act. We find deconstruction a useful praxis for these purposes. What deconstruction attempts to destroy is the claim of any rule-bound system of knowledge production to unequivocally dominate another, the attempt to close off the scholarly conversation by privileging one's own discourse over others.

### RECENT CASE EXAMPLE OF DECONSTRUCTION

*The following article is an example of how deconstruction has been used in the past by researchers in Sport Management Research. The interested reader may wish to find/download and read the article for further insights.*

The (re)presentation of 'the boxer': A discursive analysis and deconstruction. Mandlis, L. R. (2005). Masters Thesis, University of Alberta (Canada).

In his thesis Mandlis uses discourse analysis and specific Derridian deconstructive ideas to examine different aspects of the representation of boxing and boxers. This study is an example of the application of deconstruction to the study of sport. By extrapolation it demonstrates one application of deconstruction to the field of Sport Management Research.

## HYPOTHETICAL CASE STUDY

### Racial stereotypes in sport

Below is a list of stereotypes that have been associated with white and black athletes, or at least the identity of white and black in sport.

| White | Black |
| --- | --- |
| Wealthy, privileged upbringing | Poor, unprivileged upbringing |
| Well coached | Genetically gifted |
| Educated | Uneducated |
| Obedient | Wayward |
| Leader | Workhorse |

As an introductory exercise into deconstruction, think about and discuss these questions:

1. Would you fit neatly into these categories? What about your friends and family?
2. Which side tends to be more glorified in our culture? Why?
3. Where do you see faults in these stereotypes?

## CONCLUSION

By introducing deconstruction to sport management it is possible to subvert the pretensions of positive theory as a theory of knowledge production. Therefore, by supporting deconstruction it is possible to hold positive theory intellectually accountable and to make clear the fact that knowledge production is always shaped by political, ontological and epistemological assumptions. The challenge of deconstruction as a research approach is that no one *narrative* is considered dominant or superior over another. As such, deconstruction is often viewed as more a form of critique than of conclusive analysis.

## REVIEW QUESTIONS

Deconstruction seeks to locate and identify multiple interpretations within text that challenge meaning and identity. With a basic understanding now of deconstruction as an alternative to the more traditional methodologies associated with Sport Management Research, attempt to answer the following question:

■ Is there any place within Sport Management Research for deconstruction?

## SUGGESTED EXTENDED READING FOR STUDENTS

Derrida, J. (1996). *Deconstruction and pragmatism*. New York: Routledge.

Martin, J. (1990). Deconstructing organizational taboos: The suppression of gender conflict in organizations. *Organization Science, 1*, 339–359.

Saukko, P. (2003). *Doing research in cultural studies*. London: Sage.

Wortham, S. M. (1998). *Counter-institutions: Jacques Derrida and the question of the university*. New York: Fordham University Press.

# Chapter 9

# Discourse analysis and ethnomethodology

## LEARNING OUTCOMES

By the end of this chapter, you should be able to:

- understand the basic concepts of discourse analysis;
- identify some of the key strategies with which to apply discourse analysis in Sport Management Research;
- understand the basic concepts of discourse, discourse analysis and critical discourse analysis;
- identify the implications of the use of discourse analysis and critical discourse analysis methodology in sport management;
- discuss the key characteristics of discourse analysis and conversation analysis;
- discuss how these approaches differ from other qualitative approaches previously encountered;
- reflect on what these approaches offer for research and practice.

## KEY TERMS

*Discourse* – refers to the attitudes, rules, 'ways of being', actions and language used to construct a particular knowledge. Language, power and knowledge are joined. Discourse ultimately serves to control not just *what* a subject/phenomenon is but *how* they are constructed.

*Discursive practices* – discursive practices are the translation of discourses into social action; they are the enactment of discourse.

*Ethnomethodology* – a form of discourse analysis that aims to study, understand and articulate how people make sense of themselves and each other in everyday life.

## KEY THEMES

■ Can discourse analysis be used as a research methodology in Sport Management Research?

■ What is 'discourse', 'discourse analysis' and 'critical discourse analysis'?

■ What is ethnomethodology?

■ What are some of the implications of applying the analytic tools of conversation analysis and member categorization devices to Sport Management Research?

## CHAPTER OVERVIEW

This chapter explores discourse, discourse analysis, critical discourse analysis, ethnomethodology and how these can be applied to the field of Sport Management Research in useful and practical ways that can facilitate the development of practices that enhance sport management.

## DEFINING DISCOURSE AND DISCOURSE ANALYSIS

The term 'discourse' is taken up by contrasting theoretical perspectives and so has come to mean very different things. As Potter and Wetherall (1987) suggest: 'the only thing that commentators are agreed on in this area is that terminological confusions abound' (p. 6). According to Shapiro (1987), 'discourse' can be 'any systematic or disciplined way of constituting subjects, objects, and relationships' (p. 365). Parker (1992), for example, defined discourse as 'a system of statements that construct an object' (cited in Burr, 1995, p. 48). For Burr (1995) discourse analysis is 'the analysis of a text in order to reveal either the discourses operating within it or the linguistic and rhetorical devices that are used in its construction' (p. 184).

In addition to the notion of discourse, the notion of '*discursive practices*' developed by Foucault describes the linguistic practices and the use of socially charged language to produce dominant fields of knowledge. Foucault's analysis highlights the struggle between dominant social, cultural and political power groups within society. Discursive practices are the translation of discourses into social action; they are the enactment of discourse. They are the discursively inscribed, ordered regularities of behaviour that underscore discourses as social action (Fairclough, 1989).

Discourse theory (outlined below) can be seen as a useful theoretical framework and analytic approach for a critical reappraisal of the discursive domain of sport management. Discourse analysis (DA) has been criticized in a number of areas. Table 9.1 lists some of these criticisms.

## MAPPING THEORIES OF DISCOURSE

Various forms of discourse analysis exist. The most common are Foucaultian discourse analysis, critical discourse analysis and ethnomethodology (conversation analysis). These will now be discussed.

**Table 9.1** *Criticisms of discourse analysis*

- Accusations of moral nihilism: unethical acts are dismissed as having no material reality.

- Countered by argument that discourse analysis does not deny material reality, but focuses on the way our understandings of such practices are constructed through discourse.

- Voicing concerns for groups who do not consider themselves to be oppressed or disadvantaged.

- Subversion of oppressive discourses may lead to alternative suppressive discourses for other social groups.

- Difficulty of identifying interpretative repertoires when research is not independent of linguistic resources needed to construct discourse.

## Foucaultian discourse analysis

Foucault viewed discourse analysis as revealing relations of power/knowledge encoded in the social processes of language and action. Foucaultian style discourse analysis has also been referred to as genealogy, power analytics, critical hermeneutics or critical ethnography, although there are those who maintain that there are differences among these approaches. Foucault argued that discourse, knowledge and power are so closely interrelated that a field of discourse is co-extensive with a field of power. In fact, Foucault often used the phrase 'power/knowledge' with respect to discourse. Thus, using a Foucaultian perspective, it is possible to explore the links between knowledge, power and resultant discourses. An analysis of these links reveals that claims to knowledge by exponents of certain dominant discourses are, in fact, claims to power (Foucault, 1980).

All discourses, in the Foucaultian view, contain internal contradictions. Analysis of the contradictions and silences in a discourse are important elements in a Foucaultian discourse analysis. Because of the historically situated nature of all discourses, the internal contradictions 'make sense' only with respect to a specific context. This makes it problematic to claim that a discourse analysis describes 'what is really going on' within a discourse because the analyst coexists with the discourse she or he is analysing. Consequently, the purpose of discourse analysis is to describe the contradictions and puzzles as they become apparent, as a 'tool for radical political action' (Foucault, 1980, p. 205).

A Foucaultian style discourse analysis is sometimes referred to as an analytic because it seeks the conditions that make possible the analyses practised in the discipline (Kusch, 1991). Discourse analysis decomposes statements and their context-dependent interpretation into context-dependent categories called *subjects*, *concepts* and *strategies*. Foucault (1983) stressed that a discourse analysis concerns itself with the following five power/knowledge issues, exemplified by sport media's power/knowledge: first, the system of differentiations or privileged access to the discourse – more powerful sport media entities, such as Entertainment and Sports Programming Network (ESPN), may control access to discourse by selecting topics and interviewees or the time and place of the texts. Second, the types of objectives of one group of adherents over another – discourses may reflect an ESPN objective to market sports that are broadcast on its networks rather than sports contracted to a competitor's network.

Third, the means of bringing power relations into being that reveals surveillance systems, threats and dismissals – a recent example could be ESPN's influence in the collegiate sports conference realignment in the USA, as colleges were under threat of losing media coverage depending on what conference they participate in. Fourth, 'forms of institutionalization' such as the bureaucratic structures ESPN engages sports properties in, pressuring textual conformity to ESPN's agenda. Finally, the degree of rationalization required to support power arrangements. As more sports are contracted to the ESPN network, sport governing bodies tend to rationalize that they need to be on ESPN in order to attain the desired coverage.

The process of a Foucaultian style discourse analysis involves careful reading of entire bodies of text and other organizing systems (such as taxonomies, commentaries and conference transcriptions) in relation to one another, in order to interpret patterns, rules, assumptions, contradictions, silences, consequences, implications and inconsistencies. The product of a discourse analysis shows how discourses are constructed, circulated and played out. Discourse analysis includes a focus on oppression and also identifies potential discourses of resistance through which people may construct subject positions that challenge the dominant discourses. Discourse analysis may involve identification of several related discourses available to people in a given social context at a given time.

Edwards and Skinner (2009) suggested that the potential contribution of a Foucaultian style discourse analysis to the discipline of sport management is twofold: first, discourse analysis would provide an approach suitable for addressing such notions as the taken-for-granted nature of specific sport management practices; the history of sport management practices; the vested interest of authorized voices; the rules of evidence used to formulate and structure discussions; the rules of evidence used to produce explanations and the rules of which topics are dismissed from inquiry. Second, from Foucault's perspective, all discourses are merely perspectives. The aim of Foucaultian analysis is to examine the legitimacy of claims to truth by such groups as policy makers, editorial boards and researchers. Foucaultian discourse analysis constantly asks questions about how and why knowledge is constructed and by whom. From this perspective all sport management knowledge is under constant scrutiny. There are no absolute truths that are above or exempt from examination.

## FAIRCLOUGH'S CRITICAL DISCOURSE ANALYSIS (CDA)

According to Fairclough (1993), critical discourse analysis is:

> discourse analysis that aims to systematically explore the often opaque relationships of causality and determination between (a) discursive practices, events, and texts, and (b) wider social and cultural structures, relations and processes; to investigate how such practices, events and texts arise out of and are ideologically shaped by relations of power and struggles over power; and to explore how the opacity of these relationships between discourse and society is itself a factor in securing power and hegemony (p. 135).

The theoretical underpinnings of CDA bring together a wide variety of critical social theories, the Frankfurt school and other neo-Marxist scholars (Blommaert and Bulcaen, 2000).

Collectively, these theories have influenced many facets of CDA including the way power is conceptualized. Fairclough's (1993) model focuses on discourse as text. It is centred on the pivotal point that text is a concrete manifestation of discourse. Given this focus, Fairclough analyses structural and stylistic aspects within documents (e.g. paragraphs, sentences, phrases, clauses, grammar, speech acts and vocabulary) and their interactions and ties these discursive constructions (or elements of orders of discourse) to social relations. Figure 9.1 provides an overview of these aspects.

Fairclough (1992) believes there are three dimensions to a discursive event: '(1) it is spoken or written language *text*, (2) it is an *interaction* between people involving processes of producing and interpreting the text (discursive practice), and (3) it is part of a piece of *social action* (social practice)' (p. 10, emphasis in original). As such, he believes there should be three dimensions to CDA '(1) *description* of the text, (2) *interpretation* of the interaction processes and their relationship to the text, and (3) *explanation* of how the interaction process relates to the social action' (Fairclough, 1992, p. 11, emphasis in original).

The *description* dimension consists of examining the organization of the text, its structure and vocabulary while 'framing' the language of the text within the other dimensions of the analysis (since one cannot separate description and interpretation).

The aim in the *interpretation* dimension is to give a moment-by-moment analysis of how the participants produce and interpret the texts by specifying the discursive practices that are

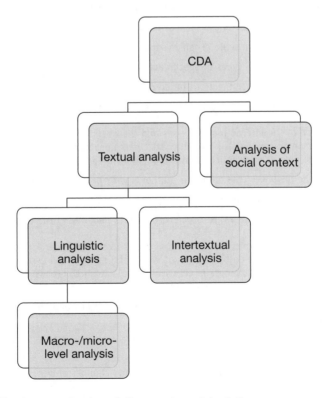

**Figure 9.1** *Elements of orders of discourse to social relations*

being used and in which combinations. This process relates the discourse event to the order of discourse used.

The aim in the *explanation* dimension is to explain the properties of the interaction by referring to its social context and assessing its contribution to social action (its effectiveness in constituting or helping to reconstitute different dimensions of the social in the interpretation phase). In this social action dimension, Fairclough's (1993) focus is political and ideological: political in that it establishes, sustains and changes power relations and ideological in that it constitutes, naturalizes, sustains and changes significations of the world. The two are not independent of each other 'for ideology is significations generated within power relations as a dimension of the exercise of power and struggle over power' (Fairclough, 1993, p. 67). In sum, he focuses on the discursive event within relations of power and domination. For a summary of Fairclough's three-dimensional analysis see Table 9.2.

**Table 9.2** *Fairclough's three-dimensional analysis*

1   *Description* of the text: examine the organization of the text, its structure and vocabulary.

* Vocabulary – individual words

* Grammar – words combined into clauses and sentences

* Cohesion – how clauses and sentences are linked together

* Text structure – large scale organizational properties of texts

* Force of utterances – types of speech acts used (promise, request, threat)

* Coherence of texts – connections based on ideological assumptions

* Intertextuality – connections to other texts, may be explicit or implicit

2   *Interpretation* of the interaction processes and their relationship to the text: give a moment-by-moment analysis of how the participants produce and interpret the texts by specifying the discursive practices that are being used and in which combinations.

* Who is the producer (the animator, author and/or principal) of the text?

* What are the social constraints as to how it is produced?

* What aspects of members' resources are used to understand the text?

3   *Explanation* of how the interaction process relates to the social action: explain the properties of the interaction by referring to its social context and assess its contribution to social action (its effectiveness in constituting or helping to reconstitute different dimensions of the social in the interpretation phase).

* Ideology – how the text constitutes, naturalizes, sustains and changes significations of the world

* Hegemony – the implicit practices that become naturalized or automated, and expose the constant struggle

* Political – how the text establishes, sustains and changes power relations

Source: Fairclough (1993)

**Table 9.3** *Fairclough's CDA*

*Strengths*

- Links discourse to material relations
- It is political; it focuses on power relations
- Reveals the impact on social relations, not the 'truth'
- Does not grant privileged status to the content of a discourse

*Weaknesses*

- Not specific enough in explaining how people reconcile contradictions by creating new discourses
- Critical research projects develop a social critique without developing a theory of action that people can draw upon to develop 'counter-hegemonic' practices in which dominant structures can be challenged

Source: Fairclough, 1995.

Fairclough's (1995) CDA is based on the premise that power operates through discourse to structure social relations. This method analyses how stylistic properties of the text are linked to material relations. For example, the method assists in examining how the communications and organizational documents from an international sports federation contribute to the power relationship with national sports federations. In this way, critical discourse analysis moves beyond the content of a text to examine the effect of discourse on reality. By firmly centring the analysis of discourse within the field of political action, CDA does not reduce its analysis to 'merely the markings of textuality', but also examines the physicality of its effects in the materiality of its practices (Foucault, 1981, p. 66; as cited in Hook, 2001, p. 537). Fairclough's method is also political for its goal is not only deconstruction but also social change. The objective of his approach is to transform society by exposing how material relations of force are linked to discourse. CDA is not without its critics. Table 9.3 indicates some of the strengths and weaknesses of this approach.

## CDA AND SPORT MANAGEMENT

There is no set questioning through which a CDA takes place. The questions asked in an analysis of a particular text depend on the research aims and the nature of the debate under analysis (Fairclough, 2003). Critical discourse analysis presents a structured methodology for analysing any text and is useful for sport management researchers who require a set approach to the analysis of discourse. The utility of the textual analysis offered by CDA lies in the depth that it can add to issues related to sport management practice.

## HYPOTHETICAL CASE STUDY: DISCOURSE ANALYSIS

Partial transcript of a public forum with key people from Australian Rugby Union (ARU) and Rugby Media

Key: Q — member of the public; BP — Bill Pulver, CEO of Australia Rugby Union

**Q:** I'd like to ask about junior development as an area of rugby growth in the heart of Sydney, and the fact that rugby league is pillaging our youth. What are you doing to expand that area and what are your plans for winning that back?

**BP:** That is such a good point and I mentioned, I think, in my comment that there were three key drivers of the game: growth in participation, growth in elite talent and growth in revenue. Unless we grow participation rates, the game is dead and it doesn't matter how well you play at the elite level, the game is dead and so you are absolutely right. And am I nervous about it? Yes, I am. The last three weeks I've had meetings with headmasters and sadly in Australia, rugby is known as a private school game and I want to change that and sevens will help to change that. Sevens will collect a way more diversified audience for our game.

But I've got two challenges in the short term. Put your hand up if you went to the last Waratah's game. [6 hands raised from 50+ in attendance] How pathetic is that? With respect, I'm sorry but that is the point, we have a rusted on rugby community that don't go and watch the games. Now unless we start growing the number of people that love this game from the grassroots level, we have a huge problem. I can go on forever about this because you're spot on strategically and I am very nervous about it. AFL and rugby league with their 1.2 and 1.3 billion dollar broadcasting relationships have just money to burn. When I go and talk to the headmasters of these schools, the AFL have already been there with grounds lined up, coaches lined up, all the gear they want and putting in place programmes for seven, eight, nine, ten, eleven year olds. And to me, strategically, the AFL are this train that is lined up with its headlight right between my eyes that's going to hit me in ten years that I'm standing here going I can't do anything to stop it. So we need initiatives at the grassroots level to deal with it, strategically it's a huge issue.

I've just announced a new structure at the ARU. I've got to try and get cost out of the ARU and we've done that to a large degree. There's one position I'm aiming to fill and we've got these state community programmes. This position is someone who is going to be the general manager of participation. That's all I want, participation. One objective: we have 320,000 participants today and the objective is to get it to 500,000 within a reasonable window. How do we do that? We just have to redirect some investment, money we don't actually have today, but we've got to find a way to do this and re-energize the younger age brackets of getting back involved in the game.

One of the problems with participation with junior level is mums are worried about the physicality of the game. I would love ultimately to see the game as being the 15-man game, sevens and touch. If you can create a non-contact form of this game, you could actually attract every single sporting enthusiast to become a potential participant. So it's a huge strategic issue, you are spot on. There is a lot of creative talk that's got to go into fixing it and we're going to dive in and try and address it.

**Q:** I'd like to come back to the sevens as well. What is being actively done to encourage people to engage more in sevens because it's not that popular, and what's with Fox Sport [broadcast partner of rugby] not showing it, what's the future there because you can easily claim, you have full stadia, you have people dressing up, you have exciting tournaments . . . but with Australian men possibly not even qualifying for the Olympic Games, the women I think are OK, but the Australian men might not even qualify, how can you engage the Australian public to be passionate about sevens and then the Commonwealth Games is the next question.

**BP:** You guys are all explaining why I have a very difficult job in everything but you're spot on. So what have we done?

Step 1: I've appointed somebody nationally accountable for sevens rugby. Anthony Eddy will have a dedicated executive focused exclusively on sevens rugby.

Step 2: And sevens has actually developed at the international level. There are nine tournaments played around the world. One of those is ours. On 12 and 13 October in the Gold Coast is a phenomenal tournament that I would ask you to support and get up there and have a fun weekend. If any of you have ever been to Hong Kong or any of these tournaments, they're great fun. You can dress up, you can do whatever you like. It's a party, but it's a party with great rugby so please get there and support it.

We need to put sevens competition structure all the way down through the age groups from juniors to seniors, to schools to a national . . . I would like to see Super Rugby sevens. I'm already talking to Super Rugby chief executives about Super Rugby competitions, topping and tailing the current XVs. So you're going to see an infrastructure put in place.

One of the other issues with sevens, I'll ask you and it's interesting, because Greg's [Greg Clarke commentator on Fox Sports, and on the panel] son is actually part of the Australian sevens, so apart from him, can anyone name another Australian men's sevens player? [three people shout out a couple names] Some of you are rusted on rugby fans, which is good. But by and large we don't have profile names in sevens and there's a bit of a policy issue that Australian Rugby is deciding you're a XVs player, you're a sevens player. Well I'm going to mix that up and in June basically in a couple of days they're going to Moscow for the World Cup of sevens. Bernard Foley is going, Matt Lucas is going and there's a third, Luke Monahan [three Super Rugby players] is going and guys like Israel Folau, guys like James O'Connor [National 15 squad member], they want to play sevens so we need to find an approach where you can mix between sevens and XVs.

And again I wish I had 50 million bucks sitting in the bank to invest in all this stuff, which I don't. But there will be a lot more time and effort going into it. The same on the women's side and really we need to put a competition structure right down through the game. The Olympics will help enormously. You touched on a really serious point we've got to qualify, speaking of the pain of the qualification process but there's a lot to do. We will get there.

Complete a basic discourse analysis by answering these questions:

a)  What word use and narratives stood out? Why?
b)  What are the underpinning attitudes, rules, etc. for this dialogue?
c)  What are the main themes?

Compare your answers with other students.

a)  What differences occurred among the analyses?
b)  What significance do those differences mean to this type of research?

One area in which CDA could have particular relevance within the Sport Management Research domain is sport policy. Policies can be broadly defined and include directives for action, or the responsibilities for action and the processes guiding the implementation of action. Critical discourse analysis aims to expose sources of domination, repression and exploitation that are entrenched in, and legitimated by policy. Thus a policy analysis goes beyond analysing the content and implementation of policies to examine how those policies reflect certain understandings of reality in the first instance.

## CRITICAL DISCOURSE ANALYSIS OF SPORT POLICY

A critical discourse analysis of sport policy should have the following characteristics:

a)  situates the policy in its discursive context;
b)  examines the multiple voices present in policy discourse, i.e. the policy actors/stakeholders and their power relationships;
c)  identifies multiple discourses exposing their relationships and interactions with each other;
d)  highlights predominant discourses;
e)  conducts multileveled analysis of texts. Analyses detailed structural aspects within the textual document (e.g. paragraphs, sentences, phrases, clauses, grammar, speech acts and vocabulary) and their interactions;
f)  exposes ideology operating through discourse (i.e. how discourse orchestrates a version of truth that structures reality);
g)  proposes a theory of action through the development of counter discourses as forms of resistance.

**RECENT CASE EXAMPLE: CRITICAL DISCOURSE ANALYSIS**

*The following article is an example of how critical discourse analysis has been used in the past by researchers in Sport Management Research. The interested reader may wish to find/download and read the article for further insights.*

> Yao Ming and masculinity in Middle America: A critical discourse analysis of racial representations in NBA game commentary. Lavelle, K. L. (2006). Unpublished dissertation. Wayne State University.

Lavelle studied the rhetorical construction of Yao Ming (7 foot 6 inches tall Chinese basketball player), specifically how representations of him function as a clash of cultures and a statement on notions of masculinity, where race is one element, in the National Basketball Association. This study was derived from the literature that talks about how race and ethnicity can shape how players are rhetorically constructed during game commentary. Lavelle utilized critical discourse analysis to examine 15 game commentaries quantitatively and qualitatively. The qualitative analysis data consisted of a thematic analysis of players, focusing on a comparison of how players were described. Lavelle concluded that the depictions of Yao reinforce his role as a model minority.

## WHAT IS ETHNOMETHODOLOGY?

Garfinkel (1967) coined the term and was the founder of ethnomethodology. In his text discussing Garfinkel's work, Heritage (1984) defined ethnomethodology as:

> the study of . . . the body of common-sense knowledge and the range of procedures and considerations by which the ordinary members of society make sense of, find their way about in, and act on the circumstances in which they find themselves. (p. 4)

The ethnomethodological perspective views social actors as accomplishing their social worlds through interaction, by means of a continuous process of intersubjective adjustment. Social realities are, therefore, regarded as action in process (Garfinkel, 1967). Ethnomethodological studies investigate social life *in situ*, in ordinary settings, examining 'the most routine, every-day, naturally occurring activities in their concrete details' (Psathas, 1995, pp. 1–2). Lee (1991) has outlined five axioms that characterize the way that an ethnomethodological approach gives a new orientation to the study of social life and social activity. The axioms are:

1   Suspending general questions (e.g. about class, socioeconomic status, cultural differences) until those characteristics of people and activities have occurred as activity or interaction that can be understood and observed by participants

**151**

in (members of) the culture or language of the community: for example, ignoring the preconceived knowledge of sport rivalry until actions depicting rivalry among fans of different teams are observed and then understood.

2    Treating social activities, such as talk (e.g. conversation, social interaction, interviews), as jointly constructed social events that are observable, rather than as the result of cognitive or linguistic choices or cultural attributions.

3    Translating the conceptually unanalysed notion of 'language forms' into an exploration (scrutiny) of how people organize their activities in and through talk and local routines of that talk without pre-empting notions of what these structures look like.

4    Accepting that the ways in which people coordinate their activities in and through talk will show the orderliness of their culture and how that is achieved, day by day, in ordinary activities. For example, the daily activities and interactions of athletes and coaches may provide an illustration of team culture.

5    Regarding culture as implanted in and built by the course of everyday actions, because that is how members of a culture experience it, not as something 'external' to and 'constraining on language'. Culture is present in ordinary activities, in knowledge and skills used and available in talk and action. (Lee, 1991, pp. 224, 225)

Ethnomethodology studies the specific interactions among participants and acknowledges that interactions are actually agents for constituting social order and reality. Gubrium and Holstein (2000) suggest that ethnomethodologists focus on how members actually 'do' social life, aiming in particular to document how they concretely construct and sustain social entities, such as gender, self and family.

Five concepts are central to ethnomethodology; these are shown in Table 9.4:

**Table 9.4** Concepts that are central to ethnomethodology

| Process | Description |
| --- | --- |
| Indexicality | The meaning of a word – indeed of all words – is dependent on its context of use. |
| Reflexivity | This is the process in ordinary conversation by which we build up meaning, order and rationality by both describing and producing action simultaneously. |
| The documentary method of interpretation | The meaning of a word is indexical, but at the same time we seek patterns to compensate for this indexicality of language that make sense. |
| The notion of member | The term member is used in ethnomethodology to describe a member of a group who has mastered the natural language of that group and does not have to think about what he or she is doing as the routines of everyday social practice are known. |
| Accountability | Accountability means that the activities whereby members produce and manage settings of organized everyday affairs are observable and reportable. |

## METHODOLOGY

According to Schegloff (1991), the basic task of the ethnomethodologist is 'to convert insistent intuition, however correct, into empirically detailed analysis' (p. 66). Lee's (1991) five principles of ethnomethodology summarize the analyst's position. *First*, an ethnomethodologist suspends belief or acceptance of social relationships between categories of people. An ethnomethodologist understands that members continually display the 'lived' reality of their relationships and their world to themselves and to others (Schegloff, 1991). *Second*, the ethnomethodologist's task is to treat interactive situations as scenes that are jointly and sequentially produced by all participants. *Third*, the ethnomethodologist sets aside formats of talk or interaction that given participants would or should use in favour of the structures of talk and interaction that they do use. *Fourth*, the assumption that the orderliness of social structures and social organization is achieved in the day-to-day ordinary activities of members and will, therefore, be available in the details of everyday events, is maintained by the ethnomethodologist. *Finally*, the ethnomethodologist understands that, for members of a society, that society's traditions, customs and mores are not sequestered from the talk and interaction, nor do they limit and constrain what those members do and say.

## THE ANALYTIC TOOLS OF ETHNOMETHODOLOGY

The key analytic tools of ethnomethodology are conversation analysis (CA) and membership categorization devices (MCDs). CA is concerned with explicating the practices social actors (e.g. sport administrators, athletes, coaches, fans, etc.) use to understand, and exhibit understanding of, everyday discourse (e.g. social media posts, team meetings, stadium cheers and jeers, etc.). Conversation analysis goes beyond a grammatical analysis of statements and relies on detailed transcripts of conversation (naturally occurring or interviews).

CA is characterized by three main features or assumptions: first, interaction is structurally organized; second, contributions to interaction are contextually oriented; and third, as a result of these two characteristics, no order of detail in interactions can be dismissed as disorderly, accidental or irrelevant (Heritage, 1984). These features are the basic foundations on which conversation analysis is built.

CA, as a branch of ethnomethodology, examines order as it is produced through talk in an achieved manner *in situ*, accomplished in and through the actual practices of social members. Hallmarks of conversation analytic work are:

- commitment to naturally occurring discourse;
- usage of a particularly detailed transcription system;
- an inductive, theoretical stance;
- a strong reliance on the conversational text;
- avoidance of non-discourse data (e.g. participant interviews) or predetermined category information (e.g. team affiliation) that is unavailable in the interaction itself.

The distinctions between discourse analysis and conversation analysis are identified in Table 9.5.

**153**

**Table 9.5** *Discourse analysis vs conversation analysis*

| Discourse analysis | Conversation analysis |
| --- | --- |
| Rules, formulas, more typical of linguistics and philosophers | More rigorously empirical and inductive |
| Categories, contingencies, grammars | Focus on what is found in data, not on what is expected to be found or would sound odd |
| Use of a small but strategic amount of data | Hesitant to make generalizations/accused of being atheoretical |
| Accused of 'premature' theory construction | Questions about whether the rules 'work' on real data |

The MCD is an analytic tool or device that describes the culturally available sets of categories into which we commonsensically divide persons. These categories are fundamental sense-making resources for members in everyday interaction.

A summary of the terminology used in MCD is highlighted in Table 9.6.

It is not argued in this book that all the approaches to textual, conversational and pictorial analysis are, in fact, similar or interchangeable. Indeed, there are certain ways in which they are divergent. Silverman (1993), for example, argues that discourse analysis (DA) and critical discourse analysis (CDA) are different from ethnomethodology and conversation analysis (CA) in that the former two analytic approaches possess the following three features:

1    They are concerned with a far broader range of activities, often related to more conventional social science concerns (e.g. gender relations, social control, etc.).
2    They do not always use analysis of ordinary conversation as a baseline for understanding talk in institutional settings.
3    Discourse analysis (and CDA) work with far less precise transcripts than CA (p. 121).

**Table 9.6** *Terminology*

| Membership categorization devices (MCDs) |
| --- |
| *Category*: any person can be labelled in many 'correct' ways |
| *MCD*: categories are seen as grouped together in collections |
| *Economy rule*: a single category may be sufficient to describe a person |
| *Consistency rule*: if one person is identified from a collection, then another person may be identified from the same collection |
| *Duplicative organization*: when categories can be heard as a 'team' hear them that way |
| *Category-bound activities*: activities may be heard as 'tied' to certain categories |
| *Standardized relational pairs* (SRPs): pairs of categories are linked together in standardized routine ways |

**154**

## QUALITY CRITERIA

The quality criteria for carrying out research using CA are set out in Table 9.7 (see p. 156). The criteria for quality investigation (assumptions) have been adapted from a number of authoritative sources (Boden, 1994; Have, 1999; Heritage, 1997; Hutchby and Wooffitt, 1998; Psathas, 1995; Silverman, 1998). The right-hand column shows, for each of the criteria, how the methods of CA were put into practice in a research study.

Ethnomethodology is offered as a contribution to an emerging body of scholarship that is directed at promoting a more rigorous and theoretically informed understanding of the conduct and reporting of ethnographic fieldwork. It clearly has unexplored potential in the field of Sport Management Research.

---

### RECENT CASE EXAMPLE: ETHNOMETHODOLOGY

*The following article is an example of how ethnomethodology has been used in the past by researchers in Sport Management Research. The interested reader may wish to find/download and read the article for further insights.*

> Toward an alternative theory of self and identity for understanding and investigating adherence to exercise and physical activity. McGannon, K. R. (2002). Doctoral thesis, University of Alberta.

McGannon developed an alternative theory of self and identity grounded in a view of language that prioritizes the process and outcome of language and how it is tied to discursive, cultural, social and institutional practices. Feminist post-structuralism 'ethnomethodology', and narrative psychology were combined to theorize women's self and identity (i.e. who they are) and implicitly, exercise behaviour as a collection of conversations they have with themselves and others or more specifically as narratives/stories spoken from subject positions within larger discourse(s).

---

## CONCLUSION

The application of discourse analysis as a methodology for Sport Management Research provides the discipline with the opportunity to construct alternative perspectives on power and knowledge. Ethnomethodology, a form of discourse analysis, is an emerging form of scholarship that promotes a more rigorous and theoretically informed understanding of the conduct and reporting of ethnographic research. It has unexplored potential for the field of Sport Management Research.

**Table 9.7** *The methodological perspective of conversation analysis*

| Assumptions | Practice in the study |
|---|---|
| CA methods were seen by Harvey Sacks as 'methods anyone could use' (Silverman, 1998) though familiarity and practice is essential for quality data transcription and analysis.<br><br>Data should be derived from naturally recurring conversation.<br><br>CA tries to describe and analyse phenomena and not explain phenomena by drawing on a theoretical framework other than the frameworks of CA itself. | Recordings must be able to be repeatedly replayed and transcribed for verification and re-examination. |

*Data-transcription assumptions*

| | |
|---|---|
| Data is recorded by audio-recordings. This original data is the only evidence from which all analysis derives.<br><br>Transcription seeks to capture the 'machinery' of conversation using the transcription.<br><br>Practice was guided by practitioner handbooks (e.g. Have, 1999; Hutchby and Wooffitt, 1998) and skills developed during the transcription and analysis.<br><br>The researcher did not impose any order.<br><br>Members were selected randomly by other than the researcher. Places were determined by where the conversations were to take place. Research settings were natural. | The original recordings were used throughout the analysis in preference to transcripts. |

*Data analysis: analytical assumptions*

| | |
|---|---|
| CA research adopts a stance of 'unmotivated looking'.<br><br>No assumptions are made regarding members' motivations, intentions, purposes; nor about their ideas, thoughts or understandings; except in so far as these can demonstrably be shown.<br><br>The researcher's analysis of what participants are doing is never based on some constructive analytic interpretation such as: 'taking the role of the other' 'presenting a self' 'being deviant' 'managing impressions' 'defining the situation'<br><br>These are set aside because they interfere with the direct examination of the phenomena of talk-in-interaction. | Phenomena were analysed in accordance with CA theory and conventions. |

*Data analysis: practical assumptions*

| | |
|---|---|
| Existing knowledge of the 'machinery of conversation', established through research on CA over the last 30 years, is accepted as a faithful description of recurrent phenomena that can be used for analysis.<br><br>The analytical task is, initially, to provide a wholly adequate analysis of how a single instance (utterance, individually or in sequence) is organized. The aim is to 'recover the machinery' that produced the interaction 'as it happened'.<br><br>This principle, or assumption, was followed so that the researcher was not part of the interpretive framework. The question of setting aside analytical interpretations such as these do not arise as they were not used. | A single instance is not usually taken as evidence of structure. Repeated instances of demonstrably similar empirical structures are admissible. |

*Data sessions and reporting*

| | |
|---|---|
| Written reports must include transcripts of the data from which the report was written. | Transcription conventions were used but some additional notations were devised to transcribe phenomena for which there is no existing symbol. |

## REVIEW QUESTIONS

Discourses are conversations and the meanings behind those conversations. Ethnomethodology is a form of discourse analysis that aims to study, understand and articulate how people make sense of themselves and each other in everyday life. With a basic understanding now of discourse analysis, critical discourse analysis and ethnomethodology, attempt to answer the following questions:

- Identify two key features of critical discourse analysis that would have particular relevance for Sport Management Research.
- What factors should the sport management researcher take into consideration before deciding to adopt ethnomethodology as a research approach?
- How can ethnomethodology be applied to Sport Management Research?

## SUGGESTED EXTENDED READING FOR STUDENTS

Blommaert, J., and Bulcaen, C. (2000). Critical discourse analysis. *Annual Review of Anthropology*, *29*, 447–466.

Fairclough, N. (2003). *Analyzing discourse: Textual analysis for social research*. New York: Routledge.

Foucault, M. (1983). The subject and power. In D. Dreyfus, P. Rabinow and M. Foucault (eds), *Beyond structuralism and hermeneutics* (2nd edn, pp. 208–226). Chicago, IL: University of Chicago Press.

Gubrium, J., and Holstein, J. (2000). Analyzing interpretive practice. In N. K. Denzin and Y. S. Lincoln (eds), *Handbook of qualitative research* (2nd edn, pp. 487–508). Thousand Oaks, CA: Sage.

## Chapter 10

# Ethnography and emerging ethnographical approaches

## LEARNING OUTCOMES

By the end of this chapter you should be able to:

- understand the basic concepts of ethnography;
- understand the definition and purpose of ethnographic research;
- be familiar with the ethnographic research process;
- understand the types of ethnographic research;
- identify key characteristics of ethnographic research designs;
- understand ethnographic research data collection techniques;
- differentiate between traditional ethnography and ethnographical research underpinned by critical and postmodern theories;
- recognize some key features of autoethnography, netnography, ethnodrama and phenomenography;
- identify applications of these methodologies to Sport Management Research.

## KEY TERMS

*Participant observation* – the researcher is immersed in the day-to-day lives of the people, or conducts one-on-one interviews with members of the group.

*Critical ethnography* – a perspective that allows a qualitative researcher to frame questions and promote action. Critical ethnography goes beyond a description of the culture to action for change, by challenging the false consciousness and ideologies exposed through the research.

*Postmodernism* – term applied to a wide-ranging set of developments in fields of research that are generally characterized as emerging from, in reaction to, or superseding, modernism.

*Netnography* – a written account resulting from fieldwork studying the cultures and communities that emerge from online, computer mediated or Internet-based communications.

*Ethnodrama* – a process to transform data into theatrical scripts and performance pieces.

*Phenomenography* – a process that is concerned with identifying people's ideas about a phenomenon, rather than proving that the actual phenomenon exists.

## KEY THEMES

- What is 'ethnography'?
- What are the implications for applying critical and postmodern theories to ethnographical research processes being undertaken in the field of sport management?

## ETHNOGRAPHIC CONCEPTS

- culture
- holistic perspective
- contextualization
- an emic perspective
- thick description
- member checking
- a nonjudgmental orientation

## CHAPTER OVERVIEW

This chapter examines the qualitative research approach of ethnography. For many years traditional ethnography has been applied to the field of sport. From the late 1990s sport researchers began to embrace ethnographic frameworks underpinned by critical and postmodern theories. The advantage for sport management researchers in applying critical and postmodern thought to ethnographic approaches is that it strengthens their own critical consciousness. This chapter will provide an introduction and overview to the concepts of ethnography, and provide some examples of critical and postmodern frameworks from which ethnographic researchers can approach the field of sport management. In addition, this chapter will highlight some emerging ethnographical methodologies and demonstrate how they can be situated in the sport management research field. Netnography, ethnodrama and phenomenography may appear on the surface to have little relation to Sport Management Research; however, this chapter will briefly cover each of these methodologies and discuss their potential applications to the field of sport management.

## WHAT IS ETHNOGRAPHY?

Ethnographic studies involve the collection and analysis of data about cultural groups. Ethnography means: 'to write about people or cultures' from the Greek words '*ethnos*' (people) and '*graphein*' (write). It is influenced by other theories such as, phenomenology, feminism, grounded theory and postmodernism.

According to Leininger (1985), ethnography can be defined as: 'the systematic process of observing, detailing, describing, documenting, and analysing the lifeways or particular patterns of a culture (or subculture) in order to grasp the lifeways or patterns of the people in their familiar environment' (p. 35). Hammersley and Atkinson (1995) indicate that:

> The ethnographer participates, overtly or covertly, in people's daily lives for an extended period of time, watching what happens, listening to what is said, asking questions; in fact collecting whatever data are available to throw light on the issues with which he or she is concerned. (p. 2)

## ORIGINS OF ETHNOGRAPHY

Ethnography has its roots in social anthropology and launched in the late nineteenth and twentieth century. It was the result of famous anthropologists such as Malinowski (1922), Boas (1928) and Mead (1928), while seeking cultural patterns and rules, exploring several non-Western cultures and the lifestyles of the people within them. Sociologists and the Chicago School of Sociology also had an influence on ethnographic methods, immersing themselves in the culture (LeCompte and Preissle, 1993). From the pioneering beginnings at the Chicago School of Sociology in the 1920s and 1930s a division occurred between ethnography as practised by social scientists and ethnographic methods used by anthropologists.

## FEATURES OF ETHNOGRAPHY

Hammersley (1990) identified that the term ethnography typically relates to social research, which consists of most of the following characteristics: (1) people's behaviours are studied in an everyday context, rather than under experimental situations developed by the investigator; (2) data is collected from various sources, with observation and interviews being the primary aspects; (3) data is gathered in an 'unstructured' manner in that it does not follow a plan. This does not imply that the research is unsystematic, rather data is collected in as raw a form, and on as wide a front, as feasible; (4) the focus is commonly a single setting or group and on a small scale; and (5) data analysis entails interpretation of the meanings and functions of human actions and is primarily conducted in the form of verbal descriptions and explanations (p. 1). These features make ethnography very applicable to many Sport Management Research contexts or settings. Tables 10.1 and 10.2 show characteristics and applications of ethnographic research, respectively.

**Table 10.1** *Characteristics of ethnographic research*

*Ethnographic research*

- Conducted in a natural context
- Involves intimate face-to-face interactions with participants
- Reflects participants' perspectives and behaviours
- Uses inductive, interactive and recursive collection of unstructured data
- Data is collected primarily through fieldwork experiences
- Uses multiple data sources including both quantitative and qualitative
- Frames all human behaviour and beliefs within a socio-political and historical context
- Uses the concept of culture as a lens through which the results are interpreted
- Places an emphasis on exploring the nature of particular social phenomena
- Investigates a small number of cases in detail
- Uses data analyses that involve the explicit interpretation of the meanings and functions of human actions that are presented through the description of themes and interpretations within the context or group setting
- Offers interpretations of people's actions and behaviours that are uncovered through the investigation of what they actually do and the reasons for doing it
- Offers a representation or interpretation of people's lives and behaviours that is neither the researcher's or the participants' but is built on the points of understanding and misunderstanding that occur between the researcher and participants
- Is necessarily partial, bound by what can be handled within a certain time, under certain specific circumstances, and from a particular perspective

 **Table 10.2** *Applications of ethnography to Sport Management Research*

*Why should researchers consider ethnography in sport management?*

- To know 'why' people behave in a certain way over a period of time
- To understand a phenomenon in its natural setting
- To know *how, when* and *why* people behave the way they do when they interact with others in a particular setting or situation (i.e. social interaction)
- To obtain data to support your understanding of the complexity of society
- To focus on studying the culture of the sport community – socio-cultural interpretation
- To focus on natural, ordinary events in natural settings – understand better the latent or hidden or non-obvious aspects of people's behaviours, attitudes, feelings and so forth
- To use multiple data collection methods over a sustained period
- To emphasise lived experiences – locating the meanings people place on the events, processes, and patterns of their lives

*Possible areas of Sport Management Research*

- Lived day-to-day experiences of sport managers
- Fan experiences on game day
- Community sport organizational behaviour

## DEVELOPMENT OF ETHNOGRAPHY

Traditional ethnography has been a research tool used for many years and emerged from a close relationship with anthropology to study traditional and non-Western societies (Chambers, 2000). Early studies associated with traditional ethnography were the work of 'Malinowski and Evans-Prichard in social anthropology and with the classic Chicago studies in urban sociology' (Chambers, 2000, p. 406). Chambers (2000) claimed the usefulness of ethnographic data grasped what is sometimes called 'the native point of view' (p. 853) with an emphasis on the 'slice of life approach' (Atkinson, Coffey and Delamont, 1999). American ethnography, however, was derived largely on the understanding of events whereas the use of ethnography in Britain was associated more with anthropology. Skinner and Edwards (2005) purported that: 'in this tradition, emphasis has been more about understanding relationships rather than activities, and research has been based more explicitly on sociology theory' (p. 407).

Regardless of its theoretical origins, ethnography is used to understand the culture of a particular group from the perspective of the group members (Tedlock, 2000; Wolcott, 1995). Tedlock described ethnography 'as an attempt to place specific encounters, events and understandings into fuller, more meaningful context' (p. 455). Many researchers portray ethnographic fieldwork involving living both with and like those who are being studied – taking part or being in a group's activities, problems, language, knowledge, rituals and social relations (Hammersley, 1992; Pedersen, 1998; Tedlock, 2000; Van Maanen, 1988): for example, volunteering in a sport franchise for several months, or long enough to understand how the sport managers, athletes, coaches, and other staff interact and behave. Ethnography provides the opportunity for exploration and investigation of the data via progressive focusing (Burns, 1997) and allows for the 'development of theory' (Hammersley and Atkinson, 1983, p. 23).

Critics of traditional ethnography (Edwards and Skinner, 2009; Fay, 1975; Habermas, 1978) are concerned about the exclusion of power from the field of study and lack of theoretical relationship that may bring about liberation of the people being investigated. It is also argued that conventional ethnography contains a certain element of neutrality in that a sport management researcher may only observe behaviours in the sport franchise, and not attempt to challenge, change or fix issues uncovered in the observation. Tedlock (2000) denotes that interpretive ethnographers deny the voice of the researcher-as-author. Moreover, the tenets of traditional ethnography have been brought into question for their validity and worth hence the emergence of other forms of ethnographic research such as critical ethnography (Skinner and Edwards, 2005).

## CRITICAL THEORY AND ETHNOGRAPHY

Critical theory is represented to a certain degree in the work of Marx, Freud and the Frankfurt School (Hammersley, 1992). The Frankfurt School allied critical theory with social theory (Gingrich, 2002). According to Edwards, Gilbert and Skinner (2002), critical theory challenges societal beliefs to achieve positive changes due to exhibited differences in status and power. Hammersley (1992) concludes that critical theory is 'grounded in an emancipatory interest in overcoming social oppression, which is clearly the category critical ethnography is intended to fall' (p. 99). This emancipation was achieved through 'enlightenment thus enabling members of oppressed groups to recognize their interests' (Hammersley, 1992,

p. 100). Hammersley denotes that: 'advocates of critical ethnography criticize conventional ethnography for adopting an inappropriate theoretical perspective that neglects oppression and its causes and for not being closely related to political practices designed to bring about emancipation' (p. 96). Table 10.3 highlights the features of critical ethnography.

Critical ethnography emphasized the use of power by the power holders and the raising of consciousness. If it was uncovered through ethnographic investigation that a certain group (e.g. women managers) were oppressed in a sport franchise by the 'good old boys club', then a critical ethnographer would seek to empower that group. Through this enlightenment it is believed 'emancipation and empowerment occurred to allow marginalized individuals and groups to become autonomous and responsible for themselves' (Hammersley, 1992, p. 100).

Examples of critical theoretical approaches to ethnography that address hegemonic practices in sport can be seen in the work of Birrell and Theberge (1994), Edwards, Skinner and O'Keefe (2000) and Sykes (1996). In an analysis of the leadership experience of women, Edwards *et al.* (2000) conducted a critical ethnography of dominant practices and discourses that exist within sporting organizations that restrict women from managing effectively. This approach provided the participants with empowerment to enable greater insights into the hegemonic practices to improve managerial techniques.

Although critical ethnography talks about empowerment of individuals in the research process and alerts us to particular types of issues and injustice, Skinner and Edwards (2005) argue 'it does not actually involve the researcher in empowering the research participants' understanding of the research issue' (p. 411). Ethnography based on postmodern thought claims to do this.

**Table 10.3** *Features of critical ethnography*

*What is critical ethnography?*

- Used by politically minded people
- Advocate for the emancipation of marginalized groups
- Seek to change society
- Identify and celebrate research bias: all research is value laden
- Challenge status-quo and ask 'why is it so?'
- Create literal dialogue with participants
- Social issues include: power, empowerment, inequity, dominance, repression, hegemony, victimization
- Collaborate actively with participants and negotiate final report
- Self-conscious about their own interpretation
- Reflexive and self-aware of their role
- Non-neutral
- Addresses issues of power, authority, emancipation, oppression and inequity
- Advocates against inequities and domination of particular groups
- Uses contradictions, imponderable, and tension

Source: Adapted from Denzin (1997)

## POSTMODERN ETHNOGRAPHY

The idea of a 'postmodern' ethnography is a hotly debated one. Denzin (1997) dismisses critics who claim that, because of their inherent narrative and cohesive features, ethnographies can never be effectively fragmented while still telling the story of a culture. According to Lindlof and Taylor (2002), a postmodern ethnography is one that blurs genres of writing and embraces marginalized voices through a disruption of institutional narratives. Denzin and Lincoln (2000) deem that 'the emergence of postmodernism in ethnographic research was useful in adding greater theoretical weight to the ethnographic research because epistemologies from previously silenced groups emerged to offer solutions to representational concerns' (p. 17). Fay (1975) agrees that there is a need for a theory that would lead people to seek to change the way they think about what others are doing (p. 91). Skinner and Edwards (2005) concur that such a theory would 'contribute to the interrelationship between knowledge as beliefs and attitudes, actions, and power relations, and by doing so offer a social rather than individualistic approach to the study of sport and sport organizations' (p. 408).

Gottschalk (1998) argues that a postmodern ethnography is more or *differently* demanding because, in addition to the essential tasks of collecting, organizing, interpreting, validating and communicating 'the data', the author needs to remain constantly and critically attentive to issues such as subjectivity, rhetorical moves, problems of voice, power, textual politics, limits to authority, truth claims and unconscious desires. A sport management researcher might alleviate this demand by paying attention to all levels and groups within a sport organization under investigation, actively seeking to empower those with the smallest voice.

Postmodern researchers are interested 'in pointing out signs of postmodern changes in the world that is still largely under modern influences' (Markula, Grant, and Dennison, 2001, p. 260). Markula *et al.* (2001) agree with other postmodernists' argument that 'today's society is constituted of multiple meanings and prefers qualitative research that allows multiple voices to emerge from the research text' (p. 260). An important aspect in incorporating postmodern ethnography as a methodology for this thesis was that it 'favors social analyses that incorporates practical or moral interests with local narratives being preferred to grand narratives', for example telling local stories of female surfers, 'as opposed to general stories' (Edwards and Skinner, 2009, p. 267). Skinner and Edwards (2005) believe that the researcher in postmodern ethnography also becomes 'encapsulated in the research, not only in the research process but also in the empowerment of the research participants' understanding of the research issue under investigation' (p. 412).

A review of sport research by Sparkes (cited in Skinner and Edwards, 2005, p. 405) suggested that 'it was only in the 1990s that the influence of critical and postmodern ethnographic frameworks began to touch on the sub-disciplines of sport'. Packwood and Sikes (1996) believe that:

> postmodernism not only focuses on the narrative of the individual but breaks down the meta-narratives into micro-narratives. This serves to allow the voices denied in meta-narrative to be heard, and the taken-for-granted truths and realities of the meta-narratives to be made problematic and thereby verified. (p. 337)

This also permits others', for example, the sponsored female surfers, voices and opinions to be heard, not just those of the surfing industry. Packwood and Sikes (1996) summarize the underlying assumptions of postmodernism by Docherty (1993) and Smart (1992) as follows:

- Postmodernism rejects a single cosmological theory – an absolute truth in the definitive story. In this type of work, there is no single story, no meta-narrative. Instead, there is a series of stories that, when put together, constitute one individual version of the myth of the research; and
- The situation, phenomenon, or event addressed through a postmodernist perspective is made sense of by its particularity within both its immediate context and its historicity (p. 342).

This means that texts do not have absolute meaning in postmodern research. Rather their meanings reside in the reality that the interpreter brings to the text by which it is read. Packwood and Sikes (1996) believe this type of research results in a 'deep reading of the text context rather than merely accepting what it is saying' (p. 343). Semerjian and Waldron (2001) agree and state that there is 'more than one way to tell a story about what we see in the world and a number of possible perspectives' (p. 440).

As critics of traditional ethnography, Edwards and Skinner (2009) were 'concerned about the exclusion of power from the field of study' (p. 262). The application of postmodern theory within an ethnographic framework in a study by Dunbar (2003) demonstrates the successful use this approach has in highlighting contradictory images of masculinity. Both these studies enable the researcher to question and disrupt taken-for-granted notions of masculinity, empowering the research participants in both studies to revisit their understanding of 'what it means to be masculine through critical reflection' (cited in Skinner and Edwards, 2005, p. 412). Another ethnographic study about senior rugby managers underpinned by ethno-graphic principles by Skinner (2001) allowed for a 'critical examination of values, beliefs, and practices being promoted by senior rugby union managers as reflective of all organizational members to be challenged' (cited in Edwards and Skinner, 2009, p. 267).

## Five tasks in ethnographical research design

According to Spradley (1980), there are five tasks in ethnographic research design, which, although appearing sequential are actually cyclical in design. These are: (1) selecting an ethnographic project; (2) collecting ethnographic data; (3) analysing ethnographic data; (4) asking ethnographic questions; and (5) writing the ethnography. All are important components of ethnographic research. Wolcott (1995) stated that ethnographic procedures require three things: a detailed description of the culture-sharing group being studied; an analysis of this group in terms of perceived themes or perspectives, and some interpretation of the group by the researcher as to meanings and generalization about the social life of human beings, in general.

## THE ETHNOGRAPHIC PROCESS

It is proposed that the ethnographic process shares many similarities with phenomenological research. Nine steps that can be used to conduct an ethnographic study have been suggested by Gay, Mills and Airasian (2009). These are:

1   Identify the purpose of the research study.
    This section should describe and explain a facet or segment of group social life as it relates to sport management.
2   Frame the study as a larger theoretical, policy, or practical problem.
    Framing the question presents a contextual framework for the research.
3   Pose initial ethnographic research questions.
    Although research questions may change in the course of the research as more is learned it is suggested that having guiding questions is a good idea.
4   Describe the overall approach and rationale for the study.
    During this stage it is recommended that a research plan be established.
5   Describe the site and sample selection.
    The site and its characteristics are described to provide context to the study. The following steps are proposed in selecting a sample:

    a)   define the population (the population consists of every individual case that possesses the characteristic that is of interest to the researcher);
    b)   determine the sampling method.

6   Describe the researcher's role.
    The role of the researcher in qualitative research has been identified elsewhere in this book (refer to Chapter 12 on Phenomenology). According to Bryman (2004), the role of the researcher is different in ethnography according to:

    a)   open field site and covert role;
    b)   open field site and overt role;
    c)   closed field site and overt role;
    d)   closed field site and covert role.

    Ethics issues are less problematic where the research takes an overt role, where the people being studied are aware the research is occurring.
7   Describe the data collection methods.
    Data collection and analysis occur simultaneously in ethnography. As understanding of the data occurs, new questions emerge. The end purpose of ethnography is the development of cultural theories.
    The *fieldwork* researcher gathers data in the setting where the participants are located and where their shared patterns can be studied. This may be in the head office, the sport facilities, in and around the sport event area, or even in online forums and chat rooms.

*Types of data*

a) emic data (data supplied by the participants);

b) etic data (ethnographer's interpretation of participants' perspectives);

c) negotiation data (information participants and researcher agree to use in a study).

There are two main methods of collecting data through ethnographic research:

a) interviewing is the most important tool;

b) participant observation is crucial to effective fieldwork, which requires an immersion in the culture:

  ■ field notes are used to check the accuracy of an ethnographer's observations;

  ■ other forms of writing used are field jottings, field diary, and field logs.

Spradley (1980) suggested a checklist:

a) extensive fieldwork by the researcher;

b) rich, detailed description – does not attempt to summarize, generalize or hypothesize. The notes capture and describe what happened to permit interpretations, and most of all, to later convey cultural meaning.

8 Describe appropriate strategies for the analysis and interpretation of data.
The data analysis follows many of the processes recommended previously for qualitative research:

a) triangulation (checking the validity by comparing sources of information);

b) patterns (checking reliability by revealing consistencies and describing matches);

c) key events (a lens through which to view a culture);

d) visual representations (maps, charts, sociograms);

e) statistics (use of non-parametric techniques);

f) crystallization (when everything falls into place);

g) ethnographic saturation;

h) managing the process.

9 Write the ethnographic account.
The written account can follow a number of forms similar to that discussed in the case study chapter (Chapter 7).

## KEY CHARACTERISTICS OF ETHNOGRAPHIC DESIGNS: REFLEXIVITY

Reflexivity is a process that has been identified previously as fundamental to qualitative research. In ethnography this means that researchers:

■ openly discuss respect for participants and sites;

■ talk about themselves;

■ share their experiences;

■ identify how their interpretations shape their discussions about sites and groups.

As with other methods ethnographic approaches have advantages and disadvantages. Table 10.4 outlines some of these advantages and disadvantages.

## Validity in ethnography

According to Burns (1997), the data collection and analysis strategies used by ethnographers in ethnographic studies maintain high internal validity for a number of reasons. First, the long-term living relationship with participants in the setting allows continual data analysis and comparison to 'refine constructs and to ensure the match between scientific categories and participant realities' (p. 324). Second, interviews with informants, which constitute a primary ethnographic data source, must be solely derived from experience or observation and 'are less abstract than many instruments used in other research designs' (p. 324). Third, the researcher's role as participant–observer, in order to acquire the reality of life experiences of participants, is found in the natural settings. Finally, ethnographic analysis embodies a process of ethnographer self-monitoring known as disciplined activity, in which the researcher continually questions and re-evaluates information and challenges his/her own opinions or biases.

## Reliability in ethnography

The scale of reliability in ethnographic research is based on replication of the study, and that two or more individuals can have comparable explanations by conforming to categories and

 **Table 10.4** Advantages and disadvantages of ethnographic research

*Advantages*

- Provides the researcher with a much more comprehensive perspective than other forms of research
- Appropriate to behaviours that are best understood by observing them within their natural environment (dynamics)
- Looks at the situation holistically
- May arrive at greater understanding of the problem than other research processes
- Can generate theories

*Disadvantages*

- Highly dependent on the researcher's observations and interpretations
- No way to check the validity of the researcher's conclusion, since numerical data is rarely provided
- Observer bias is almost impossible to eliminate
- Generalizations are almost non-existent since only a single situation is observed, leaving ambiguity in the study
- Researcher's familiarity with the field site may have an impact
- Researcher needs to be familiar with cultural jargon/language

procedures in the study (Burns, 1997). Despite replication in social sciences not always being achievable (due to changes in the setting or behaviours of members), the possibility to replicate ethnographic findings does not undermine assessments of their validity, though it may make the task more difficult.

## Trust and integrity in ethnographic research

Definite guidelines for researchers in order to gain trust and integrity in ethnographic research do not exist and, according to Neuman (1994), 'a genuine concern for and interest in others, being honest, and sharing feelings are good strategies' (p. 342). A researcher's long-term period in this study interacting with members, listening and understanding their concerns, their verbal and non-verbal language and acknowledging their cultural rules helped to develop rapport, trust, integrity and cooperation. As a sport management researcher spends more time within the sport facilities and around sport managers, coaches, players, etc., the higher the degree of trust builds, allowing the data to be checked over and over. The degree of the relationship between researcher and members is very useful in obtaining 'accurate and dependable information' (Jorgensen, 1989, p. 70) when checking of data was undertaken with informants.

## Ethical principles

It is important to note that informants are human beings who have interests, concerns and problems and researchers' values are not necessarily similar to those of informants. Fieldwork is an essential component of ethnography and researchers in the field frequently confront conflicting values and a broad range of possible choices. To illustrate: 'How will I use the data collected and will I tell the informants how it will be used?' (Spradley, 1979, p. 79). As a result, it is important for ethnographers to protect the physical, social and psychological welfare and to honour the dignity and privacy of their informants. Ethnography also entails interaction with other people such as sponsors and gatekeepers, who may have the power to grant or withhold permission to conduct interviews. The researcher must also safeguard the artefacts that are collected. Ethical questions the researcher must ask include:

- How is the research problem defined?
- Is the work justified?
- What are the risks/benefits to participants? Social, psychological, physical.
- How will participants be selected?
- Will privacy, confidentiality and anonymity be assured? How?
- How will informed consent be established?
- How can a researcher be involved yet still maintain her/his capacity for analytical scrutiny?
- Should a researcher conduct an interview in an everyday setting, even very informally, if consent is not obtained?
- How will study participants be able to control the researcher's interpretations of their experiences?

**169**

- How will the researcher handle a situation where they are asked to take sides?
- How will the researcher manage situations where antagonistic views, violence, racism or sexism threaten their presence/values?
- How will results be disseminated?

---

## RECENT CASE EXAMPLE: ETHNOGRAPHY

*The following article is an example of how ethnography has been used in the past by researchers in Sport Management Research. The interested reader may wish to find/download and read the article for further insights.*

> Co-ed adolescent soccer players in a competitive learning milieu: An ethnographic assessment of gender attitudes, perceptions and sport specific component testing. O'Donnell, F. (2004) Unpublished dissertation. University of Central Florida. 3163619

The history of association soccer dates back to the 1800s, and all indications are that prospects for the female athlete were scarce in all sports. The researcher arranged an environment where young females could train with males in a soccer setting that has all the necessary elements for the athletes to learn, improve and compete with their own gender as well as the opposite gender. The female group were noticeable underachievers in this sport and were not aware of their potential. The research methodology employed was ethnographic. The method stressed the importance of reproducing procedures that were taught to the researcher.

---

## EMERGING ETHNOGRAPHIES

This section will highlight some emerging ethnographical methodologies and demonstrate how they can be situated in the Sport Management Research field. Autoethnography, ethnodrama, and phenomenography may appear on the surface to have little relation to Sport Management Research; however, the following discussion will cover each of these methodologies and identify their potential applications to the field of sport management.

### Autoethnography

This section explores the emerging ethnographic research approach of autoethnography. One way of understanding autoethnography is to deconstruct the components of the word. In this fashion *auto* refers to the self or the autobiographical (Reed-Danahay, 1997), *ethno* to a social group, and *graphy* to the process of researching and writing (Ellis and Bochner 2000; Reed-Danahay, 1997; Whitmore, 2003).

In an autoethnography the observer is part of the subculture studied. For example, a coach may conduct an autoethnography of the coaching culture in a local basketball league. Van

Maanen (1995) states that this type of research is carried out by a native who reveals his or her own group. Autoethnography has close ties to phenomenology and hermeneutics. Ellis (2004) describes a more specific placement of autoethnography as a form of impressionistic or interpretive ethnography. Indeed, autoethnography may be viewed as both, with narrative being the more general description.

As an outgrowth of the interpretive turn (postmodernism), autoethnography is considered a form of autobiographical narrative combining evocative writing and research that display multiple levels of consciousness, generally written in first-person (Denzin and Lincoln, 1994; Ellis, 2000, 2004). Autoethnography has been acknowledged as a method of inquiry since the mid 1970s and was shaped by the ideas of feminism, post-structuralism and postmodernism (Ellis and Bochner, 2000). Much like hermeneutics, autoethnography circles among the social and cultural aspects of personal experience; and the inner self, feelings, emotions and experience, with the primary purpose of understanding a singular or multiple self, through lived experience (Ellis and Bochner, 2000).

Ellis and Bochner (2000) have advocated the use of autoethnography suggesting personal experience as an opportunity to move beyond a passionless and objective authoritative voice; autoethnography presents an opportunity to connect the personal to the cultural. The research becomes a personal account (e.g. coach) of experiences within and in relation to a particular culture (e.g. local basketball coaches) that also draws on others' lived experiences (e.g. other coaches in the league); the completed text seeks to engage the readers and draws them into the experiences of the author and other participants. The coach has the opportunity to relay both his/her personal feelings and experience as part of the local basketball culture and other coaches' perspectives through discussions and interviews. Ellis and Bochner have also suggested that autoethnography asks readers 'to become co-participants, engaging the storyline morally, emotionally, aesthetically, and intellectually' (2000, p. 745). Other scholars have also suggested that autoethnography must be considered a valid form of reporting the social (Denzin and Lincoln, 2002); this same plea has been made specifically within the study of sport (Denison and Rinehart, 2000; Holt, 2003; Sparkes, 2000). Spry (2001) writes that: 'Autoethnography can be defined as a self-narrative that critiques the situatedness of self with others in social contexts' (p. 710).

Blurring the distinction between self and other, autoethnography is a form of research that provides opportunity for the researchers to incorporate their own life experiences with the experiences of those being studied (Reed-Danahay, 1997). Autoethnography moves beyond self-reflexivity within an ethnographic study, encouraging researchers to write about their own experiences of the social phenomena and not solely their experiences of recording the culture. As Reed-Danahay (1997) argues:

> Autoethnography is defined as a form of self-narrative that places the self within a social context. It is both a method and a text, as in the case of ethnography . . . [Autoethnography] can be done by an autobiographer who places the story of his or her life within a story of the social context in which it occurs. (p. 9)

Autoethnography emerged in the 1980s in the social sciences and more recently in the study of sport and physical education (Holt, 2003). Many evolving research methods fall under the umbrella of autoethnography: personal narratives, narratives of the self and ethnographic short stories (Ellis and Bochner, 2000). While providing unique opportunities to share personal experiences, autoethnography can be extremely difficult to undertake for a number of reasons not the least of those being the willingness of the researcher to self-analyse. As Ellis and Bochner (2000) state: 'The self-questioning autoethnography demands is extremely difficult. So is confronting things about yourself that are less than flattering . . . Honest autoethnographic exploration generates a lot of fears and doubts – and emotional pain' (p. 738).

Sparkes (2002) has suggested that in autoethnography, 'it is made clear that the author "was there" in the action, that the story is based on "real" people, "real" events, and "data" that were collected in various ways' (p. 3). Furthermore, a critical analysis of one's own experiences of the social phenomenon under study works to locate the writer/researcher as a living and breathing participant, a researcher that physically coached in the local basketball league under investigation.

One goal of autoethnography is to bring forward conversations through stories about personal, emotional experiences. What distinguishes autoethnography from other types of narratives is the intent to write about self (or multiple selves in the context of culture) (Ellis, 2004; Richardson, 2000).

Sparkes (2002) argues that alternative representation practices, such as autoethnographies, poetic representations and ethnodramas, offer insight into sport and physical activity by privileging the lived body.

## Methodology

There is much debate regarding the methodology of autoethnography and whether it constitutes scientific research. The use of self as the only data source can be problematic in this regard. Ellis (1995) argues that a story could be considered scholarly if it makes the reader believe that the experience is authentic, believable and possible. The intended purpose of autoethnography is to provide the opportunity for the reader and author to become co-participants in the recorded experience. There are also multiple warning signs, skills and difficulties that are experienced or needed in writing ethnography (Ellis and Bochner, 2000). Researchers must be adept at identifying pertinent details, introspection, descriptive and compelling writing, and confronting things about themselves that may be less than flattering. What if the coach, as the researcher, discovers they are a source of oppressing minority coaches in the same league? Will he or she be completely forthcoming in the write-up? Also, the researcher must handle the vulnerability of revealing oneself to a greater audience. The use of self as the source of data can be restrictive, yet a powerful aspect of unpacking the many layers involved in the study of a particular culture or social context. Tierney (1998) explains that autoethnography is intended to confront dominant forms of representation and power in an attempt to reclaim marginalized representational spaces.

## Data collection

Autoethnographic data collection subscribes to the dualistic nature of exploring oneself within culture, and then reflective introspection of the expressed embodiment of that culture in oneself (Foley, 2002). In autoethnographic research, the researcher may begin with the question, what is it that I really want to know and why? This framework provides a more concise description and direction for the type of data to collect, where to collect it, and whom to collect it from. In autoethnographic data collection, all of the considerations of ethnographic fieldwork are applicable as long as it adds useful information to the study (Nilan, 2002). Interviews, artefacts, sketches, field notes and photographs can all be part of autoethnographic research (Tomaselli, 2003).

The ultimate goal of self-study research is to produce literary representations and to add value to readers of our research. With this in mind, data collection tools vary greatly in self-narrative research and autobiographical studies. To ensure proper validity in an autoethnography, Feldman (2003) has developed four criteria upon which data collection are based:

1    Provide clear and detailed description of how we collect data and make explicit what counts as data in our work.
2    Provide clear and detailed descriptions of how we constructed the representation from our data. What specifics about the data led us to make this assumption?
3    Extend triangulation beyond multiple sources of data to include explorations of multiple ways to represent the same self-study.
4    Provide evidence that the research changed or evolved the educator and summarize its value to the profession. This can convince readers of the study's significance and validity. (pp. 27–28)

## Data analysis

In autoethnography, reflective analysis is an ongoing part of the data collection process (Ellis, 1999). The lived experience of the researcher is fundamental to understanding the experience as lived. The difficulty with this 'anything goes' approach to data analysis fuels the ongoing debate between traditional positivistic qualitative inquiry and postmodern, contemporary qualitative research. Other methods of data analysis specifically useful in autoethnography include collaboration, emotional recall and reflective field notes.

The analysis of data begins the moment the researcher perceives the information. In an autoethnography the analysis of data is an ongoing event, developing and crystallizing over time. With each rereading of the personal reflexive journal, each examination of a written artefact, and with further introspection and self-analysis, the process and clarity of the research is enriched. These processes form the analysis of data in a qualitative study of an autoethnographical nature. The gathering and analysis of data go hand in hand as theories and themes emerge during the study. The reflection involved by the researcher consistently shapes and forms the articulation of the experiences of the researcher in a self-study.

Ellis and Bochner (2000) assert that the analysis of data in a personal narrative involves a process where the researcher emotionally recalls the events of the past. The researcher looks back on specific, memorable episodes and experiences paying particular attention to the emotions and physical surroundings during the recollection. Emotional recall is expressed through writing that includes thoughts, events, dialogue and physical details of the particular event. Methods of data analysis specifically utilized in autoethnography include collaboration, emotional recall and reflective field notes. Collaboration in autoethnographic research relates to understanding the phenomenon studied by those involved. Reflective journals are also a key element.

Table 10.5 outlines some of the advantages and disadvantages of autoethnography.

### Validity and reliability

The inclusion of the lived experiences of others seeks to address issues of validity and reliability. Such considerations are often the crux of opposition toward autoethnographic research (Denzin, 1997; Ellis and Bochner, 2000; Sparkes, 2000). In the case of autoethnography, validity has been usefully defined by Ellis and Bochner as the seeking of 'verisimilitude', meaning that the work:

> evokes in readers a feeling that the experience described is lifelike, believable, and possible. . . [Validity might also be judged by] whether it helps readers communicate with others different from themselves, or offers a way to improve the lives of participants and readers, or even [the researcher's] own. (p. 751)

**Table 10.5** *Advantages and disadvantages of autoethnography*

*Advantages*

- Rather than maintain a disconnected objective position, the narrative and subjectivity of the researcher fashion autoethnographic writing as 'creative non-fiction' (Richardson, 2000)
- The reader is granted permission into the intricate life of another and in adding their own life experience the study becomes more personal and effective
- In autoethnographic research, the author commits to researcher subjectivity and uses an introspective lens in writing personal narrative history, often confronting hidden emotional content

*Disadvantages*

- The author must skilfully capture and communicate narrative voice
- Shallow introspection will directly influence the impact and persuasiveness of the narrative and can undermine the credibility of proposed conclusions
- Narcissistic use of 'I' in social science discourse
- Difficulty in any autoethnographic study lies in the attempt to reclaim or recollect self and story reflexively
- Autoethnography is still a contested methodological approach
- Autoethnographic study is more fiction than fact
- Autoethnography is self-indulgent, narcissistic and academic 'navel-gazing'

Source: Sparkes (2000)

Reliability within an autoethnographic study can be sought through feedback from the other participants included in the research: for example, the coach sharing the field notes with other coaches and allowing them to provide input. Ellis and Bochner (2000) have suggested that '[w]hen other people are involved, you might take your work back to them and give them a chance to comment, add materials, change their minds, and offer their interpretations' ( p. 751). With inclusion of the 'self' in the research, reliability is unorthodox as compared to traditional, positivist definitions that have previously been applied to qualitative research. To a certain degree, there must be some 'letting go' of traditional, evaluative approaches to the notions of validity and reliability. As Holt (2003) has argued:

> Describing investigator responsiveness during the research process would be a constructive approach to validity, as opposed to the inclusion of evaluative checks to establish the trustworthiness of completed research (e.g. an external audit) . . . Constructive approaches to validity and reliability would be more appropriate criteria to judge autoethnography than the post-hoc imposition of evaluative techniques associated with the parallel perspective. (pp. 11–12)

Ellis (2004, 2005) suggested that validity is still important in interpretive ethnography, and requires some conceptual reframing for autoethnographic inquiry. For her, the question is how to judge interpretive or impressionist inquiry. She suggests several questions for assessing quality including:

1   Do the stories 'ring true' to the audience?
2   Do the stories resonate with the lives of the researcher and readers?
3   Are the accounts plausible and coherent?
4   Does the author make claim to a single standard of truth or leave open the possibility of multiple interpretations and truths as is inherent in autoethnography?
5   Is the whole person taken into account?
6   Does the work communicate with others?
7   Is the resulting story useful in helping others?

Autoethnography is not concerned with generalizability, but rather with understanding the unique experiences of cultural groups or members.

## Autoethnography in sport management

Autoethnography is now an acceptable research approach in sport sociology mainly due to the work of Sparkes (2002); however, the opportunity exists for sport management to embrace the approach.

---

**RECENT CASE EXAMPLE: AUTOETHNOGRAPHY**

*The following article is an example of how autoethnography has been used in the past by researchers in Sport Management Research. The interested reader may wish to find/download and read the article for further insights.*

> Sport management, gender and the 'bigger picture': Challenging changes in Higher Education – A partial auto/ethnographical account. Humberstone, B. (2009). *Sport Management Review, 12,* 255–262.

This article focused mainly on the author's experience of Higher Education and of a module concerned with gender, difference, sport and leisure made available to students studying for sport and leisure management degrees. It reviews the changed nature of the curriculum in the shifting socio-economic climate, suggesting that the neoliberal turn influencing Higher Education in the UK is reinforcing an organizational (university) culture that is counter-productive to fostering critical gender and race awareness in both staff and students within restructured sport management programmes. The approach adopted in this paper is partly auto/ethnographic and as such, on occasion, it looks at the previous research and current experiences through the eyes and emotions of a senior woman academic located within a changing 'new' university culture. Auto/ethnography as research approach and autobiography as learning medium are considered.

---

## Netnography

Netnography is defined by Kozinets (1998) as:

> a written account resulting from fieldwork studying the cultures and communities that emerge from online, computer mediated, or Internet-based communications, where both the field work and the textual account are methodologically informed by the traditions and techniques of cultural anthropology. (p. 6)

A main difference between netnography and traditional ethnography is that netnography 'is based primarily upon the observation of textual discourse, an important difference from the balancing of discourse and observed behaviour that occurs during in-person ethnography' (Kozinets, 2002, p. 7). This raises some significant issues, mainly: how does the netnographer determine the trustworthiness – not to mention the age, gender, race, true sport team affiliation, etc. – of their informants?

In essence, this approach turns a potential problem of netnography (lack of access to informants' non-verbal cues, including their physical appearance) into a potential asset. If, as mentioned above, ethnographic studies always reflect 'differences and similarities between participants and scholars in terms of class, gender, race, culture or subculture, educational background, age, etc.' (Seiter, Borchers, Kreutzner, and Warth, 1989, p. 227), then netnography's tendency to obscure these variables may produce research uncomplicated by issues of class, gender and race. Most Internet and Usenet posts betray no information about the poster's age, gender or race.

Therefore, the focus of netnography is on what is written, not on who does the writing. It is suggested that one way for dealing with netnography's reliance on textual discourse as opposed to observed behaviour is simply to develop an understanding of the online community and its leaders, its rank-and-file members, its rhetorical style and its codes and mores. After extensive exposure, a netnographer will develop a sense of whether a particular posting is valid and reliable. As Kozinets (1998) suggests, netnographers must always be aware that:

> the limitations and requirements of producing and communicating textual information obviously structure virtual relationships in many ways, including: eliminating and simulating physicality and body (e.g. body language has been virtually replaced by (deliberately) shared (emot)icons), privileging verbal-rational states and skills over nonverbal-emotional ones, and allowing more 'pre-editing' of expressed thoughts and thus more opportunities for strategic self-presentation efforts. (p. 3)

He adds that in the end, good netnography is built on the same foundation as good ethnography: 'persistent observation, gaining rapport and trust, triangulating across sites and sources, using good interview techniques, and researcher introspection' (p. 7).

Table 10.6 outlines some of the advantages and disadvantages of using netnography.

## Ethics and netnography

Research ethics may be one of the most significant disparities between traditional ethnography and netnography. Ethical concerns over netnography turn on contentious and still largely unsettled concerns about whether online forums are to be considered a private or a public site, and about what constitutes informed consent in cyberspace (see Paccagnella, 1997). In a major shift from traditional methods, netnography uses cultural information that is not given specifically, and in confidence, to the sport management researcher. The sport consumers who originally created the data do not necessarily intend or welcome its use in research representations.

## Applications of netnography to Sport Management Research

The sport management researcher interested in applying netnographical methodologies to their research first needs to determine whether or not a viable and functioning online community exists from within which to conduct the research study.

**Table 10.6** *Advantages and disadvantages of netnography*

*Advantages*

- Large sample possible quickly
- Less obtrusive compared to surveys, focus groups and personal interviews
- Performed using observations in a context that is not fabricated by the sport management researcher
- Less costly and timelier than focus groups and personal interviews
- It is a naturalistic and unobtrusive technique
- Immediate analysis
- Transcripts easily available
- Sensitive topics can be researched

*Disadvantages*

- The lack of informant identifiers present in the online context that leads to difficulty generalizing results to groups outside the online community sample
- Narrow focus on online communities
- Inability to offer the full and rich detail of lived human experience
- The need for researcher interpretive skills
- Loss of non-verbals
- Loss of intangibles (silence, tone of voice)
- Compensate with emoticons :-)
- Cookies controversy
- Reliability and integrity of information
- Shoulder surfing distortions
- Information overload
- Netnography is still in its infancy
- Ethical concerns

## RESEARCH CASE EXAMPLE: NETNOGRAPHY

*The following article is an example of how netnography has been used in the past by researchers in Sport Management Research. The interested reader may wish to find/download and read the article for further insights.*

> Wrestling with the audience: Fan culture on the Internet. Weisberg, D. (2005). Unpublished dissertation. Northwestern University. 3177825

This study considers the culture of the 'Internet Wrestling Community', a segment of the professional wrestling audience that pursues an aspect of its fandom online. The study uses the methodology of Internet ethnography, or 'netnography'. Netnography adapts many traditional methods of sociology and cultural anthropology to meet the research opportunities and challenges presented by online communities and Internet data. Specifically, the study's primary data consists of postings culled from the Usenet group rec.sport.pro-wrestling and from wrestling-related websites. This data was supplemented with open-ended telephone interviews with 11 prominent members of the Internet Wrestling Community.

## What is ethnodrama?

The term ethnodrama refers to a recent trend in ethnography that presents research as a performance text. This ethnographic genre is also known as ethnoperformance, and performance and reflexive anthropology (Denzin, 1991). Ethnodrama employs traditional techniques to mount a performance event as an alternative mode of research representation, with actors portraying actual research participants.

The purpose of an ethnodrama is not to entertain, but to encourage critical thinking and questioning. Denzin (1991) outlines five forms of performance text:

1    dramatic texts (rituals, poems, and plays meant to be performed);
2    natural texts (transcriptions of everyday conversations);
3    performance science texts (fieldwork notes and interviews);
4    improvisational; and
5    critical ethnodramas (the merging of natural script dialogues with dramatized scenes and the use of composite characters).

### Ethnodrama and the research process

Traditionally qualitative research involves note taking, observations, interviews, transcripts, coding, triangulation, etc. and the transformation, selection, interpretation and perceptions of the researcher. These methodological approaches and issues readily transfer into the ethnodrama research design.

SCRIPTING AN ETHNODRAMA

The process of scripting an ethnodrama involves including as much verbatim narrative as possible (Mienczakowski and Morgan, 1993). This allows the performance text to attempt to create a high degree of 'vraisemblance' or 'semblance of truth' (Mienczakowski, 2001). By inviting 'informants' to validate the research by attending scripting sessions, rehearsals, group readings and preview performances, Mienczakowski used feedback from the 'informants' to edit and rewrite the script.

Post-performance discussions with the audience also allow the researcher to 'renegotiate' the ethnodrama's meaning after every performance. According to Mienczakowski (2001), this high level of communication and cooperation between researcher, informant and audience make an ethnodrama approach reflexive, polyvocal and accessible to a broad audience.

**179**

THE ROLE OF THE AUDIENCE IN AN ETHNODRAMA

The ethnodrama is the culminating piece to the research. In recent years, various researchers have recognized that they are pursuing the same ends – voicing the marginalized experience – albeit through different lenses. In the late 1980s and early 1990s, sociologists began turning ethnographic research into performances while theatre artists began to turn to ethnographies for performance material (McCall, 2000).

## Ethical concerns and limitations of ethnodrama

According to Saldana (2005), 'theatre's primary goal is neither to educate nor to enlighten. Theatre's primary goal is to *entertain*' (p. 141). This poses a dilemma for the ethnodramatist. Is it possible for ethnodrama to be widely accepted as a valid and viable methodology for data presentation or is it just entertainment? There are also ethical concerns surrounding the participants themselves, relating to issues of confidentiality and anonymity. It is essential, therefore, that all participants consent to all the content in the performance, and that they are fully aware of the implications of being in the performance, if that is the approach taken (Saldana, 1998, 2005).

## Ethnodrama and Sport Management Research

Potentially, ethnodrama has the ability to demonstrate that the embodiment of human experience through artistic means can enhance the understanding of the experiences of sport managers, and can situate the experience within a recognizable context that also has the facility to satisfy the 'entertainment' component of theatre.

---

### RECENT CASE EXAMPLE: ETHNODRAMA

*The following article is an example of how ethnodrama has been used in the past by researchers in Sport Management Research. The interested reader may wish to find/download and read the article for further insights.*

> A test of ethical behaviour: A study of ethics education as ethnodrama with under-graduate sport management students. Edwards, A. (2011). Unpublished research.

The purpose of this study was to examine the perceptions and reactions of students as they participated in an ethnodrama that was based on a lecture about ethics in sport manage-ment. Twenty-two undergraduate sport management students discussed and journaled their reactions, feelings and experiences as they participated in writing an ethnodrama on the topic of ethical behaviour. Results of this study showed that the use of ethnodrama in lectures can be a catalyst for both student voice and the development of ethical standards.

---

## What is phenomenography?

Phenomenography is a method that identifies people's ideas about a phenomenon, as opposed to proving that the actual phenomenon exists. Instead of proving that some fans have unrelenting loyalty to a certain team, phenomenography may seek to understand why fans identify themselves with a certain team. Through this approach the researcher begins to formulate an understanding of the specific ways in which these understandings form similarities and differences among people. Phenomenography attempts to identify and describe, as faithfully as possible, the individual's conceptions of some aspect of reality (Sandberg, 1995). In this way, it attempts to bring all conceptions to light and tries to describe them. The phenomenographer seeks to understand, systematize and order these conceptions in relation to each other, thus arriving at a view of the whole picture of the phenomenon, by describing the range of variation among its subjects (Svensson, 1994).

### Phenomenographic research

Phenomenographic research is centred on the variation in experiencing phenomena, and describing phenomena as others see them (Hasselgren and Beach, 1996). The variations in experiences are teased out from individual conversations, and used to exemplify different 'categories of description', which are collectively expressed as 'conceptions'. Conceptions have been variously described as a 'way of seeing something, a qualitative relationship between an individual and some phenomenon' (Johansson, Marton and Svensson, 1985, p. 236), as the ways in which individuals experience the meaning of something (Svennson, 1994), and as 'people's ways of experiencing a specific aspect of reality' (Sandberg, 1997, p. 203). The central aim of phenomenographic research is its attempt to uncover and describe qualitatively different ways people perceive, experience and understand various aspects of phenomena in the world as they see it. Phenomenography is therefore primarily concerned with identifying and understanding the relationship between the person and the phenomenon being studied.

### Phenomenography and Sport Management Research

The methods for conducting phenomenographical research may vary depending on the phenomena under investigation. The researcher will research and adopt those methods appropriate to the research study. This said, in phenomenography, sport management researchers should try to describe, analyse and understand how people think about particular phenomena. This is not about describing how reality 'is', but how reality is perceived by that person. For the sport management researcher the opportunities are boundless. For example, the following could be considered:

- How does the sport manager perceive their organization's performance in the hosting of a major sporting event?
- How does the sport manager evaluate their performance as manager of a major sporting event?

■ Did the sport manager identify problems in the event that were not recognized elsewhere?

Phenomenographic approaches are appropriate for research in the field of sport management; however, to date they have not been applied. The challenge for sport management researchers is to engage with the method and demonstrate that new sport management knowledge can be generated from this approach.

---

### RESEARCH CASE EXAMPLE: PHENOMENOGRAPHY

*The following article is an example of how phenomenography has been used in the past by researchers in Sport Management Research. The interested reader may wish to find/download and read the article for further insights.*

> Parents' conceptions of the influences of participation in a sports programme on their children and adolescents with physical disabilities. Kristèn, L., Patriksson, G., and Fridlund, B. (2003). *European Physical Education Review*, 9(1), 23–41.

This study used phenomenography to describe 20 parents' conceptions of the influences of participation in a sports programme on children with physical disabilities aged 9–15. The study found that parents regarded sports as a means for their children to participate in society and learn about health.

---

## CONCLUSION

Traditional ethnography's approach to such areas of study as sport management has a number of criticisms and weaknesses. More recent discourses such as critical and postmodern theories can be applied to the ethnographic method to broaden the field of ethnography by accentuating awareness of research practices, drawing attention to the role of power relations in the construction of reality, problematizing the role of the researcher as subject and providing the potential to empower the research participants understanding of the research issue under investigation. In endeavouring to emulate rigorous standards of research, sport management researchers should be encouraged to take more methodological 'risks' and embrace more eclectic research approaches. Critical and postmodern research approaches offer these opportunities. Moreover, if sport management researchers embrace critical and postmodern thought it provides them with a theoretical framework to question the social, historical and political forces that play a role in shaping social reality.

The three emerging research methodologies discussed in this chapter may have different output and appearance, but they are related in their connection to ethnography and its focus on the experience of the research participant. In many ways these are research approaches that will be taken on by the next generation of sport management researchers. The discipline can only benefit by sport management researchers embracing these new and emerging ethnographies to understand sport management practice.

## HYPOTHETICAL CASE: ETHNOGRAPHY ACTIVITY

One part of ethnographic methodology is non-participative observation. This activity focuses on non-verbal communicative behaviours.

To complete this activity, attend a sporting event with your classmates. Follow these steps:

A   Decide what type of non-verbal behaviour you would observe: use of space, colours, types of clothing, gestures, facial expressions, manner of greeting, vocal qualities, touch, etc.

B   Watch the fans at the sport event and record all observations of non-verbal behaviour of your choosing. You should only observe the non-verbal communicative behaviour you have chosen. Try not to let the verbal communication interfere with your observations of the non-verbal communicative behaviour. (You might want to watch how they work to complement or contradict the other.)

C   Take notes on your observation, recording different and similar behaviours and the frequency of their occurrences. Remember while observing to vary from a wide angle to a narrow angle focus.

D   When the event has ended, look over your field notes. Think about what you have observed and what your interpretations are of your findings. Be as descriptive as possible, and then infer meaning or interpret what the nonverbal communicative behaviour might mean in this particular context.

E   Get together with other people to discuss their findings and interpretations.

F   Answer these questions:

   1   What is the meaning within the context?
   2   Can you see any patterns of behaviours?
   3   Are there any themes or categories you can classify the behaviours into?
   4   What do these say about the organization and its culture?
   5   Discuss what are the limitations to this type of research procedure?
   6   What is your reaction to the experience?
      a)   Were you surprised at your findings?
      b)   Or were they expected?

## REVIEW QUESTIONS

Ethnography is a qualitative research methodology aimed at describing and analysing the practices and beliefs of cultures and communities. With a basic understanding now of ethnography, attempt to answer the following questions:

■   Is there any place within Sport Management Research for ethnography underpinned by critical and postmodern theories?

Each of the emerging ethnographies discussed in this chapter embraces this as a basic tenet while adopting a unique methodological approach that has significant relevance to Sport Management Research. With a basic understanding now of these emerging ethnographies, attempt to answer the following questions:

- Is there any place within Sport Management Research for netnography?
- Discuss the positive and negative features of an ethnodramatic approach to a Sport Management Research question.
- Provide other examples of how phenomenographic approaches to Sport Management Research could be applied.

## SUGGESTED EXTENDED READING FOR STUDENTS

Denzin, N. K., and Lincoln, Y. S. (eds). (2002). *The qualitative inquiry reader*. Thousand Oaks, CA: Sage.

Edwards, A., Skinner, J., and O'Keefe, L. (2000). Women sport managers. *International Review of Women and Leadership*, 6(2), 48–58.

Ellis, C. (2004). *The ethnographic I: A methodological novel about authoethnography*. Walnut Creek, CA: Altamira Press.

Gay, L. R., Mills, G. E., and Airasian, P. (2009). *Educational research: Competencies for analysis and applications* (9th edn). Upper Saddle River, NJ: Pearson Merrill.

Holt, N. (2003). Representation, legitimation, and autoethnography: An autoethnographic writing story. *International Journal of Qualitative Methods*, 2(1), Article 2.

Kozinets, R. V. (1998). On netnography: Initial reflections on consumer investigations of cyberculture. In J. Alba and W. Hutchinson (eds), *Advances in consumer research Vol. 25* (pp. 366–371). Provo, UT: Association for Consumer Research.

Mienczakowski, J. (2001). Ethnodrama: Performed research – limitations and potential. In P. Atkinson, A. Coffey, S. Delamont, J. Lofland, and L. Lofland (eds), *Handbook of ethnography* (pp. 468–476). London: Sage.

Paccagnella, L. (1997). Getting the seats of your pants dirty: Strategies for ethnographic research on virtual communities. *Journal of Computer-Mediated Communication*, *3*, 1. Available at: http://jcmc.indiana.edu/vol3/issue1/paccagnella.html (accessed 2 February 2014).

Saldana, J. (2005). *Ethnodrama: An anthology of reality theatre*. Walnut Creek CA: Alta Mira Press.

# Chapter 11

# Gender as a methodology in Sport Management Research

## LEARNING OUTCOMES

By the end of this chapter, you should be able to:

- understand the basic concepts of feminism;
- identify the implications of the use of feminist methodology in sport management;
- recognize some key features of 'queer theory';
- identify some strategies with which to apply feminist and queer methodology to Sport Management Research.

## KEY TERMS

*Feminism* – theories and philosophies concerned with issues of gender difference and which advocate women's rights and interests.

*Queer theory* – calls into question 'essential' sexed, gendered and sexual identities, striving to destabilize discursive constructions of sexuality that come to be accepted as 'natural' and that maintain a dominant/subordinate power relationship.

## KEY THEMES

- Is there a distinctive feminist methodology?
- What is queer theory?

## CHAPTER OVERVIEW

This chapter explores gender research methodologies and their application to sport management, in particular feminist and queer theories. The first section argues that feminist methodologies offer the sport management researcher scope to investigate issues specifically related to gender, and the impact these issues may have on the sport management environment. The second section of this chapter discusses how queer theory has the potential to be utilized in Sport Management Research.

## FEMINISM DEFINED

Doering (1992) defines feminism as 'a world view that values women and confronts systematic injustices based on gender' (p. 26). Feminist theory and research are focused on women with a major emphasis on class and race bias. Feminist theories have progressed by placing gender first, by including women in the dialogue of social and political theory and by raising awareness of women's needs and the oppression of women. The purpose of feminist research is to create a social system that represents equality.

## ORIGINS OF FEMINIST THEORY

Feminist theory has its origins in the political activism of the 1960s and 1970s, generally referred to as the second wave of feminism; the first wave being centred in the suffrage movement of the late nineteenth and early twentieth centuries. The second wave of feminism sought equality and an end to discrimination. Although the activism of the 1970s has been somewhat tempered, feminism, as an academic focus, has developed throughout the 1980s and 1990s, and into the twenty-first century, coexisting alongside what has been called the third wave of feminism, which arose as a result of perceived failures of the second wave. This third wave of feminism, with its origins in the 1980s, seeks to challenge existentialist definitions of femininity and accepted views of what is or is not good for women. Table 11.1 outlines briefly this development of feminist theory.

**Table 11.1** Stages of the development of feminist theory

- First wave – rights
- Second wave – anti-essentialism, equality
- Third wave – beyond gender, class, power
- Neo-Marxist materialist feminisms
- Queer theory – othered spaces
- Womanism and third-world feminism – beyond gender, race, class, power

## WHAT IS FEMINIST METHODOLOGY?

According to Mies (1991) the emergence of feminist methodology 'arose out of [women's] frustration at the realization that women's lives, their history, their struggles, their ideas constitute no part of dominant science' (p. 66).

Defining feminist research is far from clear-cut, with van Zoonen (1994) noting 'the issue of what exactly constitutes feminist research has been a subject of debate since the late 1970s' (p. 127). Feminist research is in 'an emergent state' (Olesen, 2000, p. 215). It has also proven to be resistant to definitions revealing itself as 'highly diversified, enormously dynamic' with competing models of thought and divergent methodological and analytic approaches jostling and at times blurring and merging (Olesen, 2000, p. 215). This stems from the differing strains of feminism that have evolved in the contemporary period embracing a multitude of variants ranging from liberal feminism to radical feminism. Consequently, feminist research has attempted to seek out methods receptive to the diversity of female experience, the multiple identities women take on (Olesen, 2000) and the plurality of subjectivities women experience. Feminist researchers and theorists draw on a range of methodologies from the social sciences, the humanities and literary theory. Postmodernism, deconstruction theory and poststructuralist theory have also led to a re-examination of the researcher's role, calling upon them to exercise 'unremitting reflexivity' (Olesen, 2000, p. 236). According to DeVault (1996):

> feminist methodologists do not use or prescribe any single research method; rather, they are united through various efforts to include women's lives and concerns in accounts of society, to minimize the harms of research and to support changes that will improve women's status. (p. 29)

Feminist research has thus evolved along with feminism to be characterized by diversity and complexity with no specific methodological or research orthodoxy prevailing. It is, however, marked by a number of fundamental precepts. Of fundamental importance in feminist research is a direct engagement with the question of gender such that research phenomena are 'studied in a "gendered", rather than a gender-blind or gender-neutral perspective' (Lundgren, 1995, p. 3).

Fine (cited in Gatenby and Humphries, 1996, pp. 77–78) details five epistemological and methodological commitments of feminist research. The *first* of Fine's precepts was labelled 'women's problematic' by which she means that for research to be considered feminist it must not only focus on gender but it must make women's experiences central to the research and seek to understand the way in which women make sense of concepts relevant to the research. For example, taking women's perspective when investigating the portrayal of women in sport media. The *second* of Fine's precepts for feminist research is 'women's ways of knowing', which is a twofold process. In the first instance the research must value women's ways of knowing by encouraging women to describe their own experiences and must respect their truths. Asking woman sport figures their opinion on how they are perceived and how they perceive other women in sport media helps to satisfy this precept. But second, researchers must address their own experiences and knowledge, and as van Zoonen (1994) terms it, radically politicize the research process by reflexively interrogating their own role, standpoint epistemologies, research praxis and position of power. Therefore, a sport management researcher must openly and honestly explore and explain any preconceptions and perceptions they have about women in sport media.

Fine's *third* requirement of feminist research is a focus on 'feminist synalytics', which she describes as a blend of analysis and synthesis to facilitate new understanding that supersedes 'the usual male-defined definitions' (cited in Gatenby and Humphries, 1993, pp. 77–78). Her *fourth* tenet is that of 'revolutionary pragmatism' – a call for research that is of practical value and that is either the basis for a call for change or can, as Olesen (cited in Olesen, 2000) argued, 'set the stage for other research, other actions, and policy that transcend and transform' (p. 215). It may at its most basic be simply 'helping the silent to speak [and] consciousness raising' (Dervin, cited in van Zoonen, 1994, p. 128), but whatever the desired outcomes, there is clear agreement that a feminist methodology entails a commitment to change, be that at the micro or at the macro level. The end result may be a reduction in the sex appeal of women in sport media, moving towards depicting woman as athletes and not sex objects. This commitment aligns with the fact that, 'feminism is first and last a political movement concerned with practical issues' (Alcoff and Potter, 1993, p. 2).

The *final* 'epistemological and methodological' commitment from Fine is that of 'methodological integrity', which refers to the necessity to utilize diverse methods and perspectives (cited in Gatenby and Humphries, 1993, pp. 77–78). In this criterion, Fine is in agreement with numerous other theorists such as Reinharz (cited in McCarl Nielsen, 1990, p. 6) for example, who describe feminist research as multi-methodological.

Ever conscious of the epistemological issues at play in feminist methodology and sensitive to all stages of the research process, Stanley and Wise (1993) suggested that:

> There are a number of key areas of the research process in which we think precepts drawn from feminist epistemology need to be integrated: in the researcher/ researched relationship; in emotion as an aspect of the research process that, like any, other aspect, can be analytically interrogated; in critically unpacking conceptualizations of 'objectivity' and 'subjectivity' as binaries or dichotomies; in the processes by which 'understanding' and 'conclusions' are reached; in the existence and management of the different 'realities' or versions held by researchers and researched and in issues surrounding authority and power in research, but also and perhaps more crucially in written representations of research. (p. 189)

## FEMINIST ETHICAL CONCERNS AS THEY RELATE TO METHODOLOGY

Thompson (1992) summarizes ethical concerns in feminist research into two areas. She believes we should first ask whether the research is either exploitative or empowering of participants and others, and then ask how oppressive objectification of participants can be avoided given that any method has the potential to be oppressive. Meeting these ethical concerns is not simple or straightforward, and feminist researchers have sometimes reported the challenges of carrying out completely ethical research on feminist terms (Maguire, 1987).

## FEMINIST THEORY MAKING

Maria Lugones and Elizabeth Spelman (1983) suggest that the following criteria are important in feminist theory making: (1) the theory or account can be helpful if it enables one to see how parts of one's life fit together; (2) a useful theory will help one locate oneself concretely in the world; (3) a theory or account not only ought to accurately locate one in the world, but also enable one to think about the extent to which one is responsible for not being in that location; (4) a theory that is useful will provide criteria for change and make suggestions for modes of resistance that don't merely reflect the situation and values of the theorizer (p. 482).

## FEMINIST THEORY AND SPORT MANAGEMENT

Recent sport management related feminist research studies have covered a diversity of topics. Brown (2007) utilized socio-legal, legal-geographic and feminist sports theory to examine increased participation of women in elite sport in a patchwork case study on four nations: Canada, the United States of America, the Islamic Republic of Iran and Australia. Vander Kloet (2005) utilized feminist post-structuralism to explore lifeguarding, subjectivity, equity and the public provision of public leisure through interviews with lifeguards. Scrogum (2005) explored the experiences of women who played rugby. Women took part in three focus groups to discuss their experiences in rugby and the meanings they attributed to them. Although not explicitly utilizing feminist theory, Farrell (2006) investigated female consumption of women's basketball through the voices and perspectives of female spectators of men's basketball. From a theoretical perspective, the following two studies provide a valuable starting point for research from a feminist perspective.

First, 'Sport and Traditions of Feminist Theory' (Burke, 2001) involves a philosophical examination of the opportunities that are offered to females who seek authority in sporting participation, by an examination of the ideas that emanate from various streams of feminist thought. Second, 'Getting girls in the game: A qualitative analysis of urban sport programs' (Cooky, 2006) discusses three of the four major theoretical approaches to the study of sex/gender: feminist interaction theory, feminist structural theories of the gender order and feminist theories of the cultural/symbolic order, including the foundations and concepts of the approach and how the theories can help elucidate understandings of girls and women in sports.

### RECENT CASE EXAMPLE: FEMINISM

*The following article is an example of how feminism has been used in the past by researchers in Sport Management Research. The interested reader may wish to find/download and read the article for further insights.*

Can gender equity be more equitable?: Promoting an alternative frame for sport management research, education, and practice. Shaw, S. and Frisby, W. (2006). *Journal of Sport Management, 20*(4), 2–24.

Shaw and Frisby suggest that gender research in sport management has been dominated by liberal feminist theory, which does little to challenge or alter dominant gendered discourses and power structures within sport organizations. In their paper, the limitations of three existing conceptual frames for understanding gender equity are discussed. A fourth frame is proposed that builds on the work of Ely and Meyerson (2000), Meyerson and Kolb (2000), and Rao, Stuart, and Kelleher (1999). The authors argue that the fourth frame, based on post-structural feminist theory, provides an important alternative, addressing the complexities of gender relations in sport organizations through the processes of critique, narrative revision and experimentation. They extend the fourth frame by considering two additional elements: (a) the intersection of gender with other aspects of diversity and (b) a deconstruction of the traditional discourses that pit gender equity against organizational effectiveness using Bauman's (2001) concept of moral sensitivity. The implications of the fourth frame are then discussed in relation to sport management teaching, research and practice.

## WHAT IS QUEER THEORY?

Queer theory seeks to deconstruct hegemonic notions of sexuality and gender. Queer theorists examine how traditional definitions of gender identity (masculine vs feminine) and sexuality (heterosexual vs homosexual) break down, overlap, misrepresent or do not adequately explain the dynamic range of human sexuality in a text. It calls into question the 'naturalness' of heterosexuality and the notion of stable sexualities. Jagose (1996) suggests that the evolution of queer theory is 'a product of specific cultural and theoretical pressures with increasingly structured debates . . . about questions of lesbian and gay identity' (p. 76). Though difficult to define as it is ever evolving, queer theory calls into question 'essential' sexed, gendered and sexual identities, striving to destabilize discursive constructions of sexuality that come to be accepted as 'natural' and that maintain a dominant/subordinate power relationship (Halperin 1995; Jagose 1996).

Queer theory also claims diversity through its intended inclusion of gay, lesbian, bisexual, transgendered and transsexual persons, and really any subject (even heterosexual) that somehow deviates from normative definitions of (sexual) desire; it purports to be inclusive of any one who feels marginalized from the norm – be it a result of sexuality, intellect, culture, etc. (Giffney, 2004). Queer theory is a contested term that is sometimes used as a catchall for marginalized sexual groups, or as a radical new theory that has emerged out of lesbian and gay studies. Queer theory has been critiqued by some as not being inclusive of other forms of difference, for example, race or gender.

Gamson (2000) argues that 'queer studies is largely a deconstructive enterprise, taking apart the view of a self-defined by something at its core, be it sexual desire, race, gender, nation, or class' (p. 348). He goes on to say, 'Queer marks an identity that, defined as it is by a deviation from sex and gender norms either by the self inside or by specific behaviors, is always in flux' (p. 349).

The distinction between queer identity and queer theory is important. We understand queer as a way of reading an action, behaviour or characteristic, so that queer can remain a fluid, dynamic term. Beemyn and Eliason (1996) write that queer theory must 'be flexible enough to accommodate all people who identify as queer' (p. 3). Beemyn and Eliason (1996) go on to argue, 'queer theory has the potential to be inclusive of race, gender, sexuality, and other areas of identity by calling attention to the distinctions between identities, communities, and cultures, rather than ignoring these differences or pretending that they don't exist' (p. 165). Krane (2001) argues that queer theory has moved beyond lesbian and gay studies because, 'queer theory seeks to avoid privileging one component of identity over another' (p. 404).

This may also be the opinion of Tierney (1997) who sees queer theory as seeking 'to interrogate terms such as gender and race so that the norms of our lives are reconfigured' (p. 37). Table 11.2 lists some of the generally accepted features of queer theory.

Queer theory calls into question understandings of identity categories and operations of power; it seeks to destabilize accepted gender and identity constructs through individual acts of resistance/subversion. Queer theorists raise questions that other researchers may not about identity categories. Examples of these types of questions are presented in Table 11.3.

**Table 11.2** *Features of queer theory*

*Queer theory*

- Gender and sex are socially constructed
- Deconstructs gender and sexuality/gender norms
- Rejects biological theories of sexual identity
- Questions the usefulness of sexual and gender categories
- Challenges the taken-for-granted binaries of gender and sexuality
- Opens up for debate and discussion the very notions of what constitutes maleness and femaleness as well as sexualities
- Gender and sex binary serves to *acknowledge* sexual differences and also operates to *contain* and *regulate* these identities
- Once such categories are formulated, various institutions – parents, families, medicine, social work, the law, mental health and criminal justice systems – regulate and police them
- Identity politics and social movements

**Table 11.3** *Questions asked by queer theorists*

*Questions queer theorists ask*

- Who do these categories serve?
- Who do these categories include and who do they exclude?
- Who has the power to define the categories?
- How are the categories policed?
- How do these categories change over time and over cultures?

## CRITICISMS OF QUEER THEORY

Critics of queer still find it problematic that queer is used. Butler (1991) argues that:

> it remains politically necessary to lay claim to 'women', 'queer', 'gay', and 'lesbian', precisely because of the way these terms, as it were, lay their claim on us prior to our full knowing. Laying claim to such terms in reverse will be necessary to refute homophobic deployments of the terms in law, public policy, on the street, in 'private' life. (p. 229)

Other criticisms of queer theory appear in Table 11.4.

**Table 11.4** Criticisms of queer theory

- It fails to consider the reality of structural power (class, patriarchy, race/ethnicity, ability
- It simply (re)named and then (re)constructed typical power relations despite its claims of diversity
- While some writers argue that queer theory is actually too inclusive because it renders difference invisible, others argue that it is not inclusive enough
- Sexual identity is a false construct created to categorize deviant behaviour and to promote a dominant sexuality
- Existing queer theory, despite attempts to avoid normativity, harbours a normative discourse around race, sexuality and class
- It must provide a framework in which to challenge racist, misogynist and other oppressive perspectives/discourse/norms, as well as those that are heterosexist and homophobic

## SPORT AND QUEER THEORY

Although not yet used in a sport management context queer theory as a research method has been applied in sport studies. Davidson and Shogan (1998) urge scholars to consider a queer theoretical perspective that would deconstruct sexuality and dominant ideologies within sport. More recently, Abdel-Shehid (2005) has explored the possibility of analysing sport through a queer lens, and more specifically of deconstructing black masculinity, its link to heterosexuality and the sexualization of black athletes. Abdel-Shehid has proposed that deconstructing sport using 'black queer theory' would engage questions of visibility and recognition and would provide an alternative reading of sport culture and black masculinity.

## RECENT CASE EXAMPLE: QUEER THEORY

*The following article is an example of how queer theory has been used in the past by researchers in Sport Management Research. The interested reader may wish to find/download and read the article for further insights.*

> Gender, sexuality, and the body: Exploring the lived experiences of gay and queer marathoners. Bridel, W. (2006). Doctoral dissertation. University of Ottawa (Canada).

Bridel's study explored the experiences of 12 gay and queer males within the sport of marathoning. Working within an anti-positivist paradigm that draws on *queer* and post-structuralist gender theories, as well as a Foucaultian perspective of the body, Bridel investigated subjects' discursive constructions of sexuality, gender and the body within the context of this individual sport milieu. In focusing specifically on an individual sporting space, this study added a unique perspective to the growing body of knowledge related to gay men in sport.

## HYPOTHETICAL CASE STUDY

### Standpoint theory and the 2012 London Olympic Games legacy

Standpoint theory is a branch of feminist theory. It assumes there is no single objective truth and 'reality' is structured by gender, class, race and sexual orientation. Standpoint theory focuses on oppressed groups and is about the different ways each person experiences situations. Our perceptions are influenced by our position in society, and by power relations. An example you may be able to understand: Ever been on a date and one of you is having a great time, and the other can hardly wait for the evening to end?

A significant part of the 2012 London Olympic Games legacy plan was the regeneration of East London. With both private and public support, almost £1 billion was provided to the Olympic Delivery Authority for regeneration of infrastructure and facilities. The transformation of East London was significant, with Queen Elizabeth Olympic Park as the centrepiece attraction to offer world-class sport venues to the local community. Over £7 billion in new contracts to build or renew housing and commercial districts was also awarded. The regeneration of East London is a tremendous opportunity to increase both social and economic benefits to the local community and the Greater London area for years to come.

Using your own knowledge and experiences, attempt to view the East London regeneration legacy from the eyes of other groups than those who benefited from the regeneration project, especially marginalized groups.

1   What other groups/people's view point did you consider when analysing the story? Is the regeneration a good thing for all groups/people?

**193**

2    What experiences, values and beliefs that you hold led to uncovering any bias the organizing committee may have towards certain groups?

3    Choose one marginalized group, and outline a version of the story from their point of view.

## CONCLUSION

Gender approaches have much to offer the sport management researcher. The overarching goal of this form of research is to identify the ways in which multiple forms of oppression impact the lives of women and those of alternate sexual orientation.

## REVIEW QUESTIONS

With a basic understanding now of feminist and queer theories, attempt to answer the following questions:

- Is the gender of the researcher important in feminist research?
- Provide some examples of how 'queer theory' could be applied to Sport Management Research.

## SUGGESTED EXTENDED READING FOR STUDENTS

Cooky, C. A. (2006). Getting girls in the game: A qualitative analysis of urban sport programs. Unpublished doctoral dissertation, University of Southern California.

Gamson, J. (2000). Sexualities, queer theory, and qualitative research. In N. K. Denzin and Y. S. Lincoln (eds), *Handbook of qualitative research* (2nd edn, pp. 347–365). Thousand Oaks, CA: Sage.

Giffney, N. (2004). Denormatizing queer theory: More than (simply) lesbian and gay studies. *Feminist Theory, 5*(1), 73–78.

Scrogum, J. (2005). Binaries and bridging: A feminist analysis of women's rugby participation. Unpublished masters thesis. University of North Carolina at Greensboro.

Tierney, W. (1997). *Academic outlaws: Queer theory and cultural studies in the academy*. London: Sage.

## Chapter 12

# Narrative inquiry and the stories sport management researchers can tell

## LEARNING OUTCOMES

By the end of this chapter, you should be able to:

- understand the basic principles associated with narrative inquiry;
- articulate the purpose of narrative research;
- outline the narrative research process and its key characteristics;
- outline narrative research data collection techniques;
- identify some strategies with which to apply a narrative methodology to Sport Management Research.

## KEY TERMS

*Narrative* – the consciously formulated, premeditated and coherent account of an experience.

## KEY THEMES

- What are the implications for utilizing narrative in the field of Sport Management Research?

## CHAPTER OVERVIEW

This chapter suggests that narrative is a useful way of approaching the world of Sport Management Research. It suggests that, in combination with the process of reflection, narrative inquiry as a qualitative research methodology has the capacity to bring to the field of Sport Management Research an understanding of the unique experiences of sports managers.

## DEFINING NARRATIVE

There appears to be some disagreement about a precise definition of narrative (Riessman, 1993). There are those who suggest that narratives are simply stories about past experiences; for example, Labov (1972) described it as a partial reliving of past experiences – 'We define narrative as one method of recapitulating past experiences' (p. 359). Notably, Labov made a point of bringing his narratives to life and not allowing his audience to question his interpretation of the story. Perhaps the most concise definition of narrative research is that proposed by Smith (1981): narratives are 'verbal acts consisting of someone telling someone else that something happened' (p. 228). Polkinghorne (1988), while acknowledging that the term narrative generally can refer to any spoken or written presentation, confines his usage to the kind of organizational scheme that is expressed in story form. He uses the term to describe the process of creating a story, the internal logic of the story (its plot and theme), and also the product – the story, tale or poem as a unit.

## WHAT IS NARRATIVE INQUIRY?

Unlike more traditional research methods, narrative inquiry captures aspects of personal and human lives that cannot be 'quantified into facts and numerical data' (Clandinin and Connelly, 2000, p. 19). Advocates of narrative research claim that it is a tool that arranges experiences to make them comprehensible, memorable and shareable (Gudsmundsdottir, 1991, 1996; Casey, 1995; Clandinin and Connelly, 2000).

To give their definition to narrative inquiry, Clandinin and Connelly (2000) proffer some of its characteristics:

> narrative inquiry is a way of understanding experience. It is collaboration between researcher and participants, over time, in a place or series of places, and in social interaction with milieu. An inquirer enters this matrix in the midst and progresses in this same spirit, concluding the inquiry still in the midst of living and telling, reliving and retelling, the stories of the experiences that make up people's lives, both individual and social. Simply stated . . . narrative inquiry is stories lived and told. (p. 20)

The key element is that meaning resides within the individual, capturing and recognizing their meaning. Some will do this in chronological order, some will do it by themes. Similarly, Gartner, Latham and Merritt (2003) propose that: 'Narrative inquiry, gives permission to learners to tap into the tacit knowledge embedded in their experience as well as to learn from each other in the process. It serves as a springboard for dialogue about the deeper issues of their professional discipline that may not be easily illuminated through other methods' (p. 2).

In narrative research, researchers describe the lives of individuals, collect and tell stories about people's lives and write narratives of individual experiences. As a distinct form of qualitative research, a narrative typically focuses on studying a single person, gathering data through the collection of stories, reporting individual experiences and discussing the meaning of those experiences for the individual (Creswell, 2003). For example, a narrative inquiry on Tiger Woods might reveal his perceptions and meanings of his quick rise to the top of golf, his transgressions and their personal effects on himself, and his rise back to the top.

Researchers draw upon many techniques and sources for the collection and analysis of narrative data. For example, the Internet, autobiographies, letters, journals, ethnographic field notes, diaries, obituaries, photograph albums, poetry, newspapers, magazines, television and participant observation can be used. However, undoubtedly the most pervasive source of data is the interview. Reissman (1987) distinguished several genres in interviews: among these, she includes *habitual narratives* (events happen over and over, and consequently, there is no peak in the action) such as the routine of team practice; *hypothetical narratives* (which depict events that did not happen) such as what would have happened if a championship was won or lost; and *topic-centred* narratives (snapshots of past events that are linked thematically) such as a player switching teams several times over his or her career. Table 12.1 lists some of the advantages and disadvantages of narrative inquiry.

**Table 12.1** *Advantages and disadvantages of narrative research*

*Advantages of narratives*

1   Through narratives individuals connect experiences in a meaningful way via temporal ordering, emplotment and evaluation

2   Through narratives people share experience because they are built on the basis of social dialogue (they are always produced for an audience)

3   Because narratives are a natural and common way to construct experience they are seen as useful to:

   •   facilitate empathy between interviewers and interviewees

   •   allow interviewees to find their voice through a dialogue with the interviewer that is largely based on the interviewees' own experience

*Disadvantages of narratives*

1   Very little safeguard against bias

2   Rigorous appraisal methods are not used

3   Analysis of collected information is often subjective

4   Researchers' opinions may be mixed together with evidence

**Table 12.2** *When to use narrative designs*

*When do you use narrative designs?*

- When individuals are willing to tell their stories
- When you want to report personal experiences in a particular setting
- When you want a close bond with participants
- When participants want to process their stories
- When you have a chronology of events
- When you want to write in a literary way and develop the micro picture

**Table 12.3** *Characteristics of narrative research*

| Process | Description |
|---|---|
| Individual experiences | Interested in exploring the experiences of an individual |
| Chronology of the experiences | Researcher analyses and writes about an individual life using a time sequence or chronology of events and then orders these events in a way that makes sense to a reader |
| Collecting individual stories | A story in narrative research is a first-person oral telling or retelling of an individual, which has a beginning, middle and end. These involve a predicament, conflict, or struggle; a protagonist or character; and a sequence with implied causality (a plot) during which the predicament is resolved in some fashion. Like a novel, stories have time, place, plot and scene and use varied sources of data to comprise the data base |
| Restorying | During restorying the researcher gathers stories and analyses them for elements of the story. During this phase the researcher rewrites the story to place it in a chronological sequence so as to provide a causal link among ideas. This information includes interaction, continuity and situation. The process involves:<br>• transcription: researcher conducts the interview and transcribes the conversation from an audiotape<br>• retranscription: identifying the key elements of the story; codes used by the researcher to identify setting, characters' actions, problem and resolution in the transcript<br>• restorying: organizing the key codes into a sequence |
| Coding for themes | Themes provide the complexity of the story and add depth to the insight about understanding an individual's experiences |
| Context or setting | Describes the context or setting for the individual stories:<br>• includes the people involved in the story<br>• includes the physical setting<br>• setting may be described before events or actions, or can be woven throughout the study |
| Collaboration with participants | During this phase the inquirer actively involves the participant in the inquiry as it unfolds. The strategies include:<br>• negotiating relationships<br>• involving participants in the process of research<br>• negotiating transitions in the research process |

Source: Based on Creswell (2008)

Mishler (1995) has organized narrative studies according to three types of central research issues. First, *reference and temporal order* refers to the relationship between the order in which events actually happened and the order in which they are told in narration. Second, *textual coherence and structure* concerns the linguistic and narrative strategies on which the story is constructed. Finally, *narrative functions* deals with the broader place of the story within the greater society or culture.

According to Creswell (2008), there are key characteristics of narrative design, these are identified within Table 12.3.

Labov (1972, 1982) suggested that a 'fully formed' (narrative) includes six common elements: (1) an abstract (summary of the substance of the narrative); (2) orientation (time, place, situation, participants); (3) complicating action (sequence of events); (4) evaluation (significance and meaning of the action, attitude of the narrator); (5) resolution (what finally happened); and (6) coda (returns the perspective to the present). With these structures a teller constructs a story from a primary experience and interprets the significance of events in clauses and embedded evaluation (Reissman, 1987, p. 19).

## STEPS IN NARRATIVE RESEARCH

Creswell (2008) has provided the following steps in the narrative research in diagrammatic form. These are presented in Figure 12.1.

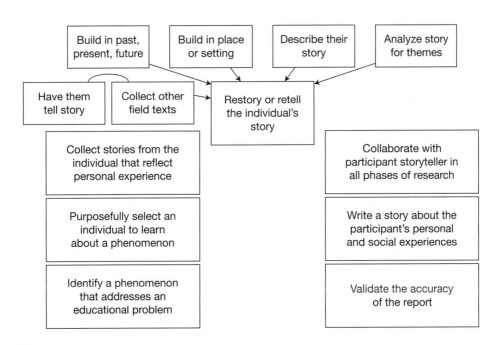

**Figure 12.1** *Steps for conducting narrative research*

Source: Creswell (2008, p. 524)

## Narrative research analysis

While some types of qualitative analysis have a standard set of procedures, narrative research does not (Riessman, 1993, p. 54). Following Riessman, Table 12.4 divides the narrative method into three stages: 'telling', 'transcribing' and 'analysing'. These stages provide an understanding of the narrative process for the sport management researcher.

## Validating narratives

Riessman (1993) acknowledged that there is no single way of evaluating narrative research. She wrote: 'There is no canonical approach in interpretive work, no recipes and formulas, and different validation procedures may be better suited to some research problems than others' (p. 69). Even so, she offered a few criteria for evaluation. First, she suggested that validation be conceived of as trustworthiness of the text. If the reader finds the text to be honest (perhaps no elaborations or misguiding in telling the story of Lance Armstrong's doping scandal), it is a starting point for a positive evaluation. Riessman further noted the persuasiveness, coherence and the pragmatic usefulness of the text as standards for evaluating the research. Noting the difficulty of establishing criteria for evaluating qualitative work, Sparkes (2002) recommends verisimilitude, rather than validity, as a starting point. The extent to which a story evokes a sense of truth within its readers is the foundation for the story's worth. Sparkes reviewed other scholars' views on evaluation as well, and included in his list of possible evaluative criteria items such as coherence, insightfulness, parsimony (Lieblich, Tuval-Mashiach, and Zilber, 1998); fairness and authenticity (Lincoln and Guba, 2000); substantive contribution, aesthetic merit, reflexivity, impact and expression of a reality (Richardson, 2000). A summary of other criteria to evaluate narrative research is provided in Table 12.5.

**Table 12.4** The narrative research process

| Process | Description |
| --- | --- |
| Telling | It is essential for the researcher to provide a facilitating context to encourage those who are interviewed to tell complete stories about important moments in their lives. Open-ended questions allow respondents to construct answers. Riessman (1993) advises a mixture of open-ended questions (to elicit narratives) and closed-ended questions or self-administered questionnaires (for later quantification). |
| Transcribing | Riessman (1993) advises that the researcher begin by getting the entire interview, including both words and selected features (crying, long pauses, laughter), on paper in a first draft. Then portions can be selected for retranscription. |
| Analyzing | Upon looking at different possibilities for reading, interpreting, and analyzing life stories and other narrative materials, two main independent dimensions emerge—those of (a) *holistic versus categorical* approaches and (b) *content versus form.* |

Source: Lieblich *et al.* (1998, p. 12)

 **Table 12.5** *How to evaluate narrative studies*

*Criteria for the evaluation of narrative studies*

*1 Width: The Comprehensiveness of Evidence.* This refers to the amount of evidence that is provided to allow the reader to make an informed judgement on the evidence and its interpretation.

*2 Coherence: The Way Different Parts of the Interpretation Create a Complete and Meaningful Picture.* Lieblich and her colleagues distinguish between internal coherence (how the parts fit together) and external coherence (how the research compares to existing theories and previous research).

*3 Insightfulness: The Sense of Innovation or Originality in the Presentation of the Story and Its Analysis.* Does this research move the reader to greater insight into his or her own life?

*4 Parsimony: The Ability to Provide an Analysis Based on a Small Number of Concepts, and Elegance or Aesthetic Appeal.* This refers to the literary merits of oral or written presentation of the story.

Source: Lieblich *et al.* (1998)

## Reliability

In narrative studies, reliability usually refers to the dependability of the data, and careful, systematic procedures to ensure the closest possible representation from the raw data stage through that of analysis and the written report are indeed necessary criteria for judging narrative work. A criticism that is launched against narrative studies on the issue of dependability – that of the truthfulness of the original narrative – however, deserves some attention.

Lysaght (2001) captures the fundamental place of the narrative in our society, saying 'narratives are said to fashion our lives, providing the structure for our day-to-day existence and they propel us into a future that is shaped by our lived experiences of them' (Lysaght, 2001, p. 64). While narratives are the fundamental means of making ourselves intelligible to one another, they provide the framework by which humans convey valuable cultural information. Values and norms on doping, cheating and other sport scandals can be passed on to future generations by storytelling or narratives. Barthes (1996) summarizes this state of affairs thus:

> The narratives of the world are without number, the narrative is present at all times, in all places, in all societies; history of narrative begins with the history of mankind, there does not exist, and never has existed, a people without narratives. (p. 1)

Narratives therefore, bind the facts of our existence together, to enable people to find meaning and continuity in seemingly complex lives (Beattie, 2000).

**RECENT CASE EXAMPLE: NARRATIVE**

*The following article is an example of how narrative has been used in the past by researchers in Sport Management Research. The interested reader may wish to find/download and read the article for further insights.*

Experiencing sport management: The use of personal narrative in sport management studies. Rinehart, R. (2005). *Journal of Sport Management, 19*, 497–522.

Rinehart argues for the use of personal narrative and personal storytelling in Sport Management Research methodology, which might result in the asking of different questions and in write-ups that could serve to invigorate sport management studies. He adds that this method of research answers different, interactionist-based questions for researchers delving into how sport management affects people and how sport managers interact with others.

## Narrative and sport management

Rinehart (2005) argued that narratives examine how lives are lived into existence, and it provides models for practitioners and scholars of sport management to model, discover, experience and use. He further suggests that:

> The possibilities for use of personal narrative within sport management are expanding all the time, as formerly discrete academic disciplines borrow from one another, creating new forms and new uses for old forms. As was pointed out earlier, sport management scholars and practitioners might gain knowledge and understanding from personal experience narratives. This type of research can provide deep understanding that could lead to structural changes in human resource management, marketing, advertising, policy studies, and leadership training for practitioners of sport management. (p. 517)

Smith and Weed (2007) propose the following orienting propositions for narrative inquiry in general, and for sport and tourism research in particular: (1) meaning is central to being human, and being human entails actively construing meaning; (2) meaning is created through narrative, and thus is a storied effort; (3) narratives are created within relationships, and thus storytelling relations are a vital condition for making narrative meaningful; (4) narratives are constructed within relationships as a result of human agency; and (5) narratives are a constitutive force. These propositions could be similarly applied to the sport management context.

## RECENT CASE EXAMPLE: NARRATIVE

*The following article is an example of how narrative has been used in the past by researchers in Sport Management Research. The interested reader may wish to find/download and read the article for further insights.*

> The potential of narrative research in sports tourism. Smith, B. and Weed, M., (2007). *Journal of Sport and Tourism, 12*(3–4), 249–269.

Narrative inquiry, as one way of theorizing and conducting qualitative research, has not been considered by researchers interested in the relationship between sport and tourism, although there is an increasing debate about the greater use of interpretive qualitative research in this area. In a modest effort to galvanize researchers and offer a direction for scholarship, this article seeks to explore narrative as one form of interpretive research. They argue an understanding of what narrative inquiry can be by laying out a theoretical basis for this kind of research, and making a case for the relevance of narrative as an alternative methodology. Next, consideration is given to conducting narrative research in sports tourism. The article closes by suggesting that narrative inquiry is a germane way of theorizing and doing research within sports tourism.

## HYPOTHETICAL CASE STUDY

Of the many inspiring stories of the 1992 Summer Olympics in Barcelona, Derek Redmond's story stands out. The British sprinter was favoured to win the 400 metre dash at the Olympic Games. Derek was injury prone, having eight surgeries on his Achilles tendon over the four years leading up to the Olympics. However, Derek was fit and confident heading into Barcelona.

Derek posted the fastest time in the quarter finals, winning his heat. In the semi-finals, Derek had a great start. However, Derek tore his hamstring as he exited the first corner, and stopped running. In obvious pain, the track officials hurried over with stretchers – but Derek waved them off and continued around the track on one leg.

Derek recalled:

> Everything I had worked for was finished. I hated everybody. I hated the world. I hated hamstrings. I hated it all. I felt so bitter that I was injured again. I told myself I had to finish. I kept hopping round. Then, with 100 metres to go, I felt a hand on my shoulder. It was my old man. (*The Guardian*, 1992)

Derek's father, Jim, had attended almost every race, and avoided security to run on the track to assist Derek to the finish line. Jim supported Derek all the way to the last few steps, where Derek hopped on one leg through the finish line. He finished.

Derek's official time was 'DNF' (did not finish) because he was aided to the finish line. Nevertheless, the 65,000 fans in attendance gave them a standing ovation in appreciation of their true Olympic spirit.

Derek won many races, but he is remembered most for his DNF.

## QUESTIONS

1   How can this short story be used as a basis of a narrative inquiry? What steps would you take to expand the story into a narrative inquiry?
2   What cultural norms and values (themes) can be extracted from this story? To what other contexts or settings can these themes be transferred?

## CONCLUSION

Narrative inquiry as a research methodology has the potential to engage the sport management researcher in the reflective practice of lived experiences. This then allows the researcher to understand the complex nature of the sport practitioner, or sport management practitioner's world. The narrative process of writing, sharing, reflecting and then analysis can work to improve sport management knowledge and practice.

## REVIEW QUESTIONS

With a basic understanding now of the key elements of narrative inquiry, attempt to answer the following questions:

■   Identify two ways in which narrative inquiry can be used in Sport Management Research.
■   Discuss the importance of critical reflection to the narrative inquiry process.

## SUGGESTED EXTENDED READING FOR STUDENTS

Edwards, A., Skinner, J., and Gilbert, K. (2004). Sport management: Varying directions towards the narrative. *Kinesiology: International Journal of Fundamental and Applied Kinesiology, 36*(2), 220–231.
Gartner, A., Latham, G., and Merritt, S. (2003). The power of narrative: transcending disciplines. Available at: http://ultibase.rmit.edu.au/Articles/dec96/gartn1.htm# (accessed 3 March 2011).
Gay, L. R., Mills, G. E., and Airasian, P. (2009). *Educational research: Competencies for analysis and applications* (9th edn). Upper Saddle River, NJ: Pearson Merrill.

Gudsmundsdottir, S. (1991). Story maker, story teller: Narrative structures in the curriculum. *Journal of Curriculum Studies, 23*(3): 207–218.

Richardson, L. (2000). Writing: A Method of Inquiry. In N. K. Denzin and Y. S. Lincoln (eds.), *Handbook of qualitative research* (2nd edn, pp. 923–948). Thousand Oaks, CA: Sage.

Rinehart, R. E. (2005). 'Experiencing' sport management: The use of personal narrative in sport management studies. *Journal of Sport Management, 19*(4), 497–522.

Sparkes, A. C. (2002). *Telling tales in sport and physical activity: A qualitative journey.* Champaign: Human Kinetics.

## Chapter 13

# Phenomenology and the lived experience of the sport management researcher

## LEARNING OUTCOMES

By the end of this chapter, you should be able to:

■ understand the basic concepts of phenomenology;
■ recognize the implications for adopting a phenomenological approach to sport management.

## KEY TERMS

*Hermeneutic phenomenology* – a phenomenological interpretation that seeks to unveil hidden meanings in phenomena.

*Theory* – a well-substantiated explanation of some aspect of the natural world; an organized system of accepted knowledge that applies in a variety of circumstances to explain a specific set of phenomena.

## KEY THEMES

■ Can phenomenology be used as a research methodology in Sport Management Research?
■ What are some of the uses of phenomenology for Sport Management Research?

## CHAPTER OVERVIEW

Phenomenology aims to investigate and comprehend the lived experience of its participants. In sport management literature, phenomenology offers researchers a different perspective while providing the opportunity to explore previously unchartered waters. This chapter will provide an introduction and overview to the major concepts of phenomenology, as well as provide some suggestions as to possible frameworks from which to apply the phenomenological methodology to Sport Management Research.

## INTRODUCTION

Defining phenomenology is complex. Phenomenology is a method of philosophical inquiry that lays stress on the impressions of a reader. The reader is the main figure to determine the meanings of a given text. The name Husserl (1931) gave to his philosophical method is phenomenology. As a methodology, phenomenology has become increasingly employed in social science research, and has the potential to be used with great effectiveness in the field of Sport Management Research.

## WHAT IS PHENOMENOLOGY?

Phenomenology describes 'how one orients to lived experience'. From a phenomenological point of view, to do research is always to 'question the way we experience the world, to want to know the world in which we live as human beings' (Van Manen, 1990, p. 5).

### Phenomenology as a philosophy

Phenomenology derives from the Greek word *phainomenon*, which means 'to show itself' (Husserl, 1931) or 'what shows itself; the self-showing; the manifest' and is 'thus the totality of what lies in the light of day or can be brought to light' (Heidegger, 1977, pp. 74–75). Phenomenology is a philosophy, or a variety of distinctive yet related philosophies. However, it is also concerned with approach and method. Husserl (1931) considered phenomenology to be all three, philosophy, approach and method. As a philosophy, phenomenologists hold differing views on epistemological and ontological questions and therefore on the way phenomena may reveal themselves through the phenomenological process. Thus, the character of phenomenology is diverse, and the assumptions inherent in the various phenomenological approaches to understanding, and the methods they advocate, differ greatly. Three main approaches have been identified in phenomenology. The key features and researchers in these areas will now be discussed briefly.

### Phenomenology as a philosophy/history

This can be viewed as three forms: transcendental, hermeneutic and existential. *Transcendental phenomenology* as methodology began with Husserl (1931) who presented an alternative way of thinking offered by positive philosophy. Instead of trying to explain minds in terms of matter, or vice versa, Husserl demanded that each experience must be taken in its own right as it shows itself and as one is conscious of it. Husserl reflected that to truly understand a phenomenon one needed to bracket oneself or suspend all biases and assumptions. He used the term Epoche to describe this bracketing of prior assumptions. In Husserl's conception, phenomenology is primarily concerned with making the structures of consciousness, and the phenomena that appear in acts of consciousness, objects of systematic reflection and analysis. Such reflection was to take place from a highly modified 'first person' viewpoint, studying phenomena not as they appear to 'my' consciousness, but to any consciousness whatsoever. For example, examining values associated with youth sports (competitiveness, sport for all, optimal development, etc.) from as many viewpoints as possible to encompass all readers' viewpoints. Husserl believed that phenomenology could thus provide a firm basis for all human knowledge, including scientific knowledge, and could establish philosophy as a 'rigorous science'.

Husserl (1931) hoped to develop a philosophy that would deepen our understanding of how objects, or phenomena, are experienced and present themselves to our consciousness. He looked to answer the question 'how do we know?' by examining and describing the world-as-experienced by the participants of the inquiry. Husserl referred to this world of lived experience as the life-world *(Lebenswelt)* (Spiegelberg, 1982). It is in this world that much is considered commonplace and taken for granted. Husserl believed that we need to explore the 'essential' features of this experienced world. He argued that lived experience should be used as a tool to gain access to experiences of phenomena in their original form, as part of an individual's everyday physical reality.

*Heidegger's existential phenomenology* reinterpreted phenomenology and its methods. His phenomenology is existential, a perspective that insists that the observer cannot be separated from the world, and that an understanding of the person cannot occur in isolation from the person's world. Heidegger (1962) saw humans as beings that experience objects in particular and individual ways, and proposed a particular form of hermeneutic phenomenology in his pursuit of the meaning of being. This new approach had a considerable influence on the development of existential phenomenology. In his hermeneutical work, Heidegger employed two notions, the hermeneutic circle and historicity of understanding. Heidegger's emphasis is on *being-in-the-world (dasein)* and how phenomena present themselves in lived experience, in human existence (van Manen, 1990). Heideggerian phenomenology asks 'what does it mean to be a person?' and holds that the answer to this is found in *dasein* or being already in the world. As such, it deals with questions of human existence by seeking the meaning of being. Heidegger was concerned with what he considered the essential philosophical (and human) question: what is it 'to be'?

*Hermeneutic phenomenology* concerns how one orients to lived experience, and van Manen (1994) suggested that it is, in a broad sense, a philosophy or *theory of the unique*. Van Manen was strongly influenced by Merleau-Ponty's philosophy. He explains how phenomenology differs from almost every other science in that it attempts to gain insightful descriptions of the way we experience the world. How do sport fans from all over the world each experience a World Cup? Max van Manen (1990) proposed:

phenomenology does not offer us the possibility of effective theory with which we can now explain and/or control the world but rather it offers us the possibility of plausible insight, which brings us in more direct contact with the world. (pp. 37–38)

Rather than seeking a judgement about facts or reality, the aim of phenomenology is to gain people's understanding, opinions and expressions of feelings. In other words, rather than generating theories or general explanation, phenomenology aims to describe the experience as it exists. And the World Cup experience will likely exist differently for different people, based on their cultural and personal experiences and interpretations of those experiences. It is about expressing thoughts and perceptions of phenomena in the form of language in speech or writing (van Manen, 1990). It is about describing the essence of the experience and a fuller understanding of the nature of the experience.

Max van Manen (1990) uses an eclectic approach that he calls 'hermeneutic phenomenology'. Based on the philosophical works of Heidegger, hermeneutic phenomenology, as outlined by van Manen (1990), is a process of exploring one's interests and understandings of a phenomenon, uncovering the essence of that phenomenon by gathering and interpreting 'raw data' from those living it, and offering implications for practice. The 'raw data' of a phenomenological study are personal experiences, often complemented with poetry, biography, art or literature. Hence the remark that hermeneutic phenomenology is 'both descriptive and interpretive' (p. 180).

Van Manen (1990) outlined the essentials of phenomenological research as: the study of lived experience; the explication of phenomena as they present themselves to consciousness, rather than as conceptualized, categorized or theorized; the study of essences of experience that asks, not 'how', but rather, what is the 'nature' of the experience; the description of experiential meanings we live as we live them, examples of which are designed to enable us to see the structure or the deeper significance of the experience being described; the human scientific study of phenomena in that it is systematic, explicit, inter-subjective, self-critical and examines structures of the lived, human world (rather than the natural world); the attentive practice of thoughtfulness whose language awakens a person to the meaning of the experience; a search for what it means to be human, which may be achieved by more deeply understanding human experience; and a poetizing activity insofar as its language reverberates in the world rather than speaking 'of' it, and so the poem itself is the result rather than a conclusion or summary of the phenomenological study. Table 13.1 outlines what phenomenologists 'do'.

Phenomenology in the field of sport management serves as a theoretical framework that privileges participants' lived experience. As such, phenomenological sport management researchers seek to learn what is central to the phenomena being studied. Research conducted from a phenomenological perspective allows participants to communicate their experience without the meaning being significantly altered by the sport management researcher, and can aid in the empowerment of participants by encouraging them to speak about their own experiences.

In general it is proposed that there are a number of *strengths* and *weaknesses* associated with phenomenological research. Some of these have been summarized in Table 13.2 (p. 211).

**Table 13.1** What phenomenologists do

*Phenomenologists*

- REJECT scientific realism (objects exist independently of our knowledge of their existence).
- DISAGREE that the empirical sciences are better methods to describe the features of the world.
- DESCRIBE the ordinary, conscious experience of things.
- OPPOSE the acceptance of unobservable things.
- REJECT naturalism and positivism.
- BELIEVE objects in the natural world, cultural world, and abstract objects (like numbers and consciousness) can be made evident and thus known.
- RECOGNIZE the role of description prior to explanation by means of causes, purposes, or grounds.
- DEBATE whether Husserl's transcendental epoche and reduction is useful or even possible.
- STUDY the 'life-world' (the taken-for-granted pattern of everyday living).

Source: www.phenomenologycenter.org/phenom.htm#2 (accessed 4 February 2014)

## Phenomenology as a research methodology

The differences between the philosophies of Husserlian and Heideggerian phenomenology impact their use as research methodologies. While Husserlian phenomenology is a descriptive methodology, Heideggerian phenomenology rests on an interpretive process. Phenomenology as a methodology is descriptive and interpretive. We shall now discuss each of these.

### Descriptive phenomenology

Descriptive phenomenology emphasizes descriptions of human experience. It insists on the careful description of ordinary conscious experience of everyday life – a description of 'things' as people experience them. These 'things' include hearing, seeing, believing, feeling, remembering, deciding, evaluating, acting, etc. A descriptive phenomenology of a participant's experience in a charity marathon may detail as many 'things' as possible in order to provide a holistic capture of the experience.

STEPS IN DESCRIPTIVE PHENOMENOLOGICAL STUDIES:

1  Bracketing – the process of identifying and holding in abeyance preconceived beliefs and opinions about the phenomenon.
2  Intuiting – the researcher remains open to the meanings attributed to the phenomenon by those who have experienced it.
3  Analysing – extracting significant statements, categorizing, and making sense of the essential meanings of the phenomenon.
4  Describing – researchers come to understand and define the phenomenon.

**Table 13.2** *Strengths and weaknesses of phenomenology*

| Strengths of phenomenology | Weaknesses of phenomenology |
| --- | --- |
| Efficient and economical data generation | Findings are difficult to generalize to a larger population |
| | Small number of participants (3–10) only |
| | Individual responses are not always independent of one another |
| | Dominant or opinionated members may overshadow the thoughts of the other group members if group interviews are conducted |
| Direct interaction with participants | Data is often difficult to analyse and summarize |
| Allows the researcher to ask for clarification and to ask immediate follow-up/probing questions | Enormous amount of data, difficult to organize and interpret |
| Allows the researcher to observe nonverbal responses that can be supportive or contradictory to the verbal responses | |
| Rich, first-person accounts in conversation and interviews | Researcher may give too much credit to the results (immediacy of a personal opinion) |
| Participants react to and build upon the responses of other participants | It is a philosophy not a research method |
| Research tool is applicable to a wide range of settings and individuals | Difficulty in describing the unique experiences AND make generalizations about the experiences at the same time |
| Results are easy to understand (in terms of people's direct opinions and statements) | Ethical issues occur due to the close relationship of participants and researcher |
| Uncovers taken-for-granted assumptions | Can be difficult to gain trust of participants |
| Writing of stories creates rich text to recreate 'lived experience' | Can be useful in reporting individual cases, but must be tentative when suggesting their extent to a general population |
| | A form of ideal abstraction detached from the world of concrete experience |

## Interpretive/hermeneutic phenomenology

Interpretive phenomenology stresses the interpretation and understanding, and not just description of, human experience. An interpretive phenomenologist would go beyond describing the 'things' of the marathon participant, and elaborate on the meanings and connections of certain 'things' (e.g. the importance of seeing family members cheering along the course).

■ Hermeneutic generally refers to the art and philosophy of interpreting the meaning of an object.
■ The goals of interpretive phenomenology are to enter another's world and to discover the practical wisdom, possibilities and understandings found there.

**211**

■ Interpretive phenomenology relies primarily on in-depth interviews with individuals who have experienced the phenomenon of interest. Sometimes uses supplementary texts, such as novels, poetry, or other artistic expressions – or the use of such materials in their conversations with the study participants.

---

### RECENT CASE EXAMPLE: INTERPRETIVE PHENOMENOLOGY

*The following article is an example of how interpretive phenomenology has been used in the past by researchers in Sport Management Research. The interested reader may wish to find/download and read the article for further insights.*

Grasping the phenomenology of sporting bodies. Hockey, J., and Collinson, J. A. (2007). *International Review for the Sociology of Sport, 42*(2), 115–131.

This phenomenology attempts to interpret the perceptions we have of the human body as it relates to the sporting experience. It discusses the embodiment of physical skills through repetitive engagement of the living world (ground, air, objects, etc.) specific to each athlete and sport.

---

Table 13.3 lists some of the contrasts between descriptive and interpretive phenomenology. Kerry and Armour (2000) argue that researchers who choose to employ an *existential phenomenological research* approach must provide sound conceptual rationale for using this specific method of inquiry. Existential phenomenological research consists of a sequence of interrelated steps.

### STEP 1 – CHOOSING A TOPIC

As described by Thomas and Pollio (2002), the first step is the researcher's decision regarding the topic of investigation.

### STEP 2 – THE BRACKETING INTERVIEW

Once a topic has been chosen and the phenomenological method has been determined to be the most appropriate approach for addressing it, the focus shifts to the participant. In order

**Table 13.3** *Features of phenomenology as a methodology*

| Descriptive | Interpretive |
| --- | --- |
| Believe it is possible to suspend personal opinion to arrive at a single, essential, descriptive presentation of a phenomenon | There are endless numbers of realities |
| Think that if there is more than one reality, that leaves doubt, ignorance, and a lack of clarity | Interpretations are all we have, because description IS an interpretive process |
| Husserl followers | Heidegger followers |

to sharpen this focus, a bracketing interview is conducted. During this interview the primary investigator is interviewed by another researcher familiar with the phenomenological research process.

The goal of the bracketing interview is for the primary investigator to identify his or her presuppositions from the very outset of the research project (Dale, 1996). Does the sport phenomenologist have biases towards certain sports, teams, competitions, etc. that may tarnish the investigation? By making biases visible, the researcher is positioned to be a good listener during the interview process and is less likely to mix his or her own beliefs with the experience of the participant.

## STEP 3 – INTERVIEWING PARTICIPANTS

The third step in the phenomenological research process is the actual phenomenological interviews. The researcher poses a single open-ended question or statement for the participants to ponder and respond to. Following this initial open-ended question, the interview follows the direction given it by the participant. The interview concludes once the participant agrees that he or she has described his or her experience in as much detail as possible and that there is nothing else that 'stood out' to him or her about the experience.

## STEP 4 – DATA ANALYSIS

After conducting and audiotaping the interview, the researcher uses analysis procedures to thematize the data. The steps of data analysis include transcribing and the hermeneutic circle.

### Step 4.1 – Transcribing

The audiotaped interviews are transcribed verbatim, paying close attention to pauses, laughter or other noticeable phenomena during the interview. Transcribing the interviews enables the researcher to begin the process of data analysis by trying to interpret parts of the text in relation to other parts.

### Step 4.2 – The hermeneutic circle

The hermeneutic circle is implemented in three ways during the interpretation of phenomenological interviews. First, the primary researcher brings his/her own interpretation of an interview to an interpretative research group, where the interview is read aloud. While the primary researcher sits and takes notes, two other members of the group take turns reading the questions and statements by the interviewer and the participant, respectively. The group provides feedback as to whether the presented thematic structures are supported by the interview data and represent clear descriptions of the participants' experiences.

Second, the hermeneutic circle functions in an 'idiographic' way, where the group or the primary researcher continuously relates parts of a single interview to the whole text. This methodological procedure is used to ensure that all parts of the text are always understood in terms of their relationship to the larger whole. Thematic descriptions of passages of a participant's interview lead to the formation of an overall thematic structure of that individual's unique experience.

The third function of the hermeneutic circle is in the analysis of each transcript in the context of all the other transcripts. This application is referred to as the 'nomothetic' (in

**213**

contrast to the 'idiographic') level of hermeneutic analysis (Pollio, Henley, and Thompson, 1997). During this step the researcher attempts to develop a single general or overall thematic structure for all of the interviews.

### STEP 5 – REPORTING FINDINGS TO PARTICIPANTS

During the last step of the phenomenological research process the focus shifts back to the participant. Here the researcher gives participants an opportunity to review the thematic structure describing their experience and provide feedback as to how accurately and completely the structure does so. This step is important in securing the study's validity (Dale, 1996).

## PHENOMENOLOGICAL 'TRADITION'

In contrast to both Husserl and Heidegger, van Manen (1990) spoke of there being no '*method*' as such if this is understood as a set of procedures, but rather of 'ways' or 'paths' leading to 'clearings'. These paths cannot be determined by fixed signposts – they need to be discovered or invented as a response to the question in hand. He spoke, however, of a 'tradition' – a set of guides and recommendations that form the basis of a principled form of enquiry. This tradition is presented as 'methodological structure' in which hermeneutic phenomenological research is seen as a dynamic interplay among six research activities. Van Manen lists these six activities as:

1    turning to a phenomenon that seriously interests us and converts us to the world;
2    investigating experience as we live it rather than as we conceptualize it;
3    reflecting on the essential themes that characterize the phenomenon;
4    describing the phenomenon through the art of writing and rewriting;
5    maintaining a strong and oriented pedagogical relation to the phenomenon;
6    balancing the research context by considering parts and the whole. (pp. 30–31)

From this perspective the source of phenomenological research is the life-world. The aim is to create a dialogue between practical concerns and lived experience through engaged reasoning and imaginative dwelling in the immediacy of the participants' worlds (van Manen, 1990).

## RESEARCH ISSUES

### Data saturation

Many qualitative researchers use the term 'data saturation' to suggest when enough data have been collected. Saturation is a term that refers to the repetition of discovered information and confirmation of previously collected data. 'An inquirer does not involve an exhaustive number of participants, but identifies when the data has revealed itself to be rich, diverse and significant enough to illuminate for readers an experience that leads to a deeper understanding of the phenomenon. The phenomenologist knows that one's own experiences are also the possible experiences of others' (van Manen 1990, p. 54).

## Phenomenological sampling

In phenomenological inquiry, purposeful sampling is commonly used. This method of sampling selects individuals for study participation based on their particular knowledge of a phenomenon, for the purpose of sharing that knowledge: for example, asking athletes on a championship winning team to describe that experience over asking any athletes (winners or not) to describe the experience.

## Issues of validity and reliability in phenomenology

In phenomenological research the term *validity* is used in a general sense. According to Polkinghorne (1989), the issue concerns the question, 'does the general structural description provide an accurate portrait of the common features and structural connections that are manifested in the examples collected?' (p. 57). The challenge for the phenomenological researcher is to convince the reader that their findings are accurate. To achieve that goal the researcher must show that their method has been applied rigorously and appropriately, and that the results are plausible and illuminating. Pollio *et al.* (1997) point out that 'only when both criteria are met does phenomenological description attain the rigour and insight that it aspires to attain' (p. 56). One way to ensure the validity of phenomenological interview data is to send participants the thematic structure that emerged from the data analysis and ask them to confirm that it accurately represents their experience.

Giorgi (1975) argued that findings from a phenomenological research project are *reliable* 'if a reader, adopting the same viewpoint as articulated by the researcher, can also see what the researcher saw, whether or not he agrees with it' (p. 93). Thus, it is the researcher's responsibility to provide the reader with as much information as possible in order to allow the reader to understand the researcher's perspective.

A phenomenological researcher expects that an overall thematic structure and understanding of participants' experiences that might emerge from another study examining the respective experience would be commensurate with the structure found in the original study. Summing up their notions about the reliability of phenomenological studies, Thomas and Pollio (2002) point out that 'in a sense, the aim of replication is to *extend*, not *repeat*, the themes and relations obtained in the original study' (p. 40, italics in original).

## PHENOMENOLOGY IN SPORT MANAGEMENT

Phenomenological research is important in sport management because sport managers are interested in human experiences and phenomenological research is a way to study human experiences. Phenomenology involves developing relationships with participants of the research process. It is believed that phenomenological research is a way for sport managers to enhance their knowledge about lived experiences, which can lead to the development or enhancement of sport management knowledge, and stimulate changes in the sport management process.

Phenomenological research is seen as a co-creation between researcher and participants rather than an observation of objects or behaviours. It is also said that phenomenology strives to bring language, perceptions and descriptions of human experience, with all types of phenomena, to enhance understanding.

Sports management researchers have already effectively utilized the phenomenological hermeneutic research method when studying human experiences. For example McAllister (2006) utilized phenomenology to explore how women administrators perceive the benefits of competitive sport experiences. Edwards and Skinner (2009) provide additional information on the application of phenomenology to sport management.

## RECENT CASE EXAMPLE: PHENOMENOLOGY

*The following article is an example of how phenomenology has been used in the past by researchers in Sport Management Research. The interested reader may wish to find/download and read the article for further insights.*

> Retired National Football League players' perceptions of financial decisions made: A phenomenological study. Karaffa, J. E. (2010). Unpublished dissertation. University of Phoenix. AAT 3417794

The purpose of this qualitative phenomenological research study was to examine the lived experiences and perceptions of 25 former National Football League (NFL) players regarding the financial decisions they made when active as players for information that could lead to an appropriate model for making good financial decisions. Determined in the qualitative phenomenological study were the influential factors identified by the participants in the study that focused on financial decisions made by former NFL players. The study revealed five themes: (1) wealth enablers, (2) wealth killers, (3) challenges, (4) attitudes and (5) wealth weak spots.

## CONCLUSION

This chapter has explored and examined the concepts and methods of phenomenology. With the aim of studying and understanding the 'lived experience', phenomenology offers sports management researchers the opportunity to delve into previously under-researched phenomena. A phenomenological research approach has value in that it critically analyses phenomena as they present in sport and sport management for deeper understanding of the universal meanings of the phenomena that occur in these fields. Phenomenology can be used to address some of the more under-explored areas in Sport Management Research such as the lived experiences of athletes attempting to excel in a non-traditional gender-specific sport, or the daily experiences of a sport manager operating at an elite level in a worldwide sporting event, where the sport management researcher seeks to understand the human condition as much as the lived experience of the phenomenon itself. For this reason, such research can lead one in the direction of uncovering the meaning of lived experience from the subjective perspectives of the persons who participate. This approach therefore has the ability to foster understanding of many of the complex and perplexing conditions in which sport managers find themselves.

## REVIEW QUESTIONS

Phenomenology seeks to identify and understand the lived experience of individuals. With a basic understanding now of phenomenology, an alternative to the more traditional methodologies associated with Sport Management Research, attempt to answer the following questions:

- Is there any place within Sport Management Research for phenomenology? Explain your reasons.
- Identify those key features of Husserl's and Heidegger's approach to phenomenology that you believe would enable an effective analysis of the lived experience of a sport manager.

## SUGGESTED EXTENDED READING FOR STUDENTS

Kerry, D. S., and Armour, K. M. (2000). Sports sciences and the promise of phenomenology: Philosophy, method, and insight. *Quest, 52*(1), 1–17.

McAllister, S. L. (2006). Women administrators' perceptions of the contribution of competitive sport experiences to their career paths and leadership practices. Unpublished doctoral dissertation, Illinois State University, Bloomington.

Thomas, S. P. and Pollio, H. R. (2002). *Listening to patients: A phenomenological approach to nursing research and practice.* New York: Springer.

van Manen, M. (1990). *Researching lived experience – Human science for an action sensitive pedagogy.* Ontario, Canada: The University of Western Ontario.

## Chapter 14

# Emerging qualitative approaches for the sport management researcher to consider

## LEARNING OUTCOMES

By the end of this chapter you should be able to:

■ recognize some key features of social network theory, whiteness studies, race/critical race theory, disability studies, visual sociology and participant authored audiovisual stories;
■ distinguish between these different emerging methodologies;
■ identify some applications of these methodologies to Sport Management Research;
■ understand the concepts of postcolonialism and globalization;
■ identify some implications of the application of postcolonialism and globalization approaches to research in sport management;
■ distinguish between postcolonialism and globalization;
■ reflect on how the process of globalization has impacted on world sport.

## KEY TERMS

*Social network* – is a social structure made of nodes (which are generally individuals or organizations) that are tied by one or more specific types of interdependency, such as values, visions, ideas, financial exchange, friendship, kinship, dislike, conflict or trade.

*Race/critical race theory* – investigates the social constructions of race and discrimination that are present in society.

*Disability studies* – an interdisciplinary field of study that is focused on the contributions, experiences, history and culture of people with disabilities.

*Visual sociology* – a research approach concerned with the visual dimensions of social life.

*Participant authored audiovisual stories* – deal with qualitative research methodology based on sound and image data, in particular with audiovisual stories authored by the research participants.

*Postcolonialism* – challenges Western science as the unique source of knowledge production and uncovers inequities related to gender, race and class resulting from the process of colonization and post-colonization.

*Globalization* – in general terms it is a means to explain the intricacy and variability of the ways in which the world is restructuring.

## KEY THEMES

■ What is social network theory?
■ What is whiteness studies?
■ What are race theory and critical race theory?
■ What is disability studies?
■ What is visual sociology?
■ What are participant authored audiovisual stories?
■ What are postcolonialism and globalization?
■ What are the potential benefits from applying these research designs to sport management contexts?
■ What are the implications for applying postcolonialism and globalization theories to Sport Management Research processes?

## CHAPTER OVERVIEW

This chapter provides an outline of some emerging issues for future Sport Management Research and demonstrates how they can be situated in the Sport Management Research field. Social network theory, whiteness studies, race and critical race studies, disability studies, visual sociology, participant authored audiovisual stories; postcolonialism and globalization are research methods that need to be considered for future research projects. Each in its own way presents opportunities for sport management knowledge to be extended through its application. This chapter briefly outlines the basic principles that underpin these approaches and suggests how they might be applied in the field of sport management.

## INTRODUCTION

Research in the field of sport management is still perceived as neutral and apolitical, which explains why sensitive issues related to race, gender and class need to evolve. A diversity of perspectives such as those outlined in this chapter equip us to meet the epistemological imperative of giving voice to subjugated knowledge and the social mandates of uncovering existing inequities and addressing the social aspects of sport.

To varying degrees, sport management researchers have been slow to embrace approaches utilized in the social sciences. However, these research approaches have the potential to become acceptable forms of research within sport management.

## SOCIAL NETWORK THEORY AND SPORT MANAGEMENT RESEARCH

### What is social network theory?

A *social network* is a social structure made of nodes that are generally individuals or organizations. The nodes are tied by one or more specific types of interdependency, such as values, visions, ideas, financial exchange, friendship, kinship, dislike, conflict or trade. The resulting structures are often very complex. Social network analysis views social relationships in terms of *nodes* and *ties*. Nodes are the individual actors (athlete, fan, administration, etc.) within the networks, and ties are the relationships between the actors. There can be many kinds of ties between the nodes. Research in a number of academic fields has shown that social networks operate on many levels, and play a critical role in determining the way problems are solved, organizations are run, and the degree to which individuals succeed in achieving their goals. In its simplest form, a social network is a map of all of the relevant ties between the nodes being studied. The network can also be used when determining the social capital of individual actors. These concepts are often displayed in a social network diagram where nodes are the points and ties are the lines.

Social network analysis (related to network theory) has emerged as a key technique in a range of disciplines: modern sociology, anthropology, sociolinguistics, geography, social psychology, communication studies, information science, organizational studies, economics and biology, as well as a popular topic of speculation and study.

For over a century people have used the social network metaphor to connote complex sets of relationships between members of social systems at all scales, from interpersonal to international. In 1954, J. A. Barnes started using the term systematically to denote patterns of ties that cut across the concepts traditionally used by the public and social scientists: bounded groups (e.g. tribes, families) and social categories (e.g. gender, ethnicity). Over time other scholars expanded the use of social networks.

### The benefits of social network analysis

Social network analysis has diverged from being a suggestive metaphor to an analytic approach to a paradigm. It has its own theoretical statements, methods, social network analysis software, and researchers. Analysts reason from whole to part; from structure to relation to individual; from behaviour to attitude. They either study whole networks (also known as complete networks), all of the ties containing specified relations in a defined population, or personal networks, (also known as egocentric networks) the ties that specified people have, such as their 'personal communities'.

The analytic tendencies that distinguish social network analysis are identified as follows:

■ There is no assumption that groups are the building blocks of society: the approach is open to studying less-bounded social systems, from non-local communities to links among web sites.

■ Rather than treating individuals (persons, organizations, states) as discrete units of analysis, it focuses on how the structure of ties affects individuals and their relationships.

■ In contrast to analyses that assume that socialization into norms determines behaviour, network analysis looks to see the extent to which the structure and composition of ties affect norms.

The shape of a social network helps determine a network's worth to its individuals. Networks that are smaller can be less useful to their members than networks with lots of loose connections (weak ties) to individuals outside the main network. On the other hand, more open networks with many weak ties and social connections, are more likely to introduce new ideas and opportunities to their members than closed networks with many redundant ties. In other words, a sport organization that discusses things with each other or hires from the same network of people already shares the same knowledge and opportunities. A sport organization with connections to other social worlds is likely to have access to a wider range of information. A sport organization may be more successful if they have connections to a variety of networks rather than many connections within a single network. Similarly, individuals can exercise influence or act as brokers within their social networks by bridging two networks that are not directly linked. This process is known as filling structural holes.

The power of social network analysis stems from its difference from traditional social scientific studies, which assume that it is the attributes of individual actors that determine whether they are friendly or unfriendly. Social network analysis produces an alternate view, where the attributes of individuals are less important than their relationships and ties with other actors within the network. This approach has turned out to be useful for explaining many real-world phenomena, but leaves less room for individual agency, the ability for individuals to influence their success, because so much of it rests within the structure of their network.

Social networks have also been used as a method for exploring ways in which organizations interact with each other, characterizing the many informal connections that link sport executives together, as well as associations and connections between individual employees at different sport organizations. To illustrate, power within sport organizations often comes more from the degree to which an individual within a network is at the centre of many relationships than an actual job title. Social networks also play a key role in recruiting in sport organizations, in business success and in job performance. Networks also provide ways for organizations to gather information, deter competition and collude in setting prices or policies.

**221**

## Applying social network theory to Sport Management Research

According to Quatman (2006), studies using social network analysis have yet to be explored in any realm of the discipline of sport management. She argues that while the idea of social influence is often implied or referred to in sport management literature on consumer behaviour, conceptual and empirical studies specifically integrating the role others play in influencing others' behaviours and attitudes are limited. Although consumer behaviour is used as the primary example here, the same critique can be applied to many of the topics of interest in the field.

Quatman (2006) identified that Sport Management Research traditionally focuses on identifying and measuring the personal attributes, attitudes and perceptions of individuals. Similarly, individuals conforming to social norms (i.e. gender, race or ethnic variables) are often used as explanatory elements for many sport management studies. Paradoxically then, Quatman suggests that individuals are often assumed to be acting in complete isolation of one another, while at the same time, individuals are construed as strong conformers to social norms. Individuals' behaviours are therefore automatically believed to be a relative function of deliberate choice based on reason, serendipitous contact or 'socially con-straining factors' (p. 11). However, Quatman highlights that individuals do not function in vacuums, whether social or environmental, and are driven to action by 'both conscious and subconscious motives' (p. 11), yet 'decision making, attitudinal formation, and other processes of interest in Sport Management Research often embrace one of these two extreme approaches taking on either an over-socialized or an under-socialized view of the world' (p. 11).

Quatman (2006) argues that the capabilities of traditional methods of research have not allowed for sufficient integration of social influence into measurement and interpretation techniques. Although sport management studies often explain philosophical and paradigmatic approaches that incorporate social interaction and processes as necessary components, conventional analytical instruments have been insufficient for testing a social reality of such complexity. She suggests:

> by providing analytical tools for overturning some of the under-socialized and over-socialized limitations of the more conventional research methods, social network techniques may indeed prove to be a valuable methodological approach for investigating even more diverse topics and domains in the field of sport management. (p. 11)

### RECENT CASE EXAMPLE: SOCIAL NETWORK

*The following article is an example of how social network has been used in the past by researchers in Sport Management Research. The interested reader may wish to find/download and read the article for further insights.*

The social construction of knowledge in the field of sport management: A social network perspective. Quatman, C. and Chelladurai, P. (2008). *Journal of Sport Management, 22*, 651–676.

The works of Kuhn (1996) and other scholars on the social construction of knowledge suggest that great insight can be gained about an academic field of study by investigating interaction patterns between and among scholars. Using a social network perspective, the intent of this study was to empirically explore the social interaction patterns among scholars in the field of sport management. A network model of co-authorship was generated using several rounds of sampling of scholars in the field and archival data collection from relevant journals. The derived network structure was then explored both visually and quantitatively for meaningful patterns. The results of the study essentially tell a story of the evolution and current state of the field's collaboration structure. Drawing on propositions from the literature on the sociology of scientific knowledge generation, the findings are discussed relative to what the obtained network structure might hold for sport management scholarship.

# WHITENESS STUDIES AND SPORT MANAGEMENT RESEARCH

## What is whiteness studies?

Whiteness studies is an interdisciplinary arena of academic inquiry focused on the cultural, historical and sociological aspects of people identified as white. Since the mid 1990s, a number of publications across many disciplines have analysed the social construction of *whiteness* as an ideology tied to social status.

A central belief of whiteness is that race is said to have been constructed by a white power structure in order to justify discrimination against non-whites. Significant areas of research include the nature of white identity and white privilege, the historical process by which a white racial identity was created and the relation of culture to white identity. A reflexive understanding of such assumptions underpins work within the field of whiteness studies.

No longer content with accepting whiteness as the norm, critical scholars have turned their attention to whiteness itself. In the field of *critical white studies*, numerous thinkers investigate such questions as:

■ How was whiteness invented and why?
■ How has the category of whiteness changed over time?
■ Can some individual people be both white and non-white at different times and what does it mean to 'pass for white'?
■ At what point does pride for being white cross the line into white power and white supremacy?
■ What can whites concerned over racial inequity or white privilege do about it?

**223**

**RECENT CASE EXAMPLE: WHITENESS STUDIES.**

*The following article is an example of how whiteness studies has been used in the past by researchers in Sport Management Research. The interested reader may wish to find/download and read the article for further insights.*

> Reality bites? The cultural politics of Generation X and youthful white masculinities in sport and popular culture in 1990s America. Kusz, K. W. (2003). Unpublished doctoral dissertation. University of Illinois at Urbana-Champaign. 3086108

In this dissertation, Kusz produces a critical conjunctural analysis of the themes and meanings articulated with a number of youthful white masculinities throughout the 1990s in American sport and popular culture that are simultaneously constituted by, and constitutive of, the Generation X discursive formation of this era. He highlights how 1990s American popular culture offers images of white males as different, victimized, marginalized, unprivileged and as both hyper-masculinized and feminized. According to Kusz, such images of white masculinity are best understood as instruments and effects of a white male backlash politics that seeks to disavow and deny the privileged position of white masculinity in order to re-secure its central, privileged and normative position within a historical conjuncture of social, cultural, political and economic changes that have threatened it. He proposes that his investigations of these various cultural productions of youthful white masculinity within American sport and popular culture during the 1990s are grounded in the ideas of the British cultural studies tradition and the relatively new field of whiteness studies.

## RACE THEORY, CRITICAL RACE THEORY AND SPORT MANAGEMENT RESEARCH

### What are race theory and critical race theory?

Race theory and critical race theory are fields of inquiry that examine the social construction of race and discrimination that are present in society. Both fields emphasize the socially constructed nature of race, consider the workings of power, and oppose the constitution of all forms of subordination. Table 14.1 lists some of the key features of critical race theory.

Most recent attention in the field of race studies has occurred in the field of critical race theory (CRT). CRT is part of the milieu of critical legal studies (CLS), as a field of inquiry that argues that preserving the interests of power, rather than the demands of principle and precedent, is the guiding force behind legal judgements. Table 14.2 lists some of the major themes in CRT writings.

Race theory and CRT share an overlapping literature with both CLS and critical theory, feminist studies and postcolonial theory.

**Table 14.1** *Features of CRT*

*Critical race theory*

- Key names: Derrick Bell, William Tate, Gloria Ladson-Billings, Richard Delgado
- Derived from critical legal studies in the 1960s
- Explores the role of race in society
- Questions racism and White privilege
- Provides a space for histories of people of colour
- Describes whiteness as a form of property
- Race goes beyond colour, it includes class
- Discussion of race: beyond semantics, back to class and inequality
- CRT derivations: queer theory, Critical Asian Scholarship

**Table 14.2** *Major themes in CRT writings*

*Critical race theory*

- A critic of liberalism
- Storytelling/counter-storytelling and 'naming one's own reality'
- Revisionist interpretations of American Civil Rights law and progress
- Applying insights from social science writing on race and racism to legal problems
- Structural determinism, how the structures of legal thought or culture influence content
- The intersections of race, sex and class
- Essentialism and anti-essentialism
- Cultural nationalism/separatism as well as empowering black nationalism, power or insurrection
- Legal institutions, critical pedagogy and minorities on the bar
- Criticism and self-criticism

Source: Delgado and Stefancic (1993)

## Applications to sport management

Race studies has emerged as an academic area of inquiry since the 1960s; however, it is only recently that race studies have attracted the attention of sport scholars. Although there have been a number of studies investigating under-representation of racial groups and racial stacking in sport, particularly in the USA context, very little ideological analysis has occurred. We would encourage sport management researchers to imbue such studies with an investigation on race studies.

CRT thought has been applied in a variety of contexts where socialized and institutionalized oppression of racial minorities has been litigated in the courts. Football (soccer) players from many countries have been the subject of racist chants and comments. Despite FIFA's attempts to develop policies to rid this racism from the game, particular problems remain. In a non-sporting context Delgado and Stefancic (1993) draw on CRT in calling for tort action for racial insults, looking to the historical action of speech and the serious psychological harm inflicted on its victims as just measure for evaluating hate speech. The application of this type of research would be useful to sport administrators.

## RECENT CASE EXAMPLE: CRITICAL RACE STUDIES

*The following article is an example of how critical race studies has been used in the past by researchers in Sport Management Research. The interested reader may wish to find/download and read the article for further insights.*

White eyes on Black bodies: History, performance, and resistance in the National Basketball Association. Griffin, R. (2008). Unpublished doctoral dissertation. University of Denver. 3320573

This research focused on the performance of black masculinity in the context of a predominantly white professional sports organization. More specifically, the purpose of this dissertation was to critically deconstruct the contemporary National Basketball Association (NBA) and to explore the embodied performance of black masculinity. To do so, the NBA was positioned as a racialized organization relying upon critical race theory (CRT). CRT and theories of performance were utilized to (re)construct black masculinity. Understandings of black masculinity were (re)constructed based upon the narrative insights gleaned from the critical ethnographic interviews of eight past black professional basketball players. Six themes emerged from the interview data including: (1) getting to the ABA/NBA, (2) speaking on the current league, (3) reflections on past and present racism in professional basketball, (4) performing progressive black masculinities, (5) speaking to younger generations, and (6) reflections on the black community. The overarching conclusions drawn from this study indicate that race and racism do in fact matter in professional basketball. Likewise, new understandings of the performance of progressive black masculinities are offered as well.

## OTHER RELATED FORMS OF SPORT MANAGEMENT INQUIRY

### Ethnic studies and Sport Management Research

*Ethnic studies* is the study of ethnicity. It developed toward the end of the twentieth century partly in response to charges that traditional disciplines had a dominant eurocentric perspective. Ethnic studies attempt to examine minority cultures on their own terms, in their own language, and according to their own value system.

From this perspective, sport managers may investigate the influence of specific ethnic groups and their position in sport within defined cultural contexts: for example, the influence of Latino players in US baseball, African football players, sport in ethnic groups and the problems of integration.

---

### RECENT CASE EXAMPLE: ETHNIC STUDIES

The following article is an example of how ethnic studies has been used in the past by researchers in Sport Management Research. The interested reader may wish to find/download and read the article for further insights.

> Along ethnic lines: A quantitative analysis of football athletes' interest in coaching as a career. Bernhard, L. (2010). Unpublished doctoral dissertation. The University of North Carolina at Chapel Hill. 1477519

This study posed two questions: first, are there any significant differences related to ethnicity in the five social cognitive career theory factors? Second, is there a significant difference between an athlete's interest and intention in the coaching career based on the ethnicity of his position as coach or coordinator? A sample of student-athletes ($N = 134$) who were members of the football team at three Division I institutions in the South-east were targeted. The results indicated differences between black and white athletes for both self-efficacy ($p = .009$) and barriers ($p < .0005$).

---

## DIASPORA STUDIES AND SPORT MANAGEMENT RESEARCH

*Diaspora studies* is an academic field that was established in the late twentieth century to study dispersed ethnic populations. These groups are referred to as diaspora peoples. The term diaspora implies forced resettlement, due to expulsion, slavery, racism or war, especially national conflict. Areas of interest in diaspora studies for sport management researchers could include sport in conflict zones such as Iraq and Afghanistan, and sport and refugees.

---

### RECENT CASE EXAMPLE: DIASPORA

The following article is an example of how diaspora studies has been used in the past by researchers in Sport Management Research. The interested reader may wish to find/download and read the article for further insights.

> Cultural identity: Sport, gender, nationalism and the Irish diaspora. Black, M. F. (1997). Unpublished doctoral dissertation. University of California, Berkeley. 9803128

**227**

This ethnography is based on fieldwork carried out in the San Francisco Bay Area between 1992 and 1996. The research was conducted on two groups of Irish-born immigrants. One group of men were part of a Gaelic football team, and the other group of women played on a soccer team. This work explores issues of cultural identity and examines how identity is invented, reinvented, negotiated and changed. The study lends support to the notion that identity is dynamic, always 'in process' (Hall, 1993). It notes how identity is mediated by sport, nationalism, gender and globalizing forces and effects. This research also demonstrates how myths of national and ethnic identity are subject to manipulation and revision. All involved struggled with the 'doubleness' of the diasporan experience, which both weakened and strengthened their sense of connection to the homeland. In leaving their homeland their Irish identities were modified or 'translated' (Hall, 1993). They forged new identities in the US without simply assimilating and losing their 'Irish' identities completely. They could no longer associate with one particular 'home' as they were now part of several 'homes'. For the men in this study Gaelic games, masculinity and nationalism were all interwoven. Although they made conscious efforts to renew and intensify their Irishness in the US, their experience in the Bay Area had changed them in that they now considered Ireland with some ambivalence. This study also indicated how the context of sport was an ideal site for examining the renegotiation of identity.

## DISABILITY STUDIES AND SPORT MANAGEMENT RESEARCH

### What is disability studies?

Disability studies is an interdisciplinary field of study that is focused on the contributions, experiences, history and culture of people with disabilities. The field of teaching and research in the area of disability is growing worldwide. It is based on the premise that disadvantage typically experienced by those who are disabled reflects primarily on the way society defines and responds to certain types of difference. The definition of disability studies is contested by those coming from different epistemologies. Table 14.3 outlines some of the major features of disability studies.

Disability studies is not without its critics. It has been suggested that the dominant social model, developed in the 1970s, has now been outgrown, and requires major developments. Disability studies has also been criticized for its failure to engage with multiple forms of oppression, such as racism, sexism or homophobia. As a relatively new discipline, it is true that as yet disability studies has seen little progress in this area. More recently, the concept of *critical disability studies* has started to emerge in the social sciences. Publications are now beginning to emerge though, and in time it is hoped that this issue will be fully engaged by researchers, including sport management researchers.

Within sport management a few studies have examined disability. However, to date studies have not studied specific sport management issues from a disabilities studies perspective.

**Table 14.3** *Defining disability studies*

*Disability studies*

- should be interdisciplinary/multidisciplinary
- should challenge the view of disability as an individual deficit or defect that can be remedied solely through medical intervention or rehabilitation by 'experts' and other service providers
- should study national and international perspectives, policies literature, culture and history with the aim of placing current ideas of disability within their broadest possible context
- should actively encourage participation in disabled students and faculty, and should ensure physical and intellectual access
- should make a priority to have leadership positions held by disabled people, at the same time it is important to create an environment where contributions from anyone who shares the above goals are welcome

Research in this area is urgently needed. The Special Olympics and Paralympics provide important fertile ground for research as opposed to ploughing back over the same farrowed fields of professional sport. Gilbert and Schantz (2008) have added to this area of Sport Management Research on disability through their publication of an edited book on the Paralympics.

## RECENT CASE EXAMPLE: DISABILITY STUDIES

The following article is an example of how disability studies has been used in the past by researchers in Sport Management Research. The interested reader may wish to find/download and read the article for further insights.

> Paralympic masculinities: Media and self-representation of athletes at the 2008 Paralympic Summer Games. Stevenson, D. (2010). Unpublished doctoral dissertation. University of Manitoba (Canada). MR69718

This study uses content analysis of newspaper articles and athlete biographical/autobiographical sources to examine the constructions of masculinity of male and female athletes at the 2008 Paralympic Summer Games in Beijing, China. Based on the socially constructed tension between disability and masculinity and the connections between sport and masculinity, this study sought examples that support or challenge the portrayal of Paralympic athletes in hegemonic masculine terms. This study finds that in the majority of cases, both sets of data sources reflect and/or reinforce the association between sport and hegemonic masculinity. This public display of masculinity indicates the athletes' attempt to attain mainstream acceptance and legitimacy as 'real' athletes as much as it does a rejection of a collective disability identity.

## VISUAL SOCIOLOGY AND SPORT MANAGEMENT RESEARCH

### What is visual sociology?

Visual sociology is an emerging field in the social sciences. Despite this, its theoretical and methodological contributions are just becoming known. Visual sociology is a research approach concerned with the visual dimensions of social life. It includes the study of all kinds of visual material and the visual social world, and uses all kinds of visual material in its methodologies such as photographs, film, tape and video to study society as well as the study of the visual artefacts of a society. Visual sociology is viewed as suited to data gathering technologies for small group interactions, ethnography and oral history.

### Theory and method

There are at least three approaches to visual sociology:

### 1 Data collection using cameras and other recording technology

In this first sense visual sociology means including and incorporating visual methods of data gathering and analysis in the work of research. Visual recording technology allows manipulation of data because they make it possible to speed up, slow down, repeat, stop and zoom in on things of interest.

In a sport management context this methodological approach is routinely utilized by venue managers as they collect visual data through security cameras, to monitor the behaviour of spectators and to observe behavioural patterns that may lead to security or safety issues. These 'observations' could be the basis for a more formalized research inquiry, if ethically approved. In this way new knowledge and understanding of facility management may evolve that assists the facility manager to better understand the behaviour of fans in their venues.

### 2 Studying visual data produced by cultures

The second approach of visual sociology is to study the visual products of society – their production, consumption and meaning. Visual images are constructed and may be deconstructed and read as texts in a variety of ways.

In a sport management context, Gilbert (2008) utilized visual sociology methods for understanding the visual culture of the Olympic Games host city of Beijing. He examined a range of visual sub-cultures including architecture, space and place, landscape, art, ceremonies, cultural displays as well as people's lives and fashion. Gilbert suggests that the possibility of conceiving the visual culture of Olympic host cities as a holistic entity raises the problem of devising broader more encompassing visual-centric methodologies for London 2012.

### 3 Communication with images and media other than words

A third approach of visual sociology is both the use of visual media to communicate sociological understandings to professional and public audiences, and also the use of visual media within sociological research itself. The research brief below is a sport example of this form of visual sociology research. In a sport management context researchers could, for example, use a combination of narrative and photographs to seek a more effective way of understanding just how facility managers see and experience their environment on game day. The importance of subjecting routine understandings and practices to detailed analysis in this way allows the lives of these 'social actors' to be analysed in a unique way and provide new understanding of their 'lived experiences'.

---

### RECENT CASE EXAMPLE: VISUAL SOCIOLOGY

*The following article is an example of how visual sociology has been used in the past by researchers in Sport Management Research. The interested reader may wish to find/download and read the article for further insights.*

> Seeing the way: Visual sociology and the distance runner's perspective. Hockey, J. and Collinson, J. A. (2006). *Visual Studies, 21*(1), 70–81.

Employing visual and autoethnographic data from a two-year research project on distance runners, this research examined the activity of seeing in relation to the activity of distance running. One of its methodological aims is to develop the linkage between visual and auto-ethnographic data in combining an observation-based narrative and sociological analysis with photographs. This combination aimed to convey to the reader not only some of the specific sub-cultural knowledge and particular ways of seeing, but also something of the runner's embodied feelings and experience of momentum en route. Via the combination of narrative and photographs the authors sought a more effective way of communicating just how distance runners see and experience their training terrain.

---

## PARTICIPANT AUTHORED AUDIOVISUAL STORIES AND SPORT MANAGEMENT RESEARCH

### What are participant authored audiovisual stories?

Participant authored audiovisual stories (PAAS) are a controversial new approach that we believe has possibilities in Sport Management Research particularly in the area of consumer behaviour and insider knowledge. PAAS deals with qualitative research methodology based on sound and image data, in particular with audiovisual stories authored by the research participants. As a research method, PAAS promises a sound platform from which to explore social phenomena, especially when what is at stake is an understanding of the relationship between the agency of subjects and their sociocultural contexts.

According to Harrison (2002) visual research is still viewed as a marginal practice. Despite its marginality, Ramella and Olmos (2005) argue that research methodologies based on sound

**231**

and image data open up a vast field of opportunities, one that is rapidly capitalizing on many of the twists and turns of societal change: from the fast development of audiovisual technologies, and the improvements in digital communications, to the growing case made in the social sciences against the hegemony of the written text and the incorporation of audiovisual languages into our everyday lives (p. 3). Ramella and Olmos go on to describe the process in the following way:

> Described in a nutshell, research participants create their own stories around a more or less determined problem. For this purpose they utilize audio-visual media, that is, video cameras or photo-cameras or a radio, just to cite some. Further, they draw on a variety of genre to organize their stories, for example, an autobiography, a documentary or a drama. According to the genre selected, stories may include personal testimonies, or fictional enactment of life episodes; they may also include stories by other people (e.g. street interviews by research participants to lay people). Here the list can be limitless. Also, being in possession of the audio-visual media provide participants ample latitude to situate themselves, and importantly, their stories. Situating a story should not be restricted to a physical location; it also means situating it socially (who else is there?), and culturally (what is in it?). (p. 3)

PAAS has been successfully utilized in many projects and offers in particular the potential for research participants to *own* the story, to express it and articulate it in close relation to their everyday life social and cultural context (Ramella and Olmos, 2005).

---

## RECENT CASE EXAMPLE: PAAS

### The Positive Futures programme project

As a social inclusion programme, Positive Futures runs over 100 multi-agency partnership projects across England and Wales. Partners include statutory (e.g. Young Offending Teams, Social Services, etc.) and voluntary agencies (e.g. youth centres, football clubs, etc.). The rationale of Positive Futures works as follows: projects attract and engage with young people, work with them – mainly on sport-based activities – and facilitate their insertion in the labour market or education.

Running alongside Positive Futures, there is a programme of research and evaluation aiming to identify and establish the value that the programme has for its main stakeholders. For this purpose, the research and evaluation programme draws on quantitative and qualitative methods, including six-monthly lead agency surveys, yearly partner agency surveys, project documentation review, case studies and PAAS. General and particular aspects of Positive Futures research and evaluation strategy appear in Ramella (2004).

The goal of PAAS in Positive Futures is to explore not just the perception of young people *about* Positive Futures, but the *relationship* between young people, Positive Futures and the local communities. More specifically, stories provide accounts of how young people position themselves in relation to their sociocultural contexts, including Positive Futures. In so doing, stories contribute to the overall research and evaluation strategy by unearthing knowledge regarding not just what taking part in such an initiative *means* to them (as intended target of the programme) but importantly, by providing insight on the extent to which it *relates to their everyday lives* (Humphreys *et al.* 2003, 2004).

## POSTCOLONIALISM AND SPORT MANAGEMENT RESEARCH

### Postcolonial ideological discourse

The term *postcolonialism* is a challenging one. Just like *post-structuralism* and *postmodernism*, it has multiple meanings and implications when used. It is also highly criticized (Viruru and Cannella, 2001). Cannella and Bailey (1999) argued that postcolonial scrutiny and insights could have potential for influencing research, perhaps even challenging Western constructions of research. 'Postcolonialism' continues to generate dissatisfaction among practitioners and detractors alike, of which some (most notably those who equate postcolonial studies with postmodernism) now suggest the term may have outlived its usefulness (see San Juan, *Beyond Postcolonial Theory*, 1998; Hardt and Negri, *Empire*, 2000).

Postcolonial study is a relatively recent ideological discourse. It represents a critical response by the former colonized to the various forms and processes of Western domination and subjugation resulting from the colonial encounter. The colonial enterprise has left former colonies suffering from wounds that appear to deepen rather than heal. In virtually every aspect of their lives, former colonized people contend with the repercussions of their encounter with European colonizers. In response, postcolonial theorists engage in discussions about a host of experiences relating to slavery and colonialism such as suppression, resistance, representation, difference, race, gender and social class. Within these broader themes, specific issues such as the primacy of the colonizer's language, religion, cultural histories, knowledge and other elements of identity over that of the local peoples is topical in the postcolonial conversation. Global sport, especially football, rugby and cricket brought by the British Empire may have transcended some of the negativity left by colonizers, and can be studied as a positive change.

Postcolonial studies, therefore, is an academic space in which to contest hegemonic ideologies and impositions, which continue to oppress and confuse formerly colonized peoples who now inhabit what is called the 'developing world' (hereafter, Third World or postcolonial societies). McConaghy (2000) suggests that while postcolonialism draws on post-structuralism and postmodernism, it does not overlap neatly with them.

### Defining postcolonialism

Postcolonialism challenges Western science as the unique source of knowledge production and uncovers inequities related to gender, race and class resulting from the process of colonization and postcolonization. This discourse is especially pertinent to sport management as it brings to the forefront these issues and makes explicit how these socially constructed categories have been used in the colonizing process, and the effect that this has had on people's lives and life opportunities.

Colonization is defined by Said (2000) as: the expansive force of a people; it is its power of reproduction; it is its enlargement and its multiplication through space; it is the subjugation of the universe or the vast part of it to that people's language, customs, ideas and laws. Postcolonialism is the process of postcolonializing. Quayson (2000) suggests that to understand this process (postcolonializing), it is necessary to disentangle the term, postcolonial, from its implicit dimension of chronological supersession, that aspect of its prefix that suggests that the colonial stage has been surpassed and left behind. It is important to highlight instead a notion of the term as a process of coming into being and of struggle against colonialism and its after-effects.

More specifically, the postcolonial approach is directed at uncovering the exclusionary effects of dominant ideologies in 'Othering' other forms of knowledge – the subjugated knowledge. Foucault (1980) defines subjugated knowledge as a whole set of knowledge that has been disqualified as inadequate to its task or insufficiently elaborated: naïve knowledge, located low down in the hierarchy, beneath the required level of cognition or scientificity.

According to Quayson (2000), postcolonialism focuses on dominant discourses and ideologies that shape the social world to look at the material effects of subjugation. Subjugation is the process by which imperialism and colonialism impose a condition of positional superiority over the colonized (Said, 2000). The process is to ground contemporary world phenomena such as immigration, unemployment, health problems, into the real world to unmask the interrelations between these phenomena and new colonial ideologies. Consequently, the researcher's aim is to 'relate modern-day phenomena to their explicit, implicit, or even potential relations, to the heritage of colonialism' (Quayson, 2000, p. 11) while decolonizing methodologies and methods (Tuhiwai Smith, 1999), aim to critique the marginalizing effect of Western science on subjugated knowledge.

Applying postcolonialism to Sport Management Research unveils the reductionist Western discourse of essentializing the 'Other' in a unique, crystallized, neutral, rational and objectivist cultural entity. As well, 'decolonializing' methodologies and methods are directed at disrupting the power relations to voice subjugated knowledge. According to Hall (1997) subjectivities emerge from: 'the different constellation of social, cultural and economic forces . . . since we are, in part, constructed as subjects through the particular layering of historical discourses, which we inhabit, then new kinds of sensibilities begin to be clearly discernible' (p. 247). Postcolonial scholarship in Sport Management Research is limited; however, important work has been produced in which issues and concerns of postcolonialism and sport are discussed.

## How can postcolonialism be articulated in Sport Management Research?

The development of postcolonial scholarship in sport management depends on our abilities to define new theories and methods to explore and understand cultural differences, and to challenge dominant culture stereotypes instead of trying to change the subaltern, as proposed by culturalist models. Also, sport issues related to racial, gendered and class discrimination need to be part of the sport management social mandate. Given this era of increasing cultural intolerance, the harmful effects of racial, gendered and social discrimination on sport management must be recognized. Postcolonial research is a theoretical perspective that moves us away from the shortcomings of cultural essentialism, since culture cannot be isolated from the broader social context within which it comes into play together with a constellation of other structural factors. This theoretical approach provides the analytic lens to examine the extent to which Sport Management Research and practice perpetuate dominance through our everyday practice. However, it should be remembered that research cannot be neutral, apolitical or ahistorical since sport management is governed by normalizing discourses and practices.

Furthermore, there is the complex question of political commitment and its relation to scholarly inquiry. Undoubtedly, it is a core issue to be addressed in sport management, and postcolonial research provides the analytical framework to perform such reflection. Nevertheless, postcolonial research warns us to distance ourselves from the expert role in acknowledging the anthropological construction of sport. Democratization of Sport Management Research can be realized by recognizing 'subjugated knowledge' as a legitimate source of theorization, adapting sport management interventions to meet the needs of people located at the margins of pluralist societies. If social justice is ever to be achieved in the sport system, voices of the subaltern have to be heard. In this sense, postcolonialism questions the appropriateness of culturist theories to correct such issues as managerial imbalances stemming from social discrepancies and neocolonial ideologies.

Finally, postcolonialism is not specifically directed at developing knowledge for the sake of knowledge. Giroux (2002) describes this strategy as the 'most retrograde academic use' (p. 98) of knowledge since it evacuates the possibilities of challenging the status quo. Anderson (2000) emphasizes that deconstructing and rewriting 'taken-for-granted' knowledge, and redefining relations of power and privilege is a step towards achieving social justice.

## RECENT CASE EXAMPLE: POSTCOLONIALISM

*The following article is an example of how postcolonialism has been used in the past by researchers in Sport Management Research. The interested reader may wish to find/download and read the article for further insights.*

> Transnational television and football in francophone Africa: The path to electronic colonization? Akindes, G. A. (2010). Unpublished doctoral dissertation. Ohio University. 3413017

This study aimed to understand and to explain how television broadcasting's political and technological changes in the late 1990s induced electronic colonialism in francophone Africa. This qualitative study was conducted in Senegal, Côte d'Ivoire, Benin, Burkina and Cameroon. It constituted at first the goal to achieve an understanding of the intricacies of football television broadcasting by public, private and transnational television broadcasters. The in-depth interviews, documents analysis and field observations provided required data to analyse transnational television broadcasting in francophone Africa within the theoretical framework of Thomas McPhail's (2006) electronic colonialism.

## From theory to method

Possibly the greatest challenge in our call for a postcolonial sport management scholarship lies in the translation of its theoretical tenets into a method of research. The following section describes a postcolonial research method that has evolved from an exploration of the dialectic between theory and research.

### Framing the research

The first distinction of a postcolonial Sport Management Research method lies in the way in which the entire research project is viewed through a political lens – a lens that attends to the micro politics and macro dynamics of power. While attending to power relations is certainly a methodological theme of other brands of research (for example, feminist research may be the most overt example), a postcolonial framing rests on an overarching mindfulness of how domination and resistance mark intercultural encounters at individual, institutional and societal levels. Thus postcolonial sport management scholarship pursues matters of how contemporary constructions of race, ethnicity and culture continue to rely on colonialist images and patterns of inclusion and exclusion within sport management settings. Careful attention to the social and historical positioning of the sport management researcher vis-à-vis research participants also is paramount to the postcolonial project.

### Linking self and society

Inherent in contemporary postcolonial efforts is the tension between self and society, the local and the global, the particularities of the hybrid moment and the universality of the colonial experience. It is our ability to understand and explain how the nature of the relationship between self and society, the contextualization of subjectivity, is critical to the progress of sport management. We suggest, therefore, that a feature of postcolonial sport management scholarship is situating human experience (or everyday reality) in the larger contexts of mediating social, economic, political and historical forces. Should ex-colonies (e.g. Kenya) continue with the same high performance goals and strive to implement a Western high performance structure, simply because the West has been successful? Or are resources better utilized elsewhere? What is the opportunity cost of Kenya funding high performance structures similar to Western society? Are gold medal marathoners actually benefiting Kenya from a Kenyan point of view, or just a Western point of view?

### Giving voice

The third feature of a postcolonial research method suggested is the deliberate decentring of dominant culture so that the worldviews of the marginalized become the starting point in knowledge construction. A postcolonial commitment results in the weaving of the perspectives and experiences of those marginalized in our society into the very fabric of sport management. Core to the postcolonial movement is the question raised by Gayatri Chakrovorty Spivak's (1988) 'Can the Subaltern speak?' At its most basic level postcolonialism demands the right to speak rather than being spoken for, and to represent oneself rather than being represented or, in the extreme cases, rather than being erased entirely.

A further opportunity for giving voice to previously subjugated voices is the liberal use of poly-vocality in research through strategies such as purposive sampling from diverse groups of participants with a range of experiences, listening carefully to the accounts of these participants, and liberally using their verbatim stories in written reports.

A basic question in postcolonial research has been posed as to whether or not white researchers can truly understand the experiences of issues such as racialization and racism. Some have argued that postcolonial studies in the field are best undertaken by minority scholars; others have argued that such matching of researchers with the researched results in marginalizing certain types of research, making, for example, racism only a concern for racialized groups. We take the position that rather than pursuing the legitimacy of our roles as sport management researchers based on one aspect of one's social identity (e.g. whiteness), one's legitimacy as a sport management researcher is based on one's ability to explicate the ways in which marginalization and racialization operate. Furthermore, acknowledging the interrelatedness of race, class and gender provides important insights for postcolonial sport management inquiry and guards against incomplete and simplistic analyses.

## Emancipatory intent

The final feature of a postcolonial research method is its open commitment to critiquing the status quo and building a more just society. We make the case for emancipatory intent. Praxis-oriented research is research committed to social change. Thus, sport management inquiry within the larger genre of an emancipatory research paradigm is committed to moving beyond the description of what 'is' to providing prescription for what 'ought' to be, and raises our level of investigation from matters of the individual to consideration of larger sociopolitical forces impacting on the common good. The goal of emancipatory sport management researchers is to foster self-reflection and deeper understanding on the part of the researched at least as much as it is to generate empirically grounded theoretical knowledge.

## Method

An important distinction of a postcolonial perspective is that there are no prescribed techniques for data collection or data analysis. In this research approach, different techniques can be drawn on depending on the focus of the inquiry, as long as they meet the criteria for scientific adequacy and rigour.

The hallmark of postcolonial scholarship is a strong research-theory dialectic that brings a particular interpretive lens to the Sport Management Research that recognizes that each life is shaped by history. This lens frames how questions are formulated, who is included in the study, how data are interpreted, the meanings derived from the data, and how research findings are communicated and applied. While we are not limited in the kinds of questions we ask, our questions are framed from a particular epistemological perspective. That is, the postcolonial lens always takes into account the context in which each life is situated, and analyses how gender, race, class and historical positioning intersect at any given moment to organize experience in the here and now.

The postcolonial methodology sketched out here promises us new and important tools for forms of transformative knowledge that have been largely overlooked within sport management scholarship and practice. With such a commitment, postcolonial sport management scholarship will permit more thoughtful attention to the issues of equity and social justice.

---

### RECENT CASE EXAMPLE: POSTCOLONIALISM

*The following article is an example of how postcolonialism has been used in the past by researchers in Sport Management Research. The interested reader may wish to find/download and read the article for further insights.*

> Women's cricket spaces: An examination of female players' experiences in Canada. Razack, S. (2009). Unpublished thesis. University of Toronto (Canada). MR71379

Presently the literature available on women's cricket is very limited. This thesis attempts to redress this gap by telling a story about the experiences of women's club cricket in Toronto and Victoria. The players' social spaces were examined, as were the intersections of gender, race and culture. Using qualitative methods, narratives were interpreted and analysed using *postcolonial*, spatial and feminist theoretical frameworks.

---

## GLOBALIZATION AND SPORT MANAGEMENT RESEARCH

### What is globalization?

Globalization research can be classified in a number of ways. Specifically, it can be characterized based on its focus on specific phenomena of globalization, i.e. economic, political or social. It is, however, important to note that in each of these categories, there are different perspectives, such as neoliberalism, Marxism, neo-Marxism, etc. Sklair (2002) identified that research on globalization can be categorized into four broad approaches: the *global polity and society*; the *world systems*; the *global capitalism*; and the *global cultural* approaches.

The *global polity and society* approach maintains that global polity and society can be achieved only in the modern age with the advancement of science, technology and industry. This body of literature is filled with discussions of the decreasing power and significance of the nation-state and the increasing significance, or actually power of, super-national and global institutions and systems of belief and value (Sklair, 2002). Global sport federations and governing bodies, such as the Internatonal Rugby Board, have existed for over a hundred years, but have increased their power and influence over national governing bodies as the desire for global competitions (e.g. Rugby World Cups) has skyrocketed. The most desirable future, according to those theorists, is the organization of global governance through some global civil society, while globalization is the most potent and necessary drive for that future.

Anthony Giddens (1990) is one of the principal voices of such arguments. Giddens characterizes globalization in terms of four dimensions: the nation-state system, the world military order, the international division of labour and the world capitalist economy. He believes globalization is a consequence of modernity itself because 'modernity is inherently globalizing' (p. 63). The philosophical assumption of this approach is essentially neoliberalism.

The next approach to globalization study is the *world-systems perspective* (Sklair, 2002). This approach is based on the distinction between core, semi-peripheral and peripheral countries in terms of their positions in the international division of labour demanded by the capitalist world-system. Based on the work of Immanuel Wallerstein (1974), social scientific research on world-systems has been developed since the 1970s. Unlike other approaches in which writers are grouped based on the tenets of their work, the world-systems school is a highly institutionalized academic enterprise. This school of thought has been the most systematic available for the analysis of the global system for more than 20 years. The world-system theory closely resembles dependency theory.

An approach that is more sophisticated than the world-system approach is the *global capitalism approach* (Sklair, 2002). For these theorists, the main driving force of globalization is the structure of the ever-more globalizing capitalism (e.g. Robinson, 1996; Ross and Trachte, 1990; Sklair, 2002). In contrast to the world-system approach that focuses on nation-state centred economics, the global capitalism approach strives toward 'a concept of the global that involves more than the relations between nation-states and explanation of national economics competing against each other' (Sklair, 2002, p. 46). Similarly, many national governing bodies cannot thrive on their own, and rely on the economic value of international competition.

The final approach to globalization research is the *global culture* approach (Sklair, 2002). Placing culture at the centre is inspired by Marshall McLuhan's (1964) notion of 'the global village', the very rapid growth of the mass media in scale and scope that has taken place over the last few decades. As sociologist John Tomlinson (1999) puts it, 'Globalization lies at the heart of modern culture; cultural practices lie at the heart of globalization' (p. 1). Huntington (1993, 1996) predicts that the source of future international conflicts lies in the cultural, rather than the political and ideological. Appadurai (1996) developed a fivefold conceptual framework of empirical research on global cultural flows. His categories include ethnoscapes (flows of people), mediascapes (flows of images and information), technoscapes (development and flows of technology), finanscapes (flows of global capital) and ideoscapes (flows of ideologies and movements).

The most widespread form of research within sport and cultural studies as well as sociology is identified as the global culture approach. We have suggested that this is a self-limiting form of research inquiry (Edwards and Skinner, 2006) and have explored the conceptions of a new world order and implications for sport management in our book entitled *Sport Empire*. In this work we explored some of the concepts in this new and controversial form of globalization research.

## Globalization: decentred?

Michael Hardt and Antonio Negri (2000), in their influential work, *Empire*, argue that we experience the irresistible and irreversible globalization of economic and cultural exchanges.

These researchers suggest that with the development of a global market and global circuits of production, we also see the materialization of a global order or a new form of sovereignty. Together with the processes of globalization, sovereignty of nation-states has weakened. Now, the money, technology, people and goods move easily across national borders and the nation-state has less power to regulate these flows. It is more and more common for athletes to seek work in overseas professional systems, and harder for domestic sport organizations to retain their services.

The governing terms of Hardt and Negri's (2000) discussion are 'Empire' and 'Multitude'. It is suggested that along with the global market and global circuits of production a new global order has emerged, a new form of sovereignty based on a new logic and structure of rule. Empire is the political subject that effectively regulates these global exchanges, the sovereign power that governs the world.

Empire does not refer to imperialism; it has no territorial centre of power and does not depend on fixed boundaries. The divisions among three Worlds (First, Second, and Third) have been unclear. It is a decentred and deterritorializing apparatus of rule that progressively incorporates the entire global realm with its open, expanding frontiers. Empire manages hybrid identities, flexible hierarchies and plural exchanges through modulating networks of command (Hardt and Negri, 2000, p. xii).

Multitude is opposed to Empire. Multitude is all those who labour and produce under capital, it is the 'class of productive singularities, the class of the operators of immaterial labor' (Hardt and Negri, 2000). The Multitude however has power that is driven by its desire for liberation from Empire's global structures and networks. Edwards and Skinner (2006) have drawn upon this theoretical framework provided by Hardt and Negri (2000) to critique the implications of a new world order on global sport management.

## Globalization research approach

Essentially, qualitative globalization research may be characterized by three commitments. First, researchers employing globalization approaches seek to understand the world through interacting with, empathizing with and interpreting the actions and perceptions of its actors. Consequently, globalization research methods are used to explore the meanings of people's worlds – the myriad personal impacts of impersonal social structures, and the nature and causes of individual behaviour. Second, globalization qualitative research involves the collection of data in natural settings, rather than in artificial contexts. Third, it tends to explore and generate theory rather than test it. Qualitative globalization methods work inductively, i.e. building up theory from observations; rather than deductively, i.e. testing theories by trying to refute their propositions.

Data generated by qualitative globalization research can provide powerful and critical insights into particular questions. It is, however, important to note that it depends on the theoretical or explanatory frames and the quality of interpretation. They can be used effectively with people or places we think are familiar to us, as well as in situations somewhat removed, geographically and otherwise, from our own. Given the interpenetrating contexts generated by globalizing phenomena, together with associated mobile, trans-local and diasporic communities, much research conducted using qualitative approaches includes the ways in which communities are both tied into and construct trans-local/transnational networks and discourses, such that while people might be organizing and acting at local spatial scales they are consistently framing their identities with reference to larger scale and global contexts.

## Globalization and sport management

The problematic that globalization theorists seek to explain, while dynamic and open-ended, not invariant, may be gleaned from an emerging series of core, linked propositions. Six propositions are highlighted as they relate to Sport Management Research:

1   Many contemporary issues in sport management cannot be explained as local interactions and must be construed as global issues. Although this claim is not unique to globalization studies, at issue is a series of sport problems e.g. doping in sport, the rise of organized crime in sport, global warming threats to sport, and the spread of infectious diseases – which are beyond the regulatory framework of the national sporting organization.

2   Globalization constitutes a structural transformation in world order. As such, sport does not exist in a vacuum separate from the social, economic and environmental context. Questions arise as to how national and international sport organizations respond to this new world order.

3   As a transformation, globalization involves a series of continuities and discontinuities with the past. In other words, there is no escaping historiography. Modern conceptions of sport organization have their foundation in the past.

4   The advent of globalization is fluid. This implies that global sport is an actor in its own right. Transnational sport organizations, national sporting bodies and local sport organizations all influence and are influenced by local and global issues. In opposition to most globalization researchers Hardt and Negri (2000) suggest we need to: 'think globally and act globally'.

5   Given shifting parameters, sport needs to adjust to evolving global structures. International sport organizations, however, are in varied positions vis-à-vis globalizing structures, and need to reinvent themselves differently according to changing global circumstances.

6   Underpinning such differences is a set of new, or deeper, tensions in world sport. For example the global trend to postmodern individualistic leisure pursuits poses a challenge for traditional sport organizations such as the IAAF and the IOC. The next generations of sport consumers are likely to challenge the hegemony of some Olympic sports with little consumer appeal. The challenge is how to respond to these global changes.

## Globalization and qualitative research method

There has been no change in research methods under contemporary globalization processes. Sullivan and Brockington (2004) note that orientations to research and to the interpretation of 'findings' – particularly in relation to certainty, to the implications of notions of difference and 'the Other', and to aspirations of objectivity – have been much affected by the intertwined theoretical fields of post-structuralism, postcolonialism and feminism (p. 3). They add that by highlighting the infusion of power in research praxis the globalization researcher acknowledges the always politically constitutive role(s) of academic engagement.

As a developing sport management research paradigm, globalization is more a potential than a refined framework, kit of tools and methods, and mode of resolving questions. The efforts to theorize sport globalization have produced an intellectual move rather than a methodological movement to investigate global sport. Globalization research does not have a clearly defined methodology. There is no one correct approach. Qualitative globalization research utilizes many of the approaches mentioned previously in this book.

---

## RECENT CASE EXAMPLE: GLOBALIZATION

*The following article is an example of how globalization has been used in the past by researchers in Sport Management Research. The interested reader may wish to find/download and read the article for further insights.*

> Globalization in professional sport: A comparison of Chinese and American basketball spectators. Menefee, W. C. (2009). Unpublished thesis. North Carolina State University. 3395233

The purpose of this research was to develop a model for cross-cultural sport spectatorship, and then to compare American and Chinese basketball spectators. Means–end theory guided the development of a conceptual framework, and structural equation modelling was used to test the relationship between focal attributes and expected consequences. Focal attributes referred to the concrete features of basketball games, while expected consequences referred to abstract motives for watching sporting events. Participants were National Basketball Association spectators in the United States and Chinese Basketball Association spectators in China. Spectators in the two countries were compared on their preferences for: Kahle's List of Values, individualism/collectivism dimensions, attributes, consequences, consequence–attribute paths and behavioural intentions. This study contributed to the growing body of literature in cross-cultural sport marketing.

---

## CONCLUSION

In articulating the postcolonial notion to sport management it has been demonstrated that the negotiation of cultural differences and meanings is the basis upon which culturally safe sport management practice can be designed. The issue is to adapt sport management practice to the needs of marginalized people by integrating marginalized knowledge in sport management scholarship. Postcolonial research provides the analytic lens to critically assess the effects of power, race, gender and social class on sport management practice; to democratize Sport Management Research and practice, and to bridge theory and practice by generating transformative sport management knowledge. In this chapter it has been argued that contemporary globalizing contexts provide opportunities for sport management globalization research. The key question that will be answered within the next few years is: does globalization constitute a research paradigm to enhance our understanding of sport management practice in changing times?

If researchers are to broaden their approach and seek knowledge through new and innovative research approaches, the emerging research issues discussed in this chapter need to be considered. Each method explored in this chapter presents its own set of unique challenges while at the same time presenting opportunities to understand social reality through different theoretical lenses.

## HYPOTHETICAL CASE STUDY

Kenya was a British colony until 1963. Many Western traditions stayed in Kenya after British rule, including sport. The British (and predominately 'white') sport of rugby was a minor and amateur sport in Kenya until the early 2000s when Kenya started to find success at the shortened code of rugby – sevens. Sevens is played on a regulation size pitch but with only seven players on each side. The increased amount of space per person demands a higher level of speed and fitness from the athletes than the 15-aside game. The reduction in players also minimizes the need for technical eight-man scrums and lineouts, which is often the largest learning curve for development of rugby nations. These differences made sevens an ideal sport for the fit and fast Kenyan athletes.

Rugby high performance development in Kenya attempts to mimic the British or Western system, with private schools and semi-professional clubs working with the national governing body. The International Rugby Board (IRB), started in Britain in the late 1800s, also pressures Kenya to conform to their 'best practices' in regards to training, recruiting, fundraising and competing. With sevens becoming an Olympic sport in 2016, Kenya has even more pressure to succeed internationally with the lure of Olympic medals outside of Athletics. Resources are now diverted from the government (by order of the Kenyan President) to the Kenya Rugby Union to pay players, compete internationally and hire Western coaches.

The players are paid a competitive wage compared to other rugby sevens playing nations, but it is 10–15 times greater than the average annual wage in Kenya (where the other nations' sevens players earn below their national average wage). Kenya competes on the British governed IRB Sevens Series, competing in nine tournaments each year. Eight of the nine tournaments are in countries currently or formally under British rule (Japan is the exception). Kenya has hired two coaches in the past two years, one from England (white) and another from South Africa (mixed race). Both coaches come from very large, successful and wealthy rugby unions and have attempted to restructure Kenya's high performance system to match their home union's systems.

## QUESTIONS

1   Of the research methodologies in this chapter, which would you choose as a lens to study Kenyan rugby? Explain why.
2   What outcome would your study have? Explore and describe? Provide awareness? Enact change?

## REVIEW QUESTIONS

Each of the emerging issues discussed in this chapter embrace a unique methodological approach that has significant relevance to Sport Management Research. With a general understanding of these emerging issues, attempt to answer the following questions:

- Is there any place within Sport Management Research for these approaches to Sport Management Research? Justify your answer.
- Discuss the positive and negative features of each approach.
- Provide examples of how two of these approaches could be applied to Sport Management Research.

## SUGGESTED EXTENDED READING FOR STUDENTS

Edwards, A., and Skinner, J. (2006). *Sport empire*. Oxford: Meyer & Meyer Sports.

Gilbert, K., and Schantz, O. J. (eds). (2008). *The Paralympic Games: Empowerment or side show?* Maidenhead: Meyer & Meyer.

Hardt, M., and Negri, A. (2000). *Empire*. Cambridge, MA: Harvard University Press.

McConaghy C. (2000). *Rethinking indigenous education: Culturalism, colonialism and the politics of knowing*. Flaxton: Post Pressed.

Quatman, C. (2006). The social construction of knowledge in the field of sport management: A social network perspective. Unpublished doctoral dissertation, The Ohio State University, Columbus.

Ramella, M., and Olmos, G. (2005). *Participant authored audiovisual stories (PAAS): Giving the camera away or giving the camera a way?* Papers in Social Research Methods: Qualitative Series no. 10, June (London School of Economics and Political Science Methodology Institute).

Spivak, G. C. (1988). Can the subaltern speak? In C. Nelson and L. Grossberg (eds), *Marxism and the interpretation of culture* (pp. 24–28). London: Macmillan.

Sullivan, S., and Brockington, D. (2004). Qualitative methods in globalisation studies: Or, saying something about the world without counting or inventing it. *CSGR Working Paper,* 139/04.

# Part 3

## Quantitative research for sport management researchers

# Chapter 15

# Research design for a quantitative study

## LEARNING OUTCOMES

By the end of this chapter you should be able to:

■ understand the different aspects relevant to designing a quantitative research study;
■ distinguish between descriptive and inferential statistics;
■ discuss the most common quantitative research designs that are used by sport management researchers;
■ identify the strengths and weaknesses of survey designs.

## KEY TERMS

*Research instrument* – an instrument is a tool for measuring, observing or documenting quantitative data.

*Descriptive statistics* – refers to the transformation of the raw data into a form that will make them easy to understand and interpret.

*Inferential statistics* – statistical techniques that make an inference about a population from observations collected from a sample. They can establish that an obtained statistical description of a sample is genuine and it is not due to chance occurrence.

*Survey* – involves selecting a sample of individual people from a given population and presenting them with a series of questions in the form of a structured questionnaire.

## KEY THEMES

■ What are the key aspects of a quantitative research design?
■ What are the most common quantitative research designs?
■ How can survey designs be used by sport management researchers?

## CHAPTER OVERVIEW

In many ways all sport managers are researchers. Sport managers are constantly engaged in solving problems in the organizational context in which they find themselves. To avoid making poor decisions sport managers need to first identify the problem at hand, collect pertinent information in relation to that problem and draw a conclusion in terms of an appropriate course of action. This chapter outlines how the sport management researcher would design their research to be able to complete the above.

## FEATURES OF QUANTITATIVE RESEARCH

Quantitative research is a type of research in which the sport management researcher decides what to study, asks specific, narrow questions, collects quantifiable data from participants, analyses these numbers using statistics and conducts the inquiry in an unbiased, objective manner. Creswell (2008) sees three main features of quantitative research that are prevalent today: (1) collecting and analysing information in a numeric form; (2) collecting scores and then using them to measure the performance or attributes of individuals and organizations; and (3) procedures and processes by which groups are compared or by which factors common to individuals or groups are related through experiments, surveys, correlation studies and other methods (p. 48).

The quantitative approach rests in certain basic assumptions in respect to knowledge and the process by which one attains knowledge. These assumptions include the following: (1) reality is objective, and it is independent of the researcher. Thus reality is something that can be studied objectively; (2) the researcher remains distant and independent of what is being researched. Unlike in qualitative research, the researcher should not be enmeshed in the process; (3) the values of the researcher do not interfere with, or become part of the research. Research should be value-free; (4) research is based primarily on deductive forms of logic; theories and hypotheses should be tested in a cause–effect order; and (5) the goal of research is to develop generalizations about a population that contribute to theory that enable the researcher to predict, explain and understand some phenomenon.

### Specifying a purpose for the research

In quantitative research, the purpose statement, research questions and hypotheses tend to be specific and narrow and seek measurable, observable data on variables. The major statements and questions of direction in a study – the purpose statement, the research questions and the hypotheses – are specific and narrow because one identifies only a few variables to study. From the study of these variables one may obtain measures or assessments on an instrument or record scores on a scale from observations.

### Collecting data

In quantitative research, the data collection tends to consist of using instruments with preset questions and responses, gathering quantifiable (numeric) data and collecting information from a large number of individuals. A simple example is an online poll embedded into ESPN.com asking readers' opinions and knowledge on various current sport stories. An instrument is a tool for measuring, observing or documenting quantitative data. It contains specific questions and response possibilities that one establishes or develops in advance of the study. Examples of instruments are survey questionnaires, standardized tests and checklists. The instruments are administered to participants and data is collected in the form of numbers. The intent of this process is to apply the results from a small number of people to a large number, a few thousand ESPN.com readers to all sport fans. The larger the number of individuals studied, the stronger the case for applying the results to a large number of people. For example, a survey sent to 500 parents of teenage football players from one club should provide a significant amount of data from which to extrapolate relevant information. It is important, however, to note that these types of polls can be misleading in relation to the assumptions of generalizability. Randomness in sampling is an assumption of generalization; hence, it is likely that ESPN would use a convenience sample, which would not represent all ESPN consumers or satisfy the condition of random sampling.

## Analysing and interpreting data

In quantitative research the data analysis tends to consist of statistical analysis. Descriptive statistics refers to the transformation of the raw data into a form that will make them easy to understand and interpret. Describing responses or observations is typically the first form of analysis. The calculations of averages, frequency distributions and percentage distributions are the most common form of summarizing data (Muijs, 2011; Zikmund, 2000). As the analysis progresses beyond the descriptive stage the sport management researcher will generally apply what are called inferential statistics. Inferential statistics take data analysis one step further than descriptive statistics by asking two related questions. First, can the description be regarded as genuine or could the results be due to chance or random happenings? Second, can the results that describe a sample be generalized to the population from which the sample was drawn? At the risk of over-simplifying, if through inferential statistics techniques we can establish that an obtained statistical description of a sample is genuine and not due to chance occurrence, then if the sample from which we drew the participants is random, or representative of the population, we can infer that what we can say about the sample can also be said about the population from which the sample is drawn.

In this light, statistical analysis consists of breaking down the data into parts to answer the research questions. Statistical procedures such as comparing groups or relating scores for individuals provide information to address the research questions or hypotheses. These results are then interpreted in light of initial predictions or prior studies. Examples of data collected by the sport management researcher that could be analysed statistically include attendance figures at different sporting events (including a more detailed demographic analysis), club membership figures and sporting participation rates.

## Reliability and validity

Sport management researchers often need to determine how precise their measurements are. The two most important aspects of precision are reliability and validity. Without reliability or validity we cannot discriminate differences in observations that are associated with measurement error from real differences. *Reliability* refers to the reproducibility or consistency of a measurement. You quantify reliability simply by taking several measurements on the same subjects. However, some measures of reliability don't require repeated measures, for example, Cronbach's alpha. Poor reliability degrades the precision of a single measurement and reduces your ability to track changes in measurements in research.

Another form of within-subject variation promoted by some statisticians is confidence intervals, which represent a 68 per cent likely range for the difference between a participant's scores in two tests. We can use confidence intervals to express how sure we are that values are going to be within a certain range. For example, a sport researcher may be able to state that they are 95 per cent confident that doping occurs in 1.5 per cent to 3.2 per cent of all athletes. Confidence intervals also allow us to determine whether a change is large enough to warrant further investigation.

## Reporting and evaluating research

In quantitative research the researcher aims to take an objective and unbiased approach, ensuring that their own biases and value systems do not influence the results. The format for a study follows a standard pattern of introduction, literature review, methods, results and discussion. The research is also reported without reference to the researcher or their personal reaction to the results achieved.

Clearly there are many studies in which the sport management researcher will obtain useful and valuable data through the use of quantitative methods. Analysis of athlete performance across a number of events, a demographic analysis of attendance figures at sporting events, even the analysis of sport merchandise consumption can provide valuable data to practitioners, which can be used to shape and develop training regimes, marketing strategies and address other specific areas of concern.

## Quantitative research designs

Creswell (2008) identifies three main types of quantitative research designs: experimental, correlational and survey.

### Experimental designs

Experimental designs are where the researcher determines whether an activity or materials make a difference in results for participants. This is done by giving one group one set of activities (the intervention) and withholding the set from another group. While very popular in the sport science discipline (training protocols, rehabilitation, supplementation, etc.), experimental designs are not very popular among sport management researchers.

## Correlational designs

Correlational designs are procedures, according to Creswell (2008), in which researchers:

> measure the degree of association (or relation) between two or more variables using the statistical procedure of correlational analysis. The degree of association, expressed as a number, indicates whether the two variables are related or whether one can predict another. (p. 60)

To accomplish this, the researcher 'studies a single group of individuals rather than two or more groups as in an experiment' (p. 60).

---

### RECENT CASE EXAMPLE: CORRELATIONAL DESIGN

*The following article is an example of how correlational research design has been used in the past by researchers in Sport Management Research. The interested reader may wish to find/download and read the article for further insights.*

> Relationships among spectator gender, motives, points of attachment, and sport preference. Robinson, M. J., and Trail, G. T. (2005). *Journal of Sport Management,* *19*(1), 58–80.

The researchers investigated the correlations among gender, motives for spectating, points of attachment (or team identification) and sport preference by surveying 669 spectators at intercollegiate contests. The study was aimed at sport marketers looking to segment the market based on the correlations.

---

## Survey designs

According to Creswell (2008) survey designs:

> seek to describe trends in a large population of individuals. In this case, a survey is a good procedure to use. Survey designs are procedures in which one administers a survey or questionnaire to a small group of people (called the sample group) to identify trends in attitudes, opinions, behaviors, or characteristics of a large group of people (the population). (p. 61)

Survey designs are often used in sport management, especially when investigating large fan or sport event participant bases.

## Survey designs

A survey involves selecting a sample of individual people from a given population and presenting them with a series of questions in the form of a structured questionnaire. Answers

**251**

are transformed into a numerical format (producing quantitative data) so you can analyse the data in terms of comparing the responses on different questions or variables, using statistical techniques. For the survey to be complete, we need to produce some kind of report of the results. Thus, key characteristics of surveys are that they focus on individuals and that individuals are part of a sample. The individuals answer a questionnaire that can produce quantitative/numerical data about each individual. The variables in the data set are then analysed to identify patterns in them or relationships between them.

There are a number of strengths and benefits associated with surveys. Some of the strengths include the ability to collect information for individuals including attitudinal data such as opinions and values about team success or sponsor engagement. When done correctly data collected from a survey can be representative of a given population and the results, within limits, can be generalized. In these cases we are therefore able to produce 'scientific' results that can be replicated and verified. We can therefore produce 'hard' data that allows us to test theories and the results can be treated with some confidence.

Similarly, there are weaknesses and criticisms of surveys. These include their tendency to reduce everything to numbers and therefore they don't capture the richness of the real world. This has led some critics to suggest that surveys don't investigate interesting questions and that the accuracy of surveys is open to question (opinion polls). Some qualitative researchers might even suggest that surveys are a barren atheoretical approach to research that may make results look solid and scientific (factual), but in reality this may not be the case.

Generalizability is considered questionable and results are often considered not very meaningful as researchers cannot establish causal connections unequivocally. This has led some to suggest that surveys can be used in some cases to prove a point or support a political stance by manipulating the sorts of answers the survey produces.

## Administering surveys

There are four main ways of administering surveys. These are the personal interview, mail, telephone and, increasingly, the Internet. The personal interview is a face-to-face interview that takes place in an agreed location, oftentimes at a stadium or sport venue. The interviewer works through a structured interview schedule and asks questions and records answers. They don't show the respondent the questions. The strengths of the personal interview include that it is the preferred method in the survey industry and is often referred to as the default option. It has certain design advantages over the other methods, especially over mail. For example, the interviewer can control (to some extent) the context of the interview, that is, who is present. The interviewer is able to build rapport with respondents and is capable of handling complex questions better than with other methods. That is, the interviewer can introduce flow sequences, different paths for different respondents and they can probe on certain responses.

The weaknesses of administering a survey face to face are that it is expensive, highly labour intensive, the interviewer can't cover large areas easily, and it is not as fast as telephone interviewing. Potential problems could arise when it comes to asking sensitive questions, particularly given the lack of anonymity. There is also the possibility of responses being susceptible to a social desirability bias and the potential for interviewer bias when asking the questions. In general, the personal interview method has advantages over other methods in terms of design and disadvantages compared to other methods with respect to implementation.

Mail surveys are (usually) mailed out with a covering letter and all instructions included. In some cases these are done as a 'leave behind' add-on to a personal interview. The respondent sees all questions, can take their time and think more deeply about answers. In general terms, mail surveys are weak on design and strong on implementation. Their strengths include the fact that they are relatively inexpensive and extensive coverage for data collection is possible. They are particularly useful for specialized populations and topics. They don't require trained interviewers and responses are free of interviewer bias. Their weaknesses are that the fieldwork process is slow and you have no control over who answers the questionnaire. Response rates tend to be lower and it is harder to get good response rates. Completion also requires a certain level of literacy although, in fact, all social surveys tend to over-represent those with greater literacy skills and more formal education.

Telephone surveys, as the name suggests, means the interview is done by telephone. There is no face-to-face contact but the interviewer asks questions and records answers as in face-to-face. The researcher can control the interview as in face-to-face in some respects to a greater degree, in some respects to a lesser degree. For example, the respondent can't look over the interviewer's shoulder at questions, but the interviewer can't control or see whether others might be present, who, although they can't hear questions, may influence the general openness of responses. These types of surveys are being increasingly used by commercial survey organizations.

The strengths of the telephone survey are that the fieldwork process can be completed quickly and efficiently. They tend to be less expensive than personal interviews and interviewers don't face any personal risk. Interviewers can also be supervised directly and performance monitored. The approach lends itself to computer assistance in various ways and facilitates direct data entry. Telephone surveys also allow for complex designs. For example, multiphase questionnaires, in which different subsamples are asked different questions, asked the questions in a different order or questions can be asked in random order. Their weaknesses are they are more expensive than mail surveys and the issue of length is important as they can't be too long as respondents can become agitated. When delivering the survey it is difficult to build rapport and as such the respondent can hang up before the interview is finished.

Surveys can also be implemented via the Internet as well as being conducted by email, or through a webpage, or a combination of both. This approach requires self-completion, so all instructions must be included and the respondent can answer in their own time. It does assume however an extensive Internet coverage of the target population, which is very common in most sport management contexts. The strengths of the Internet survey are that it is inexpensive in most instances and email surveys are amenable to the use of simple random sampling. They are good for reaching populations where all members are connected to the Internet, for example large modern sporting organizations where most have a database of their employees, fans and members (ticket buyers), and athletes. Internet surveys can also use sophisticated computer-assisted survey design features (for web-based surveys) and data entered by the respondent can be coded and set up in a database automatically. There are weaknesses with this survey method. For example, there is reduced control over timing of responses and a limited coverage of the general population. This may require specific strategies to be used to counter this problem. Finally, they often can only be used with non-probability sampling methods, as webpage surveys usually result in haphazard samples (a discussion of sampling methods follows in the next chapter). It is important to note, however, that some of these disadvantages will decrease with time.

## Procedures for conducting surveys

All survey methods may use some contact beforehand. Initial contact may be made through a letter or phone call to introduce the purpose of the survey and let the participant know it will be coming. This can make the participant feel more comfortable when it arrives. Then, at the time of the interview itself (personal interview/telephone interview) an introductory speech should be made explaining the survey and if necessary a convenient time arranged to call back. With mail and Internet surveys, a covering letter or statement should be included and you should send follow-up reminders to complete the survey at regular intervals and all questions should be asked in same way for every participant.

The key goals and requirements of all surveys are to collect reliable and valid data through sound questionnaire design, achieve high response rates to minimize potential sample bias, minimize potential biases resulting from the method and achieve an acceptable degree of efficiency. Dillman's (2007) Tailored Design Method is often applied to survey research. The theory is based on the notion of social exchange, which emphasizes the exchange of valued goods (each side of the transaction gets something out of it) and is based on key elements such as rewards, costs and trust.

*Rewards* suggest there are gains from the activity. There are attempts to reward participation by various means, for example incentives, either material or symbolic. The idea is to make the participant feel important through introductory comments, taking care with presentation, thanking them for their participation, attempting to make the participation as interesting and enjoyable as possible and offering to send them a report of results.

*Costs* refer to what is given up to attain the rewards. Attempt to minimize costs (such as time) by avoiding inconvenience and embarrassment, keeping the length of the survey in check and eliminating irrelevant questions.

*Trust* is based on the expectation that rewards will outweigh costs. You should attempt to build up trust to make the participant more likely to participate. To do this you should explain the nature of survey, emphasize the importance of study, have an open, honest approach, assure confidentiality and encourage queries. The aim is to maximize rewards and trust and to minimize costs.

Administration needs to be carefully considered with careful attention to all details. For example, the questionnaire and layout should be attractive; letters requesting participation should be personally signed; reply-paid envelopes should be supplied and regular follow-ups with participants should be done to increase the likelihood of participation. These general strategies need to be tailored to the particular circumstances facing each individual survey study. In summary, *tailored design* is about taking account of features of the particular survey situation, identifying and utilizing knowledge of sponsorship, the survey population and the nature of the survey so as to maximize the quality and quantity of responses and reduce survey error that may come from inadequate coverage, sampling, measurement and non-response.

## Reliability and validity of surveys

When designing questions and questionnaires there are important issues in question design that need to be considered. These focus primarily on reliability and validity; by *reliability* we mean whether the question is a consistent measure, and by *validity* we mean whether the question measures the concept that one is trying to measure. There are different measures of reliability. These include stability reliability, which refers to the test–retest method of measuring reliability on the same individuals; representative reliability, which asks whether the indicator provides the same results for different groups (different sub-populations, for example, age groups); and equivalence reliability, which refers to the use of multiple indicators to increase reliability and reduce the reliance on any one imperfect item. There are also different measures of validity. These include content validity, which seeks to determine whether measures contain the appropriate nominal content relating to the definition of the concept (e.g. tests of sporting ability – do they contain a full range of appropriate indicators?); criterion validity asks whether new measures of a concept correlate with established measures; and finally, constructs validity accesses whether measures behave according to theory in terms of their relationships with other variables.

The type of questions asked in a survey is important as different questions will elicit a different response. We often refer to this as the content of the questions: for example, are questions factual (objective) or attitudinal (subjective)? Factual questions can be attribute questions or behavioural questions. Attitudinal questions can be beliefs about what is true or opinions about what is desirable. In general terms we tend to use what can be classified as a *four-fold classification* in relation to the content of questions. This system includes factual (attribute) questions, attitudinal questions, belief questions and behavioural questions. There are two main types of questions. These are open-ended and closed-ended (forced choice/fixed choice) questions. Open-ended questions are good for obtaining a wide range of qualitative information: that is, the reasons for behaviour and when we don't know what answers to expect. However, they can create problems when it comes to handling the data and can result in multiple responses. Closed-ended questions have two parts. We refer to these as stem and answer categories. We also use filter questions and contingency questions.

When formatting our questions we can use a rating system. For example, this system could use any of the following formats: agree/disagree (Likert scale), importance (variety important), favour/oppose, definitely would/definitely wouldn't, semantic differential (e.g. warm/cold, good/bad – with series of numbers in between), or substantive choices (e.g. very, fairly, not very). Question formats can also ask participants to rank their responses or present vignettes to which participants may respond in a number of ways.

There are a number of key rules to consider when designing questions. You should keep the language simple and use a relaxed conversational style in questions. You should try to avoid the complex wording of questions, although this may sound impressive it may only further confuse your participants. When changing topic you should introduce the next section with a short explanation of where the questionnaire is moving to. You should try to keep the questions as short as possible, while using enough context to avoid confusion on the part of respondents, so try to ensure the questions are unambiguous. If necessary, define what you mean with examples to guide the respondents (e.g. membership of community sporting organizations). Make sure you keep the questions balanced (e.g. do you agree or disagree?). Make sure the answer categories fit linguistically with the stem of the question and generally phrase questions in the positive as negatives can be confusing. It is important to provide sufficient response categories to produce a well differentiated range of answers so avoid just yes/no or agree/disagree response categories. You need to provide variety in the types of questions used and use multiple indicators for complex concepts. It is also necessary to avoid double-barrelled questions, leading questions and threatening questions. Even when you get all of this correct don't forget to consider the introduction to the questionnaire, the initial sequence of questions and its layout and attractiveness for self-completion questionnaires. The placement of particular sections of the questionnaire can have an influence on completion rates as can the ordering of questions within particular batteries. In other words the flow and length of the questionnaire are key elements in its design. When we put this all together it may sound overwhelming but with the support of a good supervisor and the benefit of experience it becomes common practice. In summary the survey research process is shown in Figure 15.1.

Each element of the survey research process is discussed throughout the text but in the next chapter we concentrate our discussion on quantitative sampling.

---

### HYPOTHETICAL CASE STUDY

A local event company is hosting a bike tour and engages the local university to conduct an economic impact study. They have the following data from the online registration system: 55 per cent of all registrations are located in postal codes outside the local region, and 12 per cent are international. A total of 2,543 people have registered (and 94 per cent have provided a valid email address). The eight event host hotels have sold out for the three-day race weekend. The demographics from registration show that the participants are mostly male, very affluent and register for several bike races each year.

1   How would you survey the participants for the economic impact study?
2   What types of data would you need to collect from the participants? What questions would you ask on the survey?
3   How would you ensure reliable and valid results?

---

## CONCLUSION

This chapter has provided an understanding of the key elements involved in a quantitative research design. It has explained the role of surveys in the collection of quantitative data. It has been shown that a number of survey methods can be employed in the data collection process and each has its own unique set of advantages and disadvantages. The sport management researcher needs to consider these advantages and disadvantages in the context of the research problem under investigation and the resources available to them to complete the research.

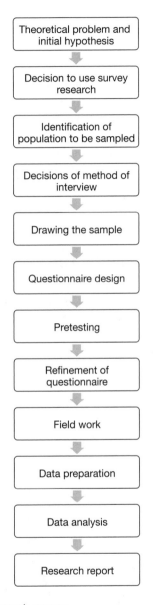

**Figure 15.1** *The survey research process*

## REVIEW QUESTIONS

Understanding how a research project should be designed is a core skill the sport management researcher requires. If your research is based on poor survey design it can result in the collection of data that can fail to answer your research question(s); given this:

- Name the key elements of a quantitative research design.
- Discuss how the failure to design a valid survey instrument could result in the collection of invalid data.

## SUGGESTED EXTENDED READING FOR STUDENTS

Creswell, J. W. (2008). *Educational research* (3rd edn). Upper Saddle River, NJ: Pearson.
Muijs, D. (2011). *Doing quantitative research in education with SPSS* (2nd edn). Thousand Oaks, CA: Sage.

## Chapter 16

# Data collection methods for a quantitative study

**LEARNING OUTCOMES**

By the end of this chapter you should be able to:

- understand what a variable is and the various scales of measurement used in quantitative research;
- discuss data collection techniques in quantitative research;
- discuss the principles of sampling and provide examples of a number of sampling techniques;
- understand the place of statistics in Sport Management Research.

**KEY TERMS**

*Variables* – anything that varies from case to case or observation to observation that can be measured.

*Population* – all members of a specified group.

*Sample* – a subset of a population.

*Subject* – a specific individual participating in a study.

*Sampling technique* – the specific method used to select a sample from a population.

**KEY THEMES**

- When is a number not a number?
- The importance of presenting data clearly so that it can be understood by the reader.
- What are the different types of data that can be collected for analysis?

## CHAPTER OVERVIEW

In a world of variability we need statistics to help us understand this variability. As such, statistical techniques perform three main functions. First, they provide ways of summarizing the information that is collected from a multitude of sources. Second, they provide a mechanism to facilitate economy of effort in research and finally, statistical techniques enable the researcher to clarify trends in vast quantities of data using a number of powerful methods (Howitt and Cramer, 2000). This chapter begins our discussion around these themes by first discussing what a variable is and the various scales of measurement used in quantitative research. The second part will discuss data collection techniques in quantitative research. Part of this process understands how to select an appropriate sample. We therefore discuss the principles of sampling and provide examples of a number of sampling techniques that can be used by the sport management researcher. The final section of the chapter will introduce some foundation statistical techniques and provide a greater understanding of the place of statistics in Sport Management Research.

## VARIABLES AND SCALES OF MEASUREMENT

In order to gain knowledge about seemingly haphazard events, statisticians collect information for variables that describe the event. A variable is anything that varies and can be measured. Data are values (measurements) that the variables can assume. Variables whose values are determined by chance are called random variables. For example, suppose a professional sporting organization studies its records over the past several years and determines that on average, three out of every 100 customers who have bought season tickets do not renew their tickets the following year. Although there is no way to predict the specific customers that will not renew their season ticket (random occurrence), the organization can adjust its marketing strategy accordingly, since the organization knows the general pattern over the long run. That is, 3 per cent of season ticket holders will not renew their tickets at the end of the season.

This concept of a variable is quite straight forward but is vital in understanding statistics. Although we indicated a variable is anything that can be measured these measurements do not have to correspond with common-sense thinking relating to measurements associated with weight, length and distance. In these cases we assign numerical values, similarly we may seek to quantify something such as attitudes towards a sports brand. In these cases we assign a form of numerical values referred to as scores that allows us to describe someone's attitude towards the sports brand. However, the gender of an individual is also a variable as it can be either male or female. It is therefore not uncommon to find different types of measurement scales. In a sport management context, however, we tend to focus on two different types of measurement. It is important to remember, however, some measurement scales are different types of numerical scores.

The two measurement scales that are commonly used in Sport Management Research are nominal categorization and score/numerical measurement. These will now be discussed.

Nominal categorization involves placing cases into named categories. Nominal implies categories and these are described in words so there are no numbers involved. There is, however, the possibility for confusion. For example, let us say we are conducting a human resource audit of a professional sporting organization. In doing this we find that the organization has 30 people with occupations you may wish to count. We may want to know how many coaches there are, or how many marketing personnel there are? The numbers in each case merely correspond to the count or frequency, the number of cases falling into each occupational category. They are not scores, they are frequencies and do not correspond to a single measurement but are the aggregate of many specific nominal measurements (Johnson and Kuby, 2011).

Score/numerical measurement is the assignment of a numerical value to a measurement. Within this measurement scale three different types of numerical scores can be generated. First, *ordinal* (or *rank*) measurement values of the numerical score tells you little other than the order of the data. It is sometimes called rank measurement since we can assign ranks to the first place-getter, second place-getter etc. These ranks have the numerical value of 1, 2, and 3, etc. Second, there is *interval* or *equal-interval* measurement. In some cases the intervals between numbers on a numerical scale are equal in size. An example of this is the distance between certain markers on a scale. In measuring distance we know the distance between 1 metre and 2 metres is the same as the distance between 4 metres and 5 metres. Finally, there is *ratio* measurement. This allows you to work out ratios between measures. Many scales have zero points that are absolute. The zero is the smallest point you can have on the scale. In these cases it is possible to work out ratios between measures. For example, a football stadium that is 20 km away is twice as far away as a football stadium that is 10 km away.

In summary and as indicated above, virtually in all practical purposes there are only two different types of measurement in statistics (1) nominal/category measurement – deciding the category the variable belongs in and (2) score/numerical measurement – the assignment of a numerical value to a measurement.

## QUANTITATIVE SAMPLING

A population in research terms can be considered the larger pool of cases from which a sample is drawn (containing all the cases that the researcher is interested in) – the target group. As such, a sample is a subset of the population or more directly a subset of cases selected from a population. An example is provided in Figure 16.1. The aim of sampling is that the sample will be *representative* of the population from which it is drawn and so we will be able to *generalize* from the sample to the population. To within certain limits of accuracy we can talk about the information we have for the sample as though it were the population. Figures obtained from samples are estimates of the characteristics of the population. With proper sampling we can calculate the extent to which the estimates are likely to be accurate and thus make inferences about the population with some confidence (Johnson and Kuby, 2011).

When trying to determine sample size there is no definitive answer to the question of how big a sample should be as it depends on various considerations. These include what is considered an acceptable size in the field of study, the level of accuracy required, the need to gain large enough numbers of important subgroups in the population and finally its cost relative to your budget. The size of population generally doesn't matter as the sampling fraction is only relevant for very small populations. As sport management researchers you may be

**Figure 16.1** *What does a sample look like?*

confronted with the possibility of a *sampling error*. The term 'sampling error' assumes the use of correct probability sampling methods and is a statistical property of samples that is quite benign. The term error refers not to a 'mistake' but to the extent to which the sample is likely to differ from the population. In other words, sampling error is the deviation of the selected sample from the true characteristics, traits, behaviours, qualities or figures of the entire population (Zikmund, 2000).

The degree of sampling error in any sample is related to the size of the sample, larger samples have smaller amounts of sampling error. For example, if a stadium has 50,000 fans (population) and you only sample ten people, there is a chance the team loyalty distribution of fans calculated from that sample will be erroneous for the population. Sampling error on its own, however, doesn't necessarily lead to bias, just imprecision, though bad sampling practices can create bias. A good rule of thumb is that a fourfold increase in sample size will halve the error. A large sample may not be a guarantee of good results as it must be combined with good sampling techniques (Bryman and Bell, 2011).

Non-sampling error can cause bias in surveys. Non-sampling error includes *coverage error,* which means having a sampling procedure that does not allow for the whole population to be covered; for example, only asking fans in the home team section of a stadium what team has their loyalty. *Non-response error* refers to systematically under- or over-representing certain groups in a sample, in turn producing an unrepresentative sample; for example, only asking fans wearing one team's apparel for their loyalty. *Measurement error* is the result of poorly designed questions that provide unreliable and/or invalid responses; for example, asking fans where they grew up and assuming that they are loyal to their hometown team. Finally, *processing error* is the result of mistakes in the coding of variables or recording of answers (Johnson and Kuby, 2011); this can be simply writing down or incorrectly transcribing the wrong team loyalty for some fans.

## Sampling assumptions

In summary the assumptions of quantitative sampling are shown in Figure 16.2.

We shall now examine in more detail some of these assumptions.

### Types of samples

Samples can be selected by either 'probability' or 'non-probability' methods. Probability samples include simple random sampling, systematic random sampling, stratified random sampling and multi-stage cluster sampling (Muijs, 2011; Chase and Brown, 2000).

In a *simple random sample* we assign a unique number to each sampling unit. We can select sampling units by using a table of random numbers. You need to list all members of the population and assign consecutive numbers to all members. It is necessary to ignore duplicates and numbers out of range when sampled. In *systematic random sampling* we select the first sample unit randomly and then select the remaining units according to the interval. It is the researcher who determines the sampling interval. For example, we select a random number, which will be known as *k*. We then get a list of people, or observe a flow of people (e.g. fans entering a stadium). We then select every *k-th* person being careful that there is no systematic rhythm to the flow or list of people. If every fourth person on the list is, say, 'rich' or 'senior' or some other consistent pattern, we would therefore need to avoid this method. The advantage of this approach is that it is very easily done. The disadvantages, however, are that it is susceptible to systematic inclusion of some subgroups and some members of the population don't have an equal chance of being included. There are also selection issues in terms of listing

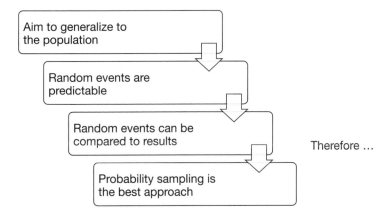

**Figure 16.2** *Assumptions of quantitative sampling*

all members of the population, determining the value of $k$, and starting at the top of the list again if the desired sample size is not reached (Thomas and Nelson, 1996).

In a *stratified random sample* proportional and non-proportional approaches can be used. Proportional means the same proportion of subgroups whereas non-proportional relates to different, often equal, proportions of subgroups. For example, we can separate our population into groups or strata that are proportionate. From here we do either a simple random sample or systematic random sample. Note you must know easily what the 'strata' are before attempting this. If your sampling frame is sorted by, say, regional sporting districts, then you're able to use this method. In sum, the researcher selects a random sample proportionate to the size of the stratum in the population (disproportionate). If the members of three regional sporting districts are 100 in region one, 150 in region two and 250 in region three, then you would randomly sample members with 20 per cent, 30 per cent and 50 per cent coming from each respective region. The advantage of this approach is you are able to achieve a representation of subgroups in the sample. The disadvantages are the identification of all members of the population can be difficult, identifying members of all subgroups can be difficult and there are selection issues; that is, the identification of relevant strata, coding subjects regarding strata and selecting randomly from within each level of the strata (Johnson and Kuby, 2011).

Finally, a *multi-stage cluster sample* is where the researcher determines the number of levels of clusters and from each level of clusters they select a sample randomly. You may choose to select subjects by using groups that have similar characteristics and in which participants can be found, let's say by sporting district, sporting club or sporting teams. For example, you get a list of 'clusters', e.g. teams within a district. You then randomly sample clusters from that list. If you have a list of, say, ten teams you then randomly sample people within those teams. This method, however, is complex and expensive. Another example might be:

1   take the population map;
2   divide it into equal clusters;
3   assign each cluster a random number;
4   select the cluster(s) on the basis of a pre-decided rule;
5   divide the selected cluster into sub-clusters;
6   repeat steps 2–5 until you get a manageable sub-cluster.

The advantage of this approach is that it is very useful when populations are large and spread over a large geographic region, as well as being convenient and expedient. The disadvantages are that representation is likely to become an issue, the assumptions of some statistical procedures can be violated, and selection issues. That is, identifying logical clusters and the average number of population members per cluster, determining the number of clusters needed, and randomly selecting necessary clusters may create problems (Muijs, 2011).

Selecting non-random samples also known as non-probability samples includes convenience sampling, snowball sampling, quota sampling and purposive sampling. *Convenience sampling* is where you find some people that are easy to find. Population elements are selected based on the judgement of the researcher, who then chooses the elements to be included because he/she believes they are representative of the population (Chase and Brown, 2000). Selection is therefore based on the availability of subjects, for example, volunteers or pre-existing sporting groups. This approach raises concerns related to representation and generalizability. *Snowball sampling* is based on finding a few participants that are relevant to your topic and asking them to refer you to more of them. For example, if you are researching drugs in sport and you are trying to understand why elite athletes may engage in this type of behaviour, an athlete who completes your survey may be able to provide access to other athletes through their networks. *Quota sampling* is where you determine what the population looks like in terms of specific qualities. You then create 'quotas' based on those qualities and select people for each quota. Selection is therefore based on the exact characteristics and quotas of subjects in the sample when it is impossible to list all members of the population. This approach does raise concerns with accessibility, representation and generalizability. *Purposive sampling* is where selection is based on the researcher's experience and knowledge of the group being sampled. They rely heavily on the experience and insight of the researcher to select participants. There is a need for clear criteria for describing and defending the sample. Again, however, there are concerns related to representation and generalizability (Muijs, 2011). In summary, types of samples are depicted in Figure 16.3.

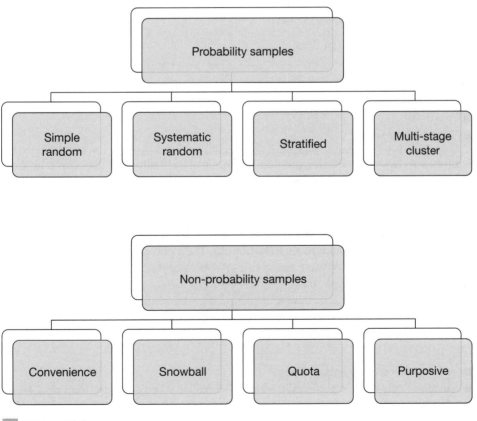

**Figure 16.3** *Types of samples*

---

## RECENT CASE EXAMPLE: DISTRIBUTION OF VARIABLES

*The following article is an example of how normal distribution has been used in the past by researchers in Sport Management Research. The interested reader may wish to find/download and read the article for further insights.*

The best and the rest: Revisiting the norm of normality of individual performance. Aguinis, H. (2012). *Personnel Psychology*, 65(1), 79–119.

This study tested a long-held assumption that individual performance follows a normal distribution. By sampling athletes, entertainers, politicians and researchers, they disproved that assumption by finding individual performance follows a power law distribution.

## MEASURES OF CENTRAL TENDENCY

In some cases however tables and diagrams can take up a large amount of space. It may therefore be more efficient to use numerical indexes to describe the distribution of variables. Numerical indexes allow large amounts of data to be described adequately using just a few techniques. The most common techniques used are:

- measures of central tendency
  - mean
  - median
  - mode
- variance
- standard deviation.

Both variance and standard deviation are measures of variability. To illustrate how these techniques are used we shall use the two sets of data in Table 16.1 as an example.

If we look at the data set we need to ask what is it telling us? Looking at the two sets of scores we can see there are major differences between the scores. They differ substantially in terms of their typical value. In one case (variable B) the scores are relatively large, in the other case the scores are much smaller (variable A). The scores also differ in their variability. Variable B seems to have a greater spread or a greater variability than the other set of scores. Each of these different features can be described using various indexes. Sport management researchers will speak about the central tendency of scores. By doing this they are raising the issue of what are the most typical and likely scores in the distribution of measurements. To repeat, measures of central tendency are:

- mean – the average score;
- median – the score in the middle when all scores are arranged in size from smallest to largest;
- mode – value of the most frequent score.

### Table 16.1 Data set

| Scores variable A | Scores variable B |
|---|---|
| 4 | 54 |
| 4 | 58 |
| 6 | 70 |
| 6 | 80 |
| 6 | 82 |
| 8 | 84 |
| 8 | 90 |
| 8 | 90 |
| 8 | 98 |
| 8 | 98 |
| 10 | 98 |

All three apply to score data, only the mode applies to categorical data. Sometimes however there is no single mode since scores jointly have the highest frequency. In this case the distribution is referred to as a bi-modal distribution. Similarly, when calculating the median it may seem straight forward when we have an odd number of scores that are all different. This is because there is no single score that corresponds to the middle score in the set of scores. However, if there is an even number of scores in the data set then sometimes the mid point will not be a single score but two scores. So, if we have two scores of 3 and 4 that fall in the middle we would say the median is 3.5. Usually the mean, median and mode will give different values of central tendency when applied to the same set of scores. It is only when the Mean = Median = Mode that the scores are symmetrically distributed. Regard big differences between the mean, median and mode as a sign that your distribution of scores is rather asymmetrical or lopsided.

The other key numerical technique for describing variables relates to the spread of scores and refers to their variability. Variability in scores can be assessed in a number of ways. For example there is the range of the data. *Range* refers to the difference between the largest and smallest scores. The range tends to ignore important information. It does not take into account all the scores in a set, merely the extreme ones. For this reason measures of the spread of variability have been developed that include the extent to which each of the scores in the set differs from the mean score of the set. One example of this is the mean deviation. *Mean deviation* highlights the extent to which each of the scores in the set differs from the mean score of the set; however, it is limited in its application and not as accurate as some other measures. The closely related concept of variance is a much more useful tool (Bryman and Bell, 2011).

*Variance* is the average of each score's squared deviation from the mean score. Variance, however, is difficult to interpret in isolation from other information about data. It is best treated comparatively, when variances of different groups of people are compared. The *standard deviation* is another standard unit of measurement in statistics. Standard deviation is the square root of the variance. In a normal curve the following rules apply to standard deviation:

- plus or minus 1 standard deviation from the mean includes 68 per cent of the scores;
- plus or minus 2 standard deviations from the mean includes 95 per cent of the scores;
- plus or minus 3 standard deviations from the mean includes 99 per cent of the scores.

The size of the standard deviation will depend on the scale of measurement in question; however, once the standard deviation is known all scores can be re-expressed in terms of the number of standard deviations they are from the mean (Thomas and Nelson, 1996).

## SHAPES OF DISTRIBUTIONS OF SCORES

### The normal curve

The normal curve describes a particular shape of a frequency curve. The normal curve is characterized by the mean, median and mode (these terms are discussed later in this chapter) being at the same point (centre of the distribution). A normal curve is highlighted in Figure 16.4 – as you can see it can be described as bell shaped and symmetrical.

In some cases the curve can be described as distorted. The main concepts that deal with distortions in the normal curve are *skewness* and *kurtosis*. Skewness is the extent to which the frequency curve is lopsided rather than symmetrical. There are special terms for left-handed and right-handed skew: a *negative skew* is when more scores are to the right of the mode than to the left. The skew is the direction of the long tail. Thus, a negative skew has more responses to the positive end of the scale – skewed by a few low scores at the negative end. A *positive skew* is when more scores are to the left of the mode than to the right. The skew is the opposite direction of the long tail. Thus, a positive skew has more responses to the negative end of the scale – skewed by a few high scores at the positive end. Kurtosis is another term used

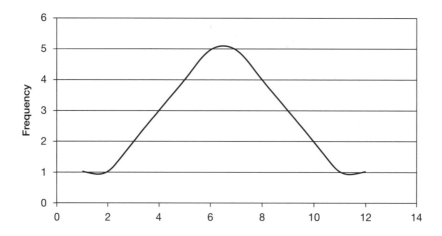

**Figure 16.4** *A normal distribution curve*

with reference to distributions. It is used to identify the degree of steepness or shallowness of a distribution. There are technical words for the different types of curves. A steep curve is called *leptokurtic* whereas a normal curve is called *mesokurtic* and a flat curve is called *platykurtic* (Johnson and Kuby, 2011).

## HYPOTHETICAL CASE STUDY

Cricket is a very popular sport around the world, especially in Commonwealth nations; however, it has not made it into the mainstream sporting calendar in the United States. The International Cricket Council (ICC) would like to conduct research on the awareness of cricket and the potential fan base (from casual to avid fans) in the United States to determine locations for hosting an international exhibition test. The USA Cricket Association recognizes 51 regional leagues and associations in eight regions.

1    How would you choose the sample for this study? Explain.
2    How could you avoid getting an erroneous or biased sample?

## CONCLUSION

This chapter has described and discussed what a variable is and the various scales of measurement used in Sport Management Research. The chapter then moved on to discuss the role of sampling in the data collection phase and its importance to collecting data that can be representative of the broader population. We discussed how samples can be representative of a given population, the possibility for sampling error, the assumptions that underpin sampling and the different types of sampling techniques. Each of these issues is a vital part of the quantitative data collection process and needs to be carefully considered. This chapter then outlined how statistical techniques can be applied to organize, review and interpret numerical data. It has shown how data can be represented to capture the key components that can help describe the data set.

## REVIEW QUESTIONS

With an understanding now of the basic functions of statistical techniques that enable the sport management researcher to clarify trends in vast quantities of data using a number of powerful methods, can you:

■    Discuss the place of statistics in Sport Management Research. Give three examples of studies in which statistical information would be critical.
■    Describe ways in which the data can be presented so that it is easily understood by the reader.

**269**

## SUGGESTED EXTENDED READING FOR STUDENTS

Bryman, A., and Bell, E. (2011). *Business research methods*. London: Oxford University Press.
Johnson, R. R., and Kuby, P. (2011). *Elementary statistics*. Boston, MA: Brooks/Cole.

# Chapter 17

# Quantitative data analysis in Sport Management Research

## LEARNING OUTCOMES

By the end of this chapter you should be able to:

- identify the basic functions of the SPSS (Statistical Package for the Social Sciences) and its application to Sport Management Research;
- describe the process of preparing and organizing your data for analysis;
- recognize how to design and present results in tables, figures, graphs and a results section.

## KEY TERMS

*SPSS* – Statistical Package for the Social Sciences.

*Code book* – a systematic record of the variables in a survey.

*Validity* – an indicator of the extent to which a test actually measures the characteristic of interest.

## KEY THEMES

- How does the SPSS support good data analysis?
- Why is good data analysis important to the sport management researcher?

## CHAPTER OVERVIEW

Sport management researchers of today have access to statistical software packages that can analyse data and provide detailed information. However, we know that good data analysis not only requires we produce figures and calculate the numerical summaries, but that we know which figures and numerical summaries to choose and how to interpret the results in plain language.

While this chapter will cover some basic procedures it will not provide a detailed account of how to use all features of statistical software packages available. Instead it will focus on one software package that is commonly used by sport management researchers: the Statistical Package for the Social Sciences (SPSS). The main emphasis of the chapter is to provide a general overview of SPSS (recognizing that each version of the software package will vary slightly) and how it can be used in the data analysis process. It will then go on to discuss the key issues of validity and reliability as they relate to data analysis.

## STATISTICAL PACKAGE FOR THE SOCIAL SCIENCES (SPSS)

According to Tukey (1977), exploratory data analysis is 'detective work' that can be both numerical and graphical in nature. Exploring and describing the data prior to and during any form of statistical analysis is invaluable for a number of reasons. These include:

1   clarity of explanation:
    ■   produces a basic understanding of the trends found in the data;
    ■   helps focus the sport management researcher on the questions to be answered;
    ■   keeps explanations logical;
2   greater effectiveness and efficiency in later confirmatory analyses. Warnings of errors or illogically and poorly performed procedures can be detected;
3   reducing ambiguity in interpretation and forcing the sport management researcher to address patterns they were hoping not to find. It can provide evidence of previously unthought-of relationships that can be pursued in later research;
4   alerting the sport management researcher to possible spurious relationships in the data produced by some anomalous scores. This gives you an indication of how robust the findings are in your analysis.

This detective work has been made easier with the development of statistical software packages such as the Statistical Package for the Social Sciences (SPSS). SPSS has three parts/windows:

■   data
    —   where you enter the data (.sav)
■   syntax
    —   where details of the analyses you are going to do are displayed (.sps)
■   viewer/output
    —   where the results are displayed (.spo)
    —   where any messages (such as errors) are displayed.

## Coding the data

A code book is a systematic record of the variables (questions) in a survey, where they are located in the data matrix and the decisions on how to code all the different answers to each question (that is, what number to assign each answer). A code book contains:

- a description of each variable;
- a short variable name – for SPSS or equivalent data analysis program;
- valid response codes for each variable and where relevant a description of the response assigned to each code;
- missing data codes for each variable;
- special features/instructions relating to the coding of the variable.

The code book usually closely follows the survey, but contains additional information (and excludes some material in the survey that is only relevant to instructing the interviewer on how to ask the questions, etc.). In sum, the code book provides a guide for coding the responses to the survey. Coding includes: (1) pre-coding: i.e., closed ended/forced choice questions, which can have a code already assigned to them on the questionnaire; (2) assigning numerical codes to pre-coded/closed-ended questions, which have fixed categories, but have not been assigned numerical codes on the questionnaire; (3) generating coding frames for open-ended questions; (4) coding the open-ended questions according to the coding frame, or (5) dealing with 'missing' data.

## Different stages of data preparation

There are four different stages involved in the data preparation phase. *Editing* involves checking completed surveys to make sure they have been filled out appropriately and that no inappropriate answers have been given, dealing with problems that are found. For example, sport management researchers often find intentional 'outliers' when receiving online survey data from event attendees asking for economic impact data, such as spending $20,000 per night on dinner while visiting the SuperBowl. You must ask yourself if this is a realistic amount, or if the respondent accidently or intentionally provided false information. *Coding* is where the researcher assigns codes to the answers (assigning numerical scores to answers/reducing all responses to a number). *Data entry* is actually keying in the numerical scores for computer analysis and *cleaning* involves checking to make sure there are no errors in the data once they have been entered into machine-readable form (entered onto the computer), and correcting any errors found. An example of this process is provided below.

## Descriptive statistics

Sport management researchers edit and code data to provide input that results in tabulated information that will answer the research questions. With this information sport management researchers logically and statistically describe the results of the research project. Within this context the term *analysis* is difficult to define because it refers to a variety of activities and processes. One form of analysis is summarizing large quantities of raw data (e.g. ratings from local residents after hosting a sport event) so the results can be interpreted (e.g. social impact of hosting that particular sport event in that region). Categorizing, or separating out the component or relevant parts of the whole data set, is also a form of analysis to make the data easily manageable. Rearranging, ordering or manipulating data may provide descriptive information that answers questions posed in the problem definition. For example, was the social impact of a sport event perceived differently among different groups in society? All forms of analysis attempt to portray consistent patterns in the data so that results may be studied and interpreted in a brief and meaningful way (Bryman and Bell, 2011; Muijs, 2011).

Descriptive statistics refers to the transformation of the raw data into a form that will make them easy to understand and interpret. Describing responses or observations is typically the first form of analysis. The calculations of averages, frequency distributions and percentage distributions are the most common form of summarizing data (Bryman and Bell, 2011). As the analysis progresses beyond the descriptive stage the sport management researcher will generally apply what are called inferential statistics. These forms of statistics are discussed later.

## Describing variables and displaying the data

### Nominal data

The sports media regularly feature statistical tables and diagrams. This makes it easier for their viewers to absorb and compare the large amounts of game data that are presented throughout the course of the telecast. For example, if we are to conduct some market research for a subscription TV provider into the type of viewer that watches the English Premier League, we might ask 100 people their age, sex, marital status, income and occupation. This would yield separate pieces of information. It is not helpful to present these 500 measurements in your report. Such unprocessed information is called *raw data*. Statistical data has to be more than describing the raw ingredients. It requires structuring it in ways that effectively communicate the major trends. If you fail to structure your data you may as well just provide copies of the completed questionnaire. There are very few rules in terms of the presentation of tables and diagrams in statistics as long as they are clear and concise and convey the major trends in the data.

One of the main characteristics of tables and diagrams for nominal data is that they have to show the frequencies of the cases in each category used. While there may be as many categories as you wish, it is not the function of statistical analysis to communicate all the data in detail; the task is to identify the major trends. For example, let us say you are researching public attitudes towards drugs in sport as you want to use this information as a reference point for developing anti-doping policies. If you ask the participants in your research their occupations you might find you have hundreds of different job occupations. Counting the frequencies with which different job titles are mentioned would result in a vast number of categories. You need to think of reducing this large number into a smaller number that captures the major trends. As 'drugs in sport' is often linked to the health of the athlete you may wish to formulate a category that is made up of those individuals involved in the health sector. Each of these separate categories could then be collapsed into one category such as 'health worker'. It is important to note there is no guiding rule for combining categories; however, the following are useful rules for using tables and diagrams for nominal data: (1) keep your number of categories low, and (2) try to make combined categories meaningful and sensible in light of the purposes of the research (Howitt and Cramer, 2000; Johnson and Kuby, 2011).

Frequencies are mainly presented in two ways:

- simple frequencies – the total number of individuals within that category;
- percentage frequencies – this is the frequency expressed as a percentage total of the frequencies (a total number of cases usually).

An example of this can be seen in Table 17.1.

Bar graphs are diagrams in which bars represent the size of each category. When using bar graphs it is important to remember the following: (1) the heights of the bars represent frequencies; (2) each bar should be clearly labelled as to the category it represents; (3) too many bars make bar charts hard to follow. An example of a bar graph is shown in Figure 17.1.

**Table 17.1** *Occupational status of research participants*

| Occupation | Frequency | Percentage frequency |
|---|---|---|
| Athletes | 17 | 21.25 |
| Coaches | 3 | 3.75 |
| Swimmers | 23 | 28.75 |
| Footballers | 20 | 25 |
| Gymnasts | 17 | 21.25 |

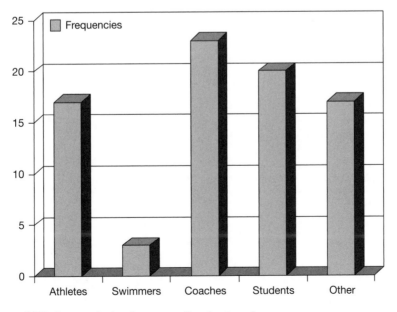

**Figure 17.1** *Bar graph showing occupational categories*

## Numerical data

The crucial consideration when deciding what tables and diagrams to use for score data is the number of separate scores recorded for the variable in question. In some cases scores can be grouped into bands or ranges of scores to allow for efficient tabulation. Table 17.2 highlights this.

Questions can be used that pre-specify just a few response alternatives. A Likert-type questionnaire is used in these circumstances. The Likert scale was invented by Rensis Likert, an educator and psychologist. It is an ordered, one-dimensional scale from which respondents choose one option that best aligns with their view. There are typically between five and seven options. A common form is an assertion, with which the person may agree or disagree to varying degrees. In scoring, numbers are usually assigned to each option such as 1 to 5. Similarly, responses that range from strongly agree to strongly disagree can be used (Howitt and Cramer, 2000; Johnson and Kuby, 2011): for example, on a scale of 1–5, with 1 'strongly disagree' and 5 'strongly agree', do you think this event is beneficial to the local community? How this information would be presented in a table is highlighted in Table 17.3.

Histograms can also be used to represent numerical data. They are similar to bar charts but without the gaps between the bars. Histograms do not represent distinct unrelated categories but different points on a numerical measurement scale. An example of a histogram is provided in Figure 17.2.

**Table 17.2** Player's age expressed as age bands

| Age range | Frequency |
| --- | --- |
| 15–18 years | 19 |
| 19–22 years | 33 |
| 23–26 years | 17 |
| 27–30 years | 22 |
| 31–34 years | 17 |
| Over 35 years | 3 |

**Table 17.3** Distribution of public attitudes on the event benefiting the local community

| Response category | Value | Frequency |
| --- | --- | --- |
| Strongly agree | 1 | 1700 |
| Agree | 2 | 1400 |
| Don't agree or disagree | 3 | 600 |
| Disagree | 4 | 200 |
| Strongly disagree | 5 | 100 |

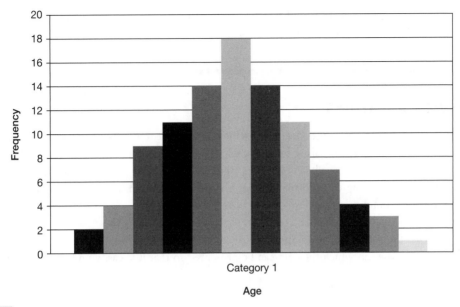

**Figure 17.2** *Histogram showing age categories*

## RECENT CASE EXAMPLE: LIKERT SCALES IN SPSS

*The following article is an example of how Likert scales were used in SPSS by researchers in Sport Management Research. The interested reader may wish to find/download and read the article for further insights.*

> Sport involvement: A conceptual and empirical analysis. Beaton, A. A., Funk, D. C., Ridinger, L., and Jordan, J. (2011). *Sport Management Review, 14*(2), 126–140.

The researchers utilized SPSS to analyse data from an online survey of running participants. Using the Psychological Continuum Model as a framework, the survey asked runners to rate various cognitive measures on a Likert scale of 1–7 (very unlikely to very likely), in addition to demographic and running behaviour questions. Unsurprisingly, they found that the longer race a person completed (from 5 km to marathon) the more allegiant they are to running. Using SPSS to segment the sample based on demographics found no differences to the allegiance – only distance run.

## CONCLUSION

This chapter has discussed the basic data analysis procedures of SPSS. It has provided examples of how data can be coded, entered into SPSS, the process to analyse the data and finally how the output from the data can be presented. It has also outlined how statistical techniques can be applied to organize, review and interpret numerical data. It has shown how data can be represented to capture the key components.

## REVIEW QUESTIONS

Good data analysis requires the sport management researcher to not only produce figures and calculate the numerical summaries, but know which figures and numerical summaries to choose and how to interpret the results in plain language. It also provides you with an understanding of ways of summarizing the information that is collected from a multitude of sources. With these points in mind:

- Discuss the place of SPSS in Sport Management Research.
- Describe ways in which the data can be presented so that it is easily understood by the reader.

## SUGGESTED EXTENDED READING FOR STUDENTS

Muijs, D. (2011). *Doing quantitative research in education with SPSS* (2nd edn). Thousand Oaks, CA: Sage.
Tukey, J. W. (1977). *Exploratory data analysis*. Reading, MA: Addison-Wesley.

# Chapter 18

# Introduction to inferential statistics

## LEARNING OUTCOMES

By the end of this chapter you should be able to:

- distinguish between independent and dependent variables;
- define the concept of a null hypothesis;
- explain the meaning of a p-value;
- explain the meaning of confidence limit.

## KEY TERMS

*Independent variable* – what the sport management researcher is manipulating.

*Dependent variable* – critical feature of behaviour of the subjects.

*Research hypothesis* – there is some relationship between the independent and dependent variables.

*Null hypothesis* – there is no relationship between the independent and dependent variables or there is no difference between means or frequencies.

*P-value* – the probability value.

*Inferential statistics* – can the description be regarded as genuine or could the results be due to chance or random happenings, and can the results that describe a sample be generalized to the population from which the sample was drawn.

## KEY THEMES

- The experimental method is a common approach to establishing facts.
- How do you express a research and null hypothesis?

## CHAPTER OVERVIEW

Inferential statistics take data analysis one step further than descriptive statistics by asking two related questions. First, can the description be regarded as genuine or could the results be due to chance or random happenings? Second, can the results that describe a sample be generalized to the population from which the sample was drawn? At the risk of over-simplifying, if through inferential statistics techniques we can establish that an obtained statistical description of a sample is genuine and not due to chance occurrence, then we can infer that what we can say about the sample can also be said about the population from which the sample is drawn. Statisticians have developed agreed-upon ways of reaching conclusions when the results of a survey are not clear cut. They apply the appropriate statistical test. Before the sport management researcher can do this, however, they need to understand some key concepts that are central to conducting inferential statistical analyses. This chapter will discuss some of the key concepts and their relationship to inferential statistics.

## INFERENTIAL STATISTICS

The following example highlights the value of inferential statistics. Suppose a sport management researcher is faced with the problem that it is assumed that prior alcohol consumption is considered to be causing a number of public disorder problems within the stadium. It is hypothesized that fans that consume alcohol for two hours before attending a football match will demonstrate significantly higher mean public disorder scores than fans who consume non-alcoholic drinks. In this case the nominal independent variable is alcoholic or non-alcoholic consumption. The interval level dependent variable is a mean public disorder score, which is measured on a scale of 0–100. The following data is produced.

- Non-alcoholic consumers have a mean public disorder score of 46.
- Alcoholic consumers have a mean public disorder score of 54.

The question we must ask is whether this difference is significant. When differences between means are very small we are confident that the differences are not significant. Similarly, when differences between means are very large we are confident that the differences are significant. However, in some cases the means may be very close together, as in the above example. So at what stage in between do we conclude that the means are different? This is where inferential statistics can be applied to reach a conclusion.

### How to determine the independent and dependent variables

A common method for establishing facts is the experimental method. The experimental method consists of the contrast between two treatment conditions. Where subjects are treated identically, except for one feature that is different – this treatment is referred to as the experimental treatment, or more commonly as the independent variable. The independent variable is what the sport management researcher is manipulating. For example, if a sport marketing executive is comparing two sales approaches to increase sales then the sales approach is the independent variable. The critical feature of behaviour of the subjects is referred to as the dependent variable, the response variable or the criterion variable. Any difference between these two conditions that we observe on the dependent variable is called the treatment effect and is usually assumed to have been caused by the experimental treatment. In essence, the dependent variable is the effect of the independent variable. In the comparison of the two sales approaches to increase sales the measure of sales is the dependent variable (Johnson and Kuby, 2011).

## The research and null hypothesis

The first step in any empirical research endeavour is to state the hypothesis. The research hypothesis ($H_1$) claims there is some relationship between the independent and dependent variables. It is usually worded in terms of:

- *differences between means* – the mean age for purchasing team merchandise will be significantly lower for males than for females;
- *relationships between variables* – the higher the disposable income of fans the greater their potential to purchase;
- *differences in frequency of occurrences* – there will be a significantly higher number of men than women who watch the English Premier League on Subscription TV.

The research hypothesis can either be one tailed or two tailed (Chase and Brown, 2000). A *one tailed research hypothesis* predicts the direction of the relationship of differences. For example, that there will be significantly more men than women who attend English Premier League matches.

A *two tailed research hypothesis* is non-directional. For example: there will be a significant gender difference in English Premier League match attendance. In this hypothesis the gender differences could be one of two possible differences. That is, more males than females or more females than males. This is therefore referred to as a two tailed hypothesis.

The null hypothesis ($H_0$) is the negation of the research hypothesis. It claims there is no relationship between the independent and dependent variables or there is no difference between means or frequencies (Chase and Brown, 2000). That is, there will be no significant gender difference in English Premier League match attendance. The null hypothesis is sometimes called the *chance hypothesis* because it claims any results obtained in an experimental or observational study are just due to chance. In statistics it is always the null hypothesis not the research hypothesis that is tested. The reason for this is quite straightforward. You can only work out the probability that a statement is true for a precisely worded statement. You cannot work out precise probability for an imprecise statement.

The null hypothesis ($H_0$) makes a precise statement: for example, that the difference between two means is zero or that the correlation (relationship) between two variables is zero. For this reason $H_0$ can be statistically tested, and the probability of it being true can be found. On the other hand, the research hypothesis ($H_1$) makes an imprecise statement. For example, one mean is greater than another or that the correlation (relationship) between variables is something other than zero. Because of this imprecise statement, the $H_1$ cannot be directly statistically tested (Chase and Brown, 2000).

How does the sport management researcher go about testing a hypothesis? Usually in a roundabout fashion that at first glance may seem unusual. For example, to find out whether Chicago Cubs fans are more aware of their team's main sponsor than non-fans, a sport management researcher will begin by claiming that the difference does not exist – that is, the null hypothesis is true. They will then conduct a statistical test to determine the extent of the difference. The probability of the null hypothesis being true is then determined from the results of the statistical test.

As these two steps are central to understanding inferential statistics we shall restate them in more technical terms.

1    To test a research hypothesis ($H_1$) you must formulate the corresponding null hypothesis ($H_0$).
2    You then conduct an inferential statistical test to determine the extent of the difference or relationships (types of inferential statistics are discussed later).
   ■ If the data from the test disagrees with the null hypothesis ($H_0$) you can reject $H_0$ and accept the $H_1$.
   ■ However, if the data is compatible with the $H_0$, then you have to accept the $H_0$ and reject the $H_1$.

As we have just stated, the $H_0$ must always be a precisely worded statement, for example:

$H_1$: Chicago Cubs fans will have significantly higher mean awareness scores than non-fans.
$H_0$: The difference between the mean awareness scores of Chicago Cubs fans and non-fans is zero.

We next have to look at how we go about proving whether $H_0$ is true or not. That is, how can we be sure the findings are genuine and not due to chance. To do this we need to understand three key concepts that underpin all inferential statistical tests. These three concepts are: the p-value (i.e. the probability of $H_0$ being true), degrees of freedom (df) and the confidence limit. We shall now discuss these concepts.

## RECENT CASE EXAMPLE: HYPOTHESIS TESTING

*The following article is an example of how hypothesis testing has been used in the past by researchers in Sport Management Research. The interested reader may wish to find/download and read the article for further insights.*

A quantitative analysis of collegiate athletic involvement and academic achievement among sport management students. Amos, C. (2013). Unpublished thesis. Liberty University. 288

The researcher tested three hypotheses relating to the academic achievement of sport management students in order to compare athletes and non-athletes. However, other data that may bias the sample was collected, such as working hours, practice and competition hours, gender, race and sport. The primary hypothesis was found to be true, that student athletes do have lower GPAs (grade point average) than non-athletes. Other hypotheses were found to be inconclusive.

## P-value

The probability value (or p-value) is the most central concept in inferential statistics. There are a number of ways of defining this notion of 'p' that can be considered precise and somewhat less precise. For example, a precise definition is that 'p' is a measure of the extent to which the obtained data agrees with $H_0$. A less precise definition is that 'p' is the probability that the obtained results are due to chance. The final aim of every inferential statistic is to produce a p-value that will allow the sport management researcher to make a decision about a null hypothesis. Being a measure of probability, the values of 'p' will lie between zero and one (Muijs, 2011; Howitt and Cramer, 2000).

In order to accurately calculate the p-value the sport management researcher has to take into consideration what is known as degrees of freedom (df), whether the $H_1$ is one tailed or two tailed, and then compare the p-value with the confidence limit. A confidence limit is an agreed probability, and if the p-value is above this limit we must accept the $H_0$ (Bluman, 2001).

## Degrees of freedom

Two important factors have a bearing on probability of the null hypothesis being true. These are:

1   whether the research hypothesis is one tailed or two tailed;
2   the number of subjects (N) sampled in the research (Muijs, 2011; Thomas and Nelson, 1996).

We discussed one and two tailed hypotheses earlier in this chapter, so we will now concentrate on the second factor: the number of subjects in the sample. It is intuitive that the greater the number of subjects sampled, the less likely you are to encounter a chance or random occurrence in your research. However, it is not mathematically correct to use N by itself to arrive at a p-value. For this, it is more appropriate to use the concept of *degrees of freedom*.

Degrees of freedom simply mean the number of scores that are free to vary within any given set. For example, if you select five numbers and write them down you would be free to vary all numbers, i.e. $df = N = 5$

If you choose five numbers and the total must be 25, then four numbers are free to vary but the fifth being the last to be chosen must be fixed. For example, $3+2+6+4+X = 25$. This can be expressed as:

$$
\begin{aligned}
\text{df} \quad &= \quad \text{N--1} \\
&= \quad 5\text{--}1 \\
&= \quad 4
\end{aligned}
$$

If you choose five numbers, the mean of which is to be 6, the same situation would be true. Four numbers could vary but once they are chosen, the fifth would be fixed. This is shown below:

$$
\begin{aligned}
\text{mean } (\bar{x}) \quad &= \quad 7+6+5+8+(x/5) \\
\text{mean} \quad &= \quad 30/5 \\
\text{mean} \quad &= \quad 6
\end{aligned}
$$

The df can be considered the corrected N. It is the number of observations minus the number of parameters being estimated.

When we select a sample for our research and find the mean, standard deviation, correlation coefficient etc. we are estimating the population parameters, that is, from the sample we are estimating the mean of the population. The parameters restrict the degrees of freedom in the sample observations. As such, when calculating 'p' (keeping in mind we must consider N, the number in our sample), we must correct for the fact that the use of any parameter has restricted the degrees of freedom of our observations (Thomas and Nelson, 1996). For example, say we want to see whether there is a difference in the mean sponsor awareness scores of Chicago Cubs fans and non-fans. Each group has an N of 10. If we apply an inferential statistical test known as an unpaired t-test (this test is discussed in Chapter 20) to measure the difference between the means of the two groups, we can say that the degrees of freedom for each group has been restricted by one parameter (i.e. the mean of each group).

In other words, while we have started out with N = 20, the fact that we are using two parameters results in the loss of two degrees of freedom. This needs to be considered in the calculation of 'p'. If we used N = 20 to calculate the p-value we may reject $H_0$, but it is possible that if df = 18 it might have resulted in $H_0$ being accepted. For other inferential statistical tests the calculation for df will vary, but will be in accordance with the rules highlighted above. Although statistical computer programs will automatically produce a p-value for you it is important that you understand the principles that underpin the calculations of the p-value.

## The confidence limit

Very small values of 'p' imply that it is very unlikely that the null hypothesis is true and so lead to the rejection of the null hypothesis and the acceptance of the research hypothesis. Not so small values of 'p' imply that it is quite possible that the null hypothesis is true and so lead to the retention of the null hypothesis and the rejection of the research hypothesis. This means there must be a cut-off value of 'p' below which the null hypothesis is rejected and the research hypothesis accepted and above which the null hypothesis is retained and the research hypothesis is rejected. The cut-off value of 'p' is known as the confidence limit (Bryman and Bell, 2011). In Sport Management Research the p-value is often set at .05. This means that if we can show that there are five chances or less out of 100 that the null hypothesis is true, then the null hypothesis is rejected and the research hypothesis is accepted. However, if you show that there are more than five chances out of 100 that the null hypothesis is true then the null hypothesis is retained and the research hypothesis is rejected.

This can be expressed in more technical terms as:

- If $p \leq 0.05$ then $H_0$ is rejected and $H_1$ is accepted (please note $\leq$ is less than or equal to).
- If $p > 0.05$ then $H_0$ is accepted and $H_1$ is rejected.

## Type 1 and type 2 errors

In hypothesis testing it is quite possible, despite accuracy of calculations, to make errors in your decisions. The sport management researcher needs to be aware of the types of error that can occur and their relationship to the whole process. When calculating 'p' and deciding whether to reject the null hypothesis there are four possible options available to choose from. Of these four decisions, two are what we call type 1 and type 2 errors. Type 1 errors occur when we reject the null hypothesis when in fact it is true. A type 2 error occurs when we accept the null hypothesis when in fact it is false. These two types of error are related and their careful consideration is important. The concern is that if you take steps to minimize a type 1 error you can immediately increase the likelihood of making a type 2 error; the reverse is also true (Muijs, 2011).

---

### HYPOTHETICAL CASE

A team is conducting research on the effect of a specific sponsor's, in this case a mobile phone company, fan engagement strategies. The team (and sponsor) would like to know if fans are more inclined to like, purchase and recommend that mobile phone provider compared to the general public since the beginning of the sponsorship engagement activities.

1   What hypotheses and null hypotheses could you test? Would each test be one-tailed or two-tailed?
2   What questions could you ask to test those hypotheses?
3   What sampling technique would you use? What groups and how many of each group?

---

## CONCLUSION

This chapter has outlined the fundamental principles that underpin the approaches sport management researchers must take in order to test the outcomes of their empirical investigations. We began by defining the nature and purpose of inferential statistics, arguing that these statistical methods go further than just describing data; they attempt to determine whether differences or relationships are really due to chance and whether they allow us to infer any such differences to populations. The chapter then led you through some key concepts that are central to conducting inferential statistical analyses. We have argued that you cannot understand hypothesis testing in inferential statistics without understanding certain key concepts and their relationship to inferential statistics.

## REVIEW QUESTIONS

Inferential statistics take data analysis one step further than descriptive statistics by asking two related questions. First, can the description be regarded as genuine or could the results be due to chance or random happenings? Second, can the results that describe a sample be generalized to the population from which the sample was drawn? With this in mind:

- Discuss when the sport management researcher would use inferential statistics.
- What are the advantages of being able to generalize from a sample?

## SUGGESTED EXTENDED READING FOR STUDENTS

Bryman, A., and Bell, E. (2011). *Business research methods.* London: Oxford University Press.
Chase, W., and Brown, F. (2000). *General statistics* (4th edn). New York: John Wiley & Sons.
Muijs, D. (2011). *Doing Quantitative Research in Education with SPSS* (2nd edn). Thousand Oaks, CA: Sage.

# Chapter 19

# Correlation and regression analysis

## LEARNING OUTCOMES

By the end of this chapter you should be able to:

- explain how the sport management researcher can explore relationships between variables;
- distinguish between a scattergram and scatterplot;
- explain the purpose of a correlation coefficient;
- define and explain Pearson product moment correlation coefficient;
- distinguish between the different types of regression analysis.

## KEY TERMS

*A correlation coefficient* – is a single numerical index that summarizes some, but not all, of the key features of a scattergram.

*Pearson product moment correlation coefficient* – identifies the closeness of fit of the points of a scattergram to the best-fitting straight line through those points and gives information about whether the slope of the scattergram is positive or negative.

*The squared correlation coefficient* – is known as the coefficient of determination.

*Regression* – allows the researcher to make predictions, and regression equations always use a predictor variable and a criterion variable.

## KEY THEMES

- What do scattergrams and scatterplots tell the sport management researcher?
- Why would a sport management researcher use regression analysis?

## CHAPTER OVERVIEW

This chapter will discuss in general terms how the relationships between two or more variables can be explained through the use of statistical techniques. In doing this it will describe some of the main graphical and tabular methods for presenting interrelationships. It will then discuss the meaningfulness and reliability of correlation coefficients and tools to measure this relationship between variables.

## INTRODUCTION

Although it is essential to be able to describe the characteristics of each variable in your research both diagrammatically and numerically, the interrelationships between variables are also an essential component of Sport Management Research. For example, membership opinion polling is something we are familiar with and the most common use of single-variable statistics that most of the population will encounter. Sport management researchers may ask a variety of questions about candidates who are seeking appointment as President of a Football Club, and voting intentions, which are reported separately. However, sport management researchers often report relationships between variables. For example, if one asks whether the voting intentions of male members and female members differ, it is really to enquire whether there is a relationship between the variable 'sex' and the variable 'voting intention'. Similarly, if one was to ask whether the popularity of the current Club President has changed over time, this really implies that there may be a relationship between the variable 'time' and the variable 'popularity' of the Club President. This is what is meant by the interrelationship between variables.

Choosing appropriate techniques to show relationships between two variables requires an understanding of the difference between nominal category data and numerical score data. The type of charts or tables you use depends on whether the variables are scores, nominal categories, or both. Where both variables take the form of numerical scores, generally the best form of graphical presentation is the *scattergram* or *scatterplot*. The values of one variable are plotted against the values on the other variable (Harnett and Soni, 1991; Johnson and Kuby, 2011; Thomas and Nelson, 1996).

A scatterplot is something you might see in a financial newspaper. The share price of say Manchester United Football Club is plotted on the Y axis and the year is plotted on the X axis. This fictitious example is shown in Figure 19.1 and we can see that if we plot the share price overtime it is dropping.

A scattergram contains the essential features of a scatterplot. That is, it is a graph representing the distribution of two variables in a sample population. One variable is plotted on the vertical axis; the second is plotted on the horizontal axis. The scores or values of each sample unit are usually represented by dots. A scattergram demonstrates the degree or tendency with which the variables occur in association with each other. A scattergram may also include a line that runs through these points (Harnett and Soni, 1991; Johnson and Kuby, 2011; Thomas and Nelson, 1996). This is called the regression line and is highlighted in Figure 19.2.

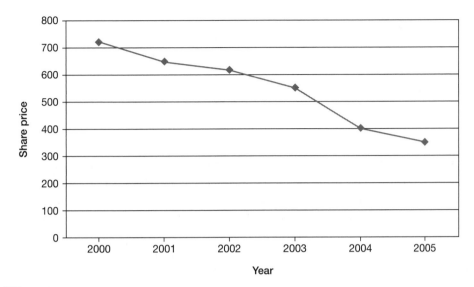

**Figure 19.1** *Share price scatterplot*

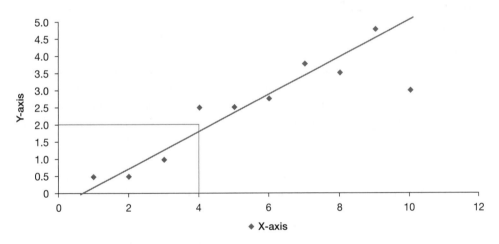

**Figure 19.2** *Scattergram example*

In Figure 19.2 the horizontal line is your X axis with the values written along it. The vertical line is your Y axis and the values as listed against this axis. The different scores are plotted and represented as squares. The point marked represents a case where the score on the X variable is 4 and on the Y variable is 2. The line that runs through these points is called the line of 'best fit'. It is a line that runs through all the data and is also called the regression line.

Sometimes, and as is the case in the above example, it is possible to see that the points on a scattergram fall more or less in a straight line. In some instances, however, it is difficult to

**Table 19.1** *Cross-tabulation/contingency table*

|  | Male | Female |
|---|---|---|
| Previously a member | f = 20 | f = 25 |
| Not previously a member | f = 30 | f = 14 |

illustrate the number of overlapping cases (i.e. the same scores) on a scattergram. Under these circumstances sport management researchers might use what is known as contingency or cross-tabulation tables in which scores are allocated into bands and expressed in frequency of occurrences. An example of a cross-tabulation/contingency table example is shown Table 19.1.

Table 19.1 simple shows the frequencies of each group and whether they have been a previous member of the club or not. If we wished we could summarize it as a percentage. We could say that 40 per cent of the males surveyed had previously been a member.

## CORRELATION COEFFICIENTS

Although a scattergram is an important tool for showing relationships between variables it is space consuming. For many purposes it is convenient to have the main features of a scattergram expressed as a single numerical index. This single numerical index is the correlation coefficient. This is a number index that summarizes some, but not all, of the key features of a scattergram. To obtain this index there are a number of underlying assumptions required (Bluman, 2001; Howitt and Cramer, 2000; Johnson and Kuby, 2011; Keppel, 1973; Wild and Seber, 2000). These are:

- related pairs – data must be collected from related pairs. For example, if you obtain a score on an X variable there must also be a score on the Y variable from the same subject;
- scale of measurement – score data;
- normality – the scores within each variable should be normally distributed;
- linearity – the relationships between two variables must be linear (that is only affected by each other);
- homoscedasticity – the variability in the scores for one variable is roughly the same at all values of the other variable. That is, it is concerned with how scores cluster uniformly around the regression line. The variability in the X scores is roughly the same variability that exists in the Y scores (Bluman, 2001; Howitt and Cramer, 2000; Johnson and Kuby, 2011; Keppel, 1973; Wild and Seber, 2000).

There are two types of correlation coefficients. Pearson product moment correlation and Spearman's rho. In this chapter we will look at Pearson's correlation. Spearman's rho will be discussed in greater detail in Chapter 21.

**290**

## Pearson product moment correlation

Pearson product moment correlation coefficient ($r$) includes two major pieces of information. These are the closeness of fit of the points of a scattergram to the best-fitting straight line through those points and information about whether the slope of the scattergram is positive or negative. By this we mean the closeness of fit of all points around the line of 'best fit' – the regression line. This is represented as a numerical index that tells us how good or bad that 'fit' is around the line. When we talk about correlation coefficients we say they have a range from +1.00 to 0.0 to −1.00. So the value can fall anywhere within this range and each value tells us something slightly different about the variables. Therefore, a correlation coefficient is made up of two parts. There is either a positive or negative sign and a numerical value between −1 and +1. The positive or negative sign tells us something about the slope of the regression line. If it is a positive sign the slope of the regression line will run from the bottom left of the scattergram to the top right corner of it. A positive sign means X and Y scores increase together (Chase and Brown, 2000; Muijs, 2011; Thomas and Nelson, 1996; Wild and Seber, 2000). For example, if ticket prices go up and attendance goes down, then there is a negative correlation, but if ticket prices go up and attendance also goes up then there is a positive correlation.

Sometimes the regression line fits perfectly along all points of the scattergram. A value of 1 (plus or minus) means the points on the scattergram lie exactly on the line of best fit – the regression line. So we can say the numerical value of the correlation coefficient (0.50, 0.42 etc.) is an index of how close the points on a scattergram fit the best-fitting straight line. The closer the index is to 1.00 (in this case plus 1) the closer the points will be to the line of best fit. If attendance rises by exactly the percentage that ticket prices increase, then there will be a +1 correlation coefficient; however, that is unlikely to occur. If the line, however, is totally vertical or horizontal that would indicate there is no variation in scores on one of the variables and so no correlation can be calculated (Chase and Brown, 2000; Thomas and Nelson, 1996; Wild and Seber, 2000).

On the other hand, if the sign is negative then the slope of the straight line goes from the upper left to the lower right of the scattergram. This would indicate a value of negative 1. A negative sign means as an X score increases a Y score decreases. A value of 0.00 means the points on the scattergram are randomly scattered around the straight line. A value of 0.50 would mean that although the points on the scattergram are generally close to the best fitting line, there is no considerable spread of these points around the straight line. A smaller correlation coefficient may suggest that other variables (e.g. win percentage, other entertainment options and opponent played) may have more of an influence on attendance than ticket price as there is too much variation to suggest ticket price alone is a primary motivation for attending a game. The correlation coefficient is merely an index of the amount of variance of the scattergram points from the straight line. Maximum variance around the straight line results in a correlation of zero. The closer the relationship between the two variables the higher the correlation coefficient, up to a maximum of 1.00 (Chase and Brown, 2000; Muijs, 2011; Thomas and Nelson, 1996; Wild and Seber, 2000).

In the formula for the correlation coefficient we use something called the *covariance*. Instead of multiplying scores by themselves, we multiply the score on one variable (X) by the score on the second variable (Y). The correlation coefficient is a measure of the *lack of variation* around a straight line though a scattergram. When we get a large positive value of covariance there is a strong positive relationship between the two variables. A large negative value indicates a negative relationship between the two variables. If there is no relationship between the variables then the covariance is zero (Bluman, 2001; Howitt and Cramer, 2000; Wild and Seber, 2000).

Another example of using the Pearson correlation coefficient may be that a sport management researcher is interested in determining the relationship between playing contact sports and the reported incidence of violence towards women. The researcher collects data from the appropriate databases and formulates the following hypotheses:

- null hypothesis: there is no relationship between playing contact sports and reported incidences of violence towards women;
- research hypothesis: there is a relationship between playing contact sports and reported incidences of violence towards women.

Before commencing it is always good practice to draw the scattergram for any correlation coefficient you are calculating as a cross-checking measure. Once the calculation is completed the researcher will need to determine statistical significance by referring to the critical value tables of correlation coefficients. Remember the sign of the correlation coefficient tells you whether the relationship is positive or negative. In order to establish how much variance is shared you need to square the correlation of coefficient. The squared correlation coefficient is known as the *coefficient of determination* (Howitt and Cramer, 2000; Muijs, 2011; Wild and Seber, 2000). For example, a correlation coefficient of 0.8 means 64 per cent of the variance is shared.

---

## RECENT CASE EXAMPLE: PEARSON CORRELATION

*The following article is an example of how Pearson correlation has been used in the past by researchers in Sport Management Research. The interested reader may wish to find/download and read the article for further insights.*

Beyond the game: Perceptions and practices of corporate social responsibility in the professional sport industry. Sheth, H., and Babiak, K. (2010). *Journal of Business Ethics*, 91(3), 433–450.

Part of this research included Pearson correlations between corporate social responsibility (CSR) and variables such as win percentage (−0.329), team revenues (0.164) and team value (−0.013). Win percentage seemed to have the only minor relationship − as teams win more, self-reported involvement in CSR decreased.

## Regression analysis

The vast majority of Sport Management Research is aimed at accounting for an event or a particular type of behaviour. Regardless of the research question, data analysis treats variables in the same way. Statistics uses numbers to find relationships between variables. It does not consider what the variables are, only the relations between the numbers.

The use of any statistical model produces two types of variability. That explained by the manipulation of, or association between variables, and that which can't be explained, unaccounted for variability or error. A general statistical model can be represented as:

| Data | = | model | + | error (residual) |
| Data | = | Explained Variability | + | Unexplained Variability |
| Aim: | | Maximize | | Minimize |

As previously discussed, good methodology plays a critical role in maximizing the variability accounted for. The best or most complex statistical analyses will not rectify problems with the data collection procedure. The statistics are a tool for the analysis of this data only. They cannot provide a miraculous cure for methodological sloppiness or errors.

The simplest model used in data analysis concerns description: how well the model is accepted as a true representation or description of behaviour or phenomena is determined by the amount of variability accounted for by the model. The size and distribution of the error evaluates this. The simplest form of a model is a single parameter where a single measure is produced. In many circumstances taking more variables into account can reduce the error term, thereby producing a better fit of the model. For example, does the number of years of experience as a sport manager contribute to the salary earned? A simple regression model is a two parameter model that works on this notion. This statistical technique allows prediction of a score on one (dependent or criterion) variable based on a score on a second (independent or predictor) variable (Bluman, 2001; Howitt and Cramer, 2000; Muijs, 2011; Wild and Seber, 2000).

So we have established that regression that allows the researcher to make predictions and regression equations always uses a *predictor variable* and a *criterion variable* (Muijs, 2011; Thomas and Nelson, 1996; Wild and Seber, 2000). When undertaking regression analysis the horizontal axis (X axis) should always be used to represent the variable from which the prediction is being made. The vertical dimension (Y axis) should always represent what is being predicted. We have previously noted, however, that a scattergram can act as a tool for prediction. If we draw a straight line as best we can through the points on a scattergram, this line could be used as a basis for making predictions. Remember this line is called the regression line. The problem with this procedure is that prediction depends on the particular line drawn through the points on a scattergram. We could all draw different lines. These subjective factors are not desirable and a method that is not influenced by subjectivity and subsequently reduces the possibility of variability would be desirable. To do this, mathematical ways of determining the regression lines have been developed (Zikmund, 2000).

The line through a set of points on a scattergram is called the regression line. The sum of deviations of the scattergram points from the regression line should be minimal. In order to specify the regression line for any scattergram, you quantify two things: first, the point at which the regression line cuts the vertical axis. It can take a positive or negative value and it is normally denoted in regression as point *a* or the intercept. Second, the slope of the regression line, which can be positive or negative, is normally denoted by the letter *b*. The slope is simply the number of units that the regression line moves up the vertical axis for each unit it moves along the horizontal axis. Prediction is the main function of regression (Muijs, 2011).

The major differences between correlation and regression are first, that regression retains the original units of measurement so direct comparison between regression analyses based on different variables is difficult. Correlation coefficients can be readily compared as they are essentially on a standardized measurement scale and free of the original units of measurements. Second, the correlation coefficient does not specify the slope of the scattergram as a regression analysis does. The correlation coefficient indicates the spread of variability of the points around the regression line in the scattergram. In other words, correlation and regression have somewhat different functions despite their close similarities. Linear regression analysis produces a line of best fit referred to as the *least squares regression equation*. This line can be thought of as a prediction line (Bluman, 2001). How linear regression could be applied to Sport Management Research could be as follows.

A group of athletes' absence from work after poor performance at the London Olympic Games was calculated in days over a six-month period. A questionnaire designed to measure the amount of positive reinforcement received by the athlete from family and friends showed no overall relationship with the amount of absence from work. However, the greater the amount of criticism received by the athlete the more the athlete was absent from work. In this case the sport management researcher could carry out a regression analysis to establish what the best prediction of absence from work would be for a person with a certain positive reinforcement score. It should be remembered though that the proper interpretation of the regression equation depends on the scattergram between the two variables showing a more or less linear (straight line) trend. If it does not show this, then the interpretations of the regression calculations for the slope and intercept will be misleading since the method assumes a straight line

## Multiple regression

In most instances it is unlikely that a single independent variable can account for the majority of the variability in a dependent variable. Generally, a number of variables contribute to any behaviour (Bluman, 2001; Howitt and Cramer, 2000; Muijs, 2011; Wild and Seber, 2000). For example, if you are considering purchasing some sporting memorabilia there are a number of factors that contribute to your decision whether to purchase or not. When more than one independent variable is used we generally are able to account for more of the variability (or components of the dependent variable) than when a single independent variable is used. When more than one independent variable is used in a regression analysis the analysis is termed multiple regression analysis. In this case the value of Y is obtained using two or more independent variables. Multiple regression takes the influence of all independent variables into account when predicting Y. In multiple regression analysis variability in the dependent variable is accounted for in the way the independent variables are related to one another and the dependent variable. In multiple regression the regression equation is the same as simple linear regression except that there are several predictors and each predictor has its own (partial) regression coefficient (Thomas and Nelson, 1996; Wild and Seber, 2000).

There are three major regression models. These are: standard/simultaneous regression, hierarchical regression and stepwise regression (Thomas and Nelson, 1996). These models differ in two ways. They differ first in the treatment of overlapping variability due to the correlation of the independent variables, and second, in terms of entry of the independent variables into the equation. In the standard/simultaneous model all independent variables enter the regression equation at once because you want to examine the relationship between the whole set of predictors and the dependent variable. In hierarchical multiple regression you determine the order of entry of the independent variables based on theoretical knowledge. In stepwise regression the number of independent variables entered and the order of entry is predetermined by statistical criteria generated by the stepwise procedure (Bluman, 2001; Howitt and Cramer, 2000; Muijs, 2011; Wild and Seber, 2000). The choice of technique depends largely on the researcher's goals. In the case of sport management it may be that a national sport marketing manager of a large fitness chain wants to determine the effect of shelf space and price on the sales of protein drinks. A random sample of 25 equal sized stores could be selected and the sales, shelf space in square metres, and price per kilogram recorded. All three regression models discussed could be applied to this research problem.

## RECENT CASE EXAMPLE: REGRESSION ANALYSIS

*The following article is an example of how regression analysis has been used in the past by researchers in Sport Management Research. The interested reader may wish to find/download and read the article for further insights.*

Expenditures on sport apparel: Creating consumer profiles through interval regression modelling. Scheerder, J., Vos, S., and Taks, M. (2011). *European Sport Management Quarterly, 11*(3), 251–274.

Ten independent (Y) variables involving demographics, behaviours and attitudes were used to predict how much money people may spend on sport apparel (the dependent or X variable). The profile with the highest probability (0.60) to purchase sport apparel was females aged 41–45, university educated, small family, intensive sport participation, partner that is involved in sport, highly favourable attitude towards sport, with many sport friends, but does not watch much sport on TV.

## CONCLUSION

This chapter discussed in general terms how the relationships between two or more variables can be explained through the use of statistical techniques. It described some of the main graphical and tabular methods for presenting interrelationships. It then discussed the meaningfulness and reliability of correlation coefficients and tools to measure this relationship between variables. It finished by providing a general discussion of multiple regression analysis.

## REVIEW QUESTIONS

In this chapter we discussed how to examine the relationships between variables. With this in mind:

- Identify how the sport management researcher can graphically and numerically represent the relationships between two variables. Prepare an example that highlights this.
- Discuss regression and how it differs from multiple regressions. Provide examples of when the sport management researcher may use regression and multiple regression techniques.

## SUGGESTED EXTENDED READING FOR STUDENTS

Chase, W., and Brown, F. (2000). *General statistics* (4th edn). New York: John Wiley & Sons.

Johnson, R. R., and Kuby, P. (2011). *Elementary statistics*. Boston, MA: Brooks/Cole.

Muijs, D. (2011). *Doing quantitative research in education with SPSS* (2nd edn). Thousand Oaks, CA: Sage.

Wild, C. J., and Seber, G. A. F. (2000). Chance *encounters: A first course in data analysis and inference*. New York: John Wiley & Sons.

## Chapter 20

# Determining difference among groups

### LEARNING OUTCOMES

By the end of this chapter you should be able to:

■ explain how the sport management researcher establishes the nature of the variable;
■ distinguish between dependent and independent variables;
■ define and identify different types of t-tests;
■ define and explain analysis of variance and repeated measures ANOVA;
■ explain the purpose of post hoc testing;
■ define and explain analysis of covariance;
■ explain when the sport management researcher would use multivariate analysis of variance.

### KEY TERMS

*Univariate statistics* – seek to measure the differences between a single variable and a fixed value.
*Bivariate statistics* – deal with the relationship between two variables.
*Multivariate statistics* – deal with complex interrelationships between two or more variables.

### KEY THEMES

■ Which inferential test is appropriate for the sport management researcher to use in a given situation?
■ How do you determine difference between groups?

## CHAPTER OVERVIEW

So far in this text we have noted that different types of data (nominal, ordinal and interval) and different types of hypothesis (differences or relationships) require different methods of analysis. In this chapter we examine the criteria we use to establish which inferential test should be chosen to effect an appropriate analysis. Inferential statistics can fall into three groups. These include: univariate, bivariate and multivariate (Harnett and Soni, 1991; Johnson and Kuby, 2011). Univariate statistics seek to measure the differences between a single variable and a fixed value. For example, the researcher may want to know whether the English Premier League viewing habits of a group of men aged 20–25 in Manchester, England is significantly different from the national average of the same sample. In this case, the single variable is the viewing habits of men located in Manchester, and the fixed value is the national average of viewing habits. Bivariate statistics deal with the relationship between two variables. Sport management researchers may be interested in gender differences in certain behaviours such as purchasing merchandise. In this case we have two variables: gender (independent variable) and purchasing behaviour (dependent variable). Gender is the nominal variable (male vs female) while purchasing behaviours is an interval level variable (say, scores on a test of intent to purchase). Multivariate statistics deals with complex interrelationships between two or more variables. Let's say we want to test whether the architectural skills of sport stadium designers are more closely related to creative styles than to intelligence. Here we have two independent variables (creative styles and intelligence) and one dependent variable (architectural skills).

## SELECTING THE RIGHT TEST

If the sport management researcher wants to know what inferential test is appropriate for a given hypothesis they need to establish the nature of the independent variable, the dependent variable and the hypothesis. How this can be done is shown in Figure 20.1. It highlights the decisions a sport management researcher must make before an appropriate inferential test can be selected.

To understand how these options are worked out we shall use the following example. We have the following hypothesis:

■ Fans who consume alcohol for two hours before attending a football match will demonstrate significantly higher mean public disorder scores than fans who consume non-alcoholic drinks.

First we need to identify the independent and dependent variables, the type of data involved in each and where applicable the number of categories per variable. For this hypothesis question we could use the data in Table 20.1.

We have established that it is a difference hypothesis as we are trying to predict a difference between the means of two different groups on the dependent variable. We also know the number of categories in the independent variable (alcoholic and non-alcoholic), so we can say there are two groups of fans to be tested. The first group consumes alcoholic drinks and the second group consumes non-alcoholic drinks. Since we have two groups in our hypothesis we know that we must apply the unpaired t-test. A t-test is used to determine whether a set

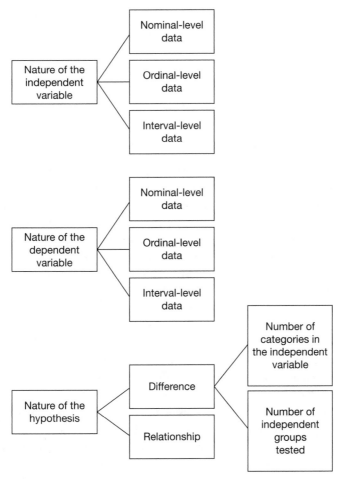

**Figure 20.1** *Selecting an inferential test*

**Table 20.1** *Variable characteristics*

| Type of variable | Type of data | Categories or scale |
|---|---|---|
| Independent variable (Type of drink consumed) | Nominal-level data | Alcoholic Non-alcoholic |
| Dependent variable (Public disorder scores) | Interval-level data | A scale of scores 0–100 |

or sets of scores are from the same population. In other words, is there a significant difference between two sets of measures? There are two main types of t-tests that will be covered in this chapter:

- repeated measures (paired t-test)
- independent groups (unpaired t-test).

## Underpinning assumptions

There are generic assumptions underlying all t-tests. These relate to the scale of measurement, that is the data should be at the interval or ratio level of measurement; the principle of random sampling, the scores should be randomly sampled from the population of interest; and the concept of normality, the scores should be normally distributed in the population (Howitt and Cramer, 2000; Johnson and Kuby, 2011). The assumption of normality is a prerequisite for many inferential statistics. The *normal curve* describes a particular shape of a frequency curve. The normal curve is characterized by the mean, median and mode being at the same point (centre of the distribution) (Bryman and Bell, 2011).

### The paired t-test

The related (correlated) t-test compares the means of two related samples of scores to see whether the means differ significantly. The related (correlated) t-test is also called the *repeated measures designs* or the *dependent t-test* (Howitt and Cramer, 2000; Johnson and Kuby, 2011). For example, a major sport technology swimsuit manufacturer developed a sharkskin swimsuit that was supposed to increase swimming efficiency. Twenty-two swimmers performed both with and without the swimsuit, and the number of metres travelled per minute was recorded. Whether the swimmer was male or female was also recorded and coded as 1 = female and 2 = male.

The manufacturer is interested in addressing the following questions. Does swimming efficiency (number of metres swum per minute) improve when the sharkskin swimsuit is used? This is a repeated measures (paired) t-test design. We can develop the following hypotheses:

- *Research hypothesis ($H_1$):* there is a significant difference in performance between swimmers wearing normal and sharkskin swimsuits.
- *Null hypothesis ($H_0$):* there is no difference in performance between swimmers wearing normal and sharkskin swimsuits.

The question is whether the mean scores in the two conditions are sufficiently different from each other to fall in the extreme 5 per cent of cases. If they do it may allow us to generalize (depending on the size of the sample) from the research findings. The key characteristic is that a group of participants is measured twice on a single variable in slightly different conditions or circumstances. The scores on this example are on the dependent variable of swimming efficiency. The independent variable refers to the various conditions in which the measurements are being taken, wearing normal or sharkskin swimsuits. If we were to conclude that the two-tailed significance is less than .05, we would accept $H_1$ and reject $H_0$. Therefore, a significant difference does exist between swimming efficiency with and without the sharkskin swimsuit. The sharkskin swimsuit significantly improves the number of metres swum per minute.

### The unpaired t-test

The independent group t-test has two additional assumptions. The first relates to the independence of groups, participants should appear in only one group and these groups are unrelated; second, there is homogeneity of variance, that is the groups should come from populations with equal variances. The unrelated t-test compares two groups of scores from two separate groups of individuals to assess whether the average score of one group is higher than that of the other group. The unrelated (uncorrelated) t-test is also called the *student t-test* or *independent t-test* (Howitt and Cramer, 2000; Johnson and Kuby, 2011).

The meaning of unrelated samples is as follows: a group of experienced sport managers may be compared with a group of inexperienced sport managers in terms of the amount of time that they take to make complex decisions. The independent variable is experience as a sport manager whereas the dependent variable is decision-making time. If we return to our previous example it may be that the sport technology manufacturer wants to know the following: does swimming efficiency (number of metres swum per minute) with and without the sharkskin swimsuit differ between male and female swimmers? This is an independent groups (unpaired) t-test. The following hypotheses may be formulated:

- *Research hypothesis (H₁)*: there is a significant difference in swimming efficiency both with and without the sharkskin swimsuit between male and female swimmers.
- *Null hypothesis (H₀)*: there is no significant difference in swimming efficiency both with and without the sharkskin swimsuit between male and female swimmers.

If we were to conclude that the two-tailed significance for *without sharkskin* swimsuit indicates that the probability is less than .05 and is not significant we would accept the null hypothesis ($H_0$) and reject the research hypothesis ($H_1$). In relation to *with-suit*, if we were to conclude that no significant differences are apparent ($p > .05$) we would again accept the null hypothesis ($H_0$) and reject the research hypothesis ($H_1$). That is, there is no significant difference in swimming efficiency between male and female swimmers either with or without the sharkskin swimsuit.

## Analysis of variance

In order to use analysis of variance (ANOVA), three general conditions must be satisfied. First, for each condition the data are normally distributed, often referred to as the *normality assumption*. Second, each condition is assumed to have the same variance, referred to as *homogeneity of variance*. When differences between groups are being considered, the size of the standard deviations between groups is important. This is referred to as homogeneity of variance and is tested with a number of different statistics. Violation of this assumption inflates the type 1 error rate (Chase and Brown, 2000). Finally it is assumed that the performance of one individual or element is not influenced by a score obtained by another individual or element; this is referred to as the *independence of observations*. The general opinion currently is that if there are equal numbers of subjects in the groups, modest violations of these assumptions are acceptable when performing ANOVA (Howitt and Cramer, 2000; Keppel, 1973; Muijs, 2011; Wild and Seber, 2000).

## Underpinning theory

The analysis of variance (ANOVA) is a general statistical technique for comparing the means of more than two treatments (levels of independent variables). It is related to the t-test and has variations corresponding to independent and repeated measure designs. ANOVA operates using the principle that each individual score can be portioned (or separated) into a number of components that are additive. The general idea underlying ANOVA is to determine whether differences between groups occur as a result of presentation of different levels of the independent variable or whether differences found are due to chance fluctuations only. The notion behind this form of analysis is that the total variability in a set of scores can be split up into a series of components, each of which can be attributed to different sources. These are within and between groups' variability. ANOVA describes the partitioning of terms such as the sum of squares. The sum of squares is the sum of the squared differences between individual scores and the mean of the group of interest. At its most general level of description the total sum of squares is divided up into a component due to differences between treatments (differences between the different levels of the independent variable) and a component that measures the variability of scores within conditions (within group variability) (Howitt and Cramer, 2000; Keppel, 1973; Muijs, 2011; Wild and Seber, 2000).

ANOVA is based on a comparison of the variability between and within treatments (Howitt and Cramer, 2000; Johnson and Kuby, 2011; Keppel, 1973; Wild and Seber, 2000). Let us consider within-treatment variability first. For any experimental condition carried out on a group of participants we would expect the scores within the condition to vary. Examples of causes of this variability are chance fluctuations, individual differences or measurement error. This gives you an estimate of the general variability within each group treatment. This provides an estimate of the sampling error and can be measured by estimating the variability of individual scores about the individual treatment mean. Now let us consider the differences between treatments. If the null hypothesis is true, the treatment means are equal. It is not expected that the obtained treatment means will be exactly equal, due to sampling error caused by general variability of scores. The amount of variability found between condition means is determined by the sampling distribution of the means (where the participants come from in the population) and how much each group differs from the total mean. This tells us about the influence of each level of the independent variable plus associated error. With this form of variability we take into account the difference between the mean for each level of the independent variable and the mean of all conditions, together with the number of participants in each of the individual groups, which is used as a weighting factor (Howitt and Cramer, 2000; Johnson and Kuby, 2011; Keppel, 1973; Wild and Seber, 2000).

**302**

In ANOVA the variability found within and between treatments is evaluated using a ratio. The key concept is that within-group variability represents the sampling error and the between-group variability represents sampling error plus the treatment effects. Therefore, under the null hypothesis, where there is no treatment effect, this value, called the F ratio or variance ratio, should be about 1.0. If there is an effect of treatment the F ratio should be greater than one (Howitt and Cramer, 2000; Johnson and Kuby, 2011; Keppel, 1973; Wild and Seber, 2000).

## The factorial analysis of variance for independent groups

A large amount of Sport Management Research is interested in results where two or more independent variables (factors) need to be examined in combination. In these cases we use more complex applications of ANOVA. Consider the following example: let us say we want to measure the way a disciplinary tribunal's attitude to a player may be influenced by the player's behaviour. The physical appearance (well dressed, not well dressed) of the player and the facial expressions used during the tribunal hearing (smiling, neutral) could be of interest. This factorial design allows the sport management researcher to find additional information concerning the way the levels of independent variables influence scores on the dependent variable. The most important aspect about a factorial design is the way the two different variables influence one another. For example, does the tribunal react differently to facial expression if the player differs in physical appearance? This is referred to as the interaction (Bluman, 2001; Howitt and Cramer, 2000; Johnson and Kuby, 2011; Keppel, 1973; Wild and Seber, 2000).

## Repeated measures ANOVA

The first point to note about repeated measures designs is that they carry an additional assumption beyond the ones we have already discussed. This assumption is called sphericity. This assumption refers to the need for the variance of the population of difference scores for any two conditions to be the same as the variance of the population difference scores for any other two conditions (Bluman, 2001; Howitt and Cramer, 2000; Johnson and Kuby, 2011; Keppel, 1973; Wild and Seber, 2000).

Repeated measures ANOVA partitions the variability into that between subjects and that within subjects. For a simple one-way repeated measures design, the between-subjects effect is simply the variation in subjects mean scores across conditions. A major source of experimental error is due to individual differences that can be controlled by using repeated measures (Keppel, 1973; Zikmund, 2000). A great deal of Sport Management Research involves studies that measure the same dependent variable more than once. For example, a sports manufacturer may want to investigate whether the packaging of a sport product has an effect on the sales of that item. Four different types of packaging have been suggested for the product. The manufacturer draws a random sample of 60 stores from the population of stores that sell that product. The product is sold at those stores for three months and then the packaging in changed. Product sales are assessed four times (quarterly) over a 12 month

**303**

period. Basically, the repeated measure is used as four levels of the independent variable, which is the packaging. The most frequent use of repeated measures involves factorial ANOVA (which has been previously discussed). In this case one or more of the factors (independent variables) are repeated measures.

According to Pedhazur (1982), repeated measures designs have some key advantages. First, they provide the sport management researcher with the opportunity to control for individual differences among participants. This is important as it is probably the largest source of variation in most research studies. Second, repeated measure designs are more economical in that fewer participants are required. Finally, repeated measure designs allow for phenomena to be studied across time. There is, however, a disadvantage with repeated measure designs that should be known. As indicated above, repeated measure designs have the additional assumption of sphericity. A failure to meet this assumption can result in an increase in type 1 error (Howitt and Cramer, 2000; Johnson and Kuby, 2011).

## Post hoc testing

We will not go into great detail about post hoc analysis other than to say that through ANOVA we may establish that a significant difference exists among the three group means. We may not know, however, whether all three groups differ. That is, do groups 1 and 2 differ from group 3 but not from each other? In these cases we can perform what is commonly referred to as a post hoc analysis. Post hoc analysis is when you search through your data for any significance. What you are looking to complete is an entire set of comparisons. This type of testing carries risks of type 1 errors. Unlike planned comparisons, post hoc tests are designed to protect against type 1 errors, given that all possible comparisons are going to be made. These tests are stricter than planned comparisons and thus it is harder to obtain significance. The more options a test offers, the stricter its determination of significance. The Scheffe post hoc test, for example, allows you to perform every possible comparison but is tough on rejecting the null hypothesis. In contrast, Tukey's significant difference test is more lenient but you are restricted in terms of the types of comparisons that can be made (Bluman, 2001; Johnson and Kuby, 2011; Keppel, 1973).

## Analysis of covariance

The aim of analysis of covariance (ANCOVA) is similar to that of ANOVA. That is, it aims to evaluate differences between groups. ANCOVA combines the features of regression analysis and ANOVA. The technique is used to statistically remove the effects of an unwanted variable (the covariate) prior to evaluating the effects between the groups. In other words, it aims to adjust the independent variable for some distractor variable – called the covariate (Johnson and Kuby, 2011; Keppel, 1973; Zikmund, 2000). Before undertaking ANCOVA it is important to ensure that all six assumptions are accounted for. These assumptions can be found in many statistics textbooks.

To highlight how this might be applied in Sport Management Research let us say we are interested in looking at whether women or men were more successful at selling corporate boxes for a professional sporting league. The researcher records sales made by 22 corporate sales representatives over a 24-month period. However, the researcher is aware that years of selling experience would also contribute to the success of the representative and considers it may be fairer to make a comparison while taking into account this added factor. Thus the dependent variable is sales in number of corporate boxes sold over a 24-month period, the independent variable is gender and the covariate is years of experience in selling corporate boxes.

## Multivariate analysis of variance

Multivariate analysis of variance (MANOVA) is a direct extension of univariate ANOVA, where instead of analysing one dependent variable, two or more are used to measure the effects on one or more categorical independent variables. MANOVA assesses the statistical significance of differences between groups on a number of different dependent variables simultaneously (Bluman, 2001; Howitt and Cramer, 2000; Johnson and Kuby, 2011; Keppel, 1973; Wild and Seber, 2000). A major aim is to determine whether the groups differ on a set of dependent variables (Keppel, 1973; Zikmund, 2000). Again, with this test there are six assumptions that first need to be met before this technique can be undertaken.

Let us say a sport management researcher is interested in comparing those members who supported the merger of a club with another club by casting a yes vote at the ballot against those who did not. Members completed a questionnaire that measured their attitudes towards the merger, their feelings about how the identity of the club may be impacted on, and their previous exposure towards the merging of two professional sporting teams. It was hypothesized that members who agreed to the merger would have more positive attitudes towards the merger, more positive feelings towards the future identity of the club and greater previous exposure to the circumstances. Therefore, the independent variable was whether the member had cast a yes vote for the merger, and the dependent variables were attitudes towards the merger, feelings towards club identity and previous exposure to the circumstances. Attitudes and feelings are measured on traditional scales with a Likert scale response format. Exposure is measured in terms of media exposure and personal experience. Conceptually and theoretically we believe these dependent variables to be related and thus MANOVA as a technique for analysis can be used.

## CONCLUSION

This chapter has examined the criteria we use to establish which inferential test should be chosen to effect an appropriate analysis. It identified the decisions a sport management researcher must make before an appropriate inferential test can be selected. In particular, it discussed the need to identify the independent and dependent variables, the type of data involved and where applicable the number of categories per variable. By doing this the sport management researcher is then able to perform the appropriate statistical analysis to the data, which will allow them to accept or reject the null hypothesis.

## RESEARCH QUESTIONS

In this chapter we examined the criteria used to establish which inferential test should be chosen to affect an appropriate analysis. With this in mind:

- Identify how the sport management researcher can determine which inferential test is appropriate for a given hypothesis.
- Discuss analysis of variance (ANOVA) and how it differs from multivariate analysis of variance (MANOVA) and analysis of covariance (ANCOVA).

## SUGGESTED EXTENDED READING FOR STUDENTS

Bluman, A. G. (2001). *Elementary statistics: A step by step approach* (4th edn). New York: McGraw-Hill.

Johnson, R. R., and Kuby, P. (2011). *Elementary statistics*. Boston, MA: Brooks/Cole.

Muijs, D. (2011). *Doing quantitative research in education with SPSS* (2nd edn). Thousand Oaks, CA: Sage.

Thomas, J. R., and Nelson, J. K. (1996). *Research methods in physical activity* (3rd edn). Champaign, IL: Human Kinetics.

Wild, C. J., and Seber, G. A. F. (2000). *Chance encounters: A first course in data analysis and inference*. New York: John Wiley & Sons.

## Chapter 21

# Chi-square and
# Spearman's rho

## LEARNING OUTCOMES

By the end of this chapter you should be able to:

- identify different types of chi-square tests;
- explain how chi-square tests benefit the sport management researcher;
- describe a situation when non-parametric tests should be used;
- distinguish between parametric statistical tests and non-parametric tests.

## KEY TERMS

*Spearman's rho* – is a non-parametric alternative to Pearson's correlation coefficient.

*Chi-square test* – is an inferential statistic used to measure the difference between an observed set of frequencies and the expected frequencies under the null hypothesis.

## KEY THEMES

- What are the different types of chi-square tests?
- When would the sport management researcher utilize non-parametric tests?

## CHAPTER OVERVIEW

When you have serious violations of the assumptions required to perform parametric statistical tests, then non-parametric tests are used. These tests however tend to be less powerful than their parametric counterparts. Examples of non-parametric statistical tests include chi-square (for frequencies) and Spearman's rho (for correlations). We shall begin by first discussing chi-square tests and then move on to a discussion of the use of Spearman's rho for correlations.

## CHI-SQUARE TESTS

The chi-square test is an inferential statistic used to measure the difference between an observed set of frequencies and the expected frequencies under the null hypothesis. This test deals with nominal-level data. It is generally used to investigate the difference between two groups (nominal-level independent variable and some dependent variable that is also at a nominal level). There are three assumptions you need to address before conducting chi-square tests. These are random sampling, independence of observations and size of expected frequencies (Harnett and Soni, 1991; Muijs, 2011; Thomas and Nelson, 1996; Wild and Seber, 2000). If a sport management researcher has several samples of data that involve frequencies rather than scores, a statistical test for frequency data must be used. The following are some examples of research of this sort:

- Male and female university students are compared in terms of wanting to be professional athletes when they leave university (Table 21.1).
- The sporting orientations of a sample of university educated men are compared with a non-tertiary educated sample.

If we refer to the sporting orientation example (Table 21.2) we are able to determine whether a preference for specific sporting orientation exists. Although the data suggests on

**Table 21.1** *Relationship between gender and wanting to be a professional athlete*

| Intention | Male | Female |
|---|---|---|
| Wants to be a professional athlete | f = 17 | f = 98 |
| Does not want to be a professional athlete | f = 67 | f = 35 |

**Table 21.2** *The relationship between sporting orientation and education*

| Orientation | Tertiary educated | Non-tertiary educated |
|---|---|---|
| Contact sports | f = 57 | f = 105 |
| Non-contact sports | f = 13 | f = 27 |
| Form sports | f = 8 | f = 17 |

casual observation that there is a preference for contact sports by both groups, we are interested primarily in whether the difference between the observed frequencies and expected frequencies is statistically significant.

In each of the previous examples, both variables consist of a relatively small number of categories. The independent variable is the sample and the dependent variable consists of one of several categories. In the case of the sporting orientation example the dependent variable categories linked to orientation include contact sports (football etc.), non-contact sports (basketball etc.) and form sports (diving etc.). So we can see the different samples are the independent variables and the different categories are the dependent variables.

Each cell contains the frequencies of the individuals in that particular sample and that particular category. So the cell that corresponds to sample 2 (middle distance runners) and category 3 (Africans) contains a frequency of 17. This means that in your data there are 17 cases of middle distance runners that are African. In other words, a cell is the intersection of a row and a column. It is important that you know how to read these tables because they are used in chi-square analysis. The statistical question based on this table is whether the distribution of frequencies in the different samples is so varied that it is unlikely that these all come from the same sample. That is, distance runners will be predominately of African descent. The population is defined by the null hypothesis that suggests there is no relationship between the independent and dependent variables. So our table is saying there is no relationship between type of race and success in particular running events. This is presented as a cross-tabulation or contingency table. An example of a cross-tabulation table based on these principles is shown in Table 21.3.

**Table 21.3** Cross-tabulation table: nationality and running event

| Category | Sample 1 – Sprinters | Sample 2 – Middle distance runners | Sample 3 – Distance runners |
|---|---|---|---|
| African Americans | 27 | 21 | 5 |
| Europeans | 19 | 20 | 19 |
| Africans | 9 | 17 | 65 |

## Types of chi-square tests

There are two forms of chi-square tests:

- *goodness of fit*, which applies to the analysis of a single categorical variable;
- *independence or relatedness*, which applies to the analysis of the relationship between two variables.

Goodness of fit could be used if you were interested in people's attitudes towards establishing a professional sport franchise in a particular city. You may want to measure the different response frequencies, for example those in favour, those against and those undecided. Your

**Table 21.4** *Attitudes towards allowing golf as an Olympic sport*

**Table 21.4** *Attitudes towards allowing golf as an Olympic sport*

| Attitude towards allowing golf as an Olympic sport | Frequency of response |
| --- | --- |
| In favour | 640 |
| Against | 1520 |
| Undecided | 2640 |

single categorical variable is 'attitude'. You would then be able to determine whether a significant difference in frequency of attitudes exists. In sum, a chi-square test for goodness of fit will allow us to determine whether differences in frequency exist across responses (Harnett and Soni, 1991; Muijs, 2011; Wild and Seber, 2000; Zikmund, 2000). If we were provided with the data as shown in Table 21.4 about the attitudes of 4,800 people towards allowing golf as an Olympic sport we could construct the appropriate hypotheses.

- *Research hypothesis* $(H_1)$: there is a significant difference in the frequency of attitudes towards allowing golf as an Olympic sport.
- *Null hypothesis* $(H_0)$: there are no significant differences in the frequency of attitudes towards allowing golf as an Olympic sport.

We could then determine whether there are significant differences in the frequency of attitudes towards allowing golf as an Olympic sport.

Independence or relatedness as a test could be used if say a publisher of a sports magazine wants to determine whether preference is dependent on the geographical location of the reader. In this case your two categorical variables are geographical location (let us say metropolitan or regional) and sport magazines (let us say Sports Illustrated or Inside Sport). What this means is that we have some observed data (observed frequencies) that we can then use to determine whether a particular preference exists (Harnett and Soni, 1991; Muijs, 2011; Wild and Seber, 2000).

Let us reshape the above example to highlight what we mean. We might want to know whether people in metropolitan or regional areas prefer Nike or Adidas athletic shoes. If we have observed data that tells us which shoes a sample of people in a metropolitan or regional area purchase we can then determine what the expected frequencies would be under the null hypothesis. These sources of information can then tell us whether a true preference exists for a particular brand of athletic shoe in these locations.

What we are interested in knowing is whether there is a particular shoe preference. We can determine this by calculating the difference between our observed frequencies and expected frequencies. Under the null hypothesis there should be no relationship between the independent and dependent variables. That is there should be no relationship between the type of shoe purchased and geographical location. To substantiate this claim we need to determine whether the difference between our observed frequencies (what we know) and our expected frequencies (what it should be) is statistically significant. This will indicate whether a preference exists in metropolitan or regional areas or both. So as a sport management researcher what we are interested in is evaluating whether the number of cases in each category (shoes) is different from what would be expected on the basis of chance. So we can see in the example we have just outlined that we have used two nominal-level categories (metropolitan or regional areas) and the type of shoe (Nike or Adidas).

Let us explore another example of independence or relatedness. Imagine a research study in which university students are asked to choose between two televised sport programmes, one violent the other non-violent. Some of the students have a history of fighting on the sporting field and others do not. The sport management researcher wants to know:

- whether there is a relationship between university students preferring to watch a violent televised sport programme and having been sanctioned for fighting on the sporting field (H$_1$);
- whether there is no relationship between university students preferring to watch a violent televised sport programme and having been sanctioned for fighting (H$_0$).

To determine whether this is true we need to know the *observed frequencies*, that is, what is our obtained data? We also need to calculate what the *expected frequencies* would be. This is what the data would be if the null hypothesis was true. There is no relationship between university students preferring to watch a violent televised sport programme and having been sanctioned for fighting.

Table 21.5 shows our observed frequencies. We can see by casual observation that the fighters (sample 1) are more likely to prefer violent sport on TV and non-fighters (sample 2) are more likely to prefer non-violent sport on TV. It is important to remember that this data has been obtained through empirical observations.

So now let us look at how we would calculate our expected frequencies. That is, the frequencies we would expect under the null hypothesis that assumes there is no relationship between university students preferring to watch a violent televised sport programme and having been sanctioned for fighting. Remember, if the null hypothesis is true, then the samples come from the same population. So samples 1 and 2 combined give an estimate of the population; remember we are still looking at the observed data.

So we assume that both samples come from the same population of data in which there is no relationship between independent and dependent variables. This implies that any difference between the samples is merely due to chance fluctuations of sampling. With chi-square we simple add together the frequencies for whatever number of samples we have. The sums are then used as an estimate of the distribution of the different categories in the population as

**Table 21.5** *Cross-tabulation table of observed frequencies*

| Categories | Sample 1 – Fighters | Sample 2 – Non-fighters |
|---|---|---|
| Violent TV sport preferred | f = 40 | f = 15 |
| Non-violent TV sport preferred | f = 30 | f = 70 |

shown below. Table 21.6 shows that 55 university students prefer violent sport on TV whereas 100 prefer non-violent sport on TV, assuming the null hypothesis.

So we now have the observed data with extra columns for row frequencies, column frequencies and overall frequencies. So in the null hypothesis defined population we would expect 55 out of every 155 to prefer violent TV sport and 100 out of the 155 to prefer the non-violent sport on TV. But we obtained 40 out of 70 preferring violent sport on TV in sample 1 and 15 out of 85 preferring violent sport on TV in sample 2. We need to know how these figures match the expectations from the population defined by the null hypothesis. To do this we need to calculate the expected frequencies of the cells in the above Table 21.5.

We do this by dividing the row frequencies by the overall frequencies and multiplying by the column frequencies. As we know sample 1 contains 70 participants; if the null hypothesis is true then we would expect 55 out of 155 of these to prefer violent sport on TV. If we do the calculation we can see that our expected frequency of those preferring violent sport on TV is 24.84 as compared to 40 in our observed data in sample 1. We can apply the same logic to sample 2, which contains 85 participants. We expect 55 out of 155 will prefer violent sport on TV and 100 out of 155 will prefer non-violent sport on TV. The expected frequency for non-fighters preferring violent sport on TV is 30.16 as opposed to 15 in our observed data.

Now if we add these two figures together, that is the sample 1 preferring violent sport on TV and those from sample 2 preferring violent sport on TV we get 55 out of 155 as we would expect. However, the expected distributions are different, 24.84 in sample 1 and 30.16 in sample 2. This may already tell us there is a relationship because our observed values of fighters are greater than the null hypothesis would suggest if no relationship between the variables was to exist. Similarly, we would expect under the null hypothesis 100 out of 155 to prefer non-violent sport on TV. Then our expected frequency for those preferring the non-violent TV sport in sample 1 is calculated the same way. Thus our expected frequency in sample 1 is 45.16 participants out of 70 are expected to prefer non-violent sport on TV. You can see that the sum of the expected frequencies for sample 1 is the same as the number of college students in that sample – 24.84 + 45.16 = 70. If we apply the formula to obtain an expected frequency for sample 2 in regards to preferring non-violent sport on TV the expected frequency is 54.84 as opposed to 70 as reflected in our observed data. Again, you can see that the sum of the expected frequencies for sample 2 is the same as the number of college students in that sample – 30.16 + 54.84 = 85.

**Table 21.6** How samples 1 and 2 are combined

| Categories | Sample 1 – Fighters | Sample 2 – Non-fighters | Row frequencies |
|---|---|---|---|
| Violent TV sport preferred | f = 40 | f = 15 | 55 |
| Non-violent TV sport preferred | f = 30 | f = 70 | 100 |
| Column frequencies | 70 | 85 | Overall frequencies = 155 |

We now have the observed and expected data and can now complete the chi-square calculation. This is in part the observed data minus the expected data and is based on the size of the difference between the observed and expected data. The smaller the observed–expected difference the more likely the null hypothesis is to be true. The larger the observed–expected difference the more likely the research hypothesis is to be true. Chi-square involves calculating the overall disparity between the observed and expected frequencies over all of the cells in the table.

The calculated value of the chi-square is compared with a table of critical values of chi-square in order to estimate the probability of obtaining our pattern of frequencies by chance. In the above example if you were to complete the calculations we would establish that the findings are significant and we can reject the null hypothesis ($H_0$) and accept the research hypothesis ($H_1$): there is a relationship between university students preferring to watch a violent televised sport programme and having been sanctioned for fighting on the sporting field ($H_1$).

---

### RECENT CASE EXAMPLE: CHI-SQUARE

*The following article is an example of how chi-square has been used in the past by researchers in Sport Management Research. The interested reader may wish to find/download and read the article for further insights.*

Sport team loyalty: Integrating relationship marketing and a hierarchy of effects. Tsiotsou, R. H. (2013). *Journal of Services Marketing, 27*(6), 458–471.

This study investigated the mediating effects of involvement, trust, self-expression and attachment to the outcome of team loyalty. The research found differences in chi-square of several models of both direct and indirect mediating effects in varying directions, which led to the conclusion of a hierarchy of effects process.

---

## SPEARMAN'S RHO

Spearman's rho is a non-parametric alternative to Pearson's correlation coefficient discussed in Chapter 19. When the requirements for a Pearson's correlation are not met, especially asymmetrical score distributions, Spearman's rho can be used. In addition, a big difference in the Pearson's and Spearman's correlation indicates that some outliers are having a greater influence on the Pearson's coefficient result; outliers have lower effect on Spearman's rho than on Pearson's *r* so in these cases it is best to use Spearman's rho (Harnett and Soni, 1991; Howitt and Cramer, 2000; Muijs, 2011; Wild and Seber, 2000).

The difference with Spearman's rho is that instead of taking scores directly from your data, the scores on a variable are ranked from smallest to largest. That is, the smallest score on variable X is given the rank of 1, the second smallest score on variable X is given the rank of 2 and so on. Similarly, the smallest score on variable Y is given the rank of 1, the second smallest score on variable Y is given the rank of 2 and so on. Then Spearman's rho is calculated like the Pearson's correlation coefficient between two sets' ranks as if the ranks were scores. The 'tied' scores are given the average of the ranks they would occupy if they were different (Howitt and Cramer, 2000; Muijs, 2011). Let us use table 21.7 to highlight what this means.

In this example the two scores of 5 are each given the rank of 2.5 because if they were slightly different they would have been given ranks 2 and 3 respectively. Similarly there are 3 scores of 9 that would have been allocated the ranks 7, 8 and 9 if the scores had been slightly different from each other. These three ranks are averaged to give an average rank of 8, which is entered as the rank for each of the three tied scores. An example of applying Spearman's rho could be if you wished to examine the relationship between athletic performance and income. The Spearman's $r$ and the Pearson's $r$ will not necessarily yield the same coefficient for the same data especially if there are a number of tied ranks. Also because $r$ is based on ranks that are not continuous or normally distributed the coefficient may differ from Pearson $r$. The Spearman $r$ is a valuable tool for special cases in which $r$ cannot or should not be used (Harnett and Soni, 1991; Howitt and Cramer, 2000; Muijs, 2011; Wild and Seber, 2000).

**Table 21.7** Ranking of a set of scores when tied

| Scores | 4 | 5 | 5 | 6 | 7 | 8 | 9 | 9 | 9 | 10 |
|--------|---|-----|-----|---|---|---|---|---|---|----|
| Ranks | 1 | 2.5 | 2.5 | 4 | 5 | 6 | 8 | 8 | 8 | 10 |

## RECENT CASE EXAMPLE: SPEARMAN'S RHO

*The following article is an example of how Spearman's rho has been used in the past by researchers in Sport Management Research. The interested reader may wish to find/download and read the article for further insights.*

Are children who play a sport or a musical instrument better at motor imagery than children who do not? Dey, A., Barnsley, N., Mohan, R., McCormick, M., McAuley, J. H., and Moseley, G. L. (2012). *British Journal of Sports Medicine, 46*(13), 923–926.

The study compared child groups (athletes, musicians, neither, both) on whether each group had better motor control. The researchers expected the data to be skewed, therefore they used Spearman's rho to compare groups. They found that being a musician or athlete had no difference in motor accuracy, but did find that children rated as 'clumsy' by their parents scored worse than other children.

## CONCLUSION

This chapter has discussed chi-square tests and the use of Spearman's rho for correlations. It was noted that the chi-square test is an inferential statistic used to measure the difference between an observed set of frequencies and the expected frequencies under the null hypothesis. This test deals with nominal-level data. The chapter then moved on to discuss Spearman's rho as a non-parametric alternative to Pearson's correlation coefficient. This test can be used when the requirements for a Pearson's correlation are not met, especially in the case of asymmetrical score distributions. Both of these non-parametric tests are used when you have serious violations of the assumptions required to perform parametric statistical tests; however, it must be remembered that these tests tend to be less powerful than their parametric counterparts.

## REVIEW QUESTIONS

In this chapter we discussed how to examine the use of non-parametric tests. With this in mind:

- Provide an example of how these types of tests can be used by the sport management researcher.
- Discuss why non-parametric tests such as chi-square and Spearman's rho tend to be less powerful than their parametric counterparts.

## SUGGESTED EXTENDED READING FOR STUDENTS

Muijs, D. (2011). *Doing quantitative research in education with SPSS* (2nd edn). Thousand Oaks, CA: Sage.

Thomas, J. R., and Nelson, J. K. (1996). *Research methods in physical activity* (3rd edn). Champaign, IL: Human Kinetics.

# Part 4

# Alternative approaches to Sport Management Research

## Chapter 22

# Mixed methods approaches to Sport Management Research

## LEARNING OUTCOMES

By the end of this chapter you should be able to:

- define a mixed methods approach to Sport Management Research;
- identify some advantages of a mixed methods approach;
- distinguish between triangulation, facilitation and complementarity;
- reflect on the appropriateness of a mixed methods approach to Sport Management Research.

## KEY TERMS

*Triangulation* – should not be considered as a single unique method, but as a metaphor with different possible meanings that can be related to a variety of different methodological problems and tasks.

*Facilitation* – how quantitative methods can be used to help qualitative methods and vice versa.

*Complementarity* – the strategy of 'complementarity' suggests that you really can't do everything with a single method. Sometimes you need to use other methods to answer the entire question. Often, however, researchers mistake this for 'more is better'.

## KEY THEMES

- How does a mixed methods approach differ from a strictly qualitative or quantitative approach?
- What are some of the main aspects of a mixed methods approach?

## CHAPTER OVERVIEW

The construction of a multi-method design requires that methodological tools are selected in regard to theoretical assumptions about the nature of the social reality under investigation. Quantitative and qualitative methods usually provide information on different levels of sociological description: quantitative analyses show phenomena on an aggregate level and can thereby allow the description of macro-social structures. Although qualitative data may also relate to phenomena on a macro-societal level, their specific strength lies in their ability to lift the veil on social micro-processes and to make visible unknown cultural phenomena. In order to formulate adequate sociological explanations of certain social phenomena it will often be necessary to combine both types of information. This chapter will discuss the distinction between quantitative and qualitative approaches and the advantages and disadvantages of employing mixed methods research. In doing this it will provide a foundation understanding of how mixed methods approaches to Sport Management Research can be employed.

## DEFINING A MIXED METHOD APPROACH

A mixed method approach to research implies that the researcher will use a combination of both quantitative and qualitative research and methodology in a single research study in order to answer the research question. This will involve using different quantitative and qualitative methods in the process of collecting and analysing the research data – often mixing the methods being used (Creswell and Plano Clark, 2007). Creswell (2008) further states that a mixed methods approach is not just a process of collecting two types of research (quantitative and qualitative) but of a process of 'merging, integrating, linking, or embedding the two "strands"' (p. 552). We discuss later in this chapter the concepts of triangulation, complementarity, and facilitation, and how these concepts aid the researcher in the process of 'mixing' research approaches to obtain a greater validity of results.

## MIXED METHODS APPROACHES TO SPORT MANAGEMENT RESEARCH

In Sport Management Research, using more than one method to study the same phenomenon has the potential to strengthen the validity of the results. A typical design might start out with a qualitative segment such as an interview, which will alert the researcher to issues that should be explored in a survey of participants, followed by the survey, which in turn is followed by semi-structured interviews to clarify some of the survey findings. A mixed method approach may also lead sport management researchers to modify or expand the research design and/or the data collection methods. To begin, let's revisit how qualitative and quantitative research can be seen. Figure 22.1 highlights some of the key areas.

Quantitative researchers seek *statistical validity*. Can you safely generalize to the population? Have you systematically excluded anyone? The expression that the 'whole is often greater than parts' is a phrase used when discussing quantitative and qualitative designs. It is a non-trivial matter to infer the behaviour of the whole from the behaviour of its parts. Quantitative research designs strive to identify and isolate specific variables (e.g. sponsor recall, likelihood

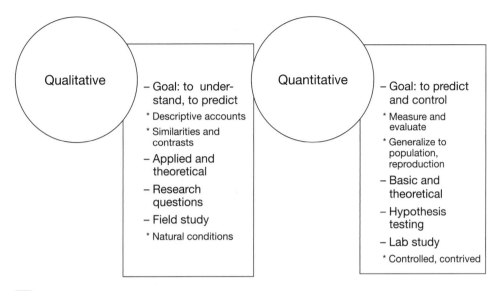

**Figure 22.1** *Features of qualitative and quantitative research*

to participate in various sports, and doping rates) within the context (seeking correlation, relationships, causality) of the study. Quantitative designs seek the accumulation of facts and causes of behaviour through careful isolation, measurement and evaluation of variables. They are about predictability and control over time. Qualitative designs however are concerned with the changing and dynamic nature of reality. That is, understanding a point in time (e.g. explaining how the sponsor's message affected purchase habits, why one chooses a certain sport, and the process by which steroids are introduced to teens).

When it comes to data collection, quantitative designs place emphasis on numerical data, measurable variables. Data is collected under controlled conditions in order to rule out the possibility that variables other than the one under study can account for the relationships identified. Quantitative research generates statistics through the use of large-scale survey research, using methods such as questionnaires or structured interviews. If a sports marketing researcher has stopped you on the streets, or you have filled in a questionnaire that has arrived through the post, this falls under the umbrella of quantitative research. This type of research reaches many more people, but the contact with those people is much quicker than it is in qualitative research. Figure 22.2 summarizes the emphasis of quantitative designs.

Qualitative research explores attitudes, behaviours and experiences through such methods as interviews or focus groups. It attempts to get an in-depth opinion from participants. As it is attitudes, behaviour and experiences that are important, fewer people take part in the research, but the contact with these people tends to last a lot longer. Qualitative researchers seek *saturation*. How many isn't the issue, it is rather, do you understand the phenomenon? Have you learned enough? Mere numbers are irrelevant: you want 'verstehen' or deep understanding. Qualitative designs, however, place emphasis on observation and interpretation. Data are collected within the context of their natural occurrence. Qualitative design focuses on a holistic view of what is being studied (via documents, case histories, observations

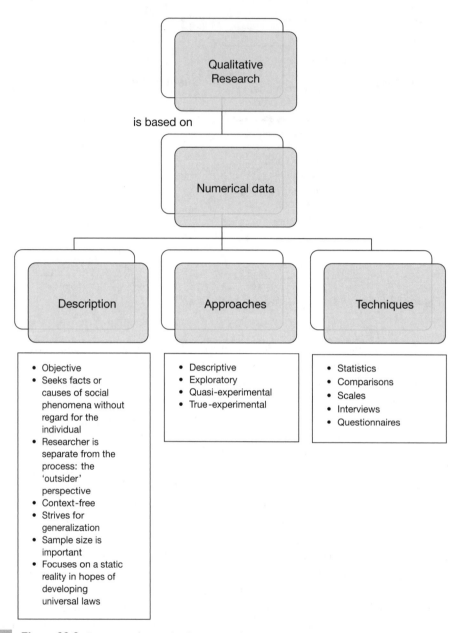

**Figure 22.2** *Features of quantitative research*

and interviews). Under the umbrella of qualitative research there are many different methodologies. Figure 22.3 summarizes the emphasis of qualitative designs and some of these methodologies.

The differences between quantitative and qualitative research are presented in Figure 22.4.

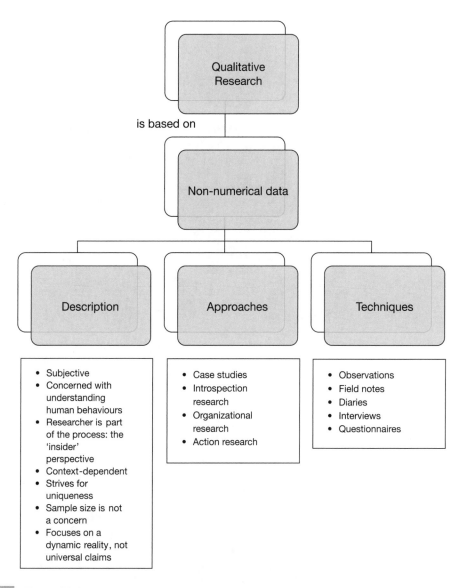

**Figure 22.3** *Features of qualitative research*

Both quantitative and qualitative research designs seek reliable and valid results. For example: quantitative reliability requires that the data are consistent or stable as indicated by the researcher's ability to replicate the findings. Will two different sport economics researchers estimate the economic impact of the Super Bowl using the same methodology and methods? Qualitative research seeks the validity of its findings as these are paramount so that the data are representative of a true and full picture of constructs under investigation. Is the researcher's portrayal of a host community's attitude towards a Super Bowl a true reflection?

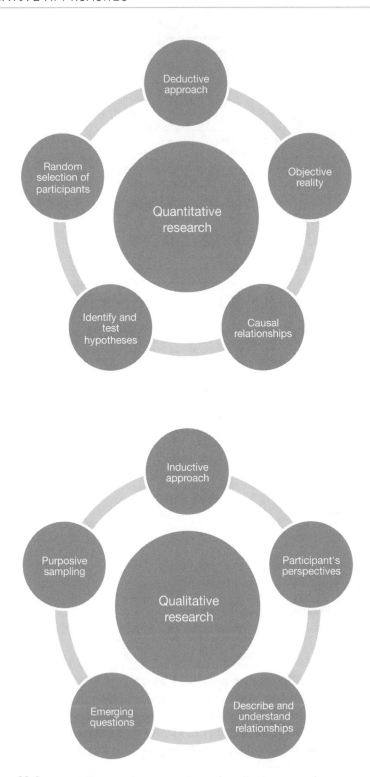

**Figure 22.4** *Some differences in quantitative and qualitative research*

There are three strategies for mixing qualitative and quantitative methods. These are:

- triangulation
- facilitation
- complementarity.

We shall now discuss each of these and their relationship to mixed methods research.

## Triangulation

The metaphor of triangulation in a mixed method approach is used in such a way that the results of qualitative and quantitative methods are regarded as analogous to the results of the single measurement operations. Normally, in describing different aspects of the same phenomenon or even different phenomena by two methods, the sport management researcher would naturally expect different results. In a true mixed method approach, qualitative and quantitative methods have to be combined in order to produce sound sociological explanations. Triangulation should not be considered as a single unique method, but as a metaphor with different possible meanings that can be related to a variety of different methodological problems and tasks. The form of 'between-method triangulation' quite often is used in sociological research, whereby qualitative and quantitative data are collected and analysed separately and the results are related to each other. If qualitative and quantitative methods are combined in this way to answer a specific research question, in principle, one of the following three outcomes may arise:

1 qualitative and quantitative results may 'converge';
2 qualitative and quantitative results may relate to different objects or phenomena, but may be 'complementary' to each other and thus can be used to 'supplement' each other;
3 qualitative and quantitative results may be 'divergent' or 'contradictory'.

Triangulation combines independent yet complementary research methods. *Simultaneous triangulation* uses both qualitative and quantitative methods at the same time. For example, survey methods and case study. *Sequential triangulation* suggests the results of one method are essential for planning the next method. For example an exploratory pilot study precedes an experimental design. This is also known as '*mixed methods*'.

Mixed methods research is therefore a style of research that uses procedures for conducting research that are typically applied in both quantitative and qualitative studies. The purpose of these designs is to build upon the synergy and strength that exists between quantitative and qualitative methods in order to more fully understand a given phenomenon than is possible using either quantitative or qualitative methods alone. Advantages of each complement the other resulting in a stronger research design, and more valid and reliable findings. The inadequacies of individual methods are minimized with threats to internal validity realized and addressed. For example, quantitative design strives to control for bias so that facts, instances and phenomena can be understood in an objective way. Qualitative approach strives to understand the perspective of participants or a situation by looking at first-hand experience to provide meaningful data.

In mixed methods research the research problem itself determines the choice of a design. For example, do we use surveys to identify specific groups of fans and conduct focus groups with them to understand their views? A series of interviews are conducted to ascertain the critical issues impacting on fans and a survey of the members is conducted using these issues as variables.

There are three characteristics that differentiate the types of mixed methods designs. These are: (1) priority is given to either quantitative or qualitative data; (2) the sequence of collecting quantitative or qualitative data; and (3) the data analysis techniques used to either combine the analysis of data or keep the two types of data separate. There are also three common designs. These are: (1) QUAL–Quan model – the exploratory mixed methods design. This is where qualitative data are collected first and are more heavily weighted; (2) QUAN–Qual model – the explanatory mixed methods design. This is where quantitative data are collected first and are more heavily weighted; and (3) QUAN–QUAL model – the triangulation mixed methods design. This is where quantitative and qualitative data are collected concurrently and both are weighted equally. The abbreviations QUAN and QUAL are obvious, however the order and capitalization is important. The first to be read or the capitalized abbreviation is the dominant perspective and is weighted more heavily. If both are capitalized, it means both are weighted equally.

We have identified nine characteristics of mixed methods designs. These characteristics are:

1   the title of the research includes terms that suggest more than one method is being used, such as:
    a)   mixed methods
    b)   integrated
    c)   triangular
    d)   quantitative–qualitative;
2   both quantitative and qualitative methods are used in the study;
3   the researcher describes the kinds of mixed methods being used;
4   the data collection section indicates narrative, numerical or both types of data are being collected;
5   the purpose statement or the research questions indicate the types of methods being used;
6   questions are stated and described for both quantitative and qualitative approaches;
7   the researcher indicates the sequencing of collecting qualitative and/or quantitative data (i.e. QUAN–Qual, QUAL–Quan or QUAN–QUAL);
8   the researcher describes both quantitative and qualitative data analysis strategies;
9   the writing is balanced in terms of quantitative and qualitative approaches.

Triangulation offers a balance between logic and stories. Qualitative research, which emphasizes exploration, understanding, contextualizing, introspection and theory construction, provides a strong base for wider quantitative measures, scaling and generalization. For example, through qualitative research, a sport manager may better be able to identify trends in sponsor activation attitudes and behaviours, and then develop quantitative scales to measure and compare those trends. Quantitative research, which emphasizes large samples, can provide an overview of an area that can reveal patterns, inconsistencies and so forth that can be further investigated with qualitative methods. For example, if one sponsor has significantly higher recall rates after an event than other sponsors, a qualitative follow-up study can identify why and how that sponsor was able to stand out. In order for triangulation to be used effectively, four principles must be adhered to. First, the research question(s) must be clearly focused. Second, the strengths and weaknesses of each chosen method must complement each other. Third, the data collection methods should be selected according to their relevance to the nature of the phenomenon being studied, and finally, a continual evaluation of the approach should be under taken during the study.

---

## RECENT CASE EXAMPLE: MIXED METHODS

*The following article is an example of how a mixed methods approach has been used in the past by researchers in Sport Management Research. The interested reader may wish to find/download and read the article for further insights.*

> Developing a method for comparing the elite sport systems and policies of nations: a mixed research methods approach. De Bosscher, V., Shibli, S., van Bottenburg, M., De Knop, P., and Truyens, J. (2010). *Journal of Sport Management, 24*(5), 567–600.

Qualitative exploration led to a conceptual model of nine 'pillars' of factors important for international sporting success. A quantitative study followed, comparing countries against each other with an objective scoring system. Qualitative data was then added to discuss contextual limitations that may have created scoring imbalances.

---

## Facilitation

Qualitative methods can be used to assist quantitative research. Similarly, quantitative methods can assist qualitative research. How this is done is highlighted in Figure 22.5.

Sale, Lohfeld and Brazil (2002), however, caution against an over-simplification of the research object in an attempt to utilize mixed methods. Or, what in actual fact may not be mixed methods at all. They pose the question, how can the results from studies using qualitative and quantitative methods appear to agree if the two paradigms are looking at different phenomena? They propose that what 'may account for seemingly concordant results could be that both are, in fact, quantitative. Conducting a frequency count on responses to open-ended questions is not qualitative research' (p. 47). It is important that the researcher therefore, if asserting that they are using a mixed methods approach, be sure of the processes

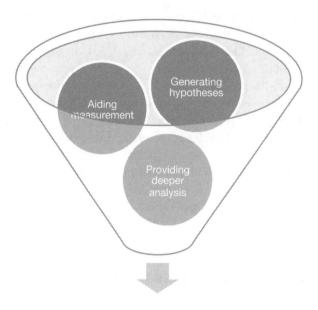

Qualitative helping quantitative

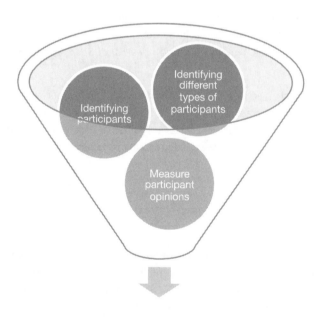

Quantitative helping qualitative

**Figure 22.5** *How qualitative and quantitative methods can assist each other*

they are following, and not merely labelling qualitative or quantitative data collection and analysis techniques as mixed methods to suit the proposed research question.

## Complementarity

In a mixed method research design the advantages of quantitative and qualitative research each complement the other resulting in a stronger research design, and more valid and reliable findings. The strategy of 'complementarity' suggests that you really can't do everything with a single method. Sometimes you need to use other methods to answer the entire question. Often, however, researchers mistake this for 'more is better'. How the strategy of complementarity emerges is highlighted in Figure 22.6.

Greene, Caracelli and Graham (1989) believe that utilizing both qualitative and quantitative methods in the same study to measure different but also overlapping facets of a phenomenon yield 'an enriched, elaborated understanding for the phenomenon. This differs from the triangulation intent in that the logic of convergence requires that the different methods assess the same conceptual phenomenon' (p. 258).

Sale *et al.* (2002) propose a method of mixing methods that does not rely on 'merely using the strengths of each method to bolster the weaknesses of the other(s), or capturing various aspects of the same phenomena' (p. 50). They start from the premise that qualitative and quantitative researchers do not study the same phenomena. However, they go on to say that

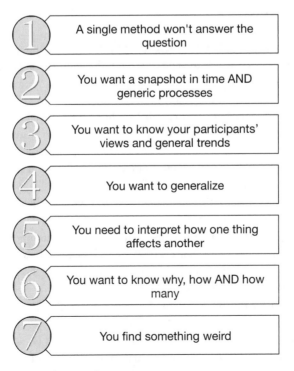

**Figure 22.6** *How complementarity emerges*

methods can be mixed in a single study if the distinction of phenomena is maintained and clarified. Translated to a sport management setting, a mixed methods study to develop a measure of burnout experienced by athletes

> could be described as a qualitative study of the lived experience of burnout to inform a quantitative measure of burnout. Although the phenomenon 'burnout' may appear the same across methods, the distinction between 'lived experience' and 'measure' reconciles the phenomenon to its respective method and paradigm. (p. 50)

In such a study, the results from one method could be used to elaborate on, help develop or inform the other method.

## How to conduct a mixed methods study

Creswell (2008) outlines the seven main steps in conducting a mixed methods study:

1   Decide whether a mixed methods study is appropriate.
    The sport management researcher needs to determine whether a mixed methods research design is appropriate to the aim of the study and the site of data collection. Apart from needing to understand the intricacies of both quantitative and qualitative design and data collection strategies, the sport management researcher will need to be able to justify a mixed methods approach to stakeholders – managers, club officials, sport practitioners etc.
2   Determine the rationale for mixing methods.
    If it is feasible and appropriate to conduct a mixed methods study, then the sport management researcher needs to articulate the rationale for collecting and analysing both quantitative and qualitative data.
3   Identify a strategy for collecting data.
    Once the sport management researcher has outlined the rationale for the study, then the procedures for collecting data will have been identified. The researcher needs to determine:
    ■   what priority will be given to quantitative and qualitative data;
    ■   what will be the sequence of data collection;
    ■   which forms of quantitative and qualitative data will be collected.
4   Develop the research questions.
    Research questions may be developed prior to starting the study, or may emerge during the course of the study. For example, in a triangulation design, the questions can be determined prior to data collection, and may be along the lines of: do the results of analysing the quantitative and qualitative data 'converge and present consistent findings or diverge and show contradictory findings?' (p. 569).
5   Collect the data.
    In a mixed method study the sequence of data collection will be determined by the design of the study. Regardless of the research design, the sport management researcher should expect that the time required may exceed that of a strictly

**330**

quantitative or qualitative study, and data collection also requires that the researcher utilizes efficient data storage, management and recording techniques.

6   Analyse the data.

Data can be analysed separately, or can be integrated as in a triangulation design. The process of data analysis will be determined by the specific type of mixed method design.

7   Write the report.

As in both a quantitative and qualitative study, the final step for the sport management researcher in a mixed methods study is to write the research report. How this is presented will be determined by how the data collection, analysis and interpretation steps have proceeded throughout the study. If these steps have proceeded separately, then the report will need to reflect this by containing distinct sections for the quantitative and qualitative methods used in the data collection, analysis and interpretation process. A triangulation design on the other hand will describe how the data collection and analysis attempts to converge both sets of data, from which the sport management researcher formulates results that attempt to answer the research question.

Figure 22.7 summarizes these steps.

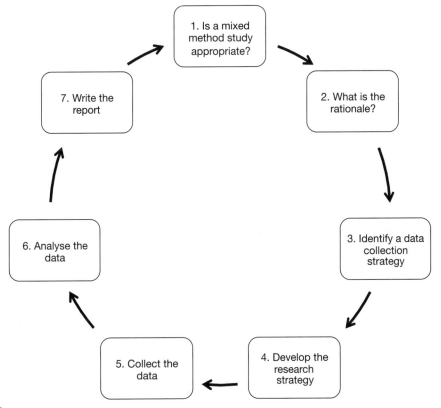

**Figure 22.7** Writing the research report

## Evaluating a mixed methods design

When evaluating a mixed methods design it is important to ask yourself eight questions. These questions are:

1   Does the study use at least one quantitative and one qualitative research strategy?
2   Does the study include a rationale for using a mixed methods design?
3   Does the study include a classification of the type of mixed methods design?
4   Does the study describe the priority given to quantitative and qualitative data collection and the sequence of their use?
5   Was the study feasible, given the amount of data to be collected and concomitant issues of resources, time and expertise?
6   Does the study include both quantitative and qualitative research questions?
7   Does the study clearly identify qualitative and quantitative data collection techniques?
8   Does the study use appropriate data analysis techniques for the type of mixed methods design?

It is important to remember that you don't mix for the sake of 'more is better'. Mixing adds to time, scope and the budget among other considerations, and as such you should consider mixing in multiple phases, not a single research project.

---

### HYPOTHETICAL CASE

You are interested in how sport event organizers communicate with volunteers. In the past, the main form of communication was physical mail and phone calls. More recently, email has more commonly been used and preferred by both parties. However, the younger generation is beginning to rely more on social media for communication than phone calls and email. As a sport event organizer, which forms of communications are critical, which are preferred, and which are a waste of time? Additionally, are there differences in the types of messages volunteers would like to receive by varying formats of communication? Furthermore, how can a sport event organizer educate its volunteer base on a specific and agreeable communication protocol?

1   What type(s) of qualitative research methods could you use (content analysis, interviews, and observation, etc.)?
2   What type of quantitative data would you collect? How would you analyse it?
3   What would be the order of a mixed methods approach? For example QUAN–qual or QUAL–quan?

---

## CONCLUSION

This chapter has examined the use of mixed methods research in sport management. It supports both quantitative and qualitative approaches, and the notion of mixed research approaches combining both quantitative and qualitative approaches. It has been suggested that by using different data collection methods at various points in the research process the research can build on the strength of each type of data collection and minimize the weaknesses of any single approach. A mixed method approach to research has the potential to increase both the validity and reliability of the data, and may also lead sport management researchers to modify or expand their data collection methods.

## REVIEW QUESTIONS

In Sport Management Research, using more than one method to study the same phenomenon has the potential to strengthen the validity of the results. It also has the potential to lead sport management researchers to modify or expand the research design and/or the data collection methods employed in the study. With this in mind:

- Discuss how a mixed methods approach can benefit the sport management researcher.
- Is there any place in Sport Management Research for a mixed methods approach?
- Provide examples of the type of sport management study where a mixed methods approach would be appropriate.
- What is the relationship between triangulation, facilitation and complementarity?

## SUGGESTED EXTENDED READING FOR STUDENTS

Creswell, J. W., and Plano Clark, V. L. (2007). *Designing and conducting mixed methods research.* Thousand Oaks, CA: Sage.

Teddlie, C., and Tashakkori, A. (2009). *Foundations of mixed methods research: Integrating quantitative and qualitative approaches in the social and behavioural sciences.* Thousand Oaks, CA: Sage.

## Chapter 23

# Research 2.0

## A framework for sport management

### LEARNING OUTCOMES

By the end of this chapter you should be able to:

- define Web 2.0;
- outline Research 2.0;
- describe the trends in Research 2.0;
- understand the use of Research 2.0 in Sport Management Research.

### KEY TERMS

*Web 2.0* – the network as platform, spanning all connected devices.

*Research 2.0* – a framework for undertaking qualitative and quantitative research in the Web 2.0 environment.

### KEY THEMES

- What is Web 2.0?
- What is Research 2.0?

## OVERVIEW

This chapter explores the potential of the Web 2.0 environment for conducting qualitative, quantitative and mixed methods research. Web 2.0 technologies create a number of new opportunities to conduct research broadly labelled as Research 2.0.

## INTRODUCTION

Web 2.0 technologies such as social networking sites and other interactive, user-driven tools have created a new environment of research, termed Research 2.0. Research 2.0 can be defined as the application of Web 2.0 technologies in shaping the next generation of research methodologies. Within the field of sport management there has been limited examination of the potential of Web 2.0 technologies in qualitative and quantitative research. Studies of research practice, including ethical and legal implications of conducting research in Web 2.0 environments, are needed to facilitate innovative use of these new technologies for Sport Management Research.

This chapter explores how Web 2.0 technologies can be applied in the research domain. The chapter also explores how qualitative and quantitative research can fit a Web 2.0 framework. In the following sections the key concepts of Web 2.0 and Research 2.0 will be examined.

## WEB 2.0

Tim O'Reilly (2005) first defined Web 2.0: 'Web 2.0 is the network as platform, spanning all connected devices; Web 2.0 applications . . . through an "architecture of participation" . . . deliver rich user experiences' (http://oreilly.com/pub/a/oreilly/time/news/2005/09/30/what-is-web-20.html, accessed 19 June 2011).

Originally, Web 1.0 was created by web designers to provide text-based information to the public. There was little opportunity for user interaction apart from email exchange. Web 2.0 is about social publishing and not just developing web pages.

Greenhow, Robelia and Hughes (2009) state that Web 2.0 provides four affordances:

1   user-defined linkages between users and content;
2   simple mechanisms to share multimedia content;
3   prominent personal profiling; and
4   Internet technology applications, enabling interfaces with services and features on other sites (p. 247).

Common elements of the Web 2.0 concept are:

■   interfaces and applications – no longer about pages and sites;
■   personalization – users can customize their experience;
■   community – users interact with one another, sometimes forming social networks;
■   creation – the platform facilitates creation, not just communication or participation;

- collaboration – creation is collaborative rather than isolated (and users can share data in different forms);
- cumulative – it's an ongoing process, where creation can be built upon. (O'Reilly, 2005)

## Characteristics of Web 2.0

A number of Web 2.0 tools and technologies such as blogs, wikis, social bookmarking, social networking, podcasting, image and video sharing, RSS (Really Simple Syndication or Rich Site Summary) feeds, Internet virtual worlds (e.g. Second Life), and content aggregators (e.g. Mashup) have been identified through the literature.

Although researchers have used online technologies for a number of years (e.g. using SurveyMonkey to implement online questionnaires, or conducting email interviews), the possibility of Web 2.0 to reshape the research landscape is an important, emergent area of investigation. The next section provides background on the development of online research practices.

## Research on the web

Basically, there are two types of Internet related studies:

1. Research about the Internet: research that deals with phenomena related to or deriving from use of the Internet itself. For instance: user demographics and rates of sport websites; quality of service in B2C services such as Ticketmaster;
2. Research through the Internet: research that employs the Internet as a platform to study issues that traditionally used to be studied through other channels. For example: sport opinion polls; fan satisfaction surveys. (Ahituv and Steimberg, 2006)

Most early research has been on computer mediated communication (CMC). The primary focus of this research was:

- email
- listservs
- instant messaging
- Internet relay chat (IRC)
- online synchronous and asynchronous interviews
- virtual focus groups. (Rathie and Given, 2010)

Some of the current literature focuses on Web 2.0 as a research environment, including what separates this emerging domain from CMC and other traditional approaches to qualitative and quantitative research in cyberspace. This distinction is known as the '*architecture of participation*' (O'Reilly, 2005, available at: http://oreilly.com/pub/a/oreilly/time/news/2005/09/30/what-is-web-20.html, accessed 19 June 2011). In this approach users are encouraged to be creators of data through use of Web 2.0 tools and techniques: for example,

**336**

creating a research-themed Twitter account to interact with fans of a particular team, league or sport.

According to Rathie and Given (2010), recent trends relevant to online research include:

■ the growth of the open source movement;
■ the emergence of collaborative tools and social media;
■ the explosion of online social networks; and
■ the importance of data gathering from multiple sources.

All these influence the practice of conducting qualitative and quantitative research online.

## Data collection

Web 2.0 is changing traditional modes of research. These changes include the use of different tools for analysis of the collected data, as well as different approaches to research ethics. Different data collection tools in Web 2.0 have been categorized into a framework based on the traditional research model of primary and secondary data sources. *Primary* research tools in Web 2.0 are those platforms that are purposefully set up for specific research objectives and *secondary* tools are those online platforms that are not explicitly meant for research but can provide access to information for research participants.

A review of literature suggests the advantages and disadvantages of Web 2.0 research as shown in Table 23.1.

In summary, Rathie and Given (2010) suggest that:

■ Web 2.0 allows for the creation of personalized research spaces. Users can compile and save personalized collections of archival holdings generated from customized searches and can classify research materials in their own ways;
■ researchers are able to save search results to be accessed from multiple locations, influence the generation of those results, or create personalized classification systems;
■ researching can happen in the same virtual space and from any appropriate physical location. Users can annotate and write notes about groups of images and access these notes and artefacts from any networked computer location;
■ Web 2.0 provides less face-to-face interaction, but it offers more possibilities for quickly connecting textually with a wide and potentially large range of people.

## RESEARCH 2.0

Currently, the concept of 'Research 2.0' is a focus for scholars as they attempt to demystify this domain; often, this literature addresses the mechanics of techniques and strategies for conducting research in Web 2.0 environments. There is limited discussion in the sport management literature that focuses on analysing this new research context or exploring the theoretical frameworks that might help researchers to develop scholarly practices for these environments.

**Table 23.1** *Advantages and disadvantages of conducting research in an online environment/Web 2.0 domain*

| Advantages | Disadvantages |
|---|---|
| Data collection at low cost | Lack of facial expressions and paralinguistic cues |
| Instantaneous | Extended time frame of user engagement in data collection |
| Efficient use for data collection | Work place interruptions prevent effective data collection |
| More participants from a range of geographic contexts | Participants may fall into typically high socio-economic and educational demographics |
| Large amounts of publicly available data | Participants who are not as 'web savvy' as Web 2.0 technologies require may be excluded from projects |
| Spatial and temporal barriers to conducting research | Software gap between computers and other devices needs to be bridged |
| Browsers are able to support different applications for data types in the same environment | Problems of coverage, measurement errors and bias, response rate and dropout rates |
| Participants could be involved in many phases of the work, from design of the project, through analysis to dissemination | Problem of bias, people who respond voluntarily to surveys on the web have different characteristics to those who choose not to participate in these surveys |
| Environment allows for the creation of personalized research spaces | |

Sources: Ferneley, Heinze and Child (2009); Greenhow, Robelia and Hughes (2009); O'Reilly (2005); Rathie and Given (2010)

## RECENT CASE EXAMPLE: WEB 2.0

*The following article is an example of how Web 2.0 has been used in the past by researchers in Sport Management Research. The interested reader may wish to find/download and read the article for further insights.*

The effect of user motives and interactivity on attitude toward a sport website. Taesoo, A. (2010). Unpublished doctoral dissertation. Florida State University College of Education.

Sport websites have become an important communication tool for companies and business, such as sport organizations, to deliver information, connect with sport consumers, generate profits, and much more. Based on uses and gratifications theory, a conceptual model of attitude towards the sport website including antecedents (user motives and interactivity) and consequence (revisit intention) was proposed. The results indicate that user motives and interactivity are significant predictors of attitude towards the sport website, which consequently influences intention to revisit a sport website.

Research 2.0 is a framework for undertaking qualitative and quantitative research in the Web 2.0 environment. This implies that we have to consider both the behavioural and technical changes that have occurred to:

- better engage respondents, participants;
- leverage their thinking to generate ideas, identify issues;
- tap into web and social media communities and discussion groups;
- access relevant up to date information.

This process involves:

- new methods of engagement (a different mindset in approaching research participants);
- the application of new technologies within existing methodologies;
- observing users, listening in on conversations. (Rathie and Given, 2010)

Although it is unlikely that this approach will ever fully replace established research techniques, this is a valuable addition to the researcher's repertoire in the digital age.

## New methods of engagement

Traditional research approaches are framed within the top-down, command and control model. Response rates continue to be a challenge. There appears to be a need to adopt new approaches to the new, collaborative nature of research. Research 2.0 provides an opportunity to tap into bottom-up, interactive communications by engaging people in different ways (Table 23.2).

**Table 23.2** *New methods of research engagement*

| Traditional research | Research 2.0 |
| --- | --- |
| • Control over feedback, dialogue | • Less control, dialogue shaped to a greater extent by audiences |
| • Participants as study objects | • Participants as stakeholders |
| • Structured feedback | • More observation |
| • Research questions identified prior to research | • Participants are enabled to suggest questions and provide true answers |

Source: Based on Rathie and Given (2010)

### Online research communities

Ferneley *et al.* (2009) suggest that online communities provide an opportunity for engagement. They further argue that there are two forms of online communities:

1   *naturally occurring online communities* (NOOCs). NOOCs consist of three basic elements:

- participants share common goals (e.g. fans want their team to be successful);
- participants mutually engage (e.g. fans cheer and jeer team transactions and performance on an online forum or social media page); and
- participants have a shared repertoire (e.g. fans sharing links, photos, insights, and stories about their team).

Trust between community members is a key enabler of community contributions. An example is the fan communities of sport teams;

2   *online research communities* (ORCs). According to Ferneley *et al.* (2009), there are key features of ORCs that differentiate them from the more traditional online communities. NOOCs tend to connect people with common interests, in ORCs the community is closed and members are selected based on specified profiles. NOOCs tend to attract people who are passionate about the subject; while this may be the case in ORCs, the aim is to ensure that the participating body represents a broader view of users rather than only brand advocates.

The nature of NOOCs means that the community is usually discovered via word of mouth or serendipity; in the case of ORCs, which are closed communities, recruitment to the community is targeted and strictly controlled. This means that NOOCs may have a much larger membership base than ORCs (Table 23.3), although engagement in ORCs tends to be much higher.

- Online communities are:
  - collaborative (bottom-up rather than top-down);
  - less controlled; and
  - participants develop a stake in the community because they can see how results are being used.
- Benefits include:
  - higher participation, engagement;
  - user-generated ideas; and
  - surfacing of unasked questions. (Ferneley *et al.*, 2009)

**Table 23.3** *Online research communities*

| Online communities are . . . | Benefits include |
|---|---|
| • collaborative (bottom-up rather than top-down) | • identifying emerging needs |
| • less controlled | • surfacing new product or service ideas |
| • participants develop a stake in the community because they can see how results are being used | • refining concepts |
| | • listening for attitudes |

Source: Ferneley *et al.* (2009)

## WHAT MAKES 2.0 DIFFERENT?

Various authors have proposed the distinctions shown in Table 23.4 in research approaches.

**Table 23.4** *Research distinctions in online approaches*

| Research 1.0 | Research 2.0 |
| --- | --- |
| Questioning | Listening |
| One-shot | Continuous |
| Quan vs Qual | Quan, Qual and Mixed |
| Transactional | Conversational |
| Representative | Targeted |
| Descriptive | Insightful |
| Scientific | Art and Science |

Ferneley *et al.* (2009), Greenhow *et al.* (2009), O'Reilly (2005)

### HYPOTHETICAL CASE EXAMPLE: RESEARCH 2.0

In the Research 2.0 world, all research stages would be executed within the web in a participatory environment. Web tools such as wikis, blogs, forums, multimedia applications and RSS feeds would help the team to conduct the study in the web. For example, a football club can research their fans through using blogs to invite them to participate in an online survey. The data collected from the study would be stored in a 'data cloud' and cloud computing through the tools and software provided by services such as Amazon Web Services (AWS) could be used for data analysis. Similarly, tools provided by a company such as Google (e.g. Google Analytics) could be used to analyse website data and generate custom reports, including the segmentation of web page visits by dimensions such as location, time of visit and referral sites from the fans.

(Based on Rathie and Given, 2010)

### Using a Web 2.0 framework

Rathie and Given (2010) define and develop the concept of Research 2.0 by drawing parallel links with Web 2.0 definitions by applying the Web 2.0 principles put forward by O'Reilly (2005). They identify the following seven elements in a framework:

- the web as a research host
- crowdsourcing

**341**

- web cloud
- perpetual beta
- mashups
- multiple interface
- the participatory research experience.

## A framework for Research 2.0

Rathie and Given (2010) have suggested the following framework for the Research 2.0 environment. These principles, first proposed by Tim O'Reilly, provide a useful lens through which researchers can examine the potential for Web 2.0 technologies in shaping the next generation of research methodologies (Table 23.5).

---

### HYPOTHETICAL CASE EXAMPLE: CROWDSOURCING

Researchers could use crowd opinions for different steps of the research process. Consumers, for example, are tagging their own content in sport fans' Community Wiki Discussion Forums. In qualitative research projects these techniques could be used for participant member checking or for inter-coder reliability checks; in quantitative projects, researchers could use these techniques to pilot a questionnaire prior to distribution or to beta-test an experimental web interface.

---

## Using the web for Research 2.0

The process of research in a web environment should be organized. We suggest the process shown in Table 23.6.

## Issues and Research 2.0

Research 2.0 presents a few challenges, such as privacy, confidentiality and other ethics issues to researchers.

### 1 Ethics

A key issue in Research 2.0 relates to *research ethics*, particularly in the areas of informed consent, confidentiality and privacy. It is the responsibility of researchers to maintain a safe environment and ensure that participants are aware of the implications for engaging in online research in public forums. For example, Web 2.0 tools can be very public. Participants must understand the implications of engaging in online research in public forums prior to answering a researcher's (or another participant's) call for commentary. Even where forums are closed

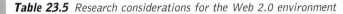 **Table 23.5** *Research considerations for the Web 2.0 environment*

| Process | Description |
| --- | --- |
| The web as a research host | Software in the Web 2.0 environment could be delivered over the web and run in a web browser (O'Reilly, 2005). In this way, data could be gathered, stored, analysed and disseminated purely in an online environment. Currently many qualitative analysis software packages (e.g. NVivo) are designed for single-use, stand-alone computing; however, the Web 2.0 environment offers new tools. |
| Crowdsourcing | The key element of Web 2.0 is '*turning the web into a kind of global brain*' (O'Reilly, 2005). Some authors have identified *crowdsourcing* where users are co-developers in the project as one of the key trends in the Web 2.0 environment. |
| Web cloud | It is argued that 'every significant Internet application to date has been backed by a specialized database' (O'Reilly, 2005). The availability of data in a web 'cloud' (e.g. blog data, temporal data of wikis, social tagging data, etc.) as a primary data source represents a significant issue in the process of data collection in Research 2.0. |
| Perpetual beta | In this new era, the creation of products is always in 'perpetual beta' (i.e. there is no final product release; instead, there is a continuous update of the software and release of newer versions). In a Research 2.0 environment data gathering is continuous in nature (i.e. data collection continues, in perpetuity). Although this may be a new way of working for many quantitative and qualitative researchers, this practice does mirror some qualitative approaches (e.g. ethnography), where the researcher lives in a community for many weeks to many years, gathering data in a very continuous way. |
| Mashups | Web 2.0 aims to syndicate and not coordinate (i.e. allow others to use the data without worrying about what will happen at the other users' end). This approach is often referred to as mashups. The data collected from blogs, wikis or forums can be mixed to conduct research. In qualitative research, this would be similar to triangulation, where data from various sources (often using different methods) are combined to provide holistic perspectives on phenomena. |
| Multiple interface | In a Web 2.0 environment, different data types are more integrated and available for collection at the same place and time. The data can then be interlinked with different data formats. Researchers should be able to connect seamlessly to the database on the Internet with any type of device and be able to view different data formats in a single device. |
| The participatory research experience | In many traditional research projects (including some web approaches, such as online questionnaires) the interaction between the participant and the researcher is generally limited to the data collection phase. In Research 2.0, participants could be involved in many phases of the work, from design of the project, through analysis and dissemination. This process is termed the 'participatory research experience'. |

**Table 23.6** *Conducting research in a web environment*

| Process | Description |
| --- | --- |
| Start with the basics | Websites such as Wikipedia and CliffsNotes can be good places to begin researching your subject. |
| Academic databases | Academic databases ERIC, HubMed, Google Scholar and Academic Search are resources that can help make search time productive. |
| Library resources | Digitized archives provide access to materials not available in physical form. |
| Knowledge and information management | A sound KIM system is important to ensure that data is recorded and able to be retrieved for analysis. |
| Check for plagiarism | Incidents of plagiarism are on the rise. Avoid copying and pasting information directly from a website into your paper or project notes unless you are quoting a person or resource. It's easy to lose track of what text you have written and what came from outside sources. |
| Use documentation resources | Use a citation format such as EndNote to help organize your work. |
| Analyse a source's validity and reliability | A lot of information online is inaccurate. Carefully check Internet resources you use in your paper or project. |
| Develop a research plan | There is a vast amount of information online. Develop a research plan to provide steps in the research process. |

to researchers and participants, only, there may be the potential for participant-to-participant breaches of privacy and confidentiality.

## 2 Credibility and trustworthiness of data

Involving participants in all phases of the work can offer modes of working that can enhance qualitative (and quantitative) practices in Web 2.0. For example, member checking of data analysis is one mechanism for ensuring the credibility of qualitative data.

---

### RECENT CASE EXAMPLE: WEB 2.0

*The following article is an example of how Web 2.0 has been used in the past by researchers in Sport Management Research. The interested reader may wish to find/download and read the article for further insights.*

Sports information in a digital age: A case study of Lehigh Athletics. McCoy, M. I. (2010). Unpublished doctoral dissertation. Lehigh University.

The digital age continues to bring sweeping changes to how college athletic sites function. This thesis examined the changes in the Lehigh Athletics website over ten years. Analysis of the website changes, interviews and other data collected revealed that the changes being made are done primarily to directly address the leading audiences and in ways that will be most appealing. Many of the changes involved incorporation of video or video technology and other new media, such as social networking sites.

## CONCLUSION

The framework proposed by Rathi and Given (2010) presents a Research 2.0 framework for undertaking qualitative and quantitative research in the Web 2.0 environment. This framework can provide sport management researchers with a reference point for future research in these environments. It is suggested, however, that this evolving field of research is a work in progress and researchers should attempt to update and familiarize themselves with new developments as they occur.

## REVIEW QUESTIONS

With a general understanding now of the potential of a Research 2.0 framework for qualitative and quantitative research in sport management, attempt to answer the following questions:

- What are some of the key ethical issues facing the sport management researcher who intends to use Research 2.0 as a framework?
- What are some of the platforms from which Research 2.0 can be undertaken?

## SUGGESTED EXTENDED READING FOR STUDENTS

Greenhow, C., Robelia, B., and Hughes, J. (2009). Web 2.0 and classroom research: What path should we take *now? Educational Researcher, 38*(4), 246–259.

Rathie, D., and Given, L. M. (2010). Research 2.0: A framework for qualitative and quantitative research in web 2.0 environments. *Proceedings of the 43rd Hawaii International Conference on System Sciences.*

# References

Abdel-Shehid, G. (2005). *Who da man? Black masculinities and sporting cultures.* Toronto, Canada: Canadian Scholars.

Adler, P. A., and Adler, P. (1987). *Membership roles in field research.* Thousand Oaks, CA: Sage.

Ahituv, N., and Steimberg, Y. (2006). The impact of the Internet on research methods: Is a new methodology being created or just a new use of existing methodologies. Working Paper No 23/2006. Available at: www.itu.dk/courses/DDKU/E2007/artikler/internet%20new%20 methods_Ahituv.pdf (accessed 18 July 2013).

Alcoff, L., and Potter, E. (1993). *Feminist epistemologies.* London: Routledge.

Altheide, D. L. (1996). *Qualitative media analysis.* Thousand Oaks, CA: Sage.

Altheide, D. L. (2000). Tracking discourse and qualitative document analysis. *Poetics, 27*(4), 287–299.

Amis, J., and Silk, M. (2005). Rupture: Promoting critical and innovative approaches to the study of sport management. *Journal of Sport Management, 19,* 355–366.

Anderson, J. M. (2000). Gender, 'race', poverty, health and discourses of health reform in the context of globalization: A postcolonial feminist perspective in policy research. *Nursing Inquiry, 7,* 220–229.

Appadurai, A. (1996). *Modernity at large: Cultural dimensions of globalization.* Minneapolis, ME: University of Minnesota Press.

Atkinson, P., Coffey, A., and Delamont, S. (1999). Ethnography: Post, past and present. *Journal of Contemporary Ethnography, 28*(5), 460–71.

Badger, T. G. (2000). Action research, change and methodological rigour. *Journal of Nursing Management, 8,* 201–207.

Barnes, J. A. (1954). Class and committees in a Norwegian island parish. *Human Relations, 7,* 39–58.

Barthes, R. (1981). *Camera lucida.* London: Vintage Press.

Barthes, R. (1996). Introduction to the structural analysis of narratives. In S. Onega and J. A. G. Landa (eds), *Narratology* (pp. 45–60). New York: Longman.

Bate, P., Khan, R., and Pye, A. (2000). Towards a culturally-sensitive approach to organizational restructuring. *Organization Science, 11*(2), 197–211.

Bauman, Z. (2001). *The Individualized Society.* Cambridge: Polity.

Beattie, V. A. (2000). The future of corporate reporting: A review article. *Irish Accounting Review, 7*(1), 1–36.

Beemyn, B., and Eliason, M. (eds) (1996). *Queer studies: A lesbian, gay, bisexual, and transgender anthology.* New York: New York University Press.

Bergen, A., and While, A. (2000). A case for case studies: Exploring the use of case study design in community nursing research. *Journal of Advanced Nursing, 31,* 926–934.

Birrell, S., and Theberge, N. (1994). Feminist resistance and transformation in sport. In M. Costa and S. Guthrie (eds), *Women and sport: Interdisciplinary perspectives* (pp. 361–376). Champaign, IL: Human Kinetics.

Bless, C., Higson-Smith, C., and Kagee, A. (2006). *Fundamentals of social research methods: An African perspective* (4th edn). Cape Town, SA: Juta & Co.

Blommaert, J., and Bulcaen, C. (2000). Critical discourse analysis. *Annual Review of Anthropology, 29*, 447–466.

Bluman, A. G. (2001). *Elementary statistics: A step by step approach* (4th edn). New York: McGraw-Hill.

Boas, F. (1928). *The dynamics of cultural transmission*. New York: Morton.

Bogdan, R. C., and Biklen, S. K. (1982). *Qualitative research for education: An introduction to theory and methods*. Toronto, Canada: Allyn & Bacon.

Bray, J., Lee, J., Smith, L. L., and Yorks, L. (2000). *Collaborative inquiry in practice: Action, reflection, and making meaning*. Thousand Oaks, CA: Sage.

Bridel, W. (2006). Gender, sexuality, and the body: Exploring the lived experiences of gay and queer marathoners. Unpublished doctoral dissertation. University of Ottawa, Canada.

Brown, D. M. (2007). *Communicating design: Developing web site documentation for design and planning*. Berkeley, CA: Peachpit.

Bryman, A. (2004). *Social research methods* (2nd edn). Oxford: Oxford University Press.

Bryman, A., and Bell, E. (2011). *Business research methods*. London: Oxford University Press.

Burke, M. (2001). Sport and traditions of feminist theory. Unpublished doctoral dissertation, Victoria University, Melbourne, Australia.

Burns, R. B. (1997). *Introduction to research methods* (3rd edn). Melbourne, Australia: Longman.

Burr, V. (1995). *An introduction to social constructionism*. London: Routledge.

Butler, J. (1991). *Gender trouble: Feminism and the subversion of identity*. New York: Routledge.

Campbell, D. T. (1966). Quasi-experimental designs for use in natural social settings. In D. T. Campbell (ed.), *Experimenting, validating, knowing: Problems of method in the social sciences*. New York: McGraw-Hill.

Cannella, G. S., and Bailey, C. (1999). Postmodern research in early childhood education. In S. Reifel (ed.), *Advances in early education and day care, Vol. 10*, (pp. 3–39). Greenwich, CN: Jai Press.

Carr, W., and Kemmis, S. (1986). *Becoming critical: Education, knowledge and action research* (Rev. edn). Geelong, Australia: Deakin University.

Casey, K. (1995). The new narrative research in education. *Review of Research in Education, 21*, 211–253.

Catelli, L. A. (1995). Action research and collaborative inquiry in a school–university partnership. *Action in Teacher Education, 16*(4), 25–38.

Chambers, E. (2000). Applied ethnography. In N. K. Denzin and Y. S. Lincoln (eds), *Handbook of qualitative research* (2nd edn, pp. 851–869). Thousand Oaks, CA: Sage.

Chase, W., and Brown, F. (2000). *General statistics* (4th edn). New York: John Wiley & Sons.

Clandinin, D. J., and Connelly, F. M. (2000). *Narrative inquiry: Experience and story in qualitative research*. San Francisco, CA: Jossey-Bass.

Coffey, A., Holbrook, B., and Atkinson, P. (1996). Qualitative data analysis: Technologies and representations. *Sociological Research Online, 1*(1). Available at: www.socresonline.org.uk/socresonline/1/1/4.html (accessed 23 March 2011).

Coghlan, D., and Brannick, T. (2001). *Doing action research in your own organisation*. London: Sage.

Coghlan, P., and Coghlan, D. (2002). Action research for operations management. *International Journal of Operations and Production Management, 22*(2), 220–240.

Collier, J., and Collier, M. (1986). *Visual anthropology: Photography as a research method*, Albuquerque, NM: University of New Mexico Press.

Cooky, C. A. (2006). Getting girls in the game: A qualitative analysis of urban sport programs. Unpublished doctoral dissertation, University of Southern California.

Creswell, J. W. (1998). *Qualitative inquiry and research design: Choosing among five traditions.* Thousand Oaks, CA: Sage.

Creswell, J. W. (2003). *Research design: Quantitative, qualitative and mixed methods approaches* (3rd edn). Thousand Oaks, CA: Sage.

Creswell, J. W. (2007). *Qualitative inquiry and research design: Choosing among five approaches* (2nd edn). Thousand Oaks, CA: Sage.

Creswell, J. W. (2008). *Educational Research.* Upper Saddle River, NJ: Pearson.

Creswell, J. W. (2009). *Research design: Quantitative, qualitative and mixed methods approaches* (4th edn). New York: Sage.

Creswell, J. W., and Plano Clark, V. L. (2007). *Designing and conducting mixed methods research.* Thousand Oaks, CA: Sage.

Creswell, J. W., and Plano Clark, V. L. (2010). *Designing and conducting mixed methods research* (2nd edn). Thousand Oaks, CA: Sage.

Crofts, K., and Bisman, J. (2010). An illustration of the use of Leximancer software for qualitative data analysis. *Qualitative Research in Accounting and Management, 7*(2), 180–207.

Dale, G. A. (1996). Existential phenomenology: Emphasizing the experience of the athlete in sport psychology research. *The Sport Psychologist, 10*(4), 307–321.

Dann, S. (2010). Redefining social marketing with contemporary commercial marketing definitions. *Journal of Business Research, 63*(1), 147–153.

Davidson, J., and Shogan, D. (1998). What's queer about studying up? A response to Messner. *Sociology of Sport Journal, 15*(4), 359–366.

De Wet, J. J., Monteith, J. De K., Steyn, H. S., and Venter, P. A. (1981). *Navorsingsmetodes in die opvoedkunde: 'n 'inleiding tot empiriesenavorsing.* Durban, SA: Butterworth.

Delgado, R., and Stefancic, J. (1993). Critical race theory: An annotated bibliography. *Virginia Law Review, 79*(2), 461–516.

Denison, J., and Rinehart, R. (2000). Imagining sociological narratives. *Sociology of Sport Journal, 17*, 1–4.

Denzin, N. K. (1989). *Interpretive interactionism.* Newbury Park, CA: Sage.

Denzin, N. K. (1991). The reflexive interview and a performative social science. *Qualitative Research, 1*(1), 23–46.

Denzin, N. K. (1994). Postmodernism and deconstruction. In D. R. Dickens and A. Fontana (eds), *Postmodernism and social inquiry.* London: Guilford Press.

Denzin, N. K. (1997). *Interpretive ethnography.* Thousand Oaks, CA: Sage.

Denzin, N. K. (2004). The war on culture, the war on truth. *Cultural Studies Critical Methodologies, 4*(2), 137–142.

Denzin, N. K, and Lincoln, Y. S. (eds). (1994). *Handbook of qualitative research.* London: Sage.

Denzin, N. K. and Lincoln, Y. S. (eds). (1998). *Collecting and interpreting qualitative materials.* Thousand Oaks, CA: Sage.

Denzin, N. K., and Lincoln, Y. S. (eds). (2000). *Handbook of qualitative research* (2nd edn). Thousand Oaks, CA: Sage.

Denzin, N. K., and Lincoln, Y. S. (eds). (2002). *The qualitative inquiry reader.* Thousand Oaks, CA: Sage.

Denzin, N. K., and Lincoln, Y. S. (eds.). (2005). *Handbook of qualitative research.* London: Sage.

Derrida, J. (1976). *Of grammatology* (G. C. Spivak, trans.). Baltimore, MD: John Hopkins University Press.

Derrida, J. (1978). *Writing and difference* (A. Bass, trans.). Chicago, IL: University of Chicago Press.

Derrida, J. (1981). *Positions* (A. Bass, trans.). Chicago, IL: University of Chicago Press.

Derrida, J. (1982). *Margins of philosophy* (A. Bass, trans.). Chicago, IL: University of Chicago Press.

Derrida, J. (1996). *Deconstruction and pragmatism.* New York: Routledge.

DeVault, M. L. (1996). Talking back to sociology: Distinctive contributions of feminist methodology. *Annual Review of Sociology, 22*, 29–50.

Dick, B. (1990). *Convergent interviewing* (version 3). Brisbane, Australia: Interchange.

Dick, B. (2000). A beginner's guide to action research. Available at: www.scu.edu.au/schools/gcm/ar/arp/guide.html (accessed 10 February 2008).

Dick, B. (2002). Action research: Action *and* research. Available at: www.uq.net.au/action_research/aip/aandr.html (accessed 22 August 2003). Southern Cross University Lismore, Australia.

Dick, B. (2014). Action research. In J. Mills & M. Birks (eds), *Qualitative methodology: A practical guide* (pp. 51–65). London: Sage.

Dillman, D. A. (2007). *Mail and Internet surveys: The tailored design method* (2nd edn). Hoboken, NJ: John Wiley & Sons.

Docherty, T. (1993). Authority, history and the question of the postmodern. In M. Biriotti and N. Miller (eds), *What is an author?* Manchester: Manchester University Press.

Doering L. (1992). Power and knowledge in nursing: A feminist poststructuralist view. *Advances in Nursing Science, 14*, 24–33.

Dunbar, R. I. M. (2003). The social brain: Mind, language and society in evolutionary perspective. *Annual Review of Anthropology, 32*, 163–181.

Edwards, A. (2011). A test of ethical behaviour: A study of ethics education as ethnodrama with undergraduate sport management students. Unpublished research.

Edwards, A., and Skinner, J. (2006). *Sport empire.* Oxford: Meyer & Meyer Sports.

Edwards, A., and Skinner, J. (2009). *Qualitative research in sport management.* Oxford: Elsevier.

Edwards, A., Gilbert, K., and Skinner, J. (2002). *Extending the boundaries: Theoretical frameworks for research in sport management.* Melbourne, Australia: Common Ground Publications.

Edwards, A., Skinner, J., and O'Keefe, L. (2000). Women sport managers. *International Review of Women and Leadership, 6*(2), 48–58.

Eisenhardt, K. M. (1989). Building theories from case study research. *Academy of Management Review, 14*(4), 532–550.

Ellis, C. (1995). *Final negotiations.* Philadelphia, PA: Temple University Press.

Ellis, C. (1999). Heartful autoethnography. *Qualitative Health Research, 9*(5), 669–683.

Ellis, C. (2000). Creating criteria: An ethnographic short story. *Qualitative Inquiry, 6*(2), 273–277.

Ellis, C. (2004). The *ethnographic I: A methodological novel about authoethnography.* Walnut Creek, CA: Altamira Press.

Ellis, C., and Bochner, A. P. (2000). Autoethnography, personal narrative, reflexivity. In N. K. Denzin and Y. S. Lincoln (eds), *Handbook of qualitative research* (2nd edn, pp. 733–779). Thousand Oaks, CA: Sage.

Ely, R. J., and Meyerson, D. E. (2000). Theories of gender in organizations: A new approach to organizational analysis and change. *Research in Organizational Behaviour, 22*, 105–153.

Fairclough, N. (1989). *Language and power.* London: Longman.

Fairclough, N. (1992). *Discourse and social change.* Cambridge: Polity Press.

Fairclough, N. (1993). Critical discourse analysis and the marketization of public discourse: The universities. *Discourse and Society, 4*(2), 133–168.

Fairclough, N. (1995). *Critical discourse analysis: The critical study of language.* New York: Longman.

Fairclough, N. (2003). *Analyzing discourse: Textual analysis for social research.* New York: Routledge.

Farrell, K. (2006). HIV on TV: Conversations with young gay men. *Sexualities, 9*(2), 193–213.

Fay, B. (1975). *Social theory and political practice.* London: Allen & Unwin.

Feldman, A. (2003). Validity and quality in self-study. *Educational Researcher, 32*, 26–28.

Ferneley, E., Heinze, A., and Child, P. (2009). *Research 2.0: Encouraging engagement in online market research communities.* Oxford: UK Academy for Information Systems (UKAIS).

Fetterman, D. M. (1989). *Ethnography: Step by step.* Thousand Oaks, CA: Sage.

Fielding, N. G., and Lee, R. M. (2002). New patterns in the adoption and use of qualitative software. *Field Methods, 14*(2), 197–216.

Fine, M. (1994). Working the hyphens: Reinventing self and other in qualitative research. In N. K. Denzin, and Y. S. Lincoln (eds), *Handbook of qualitative research* (pp. 70–82). Thousand Oaks, CA: Sage.

Foucault, M. (1980). *Power/knowledge selected interviews and other writings, 1972–77.* (C. Gordon, trans.). New York: Harvester Wheatsheaf.

Foucault, M. (1983). The subject and power. In D. Dreyfus, P. Rabinow and M. Foucault (eds), *Beyond structuralism and hermeneutics* (2nd edn, pp. 208–226). Chicago, IL: University of Chicago Press.

Franklin, R. (2012). Making waves: Contesting the lifestyle marketing and sponsorship of female surfers. Unpublished doctoral dissertation, Griffith University Queensland, Australia.

Freire, P. (1970). *Pedagogy of the oppressed.* Harmondsworth: Penguin.

Gall, M. D., Borg, W. R., and Gall, J.P. (1996). *Educational research: An introduction.* New York: Longman.

Gamson, J. (2000). Sexualities, queer theory, and qualitative research. In N. K. Denzin and Y. S. Lincoln (eds), *Handbook of qualitative research* (2nd edn, pp. 347–365). Thousand Oaks, CA: Sage.

Garfinkel, H. (1967/1999). *Studies in ethnomethodology.* Englewood Cliffs, NJ: Prentice-Hall.

Gartner, A., Latham, G., and Merritt, S. (2003). The power of narrative: transcending disciplines. Available at: http://ultibase.rmit.edu.au/Articles/dec96/gartn1.htm# (accessed 3 March 2011).

Gatenby, B., and Humphries, M. (1996). Feminist commitments in organisational communication: Participatory action research as feminist praxis. *Australian Journal of Communication, 23*(2), 73–88.

Gay, L. R., Mills, G. E., and Airasian, P. (2009). *Educational research: Competencies for analysis and applications* (9th edn). Upper Saddle River, NJ: Pearson Merrill.

Gibbs, W. W. (2007). Comment: The courage of prediction. *Conservation Magazine, 8,* 31–34.

Giddens, A. (1990). *The consequences of modernity.* Cambridge: Polity Press.

Giffney, N. (2004). Denormatizing queer theory: More than (simply) lesbian and gay studies. *Feminist Theory, 5*(1), 73–78.

Gilbert, N. (2008). *Researching social life* (3rd edn). London: Sage.

Gilbert, K., and Schantz, O. J. (eds). (2008). *The Paralympic Games: Empowerment or side show?* Maidenhead: Meyer & Meyer.

Gingrich, A. (2002). When ethnic majorities are 'dethroned'. In A. Gingrich and R. G. Fox (eds), *Anthropology, by comparison* (pp. 225–232). London: Routledge.

Giorgi, A. (1975). An application of the phenomenological method to psychology. In A. Giorgi, C. Fisher, and E. Murray (eds), *Duquesne studies in phenomenology*, Vol. 2, (pp. 82–103). Pittsburgh, PA: Duquesne University Press.

Giroux, H. A. (2002). *Breaking in to the movies: Film and the culture of politics.* Maiden, MA: Blackwell.

Gottschalk, S. (1998). Postmodern sensibilities and ethnographic possibilities. In A. Banks and S. P. Banks (eds), *Fiction and social research: By ice or fire* (pp. 205–233). Walnut Creek, CA: Altamira.

Grbich, C. (1999). *Qualitative research in health: An introduction.* Thousand Oaks, CA: Sage.

Greene, J. C., Caracelli, V. J., and Graham, W. (1989). Toward a conceptual framework for mixed-method evaluation designs. *Educational evaluation and policy analysis, 11*(3), 255–274.

Greenhow, C., Robelia, B., and Hughes, J. (2009). Web 2.0 and classroom research: What path should we take *now? Educational Researcher, 38*(4), 246–259.

Greenwood, D. J., and Levin, M. (1998). *Introduction to action research.* Thousand Oaks, CA: Sage.

Gronhaug, K., and Olson, O. (1999). Action research and knowledge creation: Merits and challenges. *Qualitative Market Research: An International Journal, 2*(1), 6–14.

Guba, E. G., and Lincoln, Y. S. (1981). *Effective evaluation: Improving the usefulness of evaluation results through responsive and naturalistic approaches.* San Francisco, CA: Jossey-Bass.

Guba, E. G., and Lincoln, Y. S. (1982). Epistemological and methodological bases of naturalistic inquiry. *Educational Technology Research and Development, 30*(4), 233–252.

Guba, E. G., and Lincoln, Y. S. (1989). *Fourth generation evaluation.* Newbury Park, CA: Sage.

Guba, E. G., and Lincoln, Y. S. (1994). Competing paradigms in qualitative research. In N. K. Denzin and Y. S. Lincoln (eds), *Handbook of qualitative research* (pp. 105–117). Thousand Oaks, CA: Sage.

Gubrium, J., and Holstein, J. (2000). Analyzing interpretive practice. In N. K. Denzin and Y. S. Lincoln (eds), *Handbook of qualitative research* (2nd edn, pp. 487–508). Thousand Oaks, CA: Sage.

Gudsmundsdottir, S. (1991). Story maker, story teller: Narrative structures in the curriculum. *Journal of Curriculum Studies, 23*(3), 207–218.

Gummesson, E. (2000). *Qualitative methods in management research* (2nd edn). Thousand Oaks, CA: Sage.

Habermas, J. (1978). *Knowledge and human interests* (J. J. Shapiro, trans.). Cambridge: Polity. (Original work published 1965).

Hall, S. (1997) The local and global: Globalization and ethnicity. In A. McClintock, A. Mufti and E. Shohat (eds), *Dangerous liaisons: Gender, nation, and postcolonial perspectives* (pp. 173–187). Minneapolis, MN: University of Minnesota Press.

Halperin, D. M. (1995). *Saint-Foucault: Towards a gay hagiography.* New York: Oxford University Press.

Hammersley, M. (1990). *Reading ethnographic research: A critical guide.* New York: Longman.

Hammersley, M. (1992). *What's wrong with ethnography: Methodological explorations.* London: Routledge.

Hammersley, M., and Atkinson, P. (1983). *Ethnography: Principles in practice.* London: Tavistock.

Hammersley, M., and Atkinson, P. (1995). *Ethnography: Principles in practice* (2nd edn, pp. 263-287). London: Routledge.

Hardt, M., and Negri, A. (2000). *Empire.* Cambridge, MA: Harvard University Press.

Harnett, D. L., and Soni, A. K. (1991). *Statistical methods for business and economics* (4th edn). New York: Addison-Wesley.

Harrison, B. (2002). Seeing health and illness worlds-using visual methods in a sociology of health and illness: A methodological review. *Sociology of Health and Illness, 24*(6), 856–872.

Hart, E. (1996). Action research as a professionalizing strategy: Issues and dilemmas. *Journal of Advanced Nursing, 23,* 454–461.

Hart, E., and Bond, M. (1995). *Action research for health and social care: A guide to practice.* Buckingham: Open University Press.

Hasselgren, B., and Beach, D. (1996). Phenomenography: A 'good-for-nothing brother' of phenomenology? Or phenomenography is what phenomenographers do when doing phenomenography. Available at: www.ped.gu.se/biorn/phgraph/misc/constr/goodno2.html (accessed 20 July 2008).

Hatch, J. A. (2002). *Doing qualitative research in education settings.* Albany, NY: State University of New York Press.

Heidegger, M. (1962). *Being and time.* New York: Harper & Row.

Heidegger, M. (1977). *The question concerning technology, and other essays.* New York: Harper & Row.

Heritage, J. (1984). *Garfinkel and ethnomethodology.* Cambridge, MA: Polity Press.

Heron, J., and Reason, P. (1997). *Qualitative inquiry.* London: Sage.

Holt, N. (2003). Representation, legitimation, and autoethnography: An autoethnographic writing story. *International Journal of Qualitative Methods, 2*(1), Article 2, 18–28.

Hook, D. (2001). The disorders of discourse. *Theoria, 1*(97), 41–68.

Howitt, D., and Cramer, D. (2000). *An introduction to statistics in psychology*. London: Prentice Hall.

Humphreys, D. R., Austin, S. A., Baumgardner, J. R., and Snelling, A. A. (2003). Precambrian zircons yield a helium diffusion age of 6,000 years. *American Geophysical Union, Fall Conference*, Abstract V32C-1047. Available at: www.icr.org/pdf/research/AGUHeliumPoster_Humphreys.pdf Abstract published in *Eos, Transactions of the American Geophysical Union* 84(46), Fall Meeting Supplement as 'Recently measured helium diffusion rate for zircon suggests inconsistency with U-Pb age for Fenton Hill granodiorite'.

Humphreys, D. R., Austin, S. A., Baumgardner, J. R., and Snelling, A. A. (2004). Helium diffusion age of 6,000 years supports accelerated nuclear decay. *Creation Research Society Quarterly*, 41(1), 1–16. Available at: www.creationresearch.org/crsq/articles/41/41_1/Helium_lo_res.pdf (accessed 12 June 2013).

Huntington, S. P. (1993). The clash of civilizations. *Foreign Affairs*, 72(3), 22–49.

Huntington, S. P. (1996). *The clash of civilizations and the remaking of world order*. New York: Simon & Schuster.

Husserl, E. (1931). *Ideas: General Introduction to Phenomenology*. New York, NY: Macmillan.

Isakhan, B. (2005). From Despotism to democracy: Reporting Iraq's January 2005 election in the Australian and Middle Eastern print media. Paper presented at the Journalism Education Australia Conference, Surfers Paradise, Australia, available at: http://live-wirez.gu.edu.au/jea (accessed 12 September 2013).

Jacob, E. R., Barnett, T., Walker, L., Cross, M., and Missen, K. (2012). Australian clinicians' views on interprofessional education for students in the rural clinical setting. *Journal of Research in Interprofessional Practice and Education*, 2(2), 219–229.

Jagose, A. M. (1996). *Queer theory: An introduction*. New York: New York University Press.

Johansson, B., Marton, F., and Svensson, L. (1985). An approach to describing learning as change between qualitatively different conceptions. In L. West & A. Pines (eds), *Cognitive structure and conceptual change* (pp. 233–257). New York: Academic Press.

Johnson, R. R., and Kuby, P. (2011). *Elementary statistics*. Boston, MA: Brooks/Cole.

Jorgensen, D. L. (1989). *Participant observation*. Newbury Park, CA: Sage.

Kemmis, S., and Grundy, S. (1997). Educational action research in Australia: Organization and practice. In S. Hollingsworth (ed.), *International action research: A casebook for educational reform* (pp. 40–48). London: Falmer Press.

Kemmis, S., and McTaggart, R. (1988). *The action research planner* (3rd rev. edn). Waurn Ponds, Australia: Deakin University.

Keppel, G. (1973). *Design and analysis: A researcher's handbook*. Englewood Cliffs, NJ: Prentice Hall.

Kerry, D. S., and Armour, K. M. (2000). Sports sciences and the promise of phenomenology: Philosophy, method, and insight. *Quest*, 52(1), 1–17.

Kozinets, R. V. (1998). On netnography: Initial reflections on consumer investigations of cyberculture. In J. Alba and W. Hutchinson (eds), *Advances in consumer research, Vol. 25*, (pp. 366–371). Provo, UT: Association for Consumer Research.

Krane, D. (2001). Disorderly progress on the frontiers of policy evaluation. *International Journal of Public Administration*, 24(1), 95–123.

Krueger, R. A. (1994). *Focus groups: A practical guide for applied research*. Thousand Oaks, CA: Sage Publications.

Kuhn, T. (1996). *The structure of scientific revolutions* (3rd edn). Chicago, IL: University of Chicago Press.

Kusch, M. (1991). *Foucault's strata and fields: An investigation into archaeological and genealogical science studies*. Dordrecht, The Netherlands: Kluwer Academic Publishers.

Labov, W. (1972). *Language in the inner city*. Philadelphia, PA: University of Pennsylvania Press.

Labov, W. (1982). Speech actions and reactions in personal narrative. In D. Tannen (ed.), *Georgetown University round table on languages and linguistics 1981: Analyzing discourse: Text and talk* (pp. 219–247). Washington, DC: Georgetown University Press.

Lather, P. (1986). Issues of validity in openly ideological research: Between a rock and a soft place. *Interchange, 17,* 63–84.

Lather, P. (1991). Deconstructing/deconstructive inquiry: The politics of knowing and being known. *Educational Theory, 41*(2), 153–173.

LeCompte, M. D., and Preissle, J. (1993). *Ethnography and qualitative design in educational research* (2nd edn). New York: Academic Press.

Lee, J. R. E. (1991). Language and culture: The linguistic analysis of culture. In G. Button (ed.), *Ethnomethodology and the human sciences* (pp. 196–226). Cambridge: Cambridge University Press.

Leininger, M. M. (ed.). (1985). *Qualitative research methods in nursing.* Orlando, FL: Grune & Stratton.

Lewins, A., Taylor, C., and Gibbs, G. (2005). *What is qualitative data analysis?* Huddersfield: School of Human and Health Sciences, University of Huddersfield.

Lewin, K. (1948). *Resolving social conflicts: Selected papers on group dynamics.* New York: Harper & Row.

Lewin, K. (1951). *Field research in social sciences.* New York: Harper & Row.

Lieblich, A., Tuval-Mashiach, R., and Zilber, R. (1998). *Narrative research.* Thousand Oaks, CA: Sage.

Lincoln, Y. S., and Guba, E. G. (1985). *Naturalistic inquiry.* Beverly Hills, CA: Sage.

Lincoln, Y. S., and Guba, E. G. (2000). Paradigmatic controversies, contradictions, and emerging confluences. In N. K. Denzin and Y. S. Lincoln (eds), *Handbook of qualitative research* (2nd edn, pp. 163–188). Thousand Oaks, CA: Sage.

Lindlof, T. R., and Taylor, B. C. (2002). *Qualitative communication research methods* (2nd edn). Thousand Oaks, CA: Sage.

Lofland, J., and Lofland, L. H. (1995). *Analyzing social settings: A guide to qualitative observation and analysis* (3rd edn). Belmont, CA: Wadsworth.

Lugones, M., and Spelman, E. (1983). Have we got a theory for you! Hypatia. 1 [special issue], *Women's Studies International Forum, 6,* 573–581.

Lundgren, E. (1995). *Feminist theory and violent empiricism.* Aldershot: Avebury.

Lysaght, P. (2001). Intelligent profiles: A model for change in women's lives. Unpublished doctoral thesis, University of Wollongong, Australia.

McAllister, S. L. (2006). Women administrators' perceptions of the contribution of competitive sport experiences to their career paths and leadership practices. Unpublished doctoral dissertation, Illinois State University, Bloomington, IN.

McCall, M. M. (2000). Performance ethnography: A brief history and some advice. In N. K. Denzin and Y. S. Lincoln (eds), *Handbook of qualitative research* (2nd edn, pp. 412–433). Thousand Oaks, CA: Sage.

McCarl-Nielsen, J. (1990). *Feminist research methods: Exemplary readings in the social sciences.* Boulder, CO: Westview.

McConaghy, C. (2000). *Rethinking indigenous education: Culturalism, colonialism and the politics of knowing.* Flaxton: Post Pressed.

McCoy, M. I. (2010). Sports information in a digital age: A case study of Lehigh Athletics. Unpublished doctoral dissertation. Lehigh University, Pennsylvania, PA.

McKenna, B. J., and Waddell, N. (2007). International political responses to the 2005 London Bombing: Epideictic discourse and public condoling. *Journal of Language and Politics, 6,* 377–399.

McLean, J. E. (1995). *Improving education through action research.* Thousand Oaks, CA: Corwin Press.

McLuhan, M. (1964). *Understanding media: The extension of man.* London: Routledge.

McMillan, A. (2004). Take-home numeracy kits for preschool children. *Australian Journal of Early Childhood, 29.* Available at: www.questia.com/googleScholar.qst?docId=5006517649 (accessed 21 August 2011).

McMillan, J., and Schumacher, S. (2006). *Research in education* (6th edn). Boston, MA: Pearson Education.

MacTaggart, R. (1991). Action research: Issues for the next decade. *Curriculum perspectives, 11*(4), 44–46.

Maguire, P. (1987). *Doing participatory research: A feminist approach.* Amherst, MA: University of Massachusetts.

Malinowski, B. (1922). *Argonauts of the Western Pacific.* New York: Dutton.

Markula, P., Grant, B., and Denison, J. (2001). Qualitative research and aging and physical activity: Multiple ways of knowing. *Journal of Aging and Physical Activity, 9,* 245–264.

Marshall, C., and Rossman, G. B. (1995). *Designing qualitative research.* Newbury Park, CA: Sage.

Martin, J. (1990). Deconstructing organizational taboos: The suppression of gender conflict in organizations. *Organization Science, 1*(4), 339–359.

Mason, J. (1996). *Qualitative researching.* London: Sage.

Maynard, M., and Purvis, J. (1994). *Methods, practice and epistemology: The debate about feminism and research.* New York: Taylor & Francis.

Maxwell, J. A. (1996). *Qualitative research design: An interactive approach.* Thousand Oaks, CA: Sage.

Mead, M. (1928). *Coming of age in Samoa.* New York: Dell.

Merriam, S. B. (1998). *Case study research in education: A qualititative approach.* San Francisco, CA: Jossey-Bass.

Meyerson, D. E., and Kolb, D. M. (2000). Moving out of the 'armchair': Developing a framework to bridge the gap between feminist theory and practice, *Organization, 7*(4), 553–571.

Michael, M. G., Fusco, S. J., and Michael, K. (2008). A research note on ethics in the emerging age of überveillance. *Computer Communications, 31*(6), 1192–1199.

Mienczakowski, J. (2001). Ethnodrama: Performed research – limitations and potential. In P. Atkinson, A. Coffey, S. Delamont, J. Lofland, and L. Lofland (eds), *Handbook of ethnography* (pp. 468–476). London: Sage.

Mienczakowski, J., and Morgan, S. (1993). *Busting: The challenge of the drought spirit.* Brisbane, Australia: Griffith University Reprographics.

Mies, M. (1991). Women's research or feminist research? The debate surrounding feminist science and methodology. In M. M. Fonow, and J. A. Cook (eds), *Beyond methodology: Feminist scholarship as lived research* (pp. 60–84). Bloomington, IN: Indiana University Press.

Miles, M. B., and Huberman, M. A. (1994). *Qualitative data analysis.* Thousand Oaks, CA: Sage.

Mintzberg, H. (1979). An emerging strategy of 'direct' research. *Administrative Science Quarterly, 24,* 580–589.

Mishler, E. G. (1995). Models of narrative analysis: A typology. *Journal of Narrative and Life History, 5*(2), 87–123.

Morse, J. M., Barrett, M., Mayan, M., Olson, K., Spiers, J., and Hon, D. (2002). Verification strategies for establishing reliability and validity in qualitative research. *International Journal of Qualitative Methods, 1*(2), 1–19.

Morse, J. M., and Richards, L. (2002). *Readme first for a user's guide to qualitative research.* Thousand Oaks, CA: Sage.

Muijs, D. (2011). *Doing quantitative research in education with SPSS* (2nd edn). Thousand Oaks, CA: Sage.

Nachimas C. F., and Nachimas, D. (1992). *Research methods in the social sciences.* New York: St Martin's Press.

Neuman, D. L. (1994). *Social research methods: Qualitative and quantitative approaches.* Boston, MA: Allyn & Bacon.

Nilan, P. (2002). Dangerous fieldwork re-examined: The question of researcher subject position. *Qualitative Research, 2,* 363–386.

Noffke, S. E., and Stevenson, R. B. (1995). *Educational action research: Becoming practically critical.* New York: Teachers College Press.

Oleson, M. E. (ed.) (2000). *Feminism, community and communication.* Binhamton, NY: The Haworth Press.

O'Reilly, T. (2005). What is Web 2.0: Design patterns and business models for the next generation of software. Available at: http://oreilly.com/pub/a/oreilly/tim/news/2005/09/30/what-is-web-20.html (accessed 19 June 2011).

Paccagnella, L. (1997). Getting the seats of your pants dirty: Strategies for ethnographic research on virtual communities. *Journal of Computer-Mediated Communication, 3*(1). Available at: http://jcmc.indiana.edu/vol3/issue1/paccagnella.html (accessed 10 January 2008).

Packwood, A., and Sikes, P. (1996). Adopting a postmodern approach to research. *International Journal of Qualitative studies in Education, 9*(3), 335–346.

Padgett, D. (2008). *Qualitative methods in social work research.* Los Angeles, CA: Sage.

Pajares, F. (2007). Self efficacy information. In T. Urden and F. Pajares (eds), *Self-efficacy beliefs of adolescents* (pp. 339–367). Charlotte, NC: Information Age Publishing.

Parker, I. (1992). *Discourse dynamics: Critical analysis for social and individual psychology.* London: Routledge

Patel, R., and Davidson, B. (2003). *Forskningsmetodikens grunder: Att planera, genomföra och rapportera en undersökning.* Lund, Sweden: Studentlitteratur.

Patton, M. Q. (1990). *Qualitative evaluation and research methods.* Newbury, CA: Sage.

Pedersen, K. (1998). Doing feminist ethnography in the wilderness around my hometown. *International Review for the Sociology of Sport, 33*(4), 393–402.

Pedhazur, E. J. (1982). *Multiple regression in behavioural research* (2nd edn). Fort Worth, TX: Holt, Rinehart & Winston.

Pierce, J. (1995). Reflections of fieldwork in a complex organization. In R. Hertz and J. Imber (eds), *Studying elites using qualitative methods* (pp. 94–110). Thousand Oaks, CA: Sage.

Polkinghorne, D. E. (1988). *Narrative knowing and the human sciences.* Albany, NY: State University of New York Press.

Polkinghorne, D. E. (1989). Phenomenological research methods. In R. S. Valle and S. Halling (eds), *Existential phenomenological perspectives in psychology* (pp. 41–60). New York: Plenum Press.

Pollio, H. R., Henley, T. B., and Thompson, C. B. (1997). *The phenomenology of everyday life.* Cambridge: Cambridge University Press.

Popkewitz, T. S. (1984). *Paradigm and ideology in educational research: The social functions of the intellectual.* Philadelphia, PA: The Falmer Press.

Potter, J., and Wetherell, M. (1987). *Discourse and social psychology: Beyond attitudes and behaviour.* London: Sage.

Psathas, G. (1995). *Conversation analysis: The study of talk-in-interaction.* Thousand Oaks, CA: Sage.

Quatman, C. (2006). The social construction of knowledge in the field of sport management: A social network perspective. Unpublished doctoral dissertation, The Ohio State University, Columbus.

Quayson A. (2000). *Postcolonialism: Theory, practice or process?* Cambridge: Polity Press.

Ramella, M. (2004). *Positive futures impact report: Engaging with young people.* London: Home Office.

Ramella, M., and Olmos, G. (2005). *Participant authored audiovisual stories (PAAS): Giving the camera away or giving the camera a way?* Papers in Social Research Methods: Qualitative Series no. 10, June (London School of Economics and Political Science Methodology Institute).

Rathie, D., and Given, L. M. (2010). Research 2.0: A Framework for Qualitative and Quantitative research in web 2.0 environments. *Proceedings of the 43rd Hawaii International Conference on System Sciences.*

Rao, A., Stuart, R., and Kelleher, D. (1999). *Gender at work: Organizational change for equality.* West Hartford, CO: Kumarian Press.

# REFERENCES

Reason, P. (1990). *Human inquiry in action: Developments in new paradigm research* (2nd edn). London: Sage.

Reason, P., and Bradbury, H. E. (2001). *Handbook of action research*. London: Sage.

Reed-Danahay, D. (1997). *Auto/ethnography: Rewriting the self and the social*. Oxford: Berg Publishing.

Reid, L. (1997). Exploring the ways that dialogue journaling affects how and why students write: An action research project. *Teaching and Change, 5*(1), 50–57.

Reinhartz, S. (1992). *Feminist methods in social research*. New York: Oxford University Press.

Richardson, L. (2000). Writing: A method of inquiry. In N. K. Denzin and Y. S. Lincoln (eds), *Handbook of qualitative research* (2nd edn, pp. 923–948). Thousand Oaks, CA: Sage.

Richardson, L., and Lockridge, E. (2004). *Travels with Ernest: Crossing the literary/sociological divide*. Walnut Creek, CA: Alta Mira Press.

Riessman, C. K. (1993). *Narrative analysis*. Newbury Park, CA: Sage.

Rinehart, R. E. (2005). 'Experiencing' sport management: The use of personal narrative in sport management studies. *Journal of Sport Management, 19*(4), 497–522.

Ritchie, J., Lewis, J., and Elam, G. (2003). Designing and selecting samples. In J. Ritchie and J. Lewis (eds), *Qualitative research practice: A guide for social sciences students and researchers* (pp. 77–109). London: Sage.

Ritchie, J., and Spencer, L. (1994). Qualitative data analysis for applied policy research. In A. Bryman and R. Burgess (eds), *Analyzing qualitative data* (pp. 173–194). London: Sage.

Robinson, W. (1996). *Promoting polyarchy*. Cambridge: Cambridge University Press.

Roche, C. (1999). *Impact assessment for development agencies: Learning to value change*. Oxford: Oxford University Press.

Rodwell, M. (1998). *Social work constructivist research*. New York: Garland.

Ross, R. J. S., and Trachte, K. C. (1990). *Global capitalism: The new Leviathan*. Albany, NY: SUNY Press.

Said, E. W. (2000). *The Edward Said Reader*, M. Bayoumi and A. Rubin (eds). New York: Vintage Books.

Saldana, J. (1998). Ethical issues in an ethnographic performance text: The dramatic impact, the juicy stuff. *Research in Drama Education, 3*(2) 181–196.

Saldana, J. (2005). *Ethnodrama: An anthology of reality theatre*. Walnut Creek, CA: Alta Mira Press.

Sale, J. E. M., Lohfeld, L. H., and Brazil, K. (2002). Revisiting the quantitative–qualitative debate: Implications for mixed-methods research. *Quality and quantity, 36*(1), 43–53.

Sandberg, J. (1995). Are phenomenographic results reliable? *Nordisk Pedagogik, 15*, 156–164.

Sandberg, J. (1997). Are phenomenographic results reliable? *Higher Education Research and Development, 16*, 203–212.

Sandelowski, M. (1996). Using qualitative methods in intervention studies. *Research in Nursing and Health, 19*, 359–364.

San Juan, E., Jr. (1998). *Beyond postcolonial theory*. New York: St Martin's Press.

Saukko, P. (2003). *Doing research in cultural studies*. London: Sage.

Schegloff, E. (1991). Reflections on talk and social structure. In D. Boden and D. H. Zimmerman (eds), *Talk and social structure: Studies in ethnomethodology and conversation analysis* (pp. 44–70). Berkeley, CA: University of California Press.

Schön, D. (1991). *The reflective practitioner* (2nd edn). San Francisco, CA: Jossey Bass.

Schwandt, T. A. (2001). *Dictionary of qualitative inquiry*. Thousand Oaks, CA: Sage.

Schwandt, T. A., and Halpern, E. S. (1988). *Linking auditing and metaevaluation: Enhancing quality in applied research*. Newbury Park, CA: Sage.

Scrogum, J. (2005). Binaries and bridging: A feminist analysis of women's rugby participation. Unpublished masters thesis. University of North Carolina at Greensboro.

Seiter, E., Borchers, H., Kreutzner, G., and Warth, E. (1989). Don't treat us like we're so stupid and naive: Toward an ethnography of soap opera viewers. In E. Seiter, H. Borchers, G. Kreutzner and E. Warth (eds), *Remote Control* (pp. 223–247). New York: Routledge.

Semerjian, T. Z., and Waldron, J. J. (2001). The journey through feminism: Theory, research, and dilemmas from the field. *The Sport Psychologist, 15*, 438–444.

Shapiro, M. J. (1987). Educational theory and recent political discourse: A new agenda for the left? *Teachers College Record, 89*(2), 171–200.

Shaw, S. and Frisby, W. (2006). Can gender equity be more equitable?: Promoting an alternative frame for sport management research, education, and practice. *Journal of Sport Management, 20*(4), 2–24.

Silverman, D. (1993). *Interpreting qualitative data: Methods for Analysing talk, text and interaction.* London: Sage.

Skinner, J. L. (2001). Environmental turbulence and its impact on strategic change and organisational culture: The case of the Queensland Rugby Union. Unpublished doctoral dissertation, Victoria University, Australia.

Skinner, J., and Edwards, A. (2005). Inventive pathways: Fresh visions for sport management research. *Journal of Sport Management, 19*(4), 404–421.

Sklair, L. (2002). *Globalization: Capitalism and its alternatives.* Oxford: Oxford University Press.

Smart, A. (1992). *Making room: Squatter clearance in Hong Kong,* Hong Kong: Centre of Asian Studies.

Smith, A., and Stewart, B. (2010). The special features of sport revisited. *Sport Management Review, 10*(1), 1–11.

Smith, A. E., and Humphreys, M. S. (2006). Evaluation of unsupervised semantic mapping of natural language with Leximancer concept mapping. *Behavior Research Methods, 38*(2), 262–279.

Smith, B. (1981). Narrative versions, narrative theories. In W. J. T. Mitchell (ed.), *On narrative* (pp. 209–232). Chicago, IL: University of Chicago Press.

Smith, B., and Weed, M. (2007). The potential of narrative research in sports tourism. *Journal of Sport and Tourism, 12*(3–4), 249–269.

Smith, R. (1993). Potentials for empowerment in critical education research. *The Australian Educational Researcher, 20*(2), 75–93.

Sparkes, A. C. (2000). Fictional representations: On difference, choice, and risk. *Sociology of Sport Journal, 19*, 1–24.

Sparkes, A. C. (2002). *Telling tales in sport and physical activity: A qualitative journey.* Champaign, IL: Human Kinetics.

Spiegelberg, H. (1982). *The phenomenological movement: A historical introduction.* Dordrecht, The Netherlands: Kluwer Academic Publishers.

Spivak, G. C. (1988). Can the subaltern speak? In C. Nelson and L. Grossberg (eds), *Marxism and the interpretation of culture* (pp. 24–28). London: Macmillan.

Spradley, J. (1979). *The ethnographic interview.* New York: Holt, Rinehart & Winston.

Spradley, J. P. (1980). *Participant observation.* New York: Holt, Rinehart & Winston.

Spry, T. (2001). Performing autoethnography: An embodied methodological praxis. *Qualitative Inquiry, 7*(6), 706–732.

Stake, R. E. (1995). *The art of case study research.* Thousand Oaks, CA: Sage.

Stake, R. (2000). Case studies. In N. K. Denzin and Y. S. Lincoln (eds), *Handbook of qualitative research* (2nd edn, pp. 435–454). Thousand Oaks, CA: Sage.

Stanley, L., and Wise, S. (1993). *Breaking out again: Feminist ontology and epistemology.* London: Routledge.

Strauss, A., and Corbin, J. (1990). *Basics of qualitative research: Grounded theory procedures and techniques.* London: Sage.

Streubert, H. J., and Carpenter, D. R. (1999). *Qualitative research in nursing: Advancing the humanistic imperative* (2nd edn). Philadelphia, PA: Lippincott.

Stringer, E. (1999). *Action research* (2nd edn). Thousand Oaks, CA: Sage.

Stringer, E., and Genat, W. J. (2004). *Action research in health*. Upper Saddle River, NJ: Pearson.

Stockwell, P., Colomb, R., Smith, A., and Wiles, J. (2009). Use of an automatic content analysis tool: A technique for seeing both local and global scope. *International Journal of Human-Computer Studies, 67*(5), 424–436.

Sullivan, S., and Brockington, D. (2004). Qualitative methods in globalisation studies: or, saying something about the world without counting or inventing it. *CSGR Working Paper,* 139/04.

Svensson, L. (1994). Theoretical foundations of phenomenography. In R. Ballantyne and C. Bruce (eds), *Phenomenography: Philosophy and practice* (pp. 9–20). Brisbane, Australia: Queensland University of Technology.

Sykes, H. (1996). Constr(i)(u)cting lesbian identities in physical education: Feminist and poststructural approaches to researching sexuality. *Quest: Journal of the National Association for Physical Education in Higher Education, 48*(4), 459–69.

Taesoo, A. (2010). The effect of user motives and interactivity on attitude toward a sport website. Unpublished doctoral dissertation. Florida State University College of Education.

Tashakkori, A., and Teddlie, C. (2003). *Handbook of mixed methods in social and behavioural research*. Thousand Oaks, CA: Sage.

Teddlie, C., and Tashakkori, A. (2009). *Foundations of mixed methods research: Integrating quantitative and qualitative approaches in the social and behavioural sciences*. Thousand Oaks, CA: Sage.

Tedlock, B. (2000). Ethnography and ethnographic representation. In N. K. Denzin and Y. S. Lincoln (eds), *Handbook of qualitative research* (2nd edn, pp. 455–486). Thousand Oaks, CA: Sage.

Tellis, W. (1997). Application of a case study methodology. *The Qualitative Report, 3*(3). Available at: www.nova.edu/ssss/QR/QR3-2/tellis1.html (accessed 4 February 2014).

Thomas, J. R., and Nelson, J. K. (1996). *Research methods in physical activity* (3rd edn). Champaign, IL: Human Kinetics.

Thomas, J. R., Nelson, J. K., and Silverman, S. J. (2005). *Research methods in physical activity*. Champaign, IL: Human Kinetics.

Thomas, S. P., and Pollio, H. R. (2002). *Listening to patients: A phenomenological approach to nursing research and practice*. New York: Springer.

Thompson, D. (1992). Against the dividing of women: Lesbian feminism and heterosexuality. *Feminism and Psychology, 2*, 387–398.

Tierney, W. (1997). *Academic outlaws: Queer theory and cultural studies in the academy*. London: Sage.

Tierney, W. G. (1998). Life history's history: Subjects foretold. *Qualitative Inquiry, 4*, 49–70.

Tomaselli, K. G. (2003). 'Dit is Die here Se Asem': The wind, its messages, and issues of auto-ethnographic methodology in the Kalahari. *Cultural Studies <=> Critical Methodologies, 3*(4), 397–428.

Tomlinson, J. (1999). Globalization and culture. Chicago, IL: University of Chicago Press.

Trochim, M. K., and Donnelly, J. P. (2008). *The research methods knowledge base* (3rd edn). Mason, OH: Cengage Learning.

Trochim, W. (1989). An introduction to concept mapping for planning and evaluation. In W. Trochim (ed.), *A Special Issue of Evaluation and Program Planning, 12*, 1–16.

Tuhiwai Smith, L. (1999). *Decolonizing methodologies: Research and indigenous peoples*. London: Zed Books.

Tukey, J. W. (1977). *Exploratory data analysis*. Reading, MA: Addison-Wesley.

Van Maanen, J. (1988). *Tales of the field: On writing ethnography*. Chicago, IL: University of Chicago Press.

Van Maanen, J. (1995). Style as theory. *Organization Science, 6*, 133–143.

Van Manen, M. (1990). *Researching lived experience: Human science for an action sensitive pedagogy*. Ontario, Canada: The University of Western Ontario.

Van Manen, M. (1994). Pedagogy, virtue, and narrative identity in teaching. *Curriculum Inquiry*, *24*(2), Summer, 135–170.

Van Zoonen, L. (1994). *Feminist media studies*. London: Sage.

Vander Kloet, M. A. (2005). Baywatch babes as recreation workers: Lifeguarding, subjectivity, equity. Masters Dissertation, University of Toronto, Canada.

Viruru, R., and Cannella, G. S. (2001). Postcolonial ethnography, young children and voice. In S. Grieshaber and G. S. Cannella (eds), *Embracing identities and early childhood education*. New York: Teachers College Press.

Wallerstein, I. (1974). *The modern world-system, I: Capitalist agriculture and the origins of the European world-economy in the sixteenth century*. New York/London: Academic Press.

Waterman, H. (1998). Embracing ambiguities and valuing ourselves: Issues of validity in action research. *Journal of Advanced Nursing*, *28*, 101–105.

Waterman, H., Tillen, D., Dickson, R., and de Konig, K. (2001). Action research: A systematic review and guidance for assessment. *Health Technology Assessment*, *5*(23), iii–157.

Webb, C. (1990). Partners in research. *Nursing Times*, *86*(32), 40–44.

Weitzman, E. A., and Miles, M. B. (1995). *Computer programs for qualitative data analysis: A software sourcebook*. Thousand Oaks, CA: Sage.

Whitmore, R. J. (2003). In search of development: An autoethnographic exploration of the Liberty Hyde Bailey Scholars Program. Unpublished doctoral dissertation, Michigan State University.

Wild, C. J., and Seber, G. A. F. (2000). *Chance encounters: A first course in data analysis and inference*. New York: John Wiley & Sons.

Willig, C. (2001). Memory work. In C. Willig (ed.), *Introducing qualitative research in psychology: Adventures in theory and method*. Buckingham: Open University Press.

Wolcott, H. F. (1995). *The art of fieldwork*. Walnut Creek, CA: AltaMira Press.

Woods, P. (1996). *Researching the art of teaching: Ethnography for educational use*. London: Routledge.

Wortham, S. M. (1998). *Counter-institutions: Jacques Derrida and the question of the university*. New York: Fordham University Press.

Yin, R. (1984). *Case study research: Design and methods* (1st edn). Beverly Hills, CA: Sage.

Yin, R. (1989). *Case study research: Design and methods* (Rev. edn). Beverly Hills, CA: Sage.

Yin, R. (1993). *Applications of case study research*. Newbury Park, CA: Sage.

Yin, R. (1994). *Case study research: Design and methods* (2nd edn). Thousand Oaks, CA: Sage.

Yin, R. K. (2003). *Case study research, design and methods* (3rd edn). Newbury Park, CA: Sage.

Yin, R. K. (2009). *Case study research, design and methods* (4th edn). Newbury Park, CA: Sage.

Zikmund, W. G. (2000). *Business research methods* (6th edn). London: The Dryden Press.

Zuber-Skerritt, O. (1992). *Action research in higher education: Examples and reflections*. London: Kogan Page.

# Index

**365**